MELANESIA: Readings on a Culture Area

Chandler Publications in ANTHROPOLOGY AND SOCIOLOGY

LEONARD BROOM, General Editor

L. L. LANGNESS, Editor

ANTHROPOLOGY

MELANESIA

READINGS ON A CULTURE AREA

EDITED BY

L. L. LANGNESS
University of Washington

and

JOHN C. WESCHLER
University of Washington

CHANDLER PUBLISHING COMPANY
An Intext Publisher • Scranton / London / Toronto

Book Design by Joseph M. Roter
Maps by Joan D. Langness and Joseph M. Roter

CONTENTS

SERIES PREFACE

Oceania, with its immense variety, has been the scene of much anthropological work since before the turn of the century. It has been a training ground for generations of anthropology students and the subject of innumerable university courses. Quite likely it will be the focus of even more attention in the immediate future. Yet, strangely, there is very little by way of text materials for the area. This series of readings is designed to provide such materials. It is hoped the readings together will provide coverage in depth, while individually providing the flexibility required for more particular interests.

NOTES ON CONTRIBUTORS

JOHN A. BARNES studied at Cambridge (B.A. 1939 in mathematics and anthropology), Cape Town, and Oxford (D. Phil. 1951 in social anthropology). He held research posts with the Rhodes-Livingstone Institute (1946–1949), St. John's College, Cambridge (1950–1953), Manchester University (Simon Fellow, 1951–1953), and Churchill College, Cambridge (1965–1966). He taught at University College, London (1949–1951), and at the London School of Economics (1954–1956). He was Professor of Anthropology at the University of Sydney (1956–1958) and the Australian National University (1958–1969), and is currently Professor of Sociology at Cambridge. Professor Barnes has done field work in Northern Rhodesia (now Zambia), Nyasaland (now Malawi), and western Norway. He is the author of *Marriage in a Changing Society* (1951), *Politics in a Changing Society* (2nd ed. 1967), and *Inquest on the Murngin* (1967). He has also written numerous articles on politics and kinship.

PAULA BROWN (GLICK) received her B.A. and M.A. in anthropology at the University of Chicago and her Ph.D. at the University of London. She has engaged in teaching and research at University College in London, the University of California at Los Angeles, the University of Wisconsin, and Cambridge University. From 1956 to 1966 she carried out research in New Guinea and the New Hebrides as Fellow of the Australian National University. She is the author of numerous articles on the Chimbu and joint author with H. C. Brookfield of *Struggle for Land* (1963) and *The People of Vila* (1969). Since 1966, she has been Professor of Anthropology at the State University of New York, Stony Brook.

RALPH N. H. BULMER trained in anthropology at Cambridge (B.A. 1952) and at the Australian National University (Ph.D. 1961). He was Lecturer and Senior Lecturer in Social Anthropology at the University of Auckland (1958–1967). Since 1968, he has been Foundation Professor of Social Anthropology at the University of Papua–New Guinea. He has written many articles and has done field work both in Lapland (1950–1951) and in the New Guinea Highlands (intermittently since 1954, working with the Kyaka Enga, and Karam).

WILLIAM H. DAVENPORT attended the University of Hawaii (B.A. 1952) and Yale University (Ph.D. 1956). He has held positions in anthropology at the Bernice P. Bishop Museum, the University of Pennsylvania, and Yale University. He is now Professor of Anthropology and Director of the Center for South Pacific Studies, University of California at Santa Cruz. Although he has worked with the Iroquois and in Jamaica, his major field work has been in the British Solomon Islands Protectorate, where he has worked in the Santa Cruz Islands, Guadalcanal, and San Cristobal. He has published extensively on the Pacific.

A. L. EPSTEIN was formerly an Officer of the Rhodes-Livingstone Institute. He worked among the Bemba and in the towns of the Northern Rhodesian (now Zambian) copperbelt. He is currently Professor of Anthropology at the Australian National University. His most recent field research has been among the Tolai of the Gazelle Peninsula of New Britain. He is the author of *Politics in an Urban African Community* (1958) and *Matupit: Land, Politics and Change Among the Tolai of New Britain* (1969). He also edited *The Craft of Social Anthropology* (1967).

BEN R. FINNEY attended the University of California, Berkeley (B.A. 1955), the University of Hawaii (M.A. 1959), and Harvard University (Ph.D. 1964). He has held positions in anthropology at the University of California in Santa Barbara, the Bernice P. Bishop Museum, and the Australian National University. He is presently Associate Professor of Anthropology, University of Hawaii. Dr. Finney has done extensive field work in French Polynesia as well as in New Guinea. In addition to articles, he has written two monographs: *Polynesian Peasants and Proletarians* (1965) and *New Guinea Entrepreneurs* (1969).

WARD H. GOODENOUGH received his Ph.D. from Yale University in 1949. Since then, he has been a member of the faculty and staff of the University Museum at the University of Pennsylvania, where he is now Professor of Anthropology and Curator of Oceanian Ethnology. He is past President of the American Ethnological Society (1962) and of the Society for Applied Anthropology (1963), and has served as Editor of the *American Anthropologist* (1966–1970). His ethnographic field work has been in Micronesia (Truk and Gilbert Islands) as well as in New Britain. His published works include *Property, Kin and Community on Truk* (1951), *Cooperation and Change* (1963), *Explorations in Cultural Anthropology* (as editor, 1964), and *Description and Comparison in Cultural Anthropology* (1970).

IAN HOGBIN was formerly Reader in Anthropology at the University of Sydney and is now continuing his distinguished career as Professorial Fellow at Macquarie University in Sydney. He was trained in anthropology by Radcliffe-Brown at Sydney and by Malinowski in London. His honors include the Wellcome Medal (1944) and the Rivers Memorial Medal (1946). He was Munro Lecturer at the University of Edinburgh (1949), Mason Lecturer at the University of Birmingham (1953), and Marett Memorial Lecturer at Exeter College, Oxford (1961). His major publications include *Law and Order in Polynesia* (1934), *Experiments in Civilization* (1939), *Transformation Scene* (1951), *Social Change* (1958), *Kinship and Marriage in a New Guinea Village* (1963), *The Kaoka Speakers: A Guadalcanal Society* (1964), and *The Island of Menstruating Men* (1970).

ROGER M. KEESING received his B.A. from Stanford University and his M.A. and Ph.D. from Harvard (Ph.D. 1965). He is currently Associate Professor of Anthropology at the University of California, Santa Cruz, where he has taught since 1965. From 1967 to 1969, Dr. Keesing was Acting Director of the Center for South Pacific Studies, and was active in the formation of the Association for Social Anthropology in Oceania. He has done extensive field research in the

British Solomon Islands, concentrating on Malaita, and has published many articles dealing with kinship and social structure.

PETER LAWRENCE attended Cambridge University, where he studied classics and anthropology (M.A. and Ph.D.). From 1949 to 1957, he was variously Research Scholar, Research Assistant, and Research Fellow at the Australian National University. From 1957 to 1960, he was Senior Lecturer in Anthropology at the Australian School of Pacific Administration, Sydney. He was Senior Lecturer in Anthropology at the University of Western Australia (1960–1963), Senior Lecturer in Social Anthropology at the University of Sydney (1963–1966). He was Professor of Anthropology and Sociology at the University of Queensland (1966–1970). He is currently Professor of Anthropology, University of Sydney. Professor Lawrence has done extensive field work in the Madang District of New Guinea, working with the Garia and Ngaing. His main works include *Road Belong Cargo* (1964) and *Gods, Ghosts and Men in Melanesia* (edited with M. J. Meggitt, 1965).

MERVYN J. MEGGITT was educated at the University of Sydney, taking his Ph.D. in anthropology in 1960. From 1955 to 1965, he was Lecturer and Senior Lecturer at the University of Sydney. He was Professor of Anthropology at the University of Michigan from 1965 to 1967. Since 1967, he has been Professor of Anthropology at Queens College of the City University of New York. A past Chairman of the Department of Anthropology, he is currently Executive Officer. Dr. Meggitt was W. M. Strong Research Fellow at the University of Sydney in 1955, and Simon Research Fellow at the University of Manchester in 1963. He has had much research experience in Central Australia, New Guinea, and Andalusia. In addition to many articles, Professor Meggitt has written *Desert People* (1962), *The Lineage System of the Mae Enga* (1965), *Gods, Ghosts and Men in Melanesia* (edited with Peter Lawrence, 1965), *Gadjari Among the Walbiri Aborigines of Central Australia* (1967), and *Pigs, Pearlshells, and Women* (edited with R. M. Glasse, 1969).

DOUGLAS L. OLIVER received his Ph.D. in ethnology from the University of Vienna in 1935. During and immediately following World War II, Dr. Oliver served on the Board of Economic Warfare, and was a consultant on Pacific Island Affairs to the Department of State and the United Nations. He was a member of the South Pacific Commission Research Council in 1949. From 1948 until the present, he has been Lecturer and subsequently Professor of Anthropology and Curator of Oceanic Ethnology at Harvard University. In 1969, Professor Oliver was appointed to the Chair of Pacific Anthropology at the University of Hawaii. Dr. Oliver has had extensive experience in the Pacific, both as a field worker and as a consultant and planner. His major field work has been in the Solomon Islands and, more recently, the Society Islands. Among his many works are *The Pacific Islands* (rev. ed. 1962), *A Solomon Island Society* (1955), *Invitation to Anthropology* (1964), and a forthcoming three-volume work on *Ancient Tahitian Society*.

ROY A. RAPPAPORT was awarded the Ph.D. from Columbia University in 1966. He was Burgess Honorary Fellow at Columbia University (1964) and John Simon Guggenheim Memorial Fellow and Senior Specialist at the East-West Center (1968–1969). He is presently Associate Professor of Anthropology at the University of Michigan. Dr. Rappaport has done archeological field work in the Society Islands and ethnographic field work in New Guinea. In addition to articles in periodicals and chapters in other books, he is the author of *Pigs for the Ancestors* (1967).

KENNETH E. READ received his M.A. from the University of Sydney (1946) and his Ph.D. from the University of London (1948). From 1950 to 1953, he was Research Fellow at the Australian National University. He was Senior Lecturer at the Australian School of Pacific Administration from 1953 to 1957. From 1958 to the present, he has been Associate Professor, Professor, and Chairman of the Department of Anthropology at the University of Washington. Professor Read was awarded a Bollingen Foundation Fellowship in 1958 and a John Simon Guggenheim Memorial Fellowship in 1966–1967. His field work has been in New Guinea, where he worked in the Markham valley (1944–1945) and the Asaro valley (1950–1952). The author of many papers, he has also written *The High Valley* (1965).

HAROLD W. SCHEFFLER received his Ph.D. from the University of Chicago in 1963. Since then, he has been Associate Professor of Anthropology at Yale University. Although Dr. Scheffler worked briefly with Northern and Plains Ojibwa, his major research activities have been in the Solomon Islands. He has worked on Choiseul, Simbo, and, most recently, Rendova Island. He is the author of *Choiseul Island Social Structure* (1965), *A Study in Structural Semantics: The Siriono Kinship System* (with F. G. Lounsbury, 1970), as well as many articles.

JAMES B. WATSON was educated at the University of Chicago (A.B. 1941, A.M. 1945, Ph.D. 1948). He has taught at Washington University, St. Louis (1947–1955), and since 1955 he has been Professor of Anthropology at the University of Washington in Seattle. From 1959 to the present, he has been Principal Investigator for the New Guinea Micro-evolution Project. Dr. Watson was Associate Editor of the *American Anthropologist* (1963–1966) and is a past President of the Central States Anthropological Society. He has also been a Consultant to the United Nations' Fund for the Development of West Irian. His principal field work has been in the Eastern Highlands District of Australian Papua–New Guinea (1953–1955 and 1963–1964). In addition to numerous articles in journals, he has contributed chapters to many books.

GERARD A. ZEGWAARD was ordained a Roman Catholic priest in 1944. He went to Merauke, New Guinea, and began missionary work in the Mimika District. In 1950–1951 he made several explorations into the Asmat area (east of Mimika) and began to work with the Asmat in 1952. In 1953, he settled in Agats, where he stayed until 1955. After nine more years in Merauke, he was assigned to Djakarta, where he presently works for the Indonesian Bishops' Conference. Father Zegwaard studied Asmat culture, especially its religious and social dimensions, as part of his missionary work, and has published extensively.

MELANESIA: Readings on a Culture Area

130°   135°   140°   145°

0°

Djajapura

W E S T
I R I A N

T E R R I T O R Y   O F
N E W
G U I N E A

Wewak

Sepik R.

Manus I.

ADMIRALTY ISLS.

BISMARCK ARCHIPELAGO

Madang

Goroka

5°

Lae

Fly R.

P A P U A

GULF OF PAPUA

Pt. Moresby

10°

Torres Str.

Darwin

CAPE
YORK
PENINSULA

GULF OF
CARPENTARIA

G R E A T   B A R R I E R   R E E F

15°

A U S T R A L I A

20°

25°

130°   135°   140°   145°   150°

Melanesia

miles

0   100   200   300

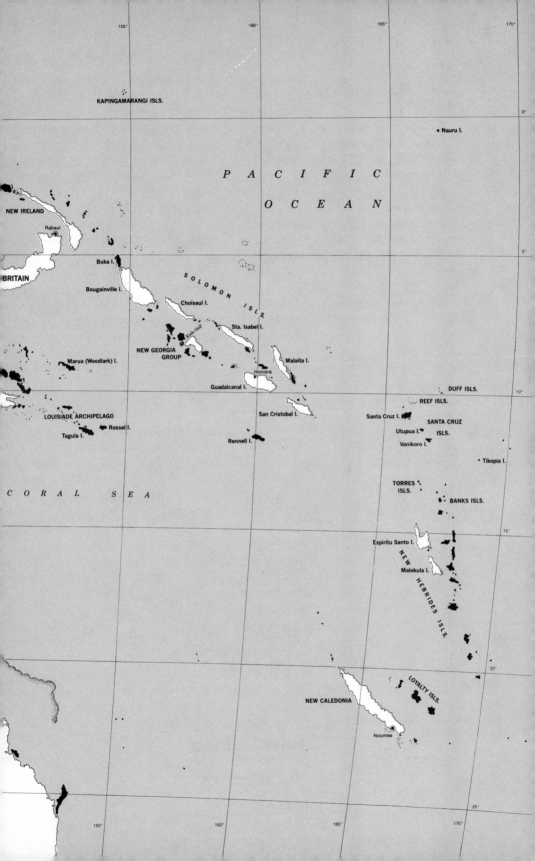

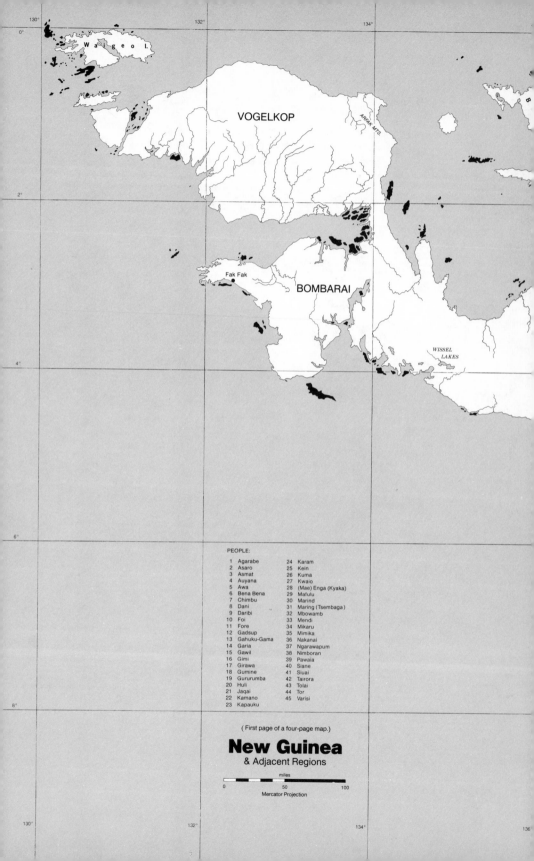

VOGELKOP

ARFAK MTS.

Wai geo I.

130°   132°   134°

0°

2°

BOMBARAI

Fak Fak

WISSEL
LAKES

4°

6°

PEOPLE:

1	Agarabe	24	Karam
2	Asaro	25	Kein
3	Asmat	26	Kuma
4	Auyana	27	Kwaio
5	Awa	28	(Mae) Enga (Kyaka)
6	Bena Bena	29	Mafulu
7	Chimbu	30	Marind
8	Dani	31	Maring (Tsembaga)
9	Daribi	32	Mbowamb
10	Foi	33	Mendi
11	Fore	34	Mikaru
12	Gadsup	35	Mimika
13	Gahuku-Gama	36	Nakanai
14	Garia	37	Ngarawapum
15	Gawil	38	Nimboran
16	Gimi	39	Pawaia
17	Girawa	40	Siane
18	Gumine	41	Siuai
19	Gururumba	42	Tairora
20	Huli	43	Tolai
21	Jaqai	44	Tor
22	Kamano	45	Varisi
23	Kapauku		

(First page of a four-page map.)

New Guinea
& Adjacent Regions

miles

0   50   100

Mercator Projection

8°

130°   132°   134°   136°

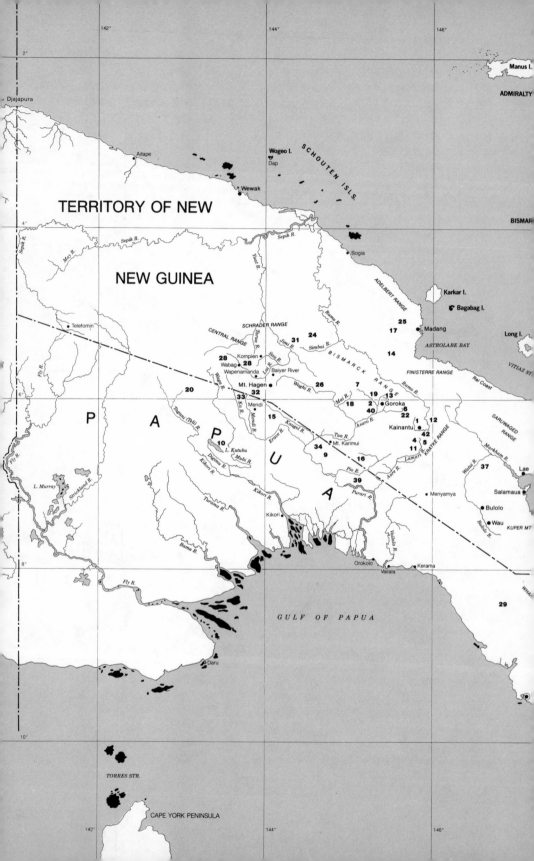

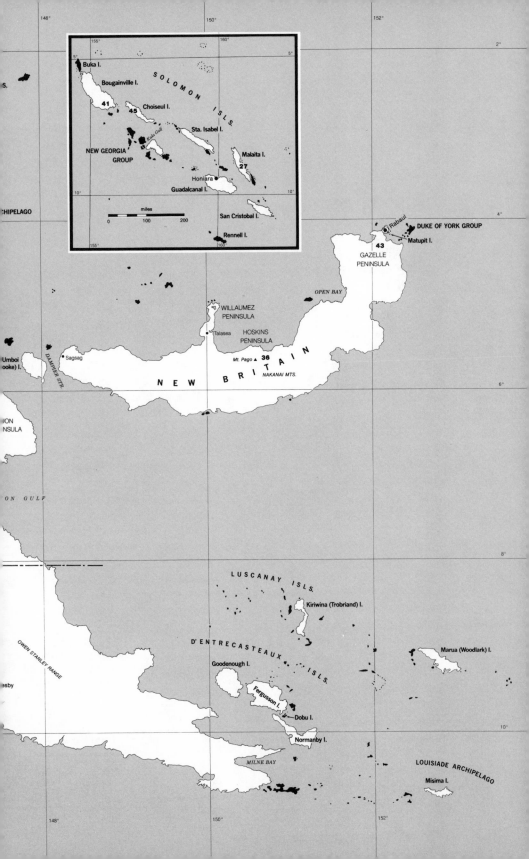

Buka I.

Bougainville I.

SOLOMON ISLS.

41

45 Choiseul I.

Sta. Isabel I.

Kula Gulf

NEW GEORGIA
GROUP

Malaita I.

27

Honiara

Guadalcanal I.

miles

0   100   200

San Cristobal I.

Rennell I.

CHIPELAGO

Rabaul DUKE OF YORK GROUP

43 Matupit I.

GAZELLE
PENINSULA

OPEN BAY

WILLAUMEZ
PENINSULA

Talasea HOSKINS
PENINSULA

Umboi
ooke) I.

Sagsag

DAMPIER STR.

Mt. Pago ▲ 36

NAKANAI MTS.

N E W   B R I T A I N

ION
NSULA

ON GULF

LUSCANAY ISLS.

Kiriwina (Trobriand) I.

D'ENTRECASTEAUX ISLS.

Marua (Woodlark) I.

OWEN STANLEY RANGE

esby

Goodenough I.

Fergusson I.

Dobu I.

Normanby I.

MILNE BAY

LOUISIADE ARCHIPELAGO

Misima I.

INTRODUCTION

Lying in the extreme western reaches of the south Pacific Ocean and immediately north and slightly to the east of the Australian continent is the culture area Melanesia. Its westernmost part is formed by the immense island of New Guinea, which, together with its offshore islands, represents the largest land mass. The Bismarck Archipelago (consisting of the large islands of New Britain and New Ireland as well as the Admiralty islands and smaller adjacent groups) lies to the east and slightly north of New Guinea. Further east and a bit to the south are the Solomons and the Santa Cruz Islands. In the eastern and southern limits of the area are the New Hebrides and New Caledonia. The islands of Fiji, although usually included in Melanesia, are discussed in a different volume of this series, *Polynesia: Readings on a Culture Area,* edited by Alan Howard (Chandler Publishing Company, 1971).

Melanesia has been prominent in anthropological studies since before the turn of the century. A. C. Haddon, W. H. R. Rivers, and C. S. Seligman began a pattern of distinguished field work with the Torres Straits Expedition of 1898. This was followed by Bronislaw Malinowski's brilliant and enduring work in the Trobriands and by Margaret Mead's pioneering research on Manus and northern New Guinea. However, these are merely reference points in a tradition which also includes Gregory Bateson, Reo Fortune, Ian Hogbin, F. E. Williams, Beatrice Blackwood, Hortense Powdermaker, Douglas Oliver, and John W. M. Whiting, to name only a few of the most distinguished.

Not all aspects of anthropology have been well represented in Melanesia. The archeology and physical anthropology of the area are still largely unknown, although in recent years there have been substantially increased efforts in these fields. Furthermore, although a large body of work in linguistics has been undertaken, mostly by members of the Summer Institute of Linguistics, the number of languages has been found to be so vast that the linguistic picture is not yet entirely clear. As answers to questions about Melanesian prehistory, physical anthropology, and languages are largely dependent on a wider Pacific and Asian perspective, these issues will be more fully treated elsewhere in this series, *Prehistory and Comparative Studies in the Pacific,* to be edited by Roger Green.

In historical times, the sailors of Portugal and Spain were the first in this part of Oceania. The Portuguese Jorge de Meneses discovered western New Guinea in 1526–1527, and Alvara de Saavedra, a Spaniard, was on its north coast the following year when he named it "Isla de Oro" (Island of Gold). From the middle of the sixteenth century to late in the eighteenth century, there was intermittent exploration by Spanish, French, German, Dutch, and British navigators. Some of the greatest names in navigation and exploration are associated with the discovery of the Solomon Islands, the Shortlands, the New Hebrides, and New Caledonia, including Cook, Bougainville, and Bligh. The British East India Company had taken possession of part of New Guinea by 1793, and in 1828 the Dutch formally took over the western half. Germany made northwest New Guinea and the Bismarck Archipelago part of a German protectorate which lasted until the end of World War I, when most of the former German colonies were mandated to the administration of Australia by the League of Nations. World War II brought the Japanese to most of Melanesia, but the United Nations mandate passed control back to Australia, with the Dutch portion, West Irian, becoming part of Indonesia in 1963. Now, questions of self-determination loom very large. But our concern here is with Melanesia as a culture area and with the forms of custom and behavior found there, not with questions of self-determination or politics.

Probably the most distinctive characteristic of Melanesia as a culture area is its immense diversity. This is true of temperature, climate, subsistence base, language, social organization, and virtually any aspect one could mention. Whereas Polynesia and Micronesia can be said to exhibit considerable cultural homogeneity, Melanesia is an area of extremes. Cannibalism existed in some parts of the New Guinea Highlands, for example, but was regarded with loathing by very similar people only a few miles away. Homosexuality, common among some groups, is virtually unknown ten miles away. Sorcery, considered almost the sole cause of illness in one part of the Highlands, is replaced by a belief in ghosts as the causative agents in others. In some areas within Melanesia, elaborate artistic traditions exist, whereas in others artistic expressions of any kind are minimal. There are groups which emphasize relationships traced through females, but more common are those which emphasize male links, and still others are difficult to classify so simply. In some areas, the sweet potato is the staple food crop; in other areas it is taro, or yams, or sago. Fish and coconuts, very important as food resources for some Melanesians, are entirely unknown to others.

The great paradox of Melanesia is that in spite of this immense variation, there is at the same time, in some important dimensions, an under-lying, equally dramatic, homogeneity. Virtually all of the people are horticulturalists, and they are, with very few exceptions, pig-raisers. Everywhere, precontact political units were relatively small. The technology was simple and basically uniform if one ignores for a moment the demands of coast and interior. There were no large urban centers, and life was lived on a daily, face-to-face level in which both food and the hazards of life were shared by all.

The phenomenon of variation around underlying homogeneity makes Melanesia potentially one of the world's greatest ethnographic laboratories, although this potential has not yet been fully realized. There have been remarkably few comparative studies and, with the rate of change accelerat-ing as it is, many opportunities have already been lost.

While change itself is a vital area for study, the possibilities for re-search in it in Melanesia are endless. The history of the area is brief and fairly well documented when compared with most areas of the world. In some areas, native groups have been reached for the first time only in recent years, thus eliminating complications which occur in studies of culture change elsewhere. A great variety of situations can be found, ranging from remote areas in the interior of New Guinea where people are occasionally just being contacted, to the sophisticated urbanized environ-ments of Honiara, Rabaul, or Port Moresby. There are places in which traditional forms of currency are still in use, and at the same time there are those which have complicated international transactions through the Papua–New Guinea Development Bank, which began operating in 1967. Politics and political change are equally diverse. Indigenous beliefs about health and illness are being challenged by the introduction of Western medicine, and traditional religious beliefs are under pressure from an exceedingly broad representation of missions. Nevertheless, just as there are pressures to change, so there are pressures to resist, or to move slowly, or even to retrogress.

The articles in this volume have been selected to present Melanesia both as a culture area and as a focus for research. Since the papers were not written specifically for this volume, it is perhaps not as well balanced as it might be. There is a surprising absence of information in the existing literature on some topics and for some areas. However, there were some difficulties in choosing which selections to use, and although an attempt was made not to include too many articles from any one geographical area, when that criterion was balanced against the content of the available articles it could not always be given priority. Thus there are more articles dealing with New Guinea than with the remainder of Melanesia. However, in view of the size of New Guinea relative to the rest of Melanesia, both in area and in population, this emphasis is not without justification. There are some obvious gaps also; that the New Hebrides and the Loyalty

Islands are not represented is a regrettable but mostly unavoidable situation. Fiji, which might have been included, is discussed in the Polynesia volume mentioned above.

In the articles which comprise this book, as the reader will perceive, there is no lack of problems or problem areas to consider. The first article poses many questions for further research, and there are such questions liberally included or suggested in the others as well. Except in the part on social structure, no effort was made to concentrate on a single problem or topic. But in Melanesia, as in Polynesia, problems of social structure have been in the vanguard of recent interest and are crucial to any appreciation of the areas in question.

The four parts in this book—Ecology and Economics, Social Structure, Social Process, and Social Change—are arbitrary, and all of the articles could easily serve more than one purpose. Thus Roger Keesing's article, although presented in the part on social structure, deals also with ancestor worship. Peter Lawrence's paper, included under the heading of social change, contains an account of traditional religion among the Garia. Paula Brown's article, in addition to materials on social structure, presents information on marriage and exchange. Ralph Bulmer's paper on the political aspects of the Moka ceremonial deals obviously with economics, and so on. We have also attempted to select materials so as to represent such things as different modes of subsistence, different types of descent, different religious systems, and different reactions to contact. There is, then, we hope, enough of a sample to whet the appetite for more information on Melanesia—one of the world's least understood and most stimulating areas for research.

PART I

ECOLOGY AND ECONOMICS

All peoples must reside on some part of the earth, but the particular portion a group inhabits necessarily influences and limits behavior in a variety of ways. In order to survive, men must devise strategies for exploiting their portion of earth. They must come to an efficient adjustment, both to the natural environment and to other human populations, and they must develop techniques for harnessing their own energies for production and distribution.

Melanesia presents a multitude of different natural environments. There are "high" islands, both continental types like New Guinea or New Caledonia, and weathered volcanic ones such as in the New Hebrides; and there are "low" types such as raised coral islands or coral atolls. Although it can be said that there are three seasons (Brookfield & Hart, 1966*), topography can modify these. Temperature, which is less important than rainfall in the tropics as a determinant of seasonality, varies less from month to month than it does from lowlands to highlands. In the highlands, local differences in altitude and the orientation and arrangement of ridges and valleys can produce microclimates which differ in degree sometimes within the same valley.

Barrau (1958) has distinguished five ecological zones and correlated types of indigenous subsistence economy in Melanesia. These are:

1. Narrow, nonmarshy coastal strips covered with herbaceous beach vegetation and small strand forest. The principal cultivated crop is the coconut palm, with supplementary gardens of taro and Polynesian arrowroot. Fishing and trade are also important.

2. Swampy lowlands covered with mangrove, sago palms, and marshy grasslands. Subsistence consists of food-gathering (sago and bruiguiera fruits), fishing, hunting, and trade. Small bush gardens of tubers are maintained on the higher ground behind the swamps.

3. Dry regions on the leeward slopes of high islands which are covered with savannah or savannah woodland, with a predominance of grasses. Shift-

---

* For full bibliographical data of works mentioned in the introduction to each part and in the Further Readings at the end of each part, see the Bibliography at the end of this volume.

ing agriculture with yams and cassava gardens is most important, requiring specialized techniques to preserve moisture in the soil. Taro is grown as a supplement in irrigated plots.

4. Foothills and mountain slopes lower than 5,000 feet covered with rainforest. Swidden or slash-and-burn cultivation of taro is predominant. Hunting, fishing, and the gathering of fruits, nuts, and wild tubers provide supplements to the staple crop.

5. Highlands areas, confined to New Guinea, where rainforest becomes mossy forest at between 5,000 and 6,500 feet. At these and higher altitudes, intensive cultivation of sweet potatoes produces the primary staple for humans and pigs. Nut pandanus, bananas, sugar cane, and assorted greens are also cultivated. Permanent gardens are drained by ditches, fertilized by composting, and fenced to protect against marauding pigs.

It is not possible here to present detailed descriptions of these five general types or to show evidence of their considerable variation, nor is it possible to present more than a brief glimpse of Melanesian economic systems. But the five papers which make up this part, together with the readings suggested at the end, should offer a substantial background for further work on this topic.

The first paper, by James B. Watson, is both fascinating and provocative. In addition to serving as a general introduction to the sweet-potato growers of the New Guinea Highlands, it also poses many different kinds of questions for students of culture. Watson explores the possibly revolutionary consequences of the recent introduction of the sweet potato to the Highlands. He suggests links of various kinds between this single innovation and aspects of demography, technology, social structure, magic, religion, mythology, and the ubiquitous ethos of male superiority in Melanesia. Although the thesis he puts forth has been challenged (Brookfield & White, 1968), the evidence presented to date is for the most part inconclusive and there are many stimulating ideas to be examined.

While almost all Melanesians rely on horticulture, in some areas hunting is still of considerable importance. Ralph Bulmer's general paper on hunting serves as more than just a description of another subsistence activity. Like Watson, Bulmer raises broad questions of man's biological and evolutionary character. How does man relate to animals, both wild and domestic? How does his behavior as a hunter relate to warfare? Is there more to hunting than simple economics? The paper also serves to introduce the reader to the fauna of New Guinea and suggests that man's alteration of his environment creates new environments for many birds, mammals, and marsupials.

The excerpts from Douglas L. Oliver's book, *A Solomon Island Society,* shift attention from the island of New Guinea and serve to demonstrate how the Siuai of Bougainville exploit available resources. There is an excellent description of how horticulture, husbandry, hunting, gathering, and fishing are integrated in the daily and annual activities of the Siuai, and the reader is given an idea of the overwhelming importance of pigs in the life of Melanesians.

Roy A. Rappaport's paper is devoted to examining the relationship between Tsembaga ritual and their environment, both physical and social, local and larger. He attempts to demonstrate that religious ritual helps to regulate such issues as the distribution of land, the size of pig herds, the amount and timing of fighting, and so on. It is a detailed and exceedingly stimulating study which so far has not been duplicated by others working in Melanesia.

The final paper, by William Davenport, is an account of a "primitive" form of currency which is the basis of a complex system of trading in the Santa Cruz Islands. As of the early 1960's, this local money had withstood the introduction of a more universal currency. It is a good example of the kind of complexity found in some Melanesian economic systems, although not as well known as Malinowski's accounts of the Kula (1920, 1922).

Melanesian economic systems appear to range from exceedingly simple, featuring hunting and gathering in addition to horticulture, as among the Kukukuku of the Eastern Highlands of New Guinea, to the very elaborate, large-scale exchange systems of the Western Highlands, to the even more complex Kula-like systems reported here from eastern Melanesia. The way is open for much further work, hopefully before the indigenous systems are lost even to memory.

1

FROM HUNTING TO
HORTICULTURE IN THE
NEW GUINEA HIGHLANDS[1]

James B. Watson

Since the discovery, in the 1920s, of the large, orderly gardens of New Guinea's Central Highlands, observers have noted the striking degree of dependence on a single crop, the sweet potato. The orderliness and scale of subsistence activities in the Highlands contrasts sharply with the food quests of lowland peoples. When ethnologists first studied Highland peoples, they found elements of clan and segmentary lineage systems. These conditions—scale, orderliness, apparent specialization of the social systems, and singularity of the interior peoples of New Guinea—have all contributed to the impression of relatively long-established cultures. It was assumed that the mountain peoples had been extremely isolated, and, considering the lateness of their discovery and the accompanying sense of surprise, they could well be thought among the most isolated peoples on earth. Certainly the mountainous interior of this great, remote island, itself epitomizing human isolation and exotic backwardness, would not suggest dynamism and sweeping change. On the contrary, the notion of a "human refuge area" might seem appropriate.

The possibility is still largely unexamined that some of the most notable characteristics of Central Highlands culture may represent a quite recent tradition. However, the tentative and provisional character of social arrangements, the compromise and opportunism of aboriginal politics, group instability—related in part, at least, to warfare—and the vagueness and individual variability of ritual and supernatural belief suggest that these people have not been settled horticulturists for very long. The stone artifacts, e.g., older types of adzes, mortars, pestles, that are turned up from time to time in streams and garden ditches are seemingly of no great age and embody no unfamiliar techniques of manufacture. Contemporary people are unable to recognize the objects as their own, however, and often consider them of supernatural origin.

Reproduced by permission of the publisher and James B. Watson from *Ethnology*, 4:295-309 (1965).

A hypothesis of a recent general migration, accounting for both the break in the lithic tradition and the fluid and unsettled character of native life, is not promising. On the basis of linguistic data, the present peoples of the Central Highlands, as far west as the Strickland Gorge or beyond, have been in the area for a long time (Wurm 1964: 96-97; McKaughan 1964: 118-119). On the other hand, what might be interpreted as unsettled social conditions, now recognized—though not in these terms—by a number of ethnologists (Pouwer 1960; Brown 1962; Barnes 1962; Langness 1964), suggest a legitimate question regarding the developments that immediately led to the modern cultures of the Highlands. Ethnologists have not, for the most part, investigated Highland development. The prehistory of the Highlands may be of intrinsic interest to only a few, but in any case it bears upon the task of interpreting the modern cultures of the area.

Evidence of the recent introduction of the sweet potato (*Ipomoea batatas*) to New Guinea is growing, and there is reason to believe that it antedates the dense populations and intensive horticulture of the area. It is reasonable to suggest that small, patrilocal bands of hunters or intermittent gardeners may have existed widely, if not generally, in the Central Highlands until two or three centuries ago.

The character of the present Highland peoples seems to be no obstacle to an hypothesis of different subsistence activities in the recent past. The native populations of the Central Highlands, though varying locally, reach impressive figures for horticultural peoples dependent principally upon root crops and stone tools—without cereals, draft animals, food storage, or the plough. The highest densities occur in the area east of the Strickland Gorge and in the Baliem Valley of Irian Barat, where populations may extend to 200-500 persons per square mile (Brookfield 1964: 23)—much greater than those of the rest of New Guinea.

Nearly all observers of the Central Highlands have recognized the sweet potato as the most important single source of subsistence. This is generally true throughout the Highlands, from east to west, though other crops and sources of protein food vary locally in importance.[2] Highland conditions generally favor much larger yields of sweet potato than of other Highland crops (Brookfield 1964: 21). The highest population densities coincide with the areas of largest sweet potato production. The dependence on this single crop is so marked in most parts of the Highlands that population in a given area becomes almost a direct function of the suitability of growing sweet potatoes (Brookfield 1964: 24).

Cultivation, however, did not develop in the Highlands only with the coming of the sweet potato. Taro (*Colocasia*) and *Pueraria lobata* (Watson 1964) are root crops that appear to have been long known and probably widespread in the Highlands. Some form of yam may have had a more limited distribution. In addition, bananas and sugar cane (Warner

1962) quite likely were grown in the Central Highlands before sweet potatoes. The age and pre-ipomoean distribution of winged beans (*Psophocarpus tetragonolobus*) is less certain, but it may be tentatively added to the list. Pre-ipomoean subsistence activities may have involved trees, such as the nut pandanus, in ways beyond their use purely as wild food sources.

How, then, is it reasonable to maintain that Highlands cultivation took on the character of intensive sedentary gardening only with the arrival of sweet potatoes? Of all the plants listed above, perhaps only yams and winged beans[3] implied tillage comparable to that of the large, carefully laid-out gardens of the present. Yams and winged beans seem both less basic and less widely cultivated in the Highlands than other food crops such as taro or *Pueraria lobata*. Furthermore, we speak of yams and winged beans in regard to large-scale, well-tilled gardens only because that is the present manner of their cultivation in some areas. If they were among the pre-ipomoean repertory of the Highlands, they may have been more roughly or casually cultivated. The "wild yams" that occur in old gardens near bush in the Eastern Highlands District may formerly have received casual or intermittent cultivation.

In a recent detailed analysis of "the distribution of the distinctive agricultural methods found in the New Guinea highlands," Brookfield (1962: 243, 247) found certain widespread characteristics, including the following: planting of a fallow cover, commonly the casuarina; the use of some form of tillage to eradicate completely the grass covering garden land; and the very infrequent employment of simple slash-and-burn techniques. He recognized variation within the Highlands, *inter alia* in the precise techniques of tillage and water control, and emphasized the methods of cultivation that attend the major crop in each of the several recognized sections of the Highlands.[4]

If we approach with an historical emphasis the full array of methods of cultivation used in any given place, including those methods applied to secondary or minor—and typically older—crops, a distinction can be made between plantings and orderly gardens. Brookfield emphasized gardens in justifying his treatment of the Highlands as unitary and in distinguishing food production there from the cultivation prevalent in the adjacent lowlands. It may well be that what I characterize as plantings correspond closely—or in the past corresponded—to swidden. Gardens, in contrast to plantings, are readily recognizable as larger, more orderly in appearance, and extensively tilled. Because of their size, gardens are necessarily outside a village, or, as from Chimbu to the Strickland Gorge, are interspersed among the homesteads of a settlement. Gardens must be extensively ditched and/or fenced to protect them from pig depredations. Small plantings, however, are located next to the house, in a small cleared patch in the bush, or in a depression inaccessible to pigs.

Gardens are often regular in shape or internal layout—the aspect that so impressed early observers. Neat, orderly rows, gridiron ditching, or a rectilinear border are common over large sections of the Highlands—partly incidental, in the opinion of Brookfield (1962: 247-248), to water control. Plantings tend to be irregular in shape and design, and the soil receives less preparatory treatment, but attention may be given to relevant factors of soil and drainage. Indeed, it is possible to predict the odd pocket of taro, carefully tucked into its special niche. Plantings are distinct from gardens, not in being unresponsive to factors of cultivation but in being responsive to a different set of factors. To describe gardens as systematically laid-out or orderly, therefore, is not to imply that plantings lack system but only that they have a different system—one apparently better suited than gardens to non-sedentary, seasonal, or intermittent cultivation.

Plantings are "casual" in respects other than their greater number and dispersion. Taro, *Pueraria lobata,* and sugar cane in the Eastern Highlands District are planted in a manner that contrasts sharply with sweet potatoes, yams, and winged beans. It is not that the former must be casually planted or that they are always so planted. Rather they lend themselves quite handily to casual planting. Taro, if planted at all in an area where the sweet potato prevails, is planted in little plots of a few to a few score cuttings each, scattered about in advantageous locations as the cuttings become available, and not after a garden has been elaborately prepared, as with sweet potatoes, yams, and beans. *P. lobata,* a very slow-growing tuber, is planted optionally, casually, and opportunistically about the dwellings, near a convenient small tree (for the vine to climb) at the edge of the bush or in the village. When planted in gardens, it is spotted about among other plants. Sugar cane nowadays is planted either formally or casually, while bananas, being admirably immune from pig damage, can be planted wherever the owner thinks they will do well, inside or outside of the village or dwelling area. Tree crops in the bush, such as the areca palm (of limited distribution in the Highlands as a domestic crop) and nut pandanus, must be added to the list of food plants that do not belong to the garden sphere.

I suggest that the sweet potato is perhaps the first plant, general in the Central Highlands, to have been intensively cultivated as a garden crop. It is quite likely that its intensive cultivation developed independently, for taro gardening would probably not have provided the proper precedents for sweet potatoes, and the limited distribution and dubious antiquity of the yam and winged bean tend to exclude them.

In their major discussion of Central Highlands prehistory, S. and R. Bulmer (1964: 47) reviewed the ethnobotanical evidence quite thoroughly, concluding:

(1) that early agriculturists in the Highlands are likely to have relied on taro and/or *Pueraria* and/or bananas, and possibly, in areas below 5,500 feet, yams;

(2) that these crops are unlikely to have supported anything approaching present population densities at between 5,000 and 6,000 feet, and can only have supported very sparse populations at higher altitudes; and (3) that major redistributions of population, particularly in the Western Highlands, have taken place since the introduction of intensive sweet potato cultivation.

While these authors do not explicitly characterize pre-ipomoean cultivation as intermittent or supplementary, they nevertheless support the late introduction of the sweet potato and refer to "the economic and social revolutions which must have followed this introduction" (S. and R. Bulmer 1964: 52). Brookfield (1964: 21-22), briefly considering pre-ipomoean cultivation, found it

plausible that taro is an older crop than sweet potato in the Highlands, but [one that] has radically different ecological requirements. . . . if [taro] was once more widespread, there must have been radical changes both in cultivation methods and in area of occupation since the general adoption of the sweet potato.

These authorities appear, broadly speaking, to confirm the association between pre-ipomoean and non-ipomoean methods of cultivation.

The planting of casuarina trees, a typical part of the fallowing cycle which Brookfield (1962: 247) recognized among modern Highlands gardeners, is said to have begun within recent memory in at least one part of the Eastern Highlands District. The trees themselves are alleged to have been introduced within the memory of both Tairora and Auyana informants. (Their memory might not exceed a hundred years in this case.) Auyana informants told S. G. Robbins that the trees came at the time of the darkness and earthquake that I have elsewhere (Watson 1963) suggested accompanied the explosion of Krakatoa in 1883. Association of the two events—the trees and the darkness—is not clear and may be fortuitous even if chronologically correct. Data are lacking for other parts of the Highlands, but if the cultivated casuarina is recent, as informants indicate, then the argument is strengthened that the modern sweet potato gardening system is also recent. It would further suggest the danger of assuming too much time for the development of horticultural elaborations as profound as that of the sweet potato.

There is still a question regarding the antiquity of domesticated pigs in the Highlands.[5] Today, the sweet potato is the principal food on which swine are fed, in addition to what they obtain from rooting about in grassland, bush, or fallow gardens. If stall-fed, what fodder was used for pre-ipomoean pigs? Quite apart from the problem of an adequate supply for both men and pigs, taro appears to be less satisfactory for pig fodder, since wild and presumably also domestic pigs seem to prefer sweet potatoes. B. and R. Craig informed me that in the Telefomin area, where taro cultivation is more important than in other parts of the Highlands, sweet potato gardens are occasionally planted primarily for pigs. Among the Awa in the Eastern Highlands District, sweet potatoes are referred to as "pig food." The preference of Highland pigs for sweet potatoes, raw or cooked, is notorious, and the use of the plant for pig fodder may have accelerated its adoption.

It might be suggested that wild, and ultimately domestic, pigs followed sweet potatoes into the area. Swine-keeping seems inconsistent with nomadism and the absence of a fixed residential base, and it can probably be taken as an index of sedentarism—though the absence of domestic pigs may not prove nomadism. Since protection for the growing plants would not be necessary without pigs, crop-planting would have involved less work. As noted above, taro planters may enjoy relative immunity from pig depredations. S. and R. Bulmer (1964: 48) report finding pigs, archeologically, only in an "almost certainly agricultural phase of western Highlands history," though they do not describe this phase as post-ipomoean.[6] Further archeological work is required in the Highlands to determine accurately the first occurrence of domestic pigs, but it is reasonable to suggest that pre-ipomoean Highlanders relied on pigs, as well as gardens, much less continuously or regularly than do the present people.

Recent work indicates that the sweet potato did not arrive in New Guinea until after Europeans had reached the southwest Pacific (Conklin 1963; Nishayama 1963; Yen 1963; S. and R. Bulmer 1964). Since early European contact with New Guinea was slight compared to the Philippines or the Spice Islands, the sweet potato probably was introduced from one or more neighboring islands. L. J. Brass, a plant ecologist with the experience of seven New Guinea expeditions, believes there is little doubt that the sweet potato reached New Guinea from the west, through bird-of-paradise hunters, traders, and other Malays. He estimates its arrival on the coast of West New Guinea (Irian Barat) about 350 years ago. If his estimate is correct, the plant may have reached the Central Highlands, and hence became a significant part of Highland subsistence, no more than three centuries ago.

Several ethnological facts suggest the recency of sweet potatoes as a crop. Sweet potatoes do not provide a focus for ritual, magic, or folklore, as surrounds taro, bananas, sugar cane, or yams. In a number of widely separated Highland cultures the ritual-conceptual context of the sweet potato is feminine, in contrast to a masculine context for bananas, sugar cane, yams, and perhaps taro. At least one Highland people, the Huli, explicitly regard the sweet potato as an introduced crop, and in their genealogies distinguish between "men of taro" and "men of sweet potato." R. M. Glasse reports that "this occurs in about the 10th ascending generation," and the people traditionally recall five or six generations prior to that. Huli legends about the spread of sweet potatoes indicate a western source and suggest that they first encountered it growing in what they regard as a wild state. Taro is still an important Huli ritual crop used in various fertility and initiation ceremonies.

The Agarabi and Tairora of the Eastern Highlands, like most Highland peoples so far described, have exceedingly shallow genealogies, and it is not surprising that they lack a tradition of pre-ipomoean men. They grow taro but usually say that they have always had sweet potatoes as well. Many varieties of cultivated plants were acknowledged to have been introduced from adjacent areas. Some informants—those with the longest list of sweet potato varieties and the best knowledge of the matter— did not assign a local origin in any single variety. All the numerous pre-contact varieties, including those which they considered the oldest, tra-ditionally reached the area from the people immediately to the west (Kamano) or, in a few instances, from still farther west. Some varieties of bananas or sugar cane were also acknowledged to have come from the outside, but others, it was insisted, had been in local hands since the beginning of things.

The case of *Pueraria lobata* may also be relevant. Until recently, this common plant of New Guinea appears to have been cultivated widely, perhaps universally, in the Central Highlands (Watson 1964), and it is still cultivated marginally in many parts, although information for much of West Irian is lacking. We cannot safely presume that its present "mar-ginal" cultivation is in all cases necessarily less than its pre-ipomoean scale of cultivation. In some places *P. lobata* is well known to individuals of all ages and is esteemed as a cultivated source of food. In the Southern Kamano-Kanite area of the Eastern Highlands District, many informants speak of it as their "number one" food, though it is not necessarily their primary food source. Nevertheless, the cultivation of *P. lobata* is waning in a number of Highland areas and has ceased altogether in others. In some villages, only older persons can identify the crop. It seems to be an earlier crop now being displaced by sweet potatoes, though this dis-placement need not be a late or post-contact phenomenon. Some Eastern Highlands District informants suggest that, if you have sweet potatoes, you do not need *P. lobata,* implying that sweet potatoes are a functional equivalent and superior substitute for the slower-growing root crop. Though differing in detail, sweet potatoes appear to have been placed in the same "tuber" category as *P. lobata* in the Gimi language, Eastern Highlands District, and perhaps in others. If the displacement of *P. lobata* is an adjustment to a superior newer tuber, that adjustment, apparently still under way, suggests a recent adoption of sweet potatoes.

As a new crop coming into the Highlands, seemingly from the north coast, sweet potatoes appear to have advanced along at least three frontiers:

(1) On the primary frontier the sweet potato reached Highland peo-ples who were already cultivators, and displaced older crops as an effi-cient food for humans and/or pigs. The Telefomin area with its taro

may be a modern remnant of this frontier, and Huli traditional history apparently recalls when the frontier included this Southern Highlands District group.

(2) The second frontier can be termed an internal frontier of horticulture (not just the sweet potato) as gardeners spread into Highland areas without previous gardening and perhaps without permanent populations. Areas of pioneer cultivation are readily recognizable today in the Western Highlands District, generally at altitudes above the safe limit for other crops but where substantial populations, dependent on the sweet potato, have recently settled. Areas recently settled by pioneer sweet potato cultivators also exist in virgin bush in the Eastern Highlands District. J. N. Warner, a plant geneticist who visited the Central Highlands in 1951, believes that the sweet potato is more recent in the west—obviously quite recent in the Wissel Lakes area. The new plant, however, may have reached the Central Highlands by more than one route from the coast, i.e., along several rivers that flow from the interior to the north.

(3) A third frontier of the sweet potato is at the southern periphery of the Highlands, where gardening practices were spread and are spreading to people who were non-horticultural. The Mikaru or Karimui peoples (Daribi, Pawaia), who speak languages distinct from those of the Highlands phylum (Wurm 1964: 79-80), serve to illustrate this frontier. According to Roy Wagner, they began sweet potato cultivation only about 60 years ago. The Daribi state that they obtained the plants and cultivation techniques from the Gumine, a Highland people north of them. Hunting is apparently still a strong tradition among the Daribi and neighboring peoples. From other peoples living on the southern fringes of the Highlands comparable data can perhaps be obtained which will support a theory of recent intensive sweet potato gardening. It is worth emphasizing that all three frontiers are still visible and suggest recent if not continuing advances.

We can only speculate that the Central Highlands were occupied by scattered bands of hunters practicing supplementary cultivation until the introduction of sweet potato cultivation. They were probably at least semi-nomadic and had few if any domestic pigs, and while comparisons can be misleading, their relation to their crops probably resembled, in a general way, that of the Siriono (Holmberg 1950). That is, the people knew and planted crops but also depended heavily on wild food sources for subsistence, and adjusted their movements as much in response to the requirements of foraging as out of concern for their plantings. They did not live in fixed or palisaded settlements, and their housing was less substantial and permanent than at present.

The wild food resources of the Highlands have been carefully reviewed by S. and R. Bulmer (1964: 48-51). More diverse than is sometimes supposed, these resources appear—especially in a forested terrain (Robbins 1963)—capable of supporting small foraging bands. The time depth of S. Bulmer's (1964b: 327) archeological material—a maximum age of some 10,000 years—makes it practically certain that people wholly ignorant of cultivation have lived in the Highlands. There can thus apparently be no argument, from a presumed paucity of wild resources, in support of the conclusion that intensively cultivated crops were essential to human occupancy.

Is a population expansion of the sort required by the present theory possible? Could scattered bands of foragers increase to become today's dense horticultural populations in the span of two or three centuries? It would have been quite possible for small band populations to reach the size of all but the largest present speech communities of the area without an extraordinary rate of population growth. (Speech communities seem to be the feasible units for consideration, since nearly all modern languages have greater time depth than the few centuries under discussion.) The Enga, including the Mae Enga, are perhaps the largest language group in New Guinea. They could have reached their present population of 100,000 in 300 years, from an initial population of 1,146 with an average annual rate of increase of 1.5 per cent (W. B. Watson, personal communication).[7]

On the same basis, a number of the small Highland speech communities could have reached their modern size starting with a tiny band or two. Some of the larger Highland speech communities, moreover, may have incorporated bands of different speech, with linguistic results that are sometimes still evident (Wurm 1964: 96-97). Wholesale accretions of aliens could make an increase rate of 1.5 per cent seem exceedingly modest. Furthermore, the coalescence and incorporation of bands, whether of the same or different speech, is both theoretically predictable and closely analogous to actual present-day occurrences with refugee groups in certain parts of the Highlands.

Two principal theories, unavoidably simplified, appear as possible explanations for the transition to sweet potatoes as a major food source:

(1) Horticulture remained, at best, the seasonal, intermittent, or supplemental practice of foraging peoples—ranging from nomadic to semi-sedentary—until sweet potato gardening was established, with concomitant changes in both population and style of life. These changes were abrupt, perhaps explosive, and recent.

(2) Pre-ipomoean horticulture, too well developed to be characterized as seasonal or supplementary, provided up to half of the food requirements for at least a majority of Highland peoples. The sweet potato displaced older crops like taro, with increasing dependence on gardens (up to the present 90 per cent or more) and less radical though recent

changes than in the first alternative. In either case, new areas became accessible to gardening and attracted pioneer cultivation of the sweet potato.

A third possibility includes both of these basic positions and suggests that Highland areas varied appreciably in their pre-ipomoean development of horticulture. Some areas, exploiting the earlier crops like taro, had been longer or more fully committed to gardening, while in others foraging predominated until the arrival of the new crop. The competitive advantages of growing sweet potatoes, especially with population pressure in grassland areas, tipped the balance toward heavy reliance on horticulture throughout the Highlands. This theory could support either "explosive" or "gradual" post-ipomoean population changes, depending upon the extensiveness of foraging areas and populations.

A slow and gradual transition to dependence upon the sweet potato as the major food resource is a logical fourth possibility. This would seem to extend the full adaptation to the new crop not only up to but probably beyond the time of European contact. Thus the sweet potato was adopted with little overt effect by a population already dense, preponderantly horticultural, and sedentary—an idea which seems to have no support among present writers, else we should expect to find more evidence than anyone has yet reported of major social and cultural readjustments still under way.

The first theory seems to be the best explanation at present. The second does not preclude some of the changes discussed in this paper but only suggests that they were less radical than in the first. A change from 50 per cent to 90 per cent reliance upon gardens for food, with a more productive crop widely adapted to Highland environments, might well prove far from negligible in the reshaping of horticultural societies and cultures in a short time. The third theory in effect postpones the issue of post-ipomoean changes in that it makes no assumption of a previous condition in the Highlands. It is simply based upon the unassailable position that we do not know enough. The fourth theory is one of either slight or slow change and, in the latter case, one that must be going on today. Surely the change is still in process, for example, with the continuing expansion of pioneer horticulturists into previously forested areas, both within and on the edge of the Highlands. But in the sense of numerous Highland peoples only now committing themselves to sweet potatoes as a major crop, or commonly remembering when there was no such commitment, this theory seems ruled out for the present.

So far we have considered the recency of the sweet potato and cultivation of prior crops, assuming a recent transition from hunting to horticulture. I would like to examine, then, the evidence for recent nonsedentary bands in the Central Highlands. One fairly obvious point may be made at the outset: the material culture of all the Highland peoples so far reported is either portable or expendable. They produce no monumental art, stone- or earthworks, large structures such as the "house *tambaran*" with carved posts, canoes, slit gongs, or the like. Their implements are simple, such as the digging stick, wooden spatula for turning the soil (in some areas), bow, arrow, shield, spear, club, and small tools and containers of bamboo, bone, chipped stone, or wood. Only the polished stone axes are of great value and not readily replaced, and these are portable. With a few excep- tions, probably all at the fringes of the Highland area, such as the Markham valley, pottery is absent or imported. The most widely and frequently used cooking vessel is a section of bamboo which usually is consumed the first time it is used on a fire. With a few exceptions such as pandanus nuts, large stores of food appear to be lacking.

At present, the chief cultural commitment to stable residence is found in the extensively fenced and ditched gardens, dwellings, pig houses, and, in some areas, watchtowers and palisades. The greatest waste in fighting, apart from the loss of life, was consequently the abandonment or destruc- tion of these works, especially when groups were driven from their land and were obliged to take refuge with a host group or establish a new settlement elsewhere. The lack of notable additional impedimenta is con- sistent with a long history of nomadism and a short one of intensive, sedentary gardening.

As a cultural complex reflecting substantial elaboration, the scale and system of Highland gardens may suggest a period of development longer than two or three hundred years—certainly an impediment to a theory of the recency of settled horticulture. In a different perspective, however, it is legitimate to question the crops of those large orderly gardens, since it is not at all clear that any of them prior to the sweet potato belonged to a garden complex such as the present one. The argument, then, re- turns to the issue of the time of arrival of sweet potatoes rather than of the time required for the development of complex gardens. We can recall the speed and completeness with which the horse was incorporated into the High Plains culture of North America. That development involved the wholesale displacement of peoples as well as a shift in subsistence patterns. On the basis of internal evidence of complexity or cultural commitment alone, the recent and rapid development of equestrian usages in the High Plains would be suspect.[8] The sweet potato garden complex, despite large-scale, intensive production of a crop in a manner impressive to the eye, is not a particularly elaborate one, and gardening implements can hardly be considered elaborate.

Sociologically, the peoples of the Highlands are diverse. Differences are often noted between the village pattern in the eastern sector of the Austra- lian Highlands and the homestead settlement pattern in the west. Villages occur again west of the Strickland. Ethnographic studies, however, reveal

certain broad tendencies among Highland peoples, including: (1) patrilineal emphasis or ideology; (2) widespread existence of clans or quasi-
clan lineage groupings; (3) importance of the sibling link; (4) a sharp
dichotomy between the sexes, often accompanied by an expressed *horror
mulieris;* (5) "looseness" of structure; (6) flexibility and relative ease of
affiliation, with consequent ramification in a fairly open system of land
rights; (7) prevalence of warfare; and (8) leadership based primarily upon
achievement and prowess rather than on lineage seniority, inheritance, or
other ascriptive qualifications. With flexible affiliation and unilineal emphasis in local group membership, it is not surprising that consanguineal
status is readily extended, when necessary, to loosely affiliated co-residents
in many parts of the Highlands.

Such general tendencies in the area suggest a common cause—either
uniform antecedent social conditions throughout the Highlands, or factors
producing convergence along common lines. If intensive horticulture, sedentarism, and related patterns have developed throughout the area within
the last two or three centuries, they could well be potent factors in producing similar contemporary societies.

There is little evidence that pre-ipomoean Highland peoples were much
more diverse than the modern peoples. S. Bulmer (1964a) has shown local
as well as temporal variety in stone tools, and S. and R. Bulmer (1964)
review the question for other artifacts. The work so far done does not
support the idea of fundamental variation in exploitative activities. It is
possible, I believe, to postulate a pre-ipomoean society from which the
modern Highland peoples could have developed.

Steward (1955) has described a type of society which he calls the patrilineal band. Service (1962: 30–31, 60) has suggested that the unit is more
appropriately termed patrilocal—drawing attention to its characteristic rule
of residence but leaving unprejudiced the question of the rule of descent.
"Patrilineal" implies more than is warranted or necessary, especially as
applied to the Central Highlands. Steward's (1955: 135) synopsis of the
ecological and demographic settings of "patrilineal" bands is nonetheless
relevant to the present case:

The factors which produce the patrilineal band are: (1) A population density
of one person or less—usually much less—per square mile, which is caused by
a hunting and gathering technology in areas of scarce wild foods; (2) An environment in which the principal food is game that is nonmigratory and scattered,
which makes it advantageous for men to remain in the general territory of their
birth; (3) Transportation restricted to human carriers; (4) The cultural-
psychological fact . . . that groups of kin who associate together intimately
tend to . . . [display] group exogamy. . . .
The scattered distribution of the game, the poor transportation, and the
general sparcity of the population make it impossible for groups that average
50 or 60 persons and that have a maximum of about 100 to 150 persons to
associate with one another frequently enough and to carry out sufficient joint
activities to maintain social cohesion. The band consists of persons who habit-

ually exploit a certain territory over which its members can conveniently range. Customary use leads to the concept of ownership. . . . The territory would . . . become divided among these patrilineal bands.

Steward (1955: 125) has reviewed the reasons for expecting bands to develop patriliny (*viz.,* "patrilocality") under such exploitative conditions. Patrilineal sentiments generally prevail in the Central Highlands today. It would seem almost impossible to deny past agnatic conditions, patrilocality in particular, without being able to ascribe present Highlands agnation to some subsequent development of extraordinary magnitude.

Steward and Service have both stressed patrilocal bands as one of the most common types of social units among primitive peoples, and Service (1962: 107–108) especially emphasizes the diversity of ecological conditions in which such systems have proven adaptive. To my knowledge, patrilocal bands have not previously been postulated for the Central Highlands, but they seem an obvious possibility. It is not the concern of this paper to debate the social order in the prehistoric or pre-ipomoean Highlands, but rather to suggest—compatible with the hypothesized horticultural revolution—a prior social order consistent with the postulated pre-ipomoean ecology and subsistence pattern and one which, given such a revolution, could have generated the present social order. Patrilocal bands meet both requirements.

According to Steward, patrilocal bands might, with remarkable ease, become clans or multilineage communities—a type widely identified with the present Central Highlands. Moreover, the transitional conditions which Steward (1955: 157-158) outlined, drawing upon the work of Gifford (1926) in California and others, are essentially those suggested in this paper with regard to the adoption of the sweet potato and intensive gardening in the Central Highlands. The first condition is "any factor that will increase population . . . to approximately one person or more per square mile—so that several bands may exist together in larger communities." Since a change such as intensive gardening alone might serve merely to reduce the area utilized by each band, a second requirement "is some factor, such as war or tribal movements, which makes for dislocation of the bands and concentrates them in large, multiband communities." The warlike competition of Central Highland societies admirably meets this requirement. In the third place, "group names, totems, ceremonies, and the like" are required to furnish ethnic identity and thus help preserve the exogamy of the group and its solidarity. Otherwise "lineages will branch off and lose their sense of relationship [and] clans will not form." Service (1962: 115-118) refers to these solidifying elements under the heading of "pan-tribal sodalities."

Multilineage communities and patriclans are widespread and well recognized in the Central Highlands. Earlier ethnographic reports suggested that highly agnatic segmentary systems might even be typical of the area. Reevaluation of Central Highland social structure, however, suggests that it should be described as "loose" or "loosely structured." Indeed, Barnes (1962) has attempted to account for the mistaken emphasis upon strict, segmentary lineage systems, and Langness (1964) has recently discussed this theme. "Looseness" can be operationally defined as referring to the low probability with which an individual's residence, marriage, land tenure, leadership, or loyalties—broadly, his group affiliation—can be predicted from knowledge of the local rule of descent. "Looseness" thus refers to an explicit or implicit lineality that is but weakly realized in its several behavioral prescriptions or implications. Calling attention to variability among jurally equivalent statuses, "loose" implies, in the Highland context, either that agnatic prescriptions or presumptions are irregularly followed, or that the regularities of certain behavior are more complex than simple unilineal rules can explain.

Present Central Highland societies appear to be neither uniformly loose nor highly lineal-agnatic. One or two societies are reported to have well-defined agnatic and segmentary systems: the Enga (Meggitt 1962: 159) with relatively tight "agnatic hierarchies" and an average of 86 per cent resident male agnates, and the Bena (Nupasafa) with 30 per cent non-agnate resident males (Langness 1964: 166). These two Highland societies are geographically distant and exist under quite different ecological and demographic conditions. Two adjacent and linguistically related peoples— the Tairora and Agarabi of the extreme eastern Highlands—differ perceptibly in the clarity and prominence of their clans. Thus at least those segments of the Central Highlands that are well known confront us with an agnatic emphasis in ideology that seems general in the whole area (and in much of the rest of New Guinea as well), but with differing degrees of lineality, or looseness, at the local level.

Is the postulated developmental sequence from recent patrilocal bands to coalescent larger communities with fixed residence supported by both ideological and sociological facts? The ubiquitous patrilineal ideology, surely a dramatic fact, is quite in keeping with other impressive region-wide uniformities of the Central Highland peoples. Can Steward's model of development—or any other—accommodate not only this fact but also the evident variability in agnation? An unbroken array of uniformly tight (or uniformly loose) agnatic structures in the Central Highlands would suggest a remarkably uniform development, but such extreme parallelism could hardly be predicted over so large an area and would be truly astonishing if it occurred. Diverse patterns of dislocation and concentration of bands could be anticipated, giving rise not only to such well known contrasts as that between village and homestead settlement, but also to a differential survival of earlier band characteristics and a differential development of typical features of lineage and clan. A late explosive growth of population and consolidation of larger groups certainly are not inconsistent with the jostling and maneuvering of uneasy neighbors and widely prevalent bellicosity. Small communities would have led a precarious socio-political existence, dependent upon flexibility and opportunism. The degree of flexibility almost certainly would have varied from one community to another, reflecting particular local circumstances, so that either system—"tight" or "loose"—need not be considered, *a priori,* anomalous for failing to fit some ideal uniformity, even assuming a similar past and similar development.

This paper has expressed the view that the Central Highlands of New Guinea have been remade within the last three centuries through the introduction of a new food plant, sweet potatoes, which, under the prevailing conditions, proved to be an innovation of radical possibilities. I have attempted to sketch the kind of sociological developments that may have occurred and to relate these to some of the problems that are recognized in interpreting Central Highlands societies. If further evidence supports the developments implied here, the Central Highlands would make an admirable place to test theories of tribalization, clan formation, and societal evolution. There is no implication that all questions about Central Highlands societies and cultures are developmental ones, but a radical reshaping of society in the recent past would certainly imply that neglect of the developmental dimension can hardly be justified.

NOTES

1. I am indebted to the Ford Foundation for a grant in 1953-55 and to the National Science Foundation for grant no. G-22676 in 1963-64 under which I have been able to carry out research in the Eastern Highlands of New Guinea, in part the basis for the present paper. My suggestions may be more particular to the eastern end of the Highlands but are thought to have some relevance as well to the Central Highlands in general. For their helpful comments on a previous draft of this paper, I would like to thank J. Barrau, N. Bowers, L. J. Brass, P. Brown, R. N. H. Bulmer, S. Bulmer, H. Cutler, R. M. Glasse, R. E. Greengo, L. L. Langness, M. J. Meggitt, P. L. Newman, K. J. Pataki, R. Rappaport, R. G. Robbins, S. G. Robbins, J. Street, A. P. Vayda, J. N. Warner, and J. P. White.

2. In the Telefomin area several peoples depend more heavily upon taro than sweet potatoes (Brookfield 1962: 243-246).

3. Winged beans are questionable as a pre-ipomoean crop in the Highlands. A Tairora legend assigns the origin of winged beans—and of pigs—to a particular spot near the village of Batainabura. In the larger context of Tairora beliefs regarding plant origins, this suggests a late appearance of the crop among these people of the Eastern Highlands. Only within recent memory has a particular large variety of the winged bean reached the Tairora from the Gadsup, a people bordering on the Markham Valley and hence the lowlands.

4. In most of the area Brookfield's characterization of agricultural methods can be assumed as dealing mainly with the cropping of sweet potatoes. In Telefomin, for example, where a different crop—taro—is dominant, the characterization also differs (Brookfield 1962: 247). This is of course reasonable since his interest is in defining the general area in terms of the methods that are of greatest present importance, especially since these are also the methods which now set the Central Highlands apart from the rest of New Guinea.

5. Interestingly enough, in certain parts of the Eastern Highlands District domestic

pigs are even now "hunted" with bow and arrow in preference to killing them by other means.

6. The final report on the bone material from S. Bulmer's two excavations has not yet appeared and may throw some light on the present question.

7. A population of 1,146 would mean eighteen to twenty bands averaging a conservative 60 members.

8. Anthropologists probably tend to err more often on the side of underestimating rate of change than the opposite.

BIBLIOGRAPHY

BARNES, J. A. 1962. African Models in the New Guinea Highlands. Man 62: 5-9.

BERNDT, R. M. 1962. Excess and Restraint: Social Control among a New Guinea Mountain People. Chicago.

BROOKFIELD, H. C. 1962. Local Study and Comparative Method: An Example from Central New Guinea. Annals of the Association of American Geographers 52: 242-254.

———— 1964. The Ecology of Highland Settlement: Some Suggestions. American Anthropologist 66: ii, 20-38.

BROOKFIELD, H. C., and P. BROWN. 1963. Struggle for Land: Agriculture and Group Territories Among the Chimbu of the New Guinea Highlands. Melbourne.

BROWN, P. 1962. Non-agnates among the Patrilineal Chimbu. Journal of the Polynesian Society 71: 57-69.

BULMER, S. 1964a. Prehistoric Stone Implements from the New Guinea Highlands. Oceania 34: 246-268.

———— 1964b. Radiocarbon Dates from New Guinea. Journal of the Polynesian Society 73: 327-328.

BULMER, S., and R. BULMER. 1964. The Prehistory of the Australian New Guinea Highlands. American Anthropologist 66: ii, 162-182.

CONKLIN, H. C. 1963. The Oceanian-African Hypothesis and the Sweet Potato. Plants and the Migrations of Pacific Peoples, ed. J. Barrau, pp. 129-133. Honolulu.

GIFFORD, E. W. 1926. Miwok Lineages and the Political Unit in Aboriginal California. American Anthropologist 28: 389-401.

HOLMBERG, A. R. 1950. Nomads of the Long Bow: The Siriono of Eastern Bolivia. Publications of the Smithsonian Institution, Institute of Social Anthropology 10: 1-104.

LANGNESS, L. L. 1964. Some Problems in the Conceptualization of Highlands Social Structures. American Anthropologist 66; ii, 162-182.

MEGGITT, M. J. 1958. The Enga of the New Guinea Highlands. Oceania 28: 253-330.

———— 1962. Growth and Decline of Agnatic Descent Groups Among the Mae Enga of the New Guinea Highlands. Ethnology 1: 158-165.

MCKAUGHAN, H. P. 1964. A study of Divergence in Four New Guinea Languages. American Anthropologist 66: ii, 98-120.

NISHAYAMA, I. 1963. The Origin of the Sweet Potato Plant. Plants and the Migrations of Pacific Peoples, ed. J. Barrau, pp. 119-128. Honolulu.

POUWER, J. 1960. Loosely Structured Societies in Netherlands New Guinea. Bijdragen tot de Taal-, Land-, en Volkenkunde 116: 109-118.

ROBBINS, R. G. 1963. Correlations of Plant Patterns and Population Migrations into the Australian New Guinea Highlands. Plants and the Migrations of Pacific Peoples, ed. J. Barrau, pp. 45-59. Honolulu.

SERVICE, E. R. 1962. Primitive Social Organization: An Evolutionary Perspective. New York.

STEWARD, J. H. 1955. Theory of Culture Change: The Methodology of Multilinear Evolution. Urbana.

WARNER, J. N. 1962. Sugar Cane: An Indigenous Papuan Cultigen. Ethnology 1: 405-411.

WATSON, J. B. 1963. Krakatoa's Echo? Journal of the Polynesian Society 72: 152-155.

———— 1964. A Previously Unreported Root Crop from the New Guinea Highlands. Ethnology 3: 1-5.

WATSON, V. 1955. Pottery in the Eastern Highlands of New Guinea. Southwestern Journal of Anthropology 11: 121-128.

WURM, S. A. 1964. Australian New Guinea Highlands Languages and the Distribution of their Typological Features. American Anthropologist 66: ii, 77-97.

YEN, D. E. 1963. Sweet Potato Variation and its Relation to Human Migration in the Pacific. Plants and the Migrations of Pacific Peoples, ed. J. Barrau, pp. 93-117. Honolulu.

2

THE STRATEGIES OF
HUNTING IN NEW GUINEA

Ralph Bulmer

In New Guinea as elsewhere a general feature of hunting is that it is a pleasurable activity. Although it often serves necessary economic and social ends, providing in many parts of New Guinea a small but still significant component of animal protein in the diet, or furnishing game animals without which ritual or ceremonial activities would be impossible or incomplete, the reports of numerous observers suggest that enthusiasm for hunting is frequently greater than its material contribution to the satisfaction of human needs would appear to warrant. It would also seem reasonable to argue that the appeal of hunting is not simply to be explained as that of a sanctioned outlet to human (and especially, male,) aggression. Hunting is a sport, a game, in which man pits himself against animate, if non-human, adversaries. It is also very frequently a competition in which the individual hunter's performance is evaluated, by himself and others, against that of his fellows. It involves concentration of attention, intellectual as well as physical effort.

I am concerned in this review with the intellectual aspect of hunting with the range and combinations of strategies which the hunters employ to locate quarry, place themselves in proximity to it, and despatch or capture it. These strategies must in their basic forms constitute a very ancient part of man's heritage, and indeed all of them he shares with non-human predators. I would argue that they probably have deep-rooted appeal in their own right, regardless of the ends they serve. It is notable that all of them are also used in war; and their analogues may be found in other fields of human activity.

The strategies of hunting must be considered firstly in relation to the kinds of game pursued, to the terrain, to the available technology and to the available manpower. However, one must also note that different strategies require different kinds of information and skill on the part of the hunter: some require elaborate and precise knowledge of animals and plants, while others do not. To understand indigenous New Guinea systems of knowledge

Reproduced by permission of A. P. Elkin, Editor of *Oceania,* and Ralph Bulmer from *Oceania,* 38:302-318 (1968).

about the natural environment one must therefore have an appreciation of
the hunting strategies adopted. Such knowledge would also appear to be
crucial to the interpretation of many aspects of New Guinea warfare, ritual,
cosmology and art.

Although there are many hundreds of brief references in the literature,
hunting in New Guinea and other parts of Melanesia has received little systematic attention from ethnographers. There are two main reasons for this.
One is that for the majority of Melanesian peoples it appears to represent
only a minor sector of the economy, being a part-time or seasonal activity
for men and boys. It is often only some men and youths in a community who
are expert hunters and spend much time in this activity. The other reason
for its neglect is that until very recent years it has been extremely difficult
for an anthropologist to obtain the zoological and botanical information he
requires in order to understand and evaluate indigenous hunting. A good
modern handbook of New Guinea birds (Rand and Gilliard 1967), intelligible to the amateur naturalist, only became available in 1967; and there
is still no comparable guide to any other group of New Guinea animals or
plants. It is also only in the last few years that the increasing scale of research in both the biological and social sciences in New Guinea has made
it possible for at least some fortunate ethnographers to enjoy collaboration
in the field with professional zoologists and botanists.

Anell (1960) provides an excellent and fully referenced discussion of the
literature on hunting technology published up to 1955. Although this
author's main interests are in trait-distributions and their culture-historical
implications, he makes a number of penetrating functional interpretations,
some of which will be discussed below. The main defects of his study reflect
inadequacies in the primary source material, notably inaccurate or inadequate identifications of the kinds of game obtained by the various techniques
described, and under-emphasis of the importance of forest hunting, particularly of arboreal mammals, as against the collective hunting methods widely
and conspicuously adopted in lowland grasslands and savannah. The present
survey, which may be read as a supplement to Anell's work, attempts to
correct these points and to take into account publications since 1955 which
contain useful information (notably Meggitt 1958: 283–6; Oosterwal 1961:
62–6; Neuhaus 1962: 70–90; Pospisil 1963: 231–48; H. Fischer 1963:
56–61, 65; S. & R. Bulmer 1964: 49–51; Serpenti 1965: 54–7; R. Bulmer
1967). Unless otherwise specified the sections on hunting technology and
strategy draw on Anell or on sources utilised by him, or on my own field
data from the Kyaka Enga (north slopes of Mt. Hagen) and Karam (Kai-
ronk Valley, Schrader Range).

GAME AVAILABLE AND ITS UTILISATION[1]

The only big-game animals in New Guinea are feral pig (*Sus scrofa pa-
puensis*)[2], descended from stock introduced, presumably by man, prior to

3,000 B.C. (S. Bulmer 1966), and three species of cassowary (*Casuarius*).[3] These are the only two kinds of creatures which grow as large as man, and they are the only ones which are dangerous if attacked, being capable of maiming or killing a hunter with their tusks or claws respectively.

Wild pig are common in many parts of New Guinea and adjacent islands up to about 5,000 ft., but they appear to be sparse or absent at higher altitudes. They seem to favour the forest edge or disturbed forest, and mixed ecological zones containing grassland, gardens and some secondary bush, rather than deep primary forest. In many lowland areas feral and domestic stock form a single breeding population, all male domestic pigs being castrated and wild boars serving the domestic sows. In some areas domestic stock is also replenished by the capture of piglets, and in extreme cases, such as that of the Tor (Oosterwal 1961: 70), pigs are not bred at all domestically, all stock kept being obtained initially by capture. Only in Highland areas where wild pigs are virtually absent do domestic pigs form distinct breeding populations.

Cassowaries of two large species (*C. casuarius* and *C. unappendiculatus*)[4], adults of which weigh up to perhaps 100 lb. are widely distributed in forest and savannah in lowland New Guinea. Dwarf cassowaries (*C. bennetti*), adults of which weigh up to 50 lb., are present in lowland and mountain forests up to 10,000 ft. However, all three species are only common in areas where human populations are very sparse; they have been eliminated from many densely settled regions, including much of the Highlands. Cassowaries are semi-domesticated in many parts of New Guinea, captured chicks being reared to adulthood for trade and slaughter, and for their plumes.

Wallabies are the most numerous terrestrial game of any size in some parts of New Guinea, but their distribution is very uneven. The literature on hunting is particularly inadequate in its failure to indicate which species or genera of wallabies are being captured, even where these are the most important category of game. The largest, the Agile Wallaby (*Protemnodon agilis*) appears to be common in sparsely populated savannah and grassland areas of southern New Guinea. The smaller scrub wallabies (*Thylogale* spp.) are widely but unevenly distributed in forest edge and grassland zones in the lowlands and restricted areas at high altitudes, but seem nowhere to be common. The small forest wallabies (*Dorcopsis* spp.) are said to have been common in the recent past in some mountain forest areas, but are now absent or very rare where human populations are intensive.

Other terrestrial mammals, present in forest and grasslands, include bandicoots (Peramelidae), echidnas (which are very rare except in restricted localities), and a wide variety of rodents.

Relatively undisturbed forest regions at all altitudes are rich in arboreal mammals, including tree-kangaroos (*Dendrolagus* spp.) cuscuses (*Phalanger* spp.), ringtail possums (*Pseudocheirus* spp.) and giant rats (e.g. *Mal-*

lomys rothschildi), and a wide range of smaller marsupials and rodents. Certain of these creatures feed on the ground as well as in the trees, e.g. some of the giant rats, the ringtail possum, *Pseudocheirus cupreus* (Brass 1964: 174) and the cuscus, *Phalanger gymnotis*, while the latter is said by local informants characteristically to have its lair in rock crevices or under tree-roots. Large fruit bats or "flying foxes" (*Pteropus* spp., *Dobsonia moluccensis*) are common in forest and well-timbered garden areas up to about 6,000 ft., and have their roosts in trees and caves. There are also many species of small bats, both insectivorous and frugivorous, in lowland and mid-mountain forest areas up to approximately the same altitude.

In lowland forests large reptiles are also significant as game, including particularly pythons and monitor lizards. Above about 4,500 ft. only the occasional small python, boiga, or agamid lizard contributes much to human diet, though the numerous small skinks are sometimes eaten, while the eggs of those which breed in subterranean colonies are considered a delicacy in some areas.

The bird fauna of New Guinea, and particularly of the forest zones, is extremely rich. Although it is only in lowland forests that large birds such as crown pigeons (*Goura* spp.), palm cockatoos (*Probosciger aterrimus*) and hornbills (*Aceros plicatus*) are numerous, relatively undisturbed forest areas at all altitudes contain a wealth of bird life which can provide a substantial source of animal protein to skilful hunters. There are no detailed studies available of the quantities of birds of different groups taken by hunters, but the author's own observations in Highlands forest areas indicate that relatively small fruit- and blossom-feeding birds (doves, honeyeaters, lorikeets) constitute the bulk of the game taken.

All these vertebrate animals, together with frogs and a very large number of invertebrate species, contribute to human diet. Plumes of many species of birds, especially birds of paradise of the genera *Paradisaea, Epimachus, Astrapia, Pteridophora* and *Lophorina,* parrots, hornbills, hawks and cassowaries, and pelts of mammals, especially certain cuscuses and tree-kangaroos, provide highly valued ornaments. Bone of cassowary, dog, pig, wallaby, tree-kangaroo and the larger fruit-bats has many technological uses. Teeth of pig, larger marsupials and especially dog are, or were formerly, used for ornaments and, in some areas, as exchange valuables; incisors of giant rats (especially *Mallomys rothschildi*) and of certain marsupials were used, before introduction of steel tools, as gravers, and pig tusks are still widely used as scrapers. Hornbill mandibles and cassowary claws are used as spear points; the maxillae and talons of these and many other birds, and mandibles or crania and other bones of many mammals, are kept as trophies in many areas and often worn as ornaments. Skins of monitor lizards and of ringtail possums (*Pseudocheirus* spp.) are used as drum-skins.

Bird plumes and to a lesser extent mammal pelts, live animals, smoked mammal and reptile carcases and other animal products, were of considerable importance in local trade or gift-exchange in pre-European times. In parts of Western and Northern New Guinea trade in bird of paradise plumes with collectors from the Indonesian Islands has a great antiquity. External trade in plumes increased enormously during the early colonial period until it was declared illegal in Australian territory in 1922 and in Netherlands New Guinea in 1931. In many regions, however, internal trade in bird of paradise plumes continues unabated and has apparently intensified in scale in many parts of New Guinea since the Central Highlands were brought under administration in the 1930's (R. Bulmer, 1962).

Economic and Social Significance of Hunting

Archaeological evidence indicates that New Guinea was occupied by man at a period before full domestication of plants and animals can plausibly be postulated (S. Bulmer, 1964). Early human populations must have lived then by hunting and gathering. However, with the exception of groups using wild sago as a staple food no contemporary or recent peoples have been described who do not rely on horticulture to provide the bulk of their diet. Pig husbandry in some form is also almost universal in New Guinea. The extent to which garden produce, or sago, and domestic pork are supplemented by wildlife in the diet varies, as a general rule, inversely with the density of the human population and the extent of deforestation and other human-induced change to the environment. At one extreme, such groups as the Pala of New Ireland (Neuhaus 1962), the Kaulong and Sengseng of S.E. New Britain (Goodale, pers. comm.), and the forest dwellers of the Arfak Mountains in West Irian (Mayr 1932) or of parts of the Saruwaged Range in the Territory of New Guinea (Van Deusen, pers. comm.), are believed to obtain a substantial proportion of the animal protein in their diet by hunting. At the other extreme, game is obtained only in negligible quantities by the dense populations of the Asaro Valley grasslands or of the lower Chimbu Valley in the Highlands. However even in these groups it seems possible that prior to European contact small vertebrate and invertebrate animals, obtained in gardens, grasslands and bush-fallow, contributed significantly to the diet of women and children.

Apart from the material reasons already noted, hunting and trapping are important to horticultural populations as a means of protecting gardens from depredations of wild pig, rodents, fruit-bats and other fauna. In many New Guinea societies game is also periodically required for ritual consumption or ceremonial distribution. In these and other contexts in which success in hunting is socially as well as economically significant, either for the individual or for the group, associated ritual observances and magic are often highly elaborated. Cases in point are the extensive hunting magic employed by the Pala of New Ireland (Neuhaus 1962: 70–90) and the ritual observances associated with cassowary hunting among the Karam of Schrader Range (R. Bulmer 1967).

Game is captured alive rather than intentionally killed under three main circumstances: firstly to keep the meat in good condition if it is not intended for immediate consumption; secondly, so that it can be ritually killed [e.g. wild boar among the people of Tor (Oosterwal 1961: 64–5) and certain other people of southern and western New Guinea; large marsupials among the Karam of the Schrader Range (R. Bulmer 1967: 25)], or die in a ritually appropriate manner [e.g. *Harpyopsis* eagle among the Kyaka Enga (R. Bulmer 1957: 225)]; thirdly, so that it can be kept domestically. In addition to the semi-domestication of feral pig and cassowary already mentioned, spotted cuscus (*Phalanger maculatus*) and occasionally other cuscuses and ringtail possums are sometimes kept as pets until such time as they are eaten. Hornbills, white cockatoos *(Cacatua galerita)* and less frequently other species of parrots are also captured, as nestlings, and kept as pets for periodic plucking. It is said that feral dog puppies are captured and tamed in some areas. Conclusive evidence of this appears to be lacking, though pre-European domestic dogs in much of interior New Guinea were certainly extremely similar in appearance and behaviour to feral populations.[5] As with the pig, it is assumed that man introduced the dog to New Guinea, though archaeological evidence for the possible date of introduction is so far lacking.

In general, hunting (with weapons) and trapping are activities for men and boys, while women and children of both sexes collect or capture small mammals, frogs and other small vertebrates and invertebrates. An exception here is that larvae of certain moths and cerambycid beetles found in sago or in timber, which are highly valued as food in many parts of New Guinea, are normally obtained by men, since this work involves use of axe or adze. Women are however often mobilized as beaters where large-scale drives are employed, and as carriers to transport the game. The place of hunting on the male side of the sexual division of labour may be related to the assignment to women of the more time-consuming activities in horticulture and sago-extraction; the fact that women are more encumbered with family and domestic duties than men; the very widespread prohibition on women using, and in some cases even handling, weapons and axes or adzes; and the very widespread New Guinea views that it is inappropriate or ridiculous, if not improper, for women to climb trees.

HUNTING

Weapons

The main traditional weapons of the hunt are the bow and arrow and the spear. Clubs and throwing-sticks are used, but less widely. Blow-pipes are known only in limited areas of West Irian and of New Britain and New Ireland, slings only in restricted areas of the Bismarck Archipelago. In any one region the many categories of arrows used typically fall into three or four functional classes: with a single palm-wood or bone point, for medium sized mammals and large birds; three- or four-pronged (with prongs often barbed) for small birds and mammals; bird-bolts with a blunt hard-wood tip, especially for birds with valuable plumes, so that these will not be damaged; and bamboo-bladed, for large game, especially pig. All the projectile weapons used (arrows, throwing spears, blow-pipe darts, throwing sticks) are accurate and efficient only at a short range. Thus getting as close as possible to the quarry is a major objective in all forms of hunting.

The Strategies

The forms of hunting in New Guinea may conveniently be classified under nine headings: stalking, ambush, luring, besetting, chase, simple drive, encircling drive, ambush-drive and trapping. I adopt these as useful descriptive categories, rather than as an entirely logical framework for the analysis of hunting systems. In fact a "grammar" of hunting could be constructed which would reduce them all to a limited number of constitutory elements, and indicate the transformations required to convert any one of them into any other. At some future stage it will probably prove valuable to undertake this exercise, either in the analysis of single well-described hunting systems, or in comparative studies. However in preliminary sorting of what are still very uneven and inadequate data, these categories are not unproductive. By using them one can point to certain types of strategy which appear to be particularly frequently used, and on which many variations, elaborations and extensions are operated.

I. *Stalking* may be defined as the covert approach by a hunter to free-moving or potentially free-moving quarry. This very simple strategy is practised to some extent throughout New Guinea in the pursuit of game of all all sizes. However, except possibly in the cases of wallaby hunting in the southern grasslands (Williams 1936: 221), and of the nocturnal hunting of forest mammals, about which very little has been reported, this appears to be an *ad hoc* strategy, adopted when game is fortuitously spotted, and not conducted with any notable expertise or with many elaborations. Thus there are no records of New Guineans using personal camouflage in stalking, and few of their daubing themselves with mud to eliminate body-odours. Although hunters are often skilled in interpreting tracks, droppings, food remnants, etc. information of this order is generally applied to other strategies—ambush, besetting or trapping. Stalking is probably most productive in bird-shooting, especially when combined with the use of decoy-calls (see luring, below). However observations in Highlands forests suggest that though birds of many different species are obtained by stalking, quantities are small as compared with those obtained by ambush. It is possible that snakes and other reptiles are largely obtained by this strategy, though information on this point is very limited. The use of hand-operated pole-snares to capture pythons and lizards has been reported from some areas.

II. *Ambush* is here applied to those strategies in which a stationary hunter waits for game to approach. Numerous variants and elaborations, appropriate to different categories of game and different routine activities on the part of certain game have been reported. Most general of all is ambush at feeding places. Pig and cassowary are shot or speared in this way, sometimes by a hunter safely out of reach in a tree (Bergman 1961: 175). Fruit-bats are shot or struck while feeding at bananas or pawpaws. However, most general of all, at least in highland areas, is the shooting of frugivorous and blossom-feeding birds (doves, small parrots, honey-eaters, flower-peckers and certain birds of paradise) at their food trees. In lowland areas hand-nets are in some places used in the same context. In mountain forest several species of birds, including some birds of paradise, are shot from ambush at drinking or bathing pools. In more open country doves (*Reinwardtoena, Macropygia* spp.) are shot at drinking pools, especially, apparently, saline pools. The valuable adult males of those birds of paradise, especially *Paradisaea* spp. which indulge in competitive, collective display, are most frequently obtained by ambush at their regular display trees, or at their display grounds. Birds of various species, especially sizable or otherwise valuable ones such as hawks or large pigeons, are ambushed at the nest, when returning to feed young (see also "besetting", below).

A frequent elaboration of ambush at feeding or watering places, display grounds or nests, is the construction of a blind or hide for the hunter, either in the branches of a tree or on the ground.

Variants and extensions of these types of ambush strategy include the use of hand-operated snares at display-trees, feeding places or nests, and, in some lowland areas, the use of bird-lime (the viscous sap of breadfruit or certain other trees, spread on perches or on sticks which are manipulated to ensnare the birds). Yet other extensions will be discussed under "luring" and "trapping" below.

Another form of ambush is the use of switches or brushes to knock down small birds or bats in their flight-lines, sometimes by a hunter concealed behind a screen in open country, or standing on a bridge above a water-course. An extension of this strategy, used in restricted areas of mainly northern New Guinea, is the hanging of nets in the flight-lines of birds or bats. At night fire is sometimes used to dazzle birds or bats so that they hit the nets.

III. *Luring* is a modified form of ambush in which the hunter not merely anticipates the voluntary movement of game in his direction, but takes action to bring this about. The two commonest forms are the use of food-bait, and the use of decoy-calls.

In Mimika and Nimboran (West Irian) and certain other areas where sago is plentiful, a sago-palm is felled and split as a bait for pig, which are then ambushed (Pouwer 1955: 39–40; Kouwenhoven 1956: 16) (See also "Ambush-drive" below.) Examples of birds being taken with bait include Little King Birds of Paradise (*Cicinnurus regius*) captured with bait and hand-operated snare (Bergman 1957: 127); Sacred Kingfisher (*Halcyon sancta*), taken with a grasshopper on a cord, used as a gorge, by Kyaka Enga boys; and herons, captured with a hook baited with a fish, on New Ireland (Neuhaus 1962: 89).

Many New Guinea peoples are highly adept at imitating bird-calls. In my own experience, although hunters not infrequently get a response from such birds as small fruit doves and cuckoo-doves (*Ptilinopus* spp., *Macropygia* spp.) by calling to them, they seldom succeed in attracting them close enough to shoot by this method, and the only species which are regularly shot with the aid of this technique are the very small mouse-babblers (*Crateroscelis* spp.) of the forest floor. However other authors report or imply successful use of this method to attract larger birds including megapodes (*Megapodius, Talegalla*) (Van Eechoud 1962: 135). In the Tor (Oosterwal 1961: 63) and some other parts of West Irian whistles of hollowed fruit are made to produce bird-calls.

Captive chicks or fledglings of many species are used to decoy their parents, e.g. cassowary (Van Eechoud, *loc. cit.*) and, in the Schrader Mountains, goshawk (*Accipiter* sp.), chestnut rail (*Rallicula forbesi*) and whistlers (*Pachycephala schlegelii*). The use of captive adult or tame birds as decoys seems, however, to be very rare.

In some areas of southern New Guinea wallabies are attracted by stamping on or striking the ground, as well as by calling (Williams 1936: 221; Serpenti 1965: 55).

Other forms of luring include the placing of perches at drinking pools, so that birds will alight in the direct line of fire of the hunter; the construction of artificial pole-tracks to lead arboreal marsupials towards the hunter (Mafulu—Williamson 1912: 190); and the reported Sepik use of fire at night to attract shags (*Phalacrocorax sulcirostris*) which are said to plummet into the flames (Rand and Gilliard 1967: 34).

IV. *Besetting* is here applied to a strategy which is in some respects the converse of ambush. In this case the quarry is at rest and, often, concealed, in its lair, roost or nest, where it is surprised by the approaching hunter. It is also an extension of stalking strategy, in that the hunter covertly approaches his quarry, but in this case he is taking advantage of prior knowledge of the animal's location and unguarded state, and its lack of opportunity to observe his approach or restricted opportunity to escape. In forest hunting this is a particularly frequent method of obtaining arboreal mammals, though many birds are also taken in this way, and it seems that it is frequently adopted in cassowary hunting and occasionally in pig hunting. Successful use of this method requires, even more than ambush strategy does, detailed knowledge of animal behaviour and the ability to interpret correctly the evidence of tracks, droppings, food remnants, browsed foliage etc. Birds and mammals are often captured by hand in this strategy, or struck down with a stick, though arrows or spears are used when appropriate.

Cassowaries are beset at the nest, pigs at their regular sleeping places (Cheesman 1949: 268). Diurnal creatures, including many birds, are captured at their roosts or nests in dusk or darkness. Certain birds of paradise (*Seleucides, Diphyllodes*) are readily taken by hand by skilled hunters using this method: in the case of *Seleucides* hunters use long climbing poles to reach the roosts (Bergman 1957: 124–7). Most arboreal mammals are nocturnal, and if captured by this method can be taken during daylight, as is the case with nocturnal birds such as owls, frogmouths, and owlet-nightjars. Those mammals which have their lairs in tree-hollows (e.g. the giant rat, *Mallomys rothschildi*) are in some cases difficult to extract and capable of injuring the hunter if tackled by hand. Smoke may be used to force them out, or hooked and pointed sticks to extract them.

Bats are obtained in day-time by being shot or struck at their roosts in caves or trees, or knocked down in caves or cave entrances with switches or brushes.

V. The *Chase* follows naturally from stalking, ambush or besetting when a creature is surprised and wounded or otherwise impeded in making its escape. Apart from this it occurs as a simple strategy, applied in an *ad hoc* way for obtaining many small, mainly terrestrial creatures, and perhaps more systematically in the capture of many arboreal mammals and reptiles. Men and boys in many parts of New Guinea are extremely agile tree-climbers, and supplement their natural agility by skilful construction and use of ladders, climbing poles and climbing-pegs driven into tree-trunks.

Extensions of this strategy include the use of dogs to flush and run down larger terrestrial game (pig, wallaby, terrestrial cuscus) and to tree arboreal mammals. In the pursuit of arboreal mammals a further extension is the systematic felling or lopping of all trees adjacent to that in which the quarry is located, so that it will not have the opportunity to escape overhead. It is unclear to what extent this was practicable before steel tools were introduced to New Guinea, but the practice is now commonly adopted in such widely separated areas as Japen Island (Cheesman 1949: 177) and the Schrader Range.

In areas of dense human population and relatively sparse population of wild mammals of any size, the chase is of negligible importance. But in heavily forested regions where human populations are small it may in some cases account for a high proportion of game captured.

VI. The term *drive* is used in the literature to describe three or four strategies all of which are elaborations or extensions of the chase and in all of which a substantial number of persons may participate.

VI*a*. *The simple drive* is where a group of hunters coordinate their efforts in flushing and chasing game, generally in a restricted area from which its escape is impeded by natural barriers. Thus in seasonally flooded areas of southern and western New Guinea advantage is taken of the concentration of animal life in limited areas above flood-level, and of the creatures' impeded movements under marshy conditions (e.g. wallaby hunting on Frederik Hendrik Island—Serpenti 1965: 54–5). When dogs are used, pig can also be effectively hunted in this way. Perhaps the prototype of the simple drive is the case of a group of small boys hunting rats in garden-fallow—the sheer fact of numbers makes the creatures' escape more difficult, but there is little else to be said in favour of this technique, which, except in the cases cited above, appears to be a strictly *ad hoc* strategy.

VI*b*. *Encircling drive* is the strategy where hunters deliberately surround game in a restricted area and converge on it. An example is cassowary and pig hunting in fairly open lowland forest, where lines of hunters converge on game which is hemmed in at the flanks by such natural barriers as rivers or cliff-faces. An alternative to closing in is to force game to attempt to escape by use of fire or dogs. This is a very widely used collective method of pig-hunting, but many other smaller grassland animals are deliberately or incidentally captured at the same time or by the same methods. Mikloucho-Maclay (D. Fischer 1956: 203–5) gives a vivid account of a fire drive on the Rai coast. On a smaller scale, when gardens are being cleared rats and other small animals are commonly obtained by this strategy.

Of all the hunting methods used in New Guinea the fire drive is undoubtedly the one with the greatest ecological significance, since the repeated burning of grasslands prevents the regeneration of forest. It is also probably the only type of hunting which is regularly organised or coordinated by members of more than one local community (see below).

VI*c*. *Ambush-drive,* as the name implies, can be seen as an extension of ambush strategy, being distinguished by its combined use of hunters in ambush and of beaters.

In some savannah areas of lowland New Guinea this is the largest-scale form of hunting, pig, wallaby and cassowary being the main game obtained. The same technique is used, but apparently more rarely, in lowland forest. In coastal and lowland areas of south-east New Guinea and in scattered parts of northern New Guinea and the Bismarck Archipelago nets are used in conjunction with the drive. In other regions ambushers wait behind screens or fences. In large drives women and boys frequently participate as beaters. To create noise rattles and, sometimes, trumpets are used, as well as the human voice. Dogs are also sometimes employed to drive game. In Schrader Range forest wallaby hunting one or two hunters conceal themselves by a wallaby track, across which they place only a low flimsy barrier. When flushed by another hunter or hunters, sometimes aided by dogs, animals seeking to escape along the track stop in confusion at the unexpected barrier and offer an easy target to the ambushers.

A special device used in parts of southern New Guinea in the drive is a "pig-fender", a loop of rattan with or without a net, attached to a pole. This enables dangerous beasts to be kept at a distance, and animals to be captured alive, for ceremonial slaughter or domestication.

An extension of the ambush-drive involves luring pigs with bait, and then driving them into nets.

VII. *Trapping* embraces two groups of strategies both of which are elaborations of ambush, the one, using unbaited traps, directly so, the other, using baited traps, deriving from ambush indirectly, through luring. The diversity and extensive use of traps and snares in Melanesia is, as Anell points out, to be related both to the fact that most New Guinea peoples are relatively sedentary horticulturalists and only part-time hunters, and to the necessity for horticultural populations to protect their crops from the depredations of wild life, especially pigs, rodents, and fruit-bats.

Apart from the hand-operated snares, lures and nets already mentioned, a wide range of trapping devices is regularly used in New Guinea. Springes (spring-snares) of many varieties are most generally and frequently used of all, particularly for birds, fruit-bats and smaller terrestrial and arboreal mammals, but also on occasion for wallaby, cassowary and even pig. For smaller creatures they are sometimes baited, and for fruit-bats they are set over bunches of ripening bananas in gardens, but for larger terrestrial and arboreal game the usual technique is simply to place them in runs. Springes are also set at the entrances to mammals' lairs and at birds' nests and at bower-birds' bowers, and at the display grounds of certain birds of paradise (e.g. *Parotia* spp.); sometimes elaborate structures are made to channel game into a springe, as in the Schrader Range technique of enclosing the whole bower of a gardner bower-bird *(Amblyornis macgregoriae)* in a hut-like structure the only entrances to which contain springes. Simple snares are widely but less intensively employed to take birds. Baited tube-snares (involving the same principle as the springe) are widely used for small rodents. Baited dead-falls and log-traps are widely used for pig, and smaller versions of the same for rodents, bandicoots and even small ground-feeding birds (e.g. pittas, which are valued for their plumes, in the lower Baiyer Valley). Baited box-traps, with and without clap-doors, and funnel-traps, are used in some areas for pig and for smaller mammals. Spring-spears or spring-poles are used in limited areas of West Irian for pig (Pospisil 1963: 241; Oosterwal 1961 : 66). Simple pit-falls are constructed for pig and in some Highlands areas for wallaby. Spiked pit-falls are widely used for pigs, and in some areas for cassowary. Spikes, of wood or bamboo, are also set in the ground, beside a lowered portion of fence, to wound and capture pigs breaking into gardens. The use of bird-lime (viscous sap of certain trees) has only been reported in restricted areas of lowland New Guinea and Bismarck Archipelago.

Hunting and the Total Ecology

With the very important exception of the use of fire as an aid in the drive, the impact of hunting on the environment is negligible as compared with the impact of horticulture. It is probably only where natural habitats have been greatly reduced by clearing and burning that hunting becomes in itself a factor significantly reducing and even eliminating animal populations. At the same time man has probably significantly influenced the balance of nature in New Guinea by more subtle methods than garden clearing and burning. Systematic utilisation of wild food plants in forest areas, such as the extensive felling of sago palms both for food and to provide breeding grounds for edible sago-grubs (Gerbrands 1962) or the husbanding of self-propagating nut pandanus groves in mountain forest, must have some consequences for other flora and for fauna. The consequences of the introduction of the pig and dog as feral creatures are at present impossible to evaluate. The question of the relationship of pig to man in New Guinea is particularly intriguing. Even as a feral beast it appears, on present evidence, to be largely symbiotic with man, favouring the disturbed ecological zones which man creates and maintains and in some areas deriving much of its sustenance from the products or by-products of gardening or sago-exploitation. Other much smaller animals which are truly symbiotic with man include certain rats of the genus *Rattus,* while several species of small birds are plentiful in garden areas or human-created grasslands but are either absent or rare in zones of natural climax vegetation. It is also possible that certain predatory birds, such as the Black Kite (*Milvus migrans*) are only present in large areas of New Guinea because man has created ecological niches for them.

Thus in much of New Guinea man is hunting the creatures which his own activities of garden-making, sago-felling and grass-burning have enabled or encouraged to live there. It has been argued by Anell (1960: 1, 10, 12) that burning-off is particularly significant in this regard, in that it not merely prevents the development of climax vegetation, but creates areas of new tender grass-shoots which attract grazing animals (? wallabies) and also facilitate the movement of hunters stalking them.

The extent of hunting is in turn regulated by both environmental and social factors. In many New Guinea societies hunting is largely a seasonal activity, undertaken when weather conditions are optimal, during slack periods in the annual horticulture cycle, or when game is required for calendrically ordered feasts or ceremonials. Both the savannah drives of lowland Papuans and intensive forest hunting by such Highlands peoples as the Karam of the Schrader Range are seasonally restricted for a combination of all three reasons. Thus while Karam hunt sporadically for arboreal mammals at all times of the year, nocturnal hunting is almost entirely restricted to the drier winter months, June to August, when clear moonlit nights offer the best opportunities to spot game. This is also the slackest period in the horticultural cycle, the season at which family parties camp in the forest to harvest pandanus nuts, and the season at which game is traditionally assembled and smoked for the feasts accompanying initiation rituals (R. Bulmer: 1967). On the other hand fowling goes on in this area throughout the year, hunters ambushing birds at the particular food-trees which are blossoming or fruiting in each season. The forms of forest hunting which require much movement are miserable and apparently unrewarding in wet periods, but the weather is less inhibiting of ambush strategies.

Although few if any New Guinea peoples are conscious conservationists, ritual restrictions on hunting or on diet probably have conservational effects in many parts of New Guinea, as for example among the Maring of the Bismarck Range (Rappaport 1967), as also do the preservation of tracts of forest or of groves of trees in cultivation areas, for religious reasons. The assertion of community monopolies over game in defined territories and in some cases of individual rights over particular highly valued creatures (e.g. birds of paradise displaying in certain trees, in many parts of the Highlands of East New Guinea) may also be significant.

CONCLUSIONS

Strategies and technology. Apart from trapping, none of the strategies described requires, in its simplest form, more than a minimum of special equipment—spears and/or clubs for those applied in hunting larger terrestrial game, and some form of lighter projectile, hand-net or hand-snare for those employed for arboreal and smaller terrestrial game which cannot be captured by hand alone. At the same time, the very general use of the bow in Melanesia undoubtedly permits greater efficiency (and in some cases personal safety) in stalking, ambush and, to a lesser extent, in other strategies. Many variants of ambush strategy, certain forms of besetting and nearly all forms of trapping require efficient artefacts for rough woodworking (construction of hides, ladders, climbing poles, digging sticks), clearing of vegetation, or construction of traps. Knowledge of net-construction permits certain variants or elaborations of ambush or ambush-drive. It is interesting that although all New Guinea peoples have quite elaborate techniques of netting used in the construction of bags and, often personal garments, the use of nets in hunting seems mainly restricted to groups who also use nets for fishing, or at least live within relatively short distances of the coast.

Use of dogs. Dogs are used to discover or flush game, and in various forms of the chase and the drive, though none of these with the exception of pig-chasing by individual hunters or small groups would appear to be entirely dependent on their use. In the different kinds of drive dogs act as substitutes or supplements for human hunters or beaters. In forest hunting they appear to be particularly useful in the chase, in running down and treeing game.[6]

Strategies and terrain. All nine classes of strategy here described are used both in forest and in open country. However, both because of terrain and because of the kinds of game available, there is a premium on ambush, besetting and luring in forest conditions, and on the drive in open country. Larger scale forms of the drive are normally only practicable in open country, and it is only in open country that fire can be employed.

Strategies and game. There are reports of the use of all nine strategies in pig hunting, though the three drive strategies, trapping, ambush and luring appear to be the most widely employed. From the rather inadequate reports of cassowary hunting all strategies except the chase appear to be used, while trapping, ambush and besetting at the nest appear to be the most widely employed. For wallaby there are no reports of besetting: the various forms of the drive seem to be the main strategies employed, though trapping is also important in forest areas. For arboreal mammals all strategies except the drive are known, but ambush and luring appear to be little used, the emphasis being on besetting and trapping.

For most small rodents and other small terrestrial mammals trapping, besetting, the chase and the two simpler forms of the drive appear to be the strategies employed. All strategies except those of the drive are significant in hunting birds other than cassowaries, but widely different ranges are applied to different groups of birds and even to different species in some instances: ambush strategies appear to be the most widely and successfully employed, but besetting, trapping and stalking are also significant, luring is of relatively minor importance, and the chase only fortuitously employed. Little is known of techniques used in hunting reptiles, but stalking and chase appear to be the main strategies.

Strategies and social grouping. All strategies except those of the drive can be operated by a single hunter. However, in those commonly utilised in forest, especially chase and besetting of arboreal mammals, the most efficient hunting unit appears to be two or three men or boys, so that while one hunter is scaling a tree his companion or companions on the ground can catch the quarry if it falls or follow it if it escapes. Hunting pig or cassowary is dangerous for a single hunter, and solo hunting also gives the quarry considerably greater chance of escape than a group of two or three hunters will permit. It is only in certain forms of drive that a large hunting group is necessary and only in the ambush-drive that a formal division of labour between beaters and hunters is present. Where large-scale encircling drives with fire are operated, parties of hunters from several villages or hamlets often coordinate their efforts. On the other hand it seems unlikely that ambush-drives, even on the largest scale, normally involve more than a single organising community since the essence of this strategy is that the actual capture or slaughter of the game is concentrated in a limited area and performed by a single coordinated group of hunters. However, this last suggestion is put forward as a hypothesis only, and needs checking against further evidence.

Diversification and elaboration of strategies. The strategies with the largest number of variant forms reported are trapping, ambush, besetting and luring. The strategy with the greatest number of elaborations would appear to be ambush: the many forms of luring, trapping and ambush-drive can be interpreted as elaborations of this.

Strategies and information about the natural environment. Biologists have commented on the skill of some New Guinea peoples as naturalists (Mayr 1932: 90; Hitchcock 1964: 369; Diamond 1966; Rand and Gilliard 1967: 19). It is probably significant that in all cases they refer to groups who do most of their hunting in the forest, and use the diversity of strategies there appropriate. The present author is at a disadvantage in having had no personal experience of New Guinea societies in lowland areas in which drives are the main forms of hunting. However, it would seem from the literature that rather little detailed knowledge of animal ecology and behaviour is required for successful use of these techniques. In contrast the strategies applied in intensive forest hunting necessitate a very great deal of accurate information on the part of the hunter. There is probably literally no limit to the knowledge of zoology and botany which is at least indirectly relevant or potentially useful to him. To give but one example: a tree or plant may have no direct use for food or technology, but the ability to recognize it and the knowledge that its blossom, fruit, foliage, epiphytes or the insects which are found in it regularly provide food for certain kinds of birds or mammals, or that it regularly provides shelter from them, are highly relevant to the hunter.

Hunting, and particularly individual and small-group hunting methods, thus place a premium on knowledge and intelligence. There is probably a reciprocal, or, in Levi-Strauss's terms, dialectical, relationship between the intellectual organisation which is required to marshall the information necessary to forest hunting and the ingenuity which New Guinea peoples have shown in adapting and elaborating universal hunting strategies. The importance of game in ritual and ceremonial contexts, and of animal life in New Guinea cosmology, folklore and art reflect this intellectual orientation.

Some authors (e.g. Diamond 1966: 1104; see also Watson 1965) have made the plausible suggestion that this "hunting-orientation" in some areas where horticulture and pig-husbandry are infinitely more important than hunting in their contribution to human diet may reflect recent change from economic and demographic conditions under which the utilisation of wild food resources was more significant than it is now. At the same time one must also note that skill in the use of weapons and in bushcraft, and the intimate knowledge of the terrain which efficiency in hunting demands, have clear survival value, both when crops fail and in times of war or other social crisis.

Finally, one may make or reiterate the obvious points that in New Guinea both hunting and warfare are male activities; that the weapons employed in the two activities are largely the same; that the basic strategies in hunting are also all employed in war, homicidal fighting and self-defence; and that there are many analogies between the ways men treat the flesh and bones of slain animals and the ways in which they treat the human dead. Thus man as a predator, or in self-defence, uses on other men the techniques and the strategies he uses on non-human animals: conversely, there is an evident tendency for man to endow those creatures that he kills or could kill in much the same way as he kills other men, with quasi-human status, and to regulate his slaughter and consumption of them accordingly (c.f. Gerbrands 1962: [v]; Bulmer 1967).

ACKNOWLEDGEMENTS

In so far as I draw on my own field experience in this paper I must acknowledge with gratitude the support of the Australian National University for my studies among the Kyaka Enga in 1955–6 and of the New Zealand University Research Grants Committee, the Golden Kiwi Lotteries Fund Scientific Research Committee, and the U.S. Public Health Service (M.H. 07957–01) for my work among the Karam of the Schrader Range in 1963–4 and 1965–6.

I am grateful to Andrew Pawley, A. B. Hooper and my wife, Susan Bulmer, for helpful comments on the first draft of this paper.

NOTES

1. An abbreviated version of these notes is being prepared for the *Encyclopaedia of Papua and New Guinea*, Melbourne University Press. No reference is here made to fishing and capture of crocodiles, turtle, dugong and other aquatic game.
2. Zoological nomenclature followed in this paper is that of Laurie and Hill (1954) for mammals and Rand and Gilliard (1967) for birds.
3. Since 1900 Rusa Deer (*Cervus timorensis*) have been introduced in several parts of West Irian and Papua, and they are now common in some lowland areas.
4. Rand and Gilliard (1967: 608-9) provide references to works which describe bird populations in different areas and ecological zones. The Archbold Expeditions reports, of which the most recent is Brass (1964) include useful information on the distribution of mammals and other fauna. Hitchcock (1964) describes the wildlife resources available to a Kuma (Wahgi Valley) community in the Highlands of East New Guinea.
5. This dog of the interior is sometimes known as *Canis familiaris hallstromi* or *C.*

hallstromi. Husson (1955: 7) remarks that pre-European domestic dogs in coastal areas were morphologically very different from the interior populations, and were probably descended from a different and more recently introduced stock. It would be interesting to know if coastal and inland domestic dogs behave differently in hunting, and to what extent they are differently employed by their owners. According to Karam (Schrader Range) informants feral and semi-domesticated dogs are particularly successful in killing wallaby (? *Dorcopsis*). Both dogs and pigs interfere with trapping by consuming game before the hunter has had a chance to recover it.

6. See footnote (5).

REFERENCES

ANELL, B. (1960): *Hunting and trapping methods in Australia and Oceania.* Studia Ethnographica Upsaliensia, XVIII.

BERGMAN, S. (1957): *Through Primitive New Guinea.* London, Robert Hale.

BERGMAN, S. (1961): *My Father is a Cannibal.* London, Robert Hale.

BRASS, L. J. (1964): "Summary of the Sixth Archbold Expedition to New Guinea", *Bulletin of the American Museum of Natural History,* Vol. 127, Art. 4.

BULMER, R. (1957): "A primitive ornithology", *Australian Museum Magazine,* Vol. XII, No. 7, pp. 224-229.

BULMER, R. (1962): "Chimbu plume traders", *Australian Natural History,* Vol. XIV, No. 1, pp. 15-19.

BULMER, R. (1967): "Why is the cassowary not a bird?", *Man* (n.s.), Vol. 2, pp. 5-25.

BULMER, S. (1964): "Radio-carbon dates from New Guinea", *Journal of the Polynesian Society,* Vol. 73, pp. 327-328.

BULMER, S. (1966): "Pig-bone from two archaeological sites in the New Guinea Highlands", *Journal of the Polynesian Society,* Vol. 75, pp. 504-505.

BULMER, S. and R. (1964): "The prehistory of the Australian New Guinea Highlands", *American Anthropologist,* Vol. 66, No. 4, Pt. 2, pp. 39-76.

CHEESMAN, E. (1949): *Six-legged snakes in New Guinea.* London, Harrap.

DIAMOND, J. M. (1966): "Zoological classification system of a primitive people", *Science,* Vol. 151, pp. 1102-1104.

FISCHER, D. (1956): *Unter Südsee-Insulanern.* Leipzig, Koehler and Amelang.

FISCHER, H. (1963): *Watut.* Braunschweig, Limbach.

GERBRANDS, A. A. (1962): *The Art of the Asmat.* New York, Museum of Primitive Art.

HITCHCOCK, W. (1964): "An introduction to the natural history of a New Guinea Highland community", *Emu,* Vol. 63, pp. 351-372.

HUSSON, A. M. (1955): "Tabel voor het determineren van de landzoogdieren van Nederlands Nieuw-Guinea", *Zoologische Bijdragen* No. 1. pp. 1-35. Leiden, Rijksmuseum van Natuurlijke Historie.

KOUWENHOVEN, W. J. H. (1956): *Nimboran: a study of social change and social economic development in a New Guinea Society.* Den Haag, Voorhoeve.

LAURIE, E. M. O. and HILL, J. E. (1954): *List of land mammals of New Guinea, Celebes and adjacent islands.* London, British Museum of Natural History.

MAYR, E. (1932): "A tenderfoot explorer in New Guinea", *Natural History,* Vol. 32, pp. 83-97.

MEGGITT, M. J. (1958): "The Enga of the New Guinea Highlands", *Oceania,* Vol. XXVIII, pp. 253-330.

NEUHAUS, Pater K. (1962): *Beiträge zur Ethnographie der Pala Mittel Neu Irland.* Kölner Ethnologische Mitteilungen, Bd. 2.

OOSTERWAL, G. (1961): *People of the Tor.* Assen, Van Gorcum.

POSPISIL, L. (1963): *Kapauku Papuan Economy.* Yale University Publications in Anthropology, No. 67.

POUWER, J. (1955): *Enkele Aspecten van de Mimika-Cultuur.* 's Gravenhage, Staatsdrukkerijen Uitgeversbedrijf.

RAND, A. L. and GILLIARD, E. T. (1967): *Handbook of New Guinea Birds.* London, Weidenfeld and Nicolson.

RAPPAPORT, R. A. (1967): "Ritual regulation of environmental relations among a New Guinea people", *Ethnology*, Vol. VI, pp. 17-30.

SERPENTI, L. M. (1965): *Cultivators in the Swamps*. Assen, Van Gorcum.

VAN EECHOUD, J. P. K. (1962): *Etnografie van de Kaowerawedj*. Verhandelingen van het Koninklijk Instituut voor Taal-, Land- en Volkenkunde, Deel 37.

WATSON, J. B. (1965): "From hunting to horticulture", *Ethnology*, Vol. IV, pp. 295-309.

WILLIAMS, F. E. (1936): *Papuans of the Trans-Fly*. Oxford, Clarendon Press.

WILLIAMSON, R. W. (1912): *The Mafulu mountain people of British New Guinea*. London, Macmillan.

3

HORTICULTURE AND HUSBANDRY
IN A SOLOMON ISLAND SOCIETY

Douglas L. Oliver

*   *   *   *

AGRICULTURE

More than half of an adult Siuai's working hours are taken up with food
—with producing, collecting, processing, and consuming it. This is an average, for women spend about ten hours daily at it and men generally much
less. These natives eat a wide variety of comestibles; but when one of them
speaks of "food" (*pao*) he is usually referring to taro. In month-long records I kept of meals eaten by representative households taro constituted
some 80 per cent by weight of everything eaten. Informants told of having
eaten a few "wild" taro during straitened times, otherwise all taro consumed is grown in their gardens.

Taro gardens are laid out on well-drained terrain where the soil is deep
and free of sand. Another technical requirement is that gardens be located
in areas of secondary growth; I did not see a single instance of primary forest being cleared for gardens. Natives say that it is too difficult even with
metal axes to cut down and remove the huge trees; but there are other
reasons why new gardens are located on old garden sites.

Taro gardens are laid out in patches fenced in to keep out pigs. These
patches are rectangular and a single patch varies from one to five thousand
square yards in area. Very rarely does one see isolated patches; they are
generally arranged in sequence, as shown in Figure 1. Taro is ready for
harvesting after about four months' growth, and planting is a continuous
process without perceptible seasonal differences in growth and yield. Added
to this is the fact that the Siuai do not know how to preserve taro and hence
must consume it within a few days after harvesting it. As soon as the
plants are harvested from a matured garden the corms are cut off just
below the stalks, for eating, and the stalks are replanted in another site

Reprinted by permission of the publishers from Douglas L. Oliver, *A Solomon Island
Society*, pp. 22-38. Cambridge, Mass.: Harvard University Press, Copyright, 1955, by
the President and Fellows of Harvard College. The figures have been renumbered to
run in sequence throughout this excerpt, and the notes have been omitted.

after their leaves have begun to rot. The gardener's ideal is to have several contiguous patches in various stages of growth. Figure 1 illustrates the technique. Patch A is completely harvested and overgrown with reeds and small trees; most of its fence timbers have already been used for firewood and those remaining are scattered and rotting. Patch B has been completely harvested of taro and now contains only a few banana and plantain trees still in bearing. Patch C contains growing taro some of which is ready for harvest. Patch D contains unripe taro in various stages of growth. Patch E has been wholly prepared for planting and contains a few plots of new taro shoots. Patch F is in process of being cleared and fenced; some trees have been felled and split for fence timbers, others have been laid on the ground to mark off plots, while still others have been strip-barked and left standing. The remaining plant rubbish is being piled and burned and the ashes scattered over the patch to enrich the soil.

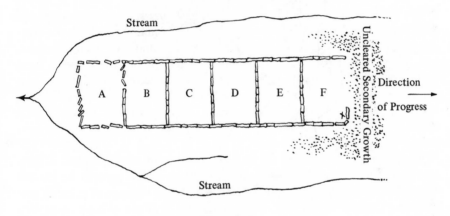

FIGURE 1

While Patch F is being cleared and fenced most efforts will be concentrated upon finishing that job; but on all other days the workers spend most of their time weeding and removing insects from Patches C and D. On all gardening days, however, before returning home a few plants are harvested from Patch C and their stalks piled up in Patch E ready for planting within the next day or so. Then natives load up with firewood by dismembering the fences or chopping up the dried trees left standing in Patch B.

Ideally this sequence will be continued as long as there is any suitable land adjoining the existing patches, and until an old patch is ready for reclaiming and planting. In hilly northeast Siuai, where suitable land is limited to the long and rather narrow interfluvial ridges, gardeners attempt to extend the patch-sequence in one direction until the old end-patch is ready for replanting (Fig. 2A). On more level terrain of central and southern Siuai the sequence follows a different pattern (Fig. 2B). In either case, natives judge that a place has lain fallow long enough when the trees on it are of a convenient size for fence-building (an interim of about six years). Their judgment might be a rationalization based upon convenience: it involves much less effort to clear land after six years than it does after three or seven or eight or more because there will be neither jungle under-growth nor over-large timbers to deal with, nor will there be a necessity for finding fence wood elsewhere. On the other hand, the natives' conception of the period of soil-replenishment might be empirically arrived at (I recorded several reports of crop failure due—according to informants—to gardeners not allowing land to remain idle long enough). Probably both of these factors are behind the native theory.

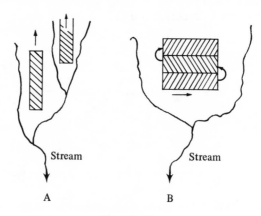

FIGURE 2

The *ideal* technique, in the northeast region, is to progress in one direc-tion for about six years and then return to the starting point and begin again. For such a process each family would require a continuous strip of fertile land about 100 feet wide and about ¼ mile long. A mapping survey of northeast Siuai indicated that such an ideal is seldom realized. Some kind of barrier—either another household's garden or an effective natural or cultural boundary—usually gets in the way.

What sometimes happens is that each household has three or four gardens, as in Figure 3.

Garden A has been deserted for three or four years; it will be replanted when Garden C is completely cultivated.

Garden B is partly harvested (at the southwest), and there is a stand of ripe taro at the northeastern end.

Garden C is being cleared and fenced in now; the gardeners plant the stalks from Garden B in the southern end of Garden C.

Firewood is collected from the southwestern end of Garden B.

I spent many days in Siuai taro patches and became deeply impressed with the rhythmic efficiency of sequence-gardening. Given their implements —ax, machete, wooden rake, and digging stick—it would be difficult to devise a more efficient procedure which would also satisfy the need for strong fences. A steel-bladed hoe would probably speed up weeding, but more complex tools and chemical insecticides would not be feasible in terms of the present economy. I learned to appreciate the labor-saving economy of sequence-gardening particularly after watching the preparation of a patch out of sequence. It happened, as it not infrequently does, that a patch was prepared at an isolated site covered with jungle past the customary growth stage. Many of the larger trees on the site had to be felled and laboriously dragged clear of the patch to avoid shading the garden

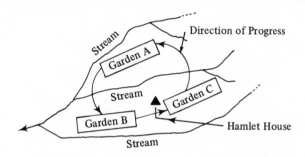

FIGURE 3

excessively, and many of the fence posts and some of the horizontal fence timbers had to be brought from elsewhere since trees of the proper size were not to be found on the site. Fence building in any case is hard work, but when heavy timbers must be carried long distances it is back-breaking, and natives so regard it. Nor do they risk failure by attempting to replant prematurely an old garden site; the thorny tangle of vines and bushes is difficult to clear and the resulting taro crop is likely to be anemic.

Fences vary in height and in thickness according to the location of the garden. Those bordering much-traveled paths are made high enough to block out the stares of strangers; those within a few hundred yards of bushhouses have to be built unusually thick and sturdy to withstand hungry domestic pigs—wild pigs being smaller and easier to fence out. It would therefore appear easier for men, who build the fences, to locate gardens farther away from settlements to permit easier fence construction. However, women have much to say about the location of gardens, and they try to avoid walking over-long distances laden, as they usually are, with crushing loads of firewood. Other factors affecting garden location will be described later on.

The taro patch is divided into plots (*nopu*) two spans wide by nine spans long (10 by 45 feet), with pathways left clear along the fences and between every two or three plots (Figure 4). These plots are marked off with logs laid on the ground, and have a number of functions. All the taro in any one plot (an average of 102 plants) is at very nearly the same stage of growth, and on the rare occasions when taro is sold the sale unit is the plotfull, which therefore provides a convenient and fairly uniform unit. Furthermore when pigs break into a patch and root up the growing plants the number of plots molested supplies a basis for indemnification—although an additional tort payment is nearly always assessed. Sociological purposes are also served by the plot layout (see below [*A Solomon Island Society*], page 264); and I am tempted to point out—although it was never rationalized to me in these terms—that delineating plots with logs cut when clearing a patch saves having to drag the logs clear of the planting.

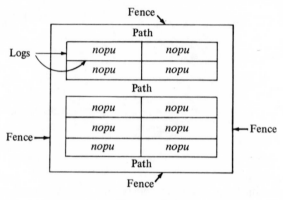

FIGURE 4

Taro occupies so prominent a place in Siuai life that one might appropriately go on for pages describing the numerous varieties grown; the exact details of planting, weeding, and harvesting; the high value placed upon it as *the* vegetable food; the feelings of deprivation natives express when they must go without it; the frequency with which it enters into conversation; the numerous metaphors for it and its use in ritual; etc. Some of this will be reported in later chapters; but rather than burden the reader with a long technical account, however justified that may be by the importance of the topic, I merely ask him to remember that Siuai natives spend more hours growing taro than in any other enterprise, that the plant comprises 80 per cent of their diet, and that it is the basis of their subsistence economy generally. If that is forgotten during consideration of more dramatic activities, then true perspective on Siuai life will have been lost.

In most taro patches natives also grow some tobacco, a dozen or so plantain and banana plants, and several yam and gourd vines trained up along the fences. Now and then one comes across a patch containing a few stalks of maize, some tomatoes, and a bush of tiny red peppers which are used as condiments. Few Siuai have yet acquired tastes for the recently introduced maize and tomatoes. Yams sometimes reach lengths of three and four feet and are pointed out as curiosities, but no special effort is made to produce or display them; because of their coarse, fibrous texture they are not rated highly as a food. Being easily roasted however they, along with plantains, are occasionally cooked and eaten as snacks by natives working in the gardens or lazing in the club-houses.

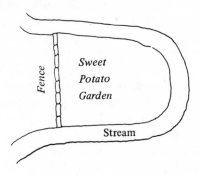

FIGURE 5

Sweet potatoes are second only to taro in Siuai diets. As their native name, *peteita,* indicates, they are of recent introduction, assertedly from Alu, but their use is expanding and even during our short stay potato acreages increased. Older people express some contempt for them, calling them pap: "children's food; not solid, strength-giving food like taro." In fact, they figure importantly only in the diets of households with mission-trained members. As a food crop sweet potatoes have several advantages: they will grow on sandy soil unsuited to taro, they require little care after planting, and they produce a higher yield per area. On the other hand they are more tempting to pigs and require sturdier fences than taro gardens do; it is said that pigs will exert greater effort to break into a sweet potato garden. Consequently natives do not waste labor by planting taro and potato in the same enclosure; in fact, they usually locate potato gardens in flood-plain valleys far away from settlements. Here, out of reach of domestic pigs, there is less danger of marauding; and if the gardener wishes to take the extra precaution of building a fence he has only to build on the landward side of a creek bend (Figure 5). Furthermore natives claim that the sandy alluvial soil is ideal for sweet potatoes.

No Siuai meal is complete without a few slivers of coconut meat or a portion of coconut oil poured over the vegetables. For special feast dishes it is indispensable—being shredded and baked with sago or mixed with boiled taro, or used to "grease" food generally, and in other ways. But far more important is the coconut's everyday use as a light repast or thirst-quencher; except for water and broth it is a Siuai's only drink. One of the compensations for anthropologizing in coconut-land is the drink of cool, slightly sweet, tangy liquid from an unripe coconut; it is not only superbly refreshing but nutritious and energy-producing. For a combination meal and drink the Siuai prefer a nut in which meat has begun to form; after cracking it and allowing the liquid to guzzle down their throats they separate the two halves and scrape out slivers of soft meat. For a more solid snack they obtain a completely dry nut and eat not only the half-inch-thick layer of meat but the spongy kernel as well. There are no sex-bound restrictions on collecting coconuts, but young boys are the ones usually sent scurrying up a palm for them. When climbing a high palm they slip a short loop of light rope around both insteps and, using that to grip the trunk, pull themselves upward with their hands by means of short hops. Coconuts are husked by jabbing them against a pointed stick stuck into the ground. Nut shredders are made of a shell or metal saw-toothed shredding blade attached to a wooden frame.

It is quite possible that some coconut palms might have "escaped" from cultivation and grown wild in parts of southern Bougainville; most of those we saw were clearly derived from native planting. If a few old palms are found standing in the wilderness, a little more searching or inquiry will establish that the place was formerly a settlement. Most palms are found near dwellings or immediately around club-houses, and show that not much thought has been given to spacing; but here and there one sees small and orderly groves. Indications are that new plantings are on the increase—stimulated partly by the Administration prescript that ten palms be planted for every newborn child, and partly by the ideas acquired at whites' plantations. There is no cash-income trade in coconuts—the only potential purchaser being a Chinese trader located on the coast one day's walk away; but judging by the frequency with which ambitious natives have to taboo their groves to accumulate nuts for feasts there is still an unfulfilled subsistence need for coconuts.

The breadfruit season lasts from early May to the middle of June and while it is in progress natives roast the fruit and eat it as a staple. It rots so quickly that it is usually eaten on the same day picked. Siuai distinguish between a large and a small variety, and prefer the latter. Most households own a few breadfruit trees and the fruit is eaten with evident enjoyment during the first few days of the season; soon however the novelty wears off and natives return to their favorite, taro. Informants tell of certain trees having been purposefully planted in past years, but I did not learn of any new plantings during our stay.

Canarium almonds leave a deeper impress on Siuai life. When they ripen, in late July and August, even garden work is forsaken for a few days to allow time for collecting nuts and extracting the kernels. Almond trees grow to heights of 100 feet or more and the nuts cluster on the outermost branches, with the result that picking them is a hazardous undertaking. Poles and ropes are used to climb the long distance to the first limbs, and then natives have to edge out to the branch ends to cut or twist loose the clusters of nuts. Now and then someone will fall, and this occasionally proves fatal.

The skill required and the danger involved add a zest to almond collecting which these usually phlegmatic natives seem to enjoy. Numbers of them will gather around a tree and yelp with admiration when a climber breaks off and drops a cluster from a topmost limb.

The kernel of a ripe canarium almond is about the size and shape of the Jordan almond. It is covered with a hard shell encased in a purplish fleshy hull. (Pigeons often eat the hull and discard the rest, littering the ground with the nuts which natives then collect.) Kernels are extracted by holding the nut on one stone and cracking it open with another. Then the kernels are either eaten whole and raw or mashed in a mortar and added to sago and taro puddings, or they may be smoked and packed away in bamboo or leaf containers for future eating or trade.

The seasonal growth of almonds, which constitute an indispenable ingredient for most special feast delicacies, results in the holding of most feasts in the months immediately succeeding nut-ripening. There is nothing inevitable about this feast cycling since properly smoked nuts will last a full year or more, but it is customary to consume the nuts within a few months after picking.

The Siuai seldom plant almond trees. They carefully avoid injuring them when clearing jungle, and build small protective fences around young trees, but the long interval between planting and fruiting appears to discourage systematic cultivation. Men will however plant a new tree to replace an old one that has to be cut to make way for a Government road.

Compared with vast areas of sago palms found in New Guinea, the few small groves scattered around the marshy places of southern Bougainville appear quite insignificant. Nevertheless, these antediluvian, giant fernlike plants do have a number of important uses for the Siuai. The starch obtained from the pith of the trunk is a substitute food staple, fronds are the principal thatching material, the broad bases of branches are used as troughs, and rotting palm stumps crawl with choice edible grubs. Sago flour is obtained by felling the palm, stripping off its outer hull, shredding the pithy center, and washing out its starch into a wooden standing-trough. A bamboo-edged adze is the shredding tool; one of the tree's own branch bases and its vegetable matting serve as washing-trough and strainer. After starch has settled in the standing-trough the water is drained off and the flour packed into cylindrical-shaped leaf containers for storage.

I could not learn whether the Siuai purposely plant sago palms, and suspect not, but I have seen them erect a crude fence around a new plant to protect it from being crushed by pigs crowding around to devour grubs and gleanings of sour sago in old stumps.

During periods of mourning, when the Siuai forego gardening, or during times of continuous rainfall, when they do not like to go to their garden because of the danger of crossing swollen creeks or the difficulty of walking along slippery paths or the cold discomfort of working in wet and mud, they reluctantly fall back upon sago for their staple; otherwise they reserve that food for their travels because of the ease of carrying and roasting it.

COLLECTING, HUNTING, AND FISHING

In addition to the plants the Siuai grow or encourage to grow for food, they collect *hari* nuts, and many kinds of edible leaves, nuts, ferns, mushrooms, and fungi from the forest. Some of these wild foods are ordinary fare, others have special uses: for example, one kind of wild yam is a rare delicacy; "pig's-wife" fern is eaten only with pork; the leaf of the *surasia* tree is a delicacy used in invalids' broth. All such foods are used as relishes —not being "solid" like taro; they constitute only a small proportion (about 2 per cent by weight) of any ordinary meal.

When food staples become scarce as a result of crop failure and sago shortage, natives ward off starvation by collecting "wild" sago, wild yams, and wild taro, but such times are infrequent and only one such "Big Hunger" was recalled by my informants, who attributed it to a prolonged drought.

Salty condiments are used extensively and are considered indispensable for the domestic meal. Natives nearer the coast make a salt by evaporating salt water; those farther inland utilize the ashes of several plants. Salt ash is kept on the smoke rack over the hearth to increase its pungency.

Collecting edible insects is only an incidental activity—if natives see them they may try to catch them; there are no special implements involved. In addition to the sago grubs, which are regarded as a delicacy, the Siuai like to eat beetles, white ants—large and small—and certain kinds of spiders.

Hunting is less haphazard. Hunting for wild pigs is in fact a serious undertaking requiring skill, persistence, and some courage. Many Siuai take sporting pleasure in hunting, even though the booty is usually small. Wild pigs and opossums are the chief quarries, but natives will shoot at tree-rats, flying foxes, and birds if they see them reasonably close.

In southern Siuai natives may go for a year or more without eating wild pig, and during my fifteen-week residence in one northern village only two wild pigs were killed by my neighbors. In villages bordering the unbroken rain forests, however, pigs are hunted more frequently and successfully, and some residents keep packs of starving dogs for the purpose.

One native I knew spent about a fifth of his working time in hunting and managed to bring in a pig or two a month.

The customary hunting method is for one man to start off with dogs and roam through the forest until the dogs find and run down an animal which is then killed by a long throwing spear made of hard limbum palm with either a plain fire-hardened point or a point of razor-sharp bamboo. (The more elaborate bone-pointed and decorated "fighting" spears are now reserved for mock battles and feasts.) Until recent years wild-pig drives involved up to a hundred men. A stockade was constructed ("like a garden fence, but not so strong"), then the hunters would unleash their dogs, form a wide circle, and converge on the stockade, rustling bushes, shouting and blowing on conch shells. Pigs driven into the stockade were then speared. Very large-scale and successful drives are said to have netted up to thirty pigs. If old tuskers were cornered they would usually attack their tormentors, and now and then a hunter or a dog would be maimed or even killed.

Opossum hunting is an adventurous outing. Two or more boys or men equip themselves with "camping" provisions—packets of sago and large quantities of betel-chewing supplies—and remain for two or three days in the forest capturing the little marsupials. After one is treed, sometimes with the help of dogs, a younger native will climb the tree and shake down the opossum while his companions wait on the ground to pounce on the stunned animal. Occasionally a live animal is brought home for a ceremony but more usually the animals are killed, eviscerated, cleaned, and smoked soon after capture. Liver, heart, and blood are promptly eaten, while the smoked carcass is usually put aside for some feast. Opossum hunters appear not to mind the short rations and rough living of the chase, but the Siuais' characteristic uneasiness about tree-climbing is apparent despite the climbers' bravado. The Siuai also set ingenious but rarely successful traps for opossum by rigging a trip-noose over an "opossum trail," a thick vine stretched between two likely trees.

Tree-rats are occasionally captured for food but I discovered few natives who had actually done so or eaten any caught by others. Soups made from flying foxes and flying mice are favorite though infrequent fare, and natives spend hours manufacturing the special four-pronged barbed arrows used in hunting these creatures. They also value their wing bones for making spear and arrow barbs.

Fishing is also an occasional pastime with many Siuai but does not add significantly to their diets. One often sees a solitary male searching for fish and eels with his bow and arrow up and down a stream, hopeful but rarely successful. Or, once a fortnight or so, women and girls will spend a few hours wading in a stream searching by hand for prawns that may hide under ledges and roots. Almost everywhere large and small basket-traps are manufactured and left in likely spots—nearly every two or three hundred feet of a stream's course will harbor one; but these remain empty for weeks at a time, and word of a catch becomes a lively conversation topic in the neighborhood. In addition to these individual and spasmodic attempts to catch fish, natives sometimes—as often as two or three times a year in communities bordering large creeks—engage in coöperative fish drives. One technique is to select a spot where the creek divides around an island, divert the water from one stream by damming, and then proceed to shoot or capture the fish and prawns left floundering in pools in the dry stream bed. In one such fish drive I witnessed, about eighty natives took part and about two hundred pounds of fish plus several hundred prawns were caught. A second large-scale fishing technique involves the use of a long seine-net carried through the wider river pools by a score or more men. Seines are made from dried and shredded bark, and are usually manufactured by several specialists working together. There were only three of these large seine-nets in all northeast Siuai during my stay, and not a single seine-drive took place.

ANIMAL HUSBANDRY

Pig-raising is vastly more important than hunting and fishing in Siuai economy. Nearly every household owns at least one pig, and most average three or four.

Domesticated pigs are fed once a day, during the late afternoon, and the rest of the time they are allowed to run free and forage. According to natives' belief, based apparently on experience, a full-grown pig must be given five to six pounds of food daily in order for it to remain properly domesticated. If fed less it will break through the strongest of fences and devour garden produce, or wander farther from home and invade the less protected potato gardens, or, worse still, it will run wild altogether in the forest. A proper diet for pigs, the Siuai consider, must be balanced and cooked like their own: a boiled taro or potato base, a portion of cooked greens, and some coconut meat. When preparing their own meals natives usually remove thick slices of peeling from taro or potatoes and cook the peel along with some taro tips for their pigs, but sometimes they feed them whole corms or tubers. This feeding is carried out with painstaking care, every animal receiving its portion on a separate basket-tray. Fully domesticated pigs do not have to be called for their daily meal; they return to the dwelling in midafternoon and clamor for it, and often remain nearby all night.

No attempt is made to pen grown pigs until they are held awaiting slaughter. At home, although the larger animals are kept outside the house, they are encouraged to stay nearby, this of course being possible only in the scattered hamlet residences, the "pig-food" houses, and not in the palisaded line villages prescribed by the Administration.

Some care is given to breeding, and a good boar is considered a very valuable resource. Sows usually farrow in thickets near their owners' dwellings; when that happens the owners close all paths to the spot and take the precaution of barring dogs. Young pigs are kept in pens alongside the dwellings; until the animals are domesticated enough to remain near home and large enough to fend for themselves, their owners believe it necessary to stay nearby at least part of each day; otherwise young animals become "lonely," natives say. During the first few months of their lives young pigs are cared for like the pets they are; their food is cooked in the pot along with their owners', and one often sees women premasticate a lump of taro or potato for sickly young animals.

It will be described later on how pigs are ritually named, "baptized," and magically treated for ailments. Here it should merely be noted that young male shoats are gelded without ceremony, as a purely practical measure— "to make them grow." Gelding is carried out with a knife (formerly with a splinter of bamboo) by splitting open the scrotum and removing the testicles. Natives take great interest in this operation and even children are allowed to try it. Pigs are also "branded" by cutting chips out of their ears; this is not an ownership mark but does serve to distinguish domestic from wild pigs (see p. 359 [in *A Solomon Island Society*]). Additional ways of distinguishing between wild and domestic pigs are known to nearly all natives. Wild pigs are smaller, thinner, quicker, more malodorous, pure "razorback"; domesticated pigs are the result of mixing native with European breeds, the latter having been introduced within recent decades by laborers returning home from white colonists' coconut plantations. Before the introduction of European strains, wild pigs were probably not very different from domestic ones—thinner and tougher, perhaps, but probably the same breed. Later on, when Siuai youths finished their terms of indenture on whites' plantations, many of them invested their earnings in European pigs and proudly carried them back home. Older natives recall those times with feeling: how great was the excitement that prevailed upon first sight of the superior animals and how longingly every adult tried to obtain one of its offspring. Disdain for the native breed, including the wild pigs, became so marked that hunting was thereby discouraged. It is certainly obvious that the new mix-breed animal is a great improvement in size and succulence over the old; but it is not all gain, for natives also state that the domesticated native pig stayed nearer home, hence did not menace gardens located farther away than a few hundred yards. It is even claimed by some older informants that during their fathers' childhoods gardens did not require fencing. Whether that be true or not, and I suspect not, the new mixed breeds possibly do rove farther afield and, being larger, probably do require sturdier garden fencing.

Killing and butchering a pig is man's work and most men can butcher quite skillfully. Some men prefer to kill an animal by strangling it—by bending its head to one side to cut off respiration. This is the tidier and more economical method because there is less loss of blood; it is used in killing a pig while a ceremony is going on. At other times the animal is killed by having its lungs caved in and heart crushed with a few hard blows of an ax-butt; this is the quicker method. When the animal is dead —or thought to be near enough dead—it is fastened to a pole and hung over a fire for singeing. After this, soot and burnt hair are scraped away with a knife and the butcher sets to work cutting the animal into twelve longitudinal strips. During the butchering the gullet is knotted near the head in order to prevent the contents of the stomach from spilling over the animal. Blood is highly valued, and is scooped up from the body cavity and placed in containers—either to be drunk at once or made into a pudding. The heart is roasted and is regarded as a great delicacy. Belly fat is also carefully saved, mixed with blood, and cooked in a pot. No attempt however is made to retain stomach or intestines.

Every settlement contains a few fowl, which fend for themselves by stealing food leavings and catching insects. They hide their eggs in the scrub, but most natives do not care for eggs anyway. Only on rare occasions do the Siuai kill and eat one of these athletic birds.

Dogs are also to be found in every settlement—almost in every house. A few of these wretched rail-thin creatures are used in hunting but the rest serve only as pets, if that is the proper word to describe the lot of these half-starved, continually kicked animals. Some households also keep a cat or two for rat-catching and for the amusement of children, and now and then natives capture and keep a cockatoo.

COOKING AND EATING

The Siuai domestic meal, the one full meal of the day, seldom varies in its main outlines: for each individual past early childhood a basic portion of three or four pounds of taro or sweet potato, along with a helping of cooked greens flavored with salt or coconut oil and, now and then, some small taste of relish—meat, fish, grubs, or other delicacy. Sometimes plantains or yams are substituted as staples for taro and sweet potato, but as already indicated they are regarded as second best, most adults insisting that taro alone gives them the feeling of stuffed satiation which should accompany every satisfactory meal. Sago is another substitute, usually eaten with the domestic meal only when some other staple is not available. Invalids are usually given vegetable or meat soups.

The Siuai vary their cooking methods with the occasion. Working in the gardens, hunting in the forests, or traveling far from home, they assuage hunger by simply roasting a plantain, a yam, or a leaf packet of sago on an open hearth. On special occasions they wrap their vegetables and relishes in leaves and bake them by covering them with hot coals. Or more elaborately, they dig a pit and place in it packets of leaf-wrapped food surrounded by hot stones; this is the favorite manner of cooking but it is laborious and hence used only for feasts. The daily meal of the household is cooked by steaming and boiling. A clay pot is wedged upright between stones on the hearth and into the pot are poured a few inches of water. Then it is filled to the brim with chunks of taro and potatoes, unpeeled plantains, small packets of greens, and any other supplement available; a covering of large leaves is fixed tightly over the top; and the pot is allowed to boil and steam until the starchy staples have reached a consistency which most Americans would find slightly underdone. This means that any meat cooked in the same pot is far tougher than stone-baked meat, and the Siuai recognize its inferiority, but the morsels of home-cooked meat are usually so minute that, natives reason, they are hardly worth while baking. Cooks sometimes use pointed sticks to test whether food is properly cooked, but usually they gauge—or more frequently mis-gauge—the time by some measure I was unable to fathom and proceed to spear out the food into basket trays. Onto each tray are placed several chunks of starchy staple, a plantain or two, a helping of greens mixed with oil, a few slivers of coconut meat, and a tidbit of the day's special relish. The solid food is then eaten by hand and washed down by drinks of broth or coconut milk. Then, after eating, comes the betel-chewing and the pipe of tobacco.

Siuai natives chew the betel mixture frequently and smoke almost continually. The betel mixture consists of areca nuts, collected from purposefully planted palms, along with catkins taken from a pepper tree, and lime obtained by burning shells collected on the southern beaches. One variety of areca nut is said to be strongly narcotic but I never noticed any native visibly affected. The Siuai say that betel-chewing staves off hunger, but they also chew it immediately after meals just for its pleasant taste. Native tobacco is smoked in trade-store pipes. It is grown in their gardens along the fences, and although some of it is sun-and-smoke-dried before use, these inveterate and hardy smokers often pick a green leaf, "cure" it over a smoky fire for a minute or two, and smoke it forthwith.

*   *   *   *

ECOLOGICAL TIME

When do all these activities take place?

If a western observer remained long enough, he would note how the sameness of the southern Bougainville climate is reflected in the sameness of Siuai life. To a visitor from the temperate zone the light breezes and clear sunny days of May-September are a welcome change from the continuous rains of October-November and the still, humid overcasts of December-April; but even if the Siuai themselves share this reaction they do not comment upon it, and in most respects it does not cause them to change their daily routines. Taro, their all-important food staple, is planted and harvested continuously so there is no basis for the agricultural cycling which structures time for so many peoples. It is true that continuous rainy spells slow down garden work and reduce natives to eating poorer and less. And it is also probably true that the mosquito-plagued days of December-April bring on more fever and hence result in less constructive work. But neither of these kinds of change has marked culture-wide ramifications. In fact, only the ripening of breadfruit and of canarium almonds provide any kind of general annual cycle. Breadfruit ripens in May-June and while its short season lasts it furnishes a welcome but quantitatively unimportant addition to the daily menu. This is also the case with almonds, which ripen in late July, but some natives forego eating this delicacy with their daily meals and use it only for feasts, and this has the effect of concentrating feasting within the few months immediately after almond picking.

The phasing of the moon is explained animistically, the new moon is greeted with ritual gestures, and bright moonlight keeps people gossiping and playing outside their huts long after nightfall; otherwise, lunar time has only minor effect on Siuai economic life. Not so with the sun. In this place of brief dawns and dusks and of ineffective man-made lighting, the rising and setting of the sun mark the start and the stopping of most activities having to do with getting a living; and throughout daylight the sun's position sets a rough kind of schedule for working and eating. But there is nothing very precise about this—the Siuai are slow starters and dawdlers, by bustling western standards. On the average day natives emerge sluggishly from their smoky huts at sunup and stand shivering and hugging themselves in shafts of sunlight for many minutes before picking their way down to a creek to bathe and make toilet. Back again at the hut, the cold remnants of yesterday's meal are divided among the children while the adults assuage hunger and sweeten breath with a chew of betel mixture followed by the first of the day's almost continuous pipe smokes. Then, some two hours after sunrise they set out for work.

Most mornings women and children go to the gardens, which are usually within a mile of the dwelling, and remain there working until midafternoon. Men and boys also go to the gardens some days but except when they are clearing a new garden site and building fences they seldom remain there as long as the women and girls. More often they will spend their working day building, repairing, manufacturing, trading, litigating, conversing, or, commonly, merely dozing. Around noontime natives eat a snack, a roasted plantain or yam if they are in the gardens, the milk and meat of a coconut, if not. Midafternoon they return home to prepare and eat the day's principal meal and feed their pigs; then they converse and visit until dark and retire into their huts to sleep.

Once in a long while this routine will be interrupted by daytime feasts and ceremonies and by all-night wakes and cremations. Or, if death strikes nearby, most work may cease for days at a time. Again, in settlements located near mission stations or possessing influential native teachers, the Sunday morning service, and sometimes even the daily one, will draw together several converts to drone out a mechanical prayer and sing a few hymns. In Methodist communities, especially, Sundays are marked by pious idleness and, consequently, frugal meals. The annual "karisimasi" (pidgin, for "Christmas") cycle and numerous Christian anniversaries have not brought about any marked change in the established flow of native activities, but the regular recurrence of "sande" is beginning to influence when and how natives do things.

Summarizing, it can be said that the annual cycle, manifested in the ripening of almonds, has some effect upon feasting; that the lunar cycle has some slight ritual and social significance; that the imported, artificial weekly cycle is beginning to have at least a negative effect on work habits; but that the main time marker is the diurnal cycle, it being divided into the period of darkness and sleep, the period of morning and early afternoon working, and the period of late afternoon eating and socializing. So much could any observer note about *when* Siuai activities take place.

4

RITUAL REGULATION OF
ENVIRONMENTAL RELATIONS
AMONG A NEW GUINEA PEOPLE[1]

Roy A. Rappaport

Most functional studies of religious behavior in anthropology have as an analytic goal the elucidation of events, processes, or relationships occurring within a social unit of some sort. The social unit is not always well defined, but in some cases it appears to be a church, that is, a group of people who entertain similar beliefs about the universe, or a congregation, a group of people who participate together in the performance of religious rituals. There have been exceptions. Thus Vayda, Leeds, and Smith (1961) and O. K. Moore (1957) have clearly perceived that the functions of religious ritual are not necessarily confined within the boundaries of a congregation or even a church. By and large, however, I believe that the following statement by Homans (1941: 172) represents fairly the dominant line of anthropological thought concerning the functions of religious ritual:

Ritual actions do not produce a practical result on the external world—that is one of the reasons why we call them ritual. But to make this statement is not to say that ritual has no function. Its function is not related to the world external to the society but to the internal constitution of the society. It gives the members of the society confidence, it dispels their anxieties, it disciplines their social organization.

No argument will be raised here against the sociological and psychological functions imputed by Homans, and many others before him, to ritual. They seem to me to be plausible. Nevertheless, in some cases at least, ritual does produce, in Homans' terms, "a practical result on the world" external not only to the social unit composed of those who participate together in ritual performances but also to the larger unit composed of those who entertain similar beliefs concerning the universe. The material presented here will show that the ritual cycles of the Tsembaga, and of

Reproduced by permission of the publisher and Roy A. Rappaport from *Ethnology*, 6:17-30 (1967).

other local territorial groups of Maring speakers living in the New Guinea interior, play an important part in regulating the relationships of these groups with both the nonhuman components of their immediate environments and the human components of their less immediate environments, that is, with other similar territorial groups. To be more specific, this regulation helps to maintain the biotic communities existing within their territories, redistributes land among people and people over land, and limits the frequency of fighting. In the absence of authoritative political statuses or offices, the ritual cycle likewise provides a means for mobilizing allies when warfare may be undertaken. It also provides a mechanism for redistributing local pig surpluses in the form of pork throughout a large regional population while helping to assure the local population of a supply of pork when its members are most in need of high quality protein.

Religious ritual may be defined, for the purposes of this paper, as the prescribed performance of conventionalized acts manifestly directed toward the involvement of nonempirical or supernatural agencies in the affairs of the actors. While this definition relies upon the formal characteristics of the performances and upon the motives for undertaking them, attention will be focused upon the empirical effects of ritual performances and sequences of ritual performances. The religious rituals to be discussed are regarded as neither more nor less than part of the behavioral repertoire employed by an aggregate of organisms in adjusting to its environment.

The data upon which this paper is based were collected during fourteen months of field work among the Tsembaga, one of about twenty local groups of Maring speakers living in the Simbai and Jimi Valleys of the Bismarck Range in the Territory of New Guinea. The size of Maring local groups varies from a little over 100 to 900. The Tsembaga, who in 1963 numbered 204 persons, are located on the south wall of the Simbai Valley. The country in which they live differs from the true highlands in being lower, generally more rugged, and more heavily forested. Tsembaga territory rises, within a total surface area of 3.2 square miles, from an elevation of 2,200 feet at the Simbai river to 7,200 feet at the ridge crest. Gardens are cut in the secondary forests up to between 5,000 and 5,400 feet, above which the area remains in primary forest. Rainfall reaches 150 inches per year.

The Tsembaga have come into contact with the outside world only recently; the first government patrol to penetrate their territory arrived in 1954. They were considered uncontrolled by the Australian government until 1962, and they remain unmissionized to this day.

The 204 Tsembaga are distributed among five putatively patrilineal clans, which are, in turn, organized into more inclusive groupings on two hierarchical levels below that of the total local group.[2] Internal political structure is highly egalitarian. There are no hereditary or elected chiefs, nor are there even "big men" who can regularly coerce or command the

support of their clansmen or co-residents in economic or forceful enterprises.

It is convenient to regard the Tsembaga as a population in the ecological
sense, that is, as one of the components of a system of trophic exchanges
taking place within a bounded area. Tsembaga territory and the biotic
community existing upon it may be conveniently viewed as an ecosystem.
While it would be permissible arbitrarily to designate the Tsembaga as a
population and their territory with its biota as an ecosystem, there are
also nonarbitrary reasons for doing so. An ecosystem is a system of material
exchanges, and the Tsembaga maintain against other human groups exclusive access to the resources within their territorial borders. Conversely,
it is from this territory alone that the Tsembaga ordinarily derive all of
their food-stuffs and most of the other materials they require for survival.
Less anthropocentrically, it may be justified to regard Tsembaga territory
with its biota as an ecosystem in view of the rather localized nature of
cyclical material exchanges in tropical rainforests.

As they are involved with the nonhuman biotic community within their
territory in a set of trophic exchanges, so do they participate in other
material relationships with other human groups external to their territory.
Genetic materials are exchanged with other groups, and certain crucial
items, such as stone axes, were in past obtained from the outside. Furthermore, in the area occupied by the Maring speakers, more than one local
group is usually involved in any process, either peaceful or warlike, through
which people are redistributed over land and land redistributed among
people.

The concept of the ecosystem, though it provides a convenient frame
for the analysis of interspecific trophic exchanges taking place within
limited geographical areas, does not comfortably accommodate intra-
specific exchanges taking place over wider geographic areas. Some sort
of geographic population model would be more useful for the analysis of
the relationship of the local ecological population to the larger regional
population of which it is a part, but we lack even a set of appropriate
terms for such a model. Suffice it here to note that the relations of the
Tsembaga to the total of other local human populations in their vicinity
are similar to the relations of local aggregates of other animals to the
totality of their species occupying broader and more or less continuous
regions. This larger, more inclusive aggregate may resemble what geneti-
cists mean by the term population, that is, an aggregate of interbreeding
organisms persisting through an indefinite number of generations and
either living or capable of living in isolation from similar aggregates of
the same species. This is the unit which survives through long periods
of time while its local ecological (*sensu stricto*) sub-units, the units more
or less independently involved in interspecific trophic exchanges such as
the Tsembaga, are ephemeral.

Since it has been asserted that the ritual cycles of the Tsembaga regulate relationships within what may be regarded as a complex system, it is necessary, before proceeding to the ritual cycle itself, to describe briefly, and where possible in quantitative terms, some aspects of the place of the Tsembaga in this system.

The Tsembaga are bush-fallowing horticulturalists. Staples include a range of root crops, taro (*Colocasia*) and sweet potatoes being most important, yams and manioc less so. In addition, a great variety of greens are raised, some of which are rich in protein. Sugar cane and some tree crops, particularly *Pandanus conoideus,* are also important.

All gardens are mixed, many of them containing all of the major root crops and many greens. Two named garden types are, however, distinguished by the crops which predominate in them. "Taro-yam gardens" were found to produce, on the basis of daily harvest records kept on entire gardens for close to one year, about 5,300,000 calories[3] per acre during their harvesting lives of 18 to 24 months; 85 per cent of their yield is harvested between 24 and 76 weeks after planting. "Sugar-sweet potato gardens" produce about 4,600,000 calories per acre during their harvesting lives, 91 per cent being taken between 24 and 76 weeks after planting. I estimated that approximately 310,000 calories per acre is expended on cutting, fencing, planting, maintaining, harvesting, and walking to and from taro-yam gardens. Sugar-sweet potato gardens required an expenditure of approximately 290,000 calories per acre.[4] These energy ratios, approximately 17:1 on taro-yam gardens and 16:1 on sugar-sweet potato gardens, compare favorably with figures reported for swidden cultivation in other regions.[5]

Intake is high in comparison with the reported dietaries of other New Guinea populations. On the basis of daily consumption records kept for ten months on four households numbering in total sixteen persons, I estimated the average daily intake of adult males to be approximately 2,600 calories, and that of adult females to be around 2,200 calories. It may be mentioned here that the Tsembaga are small and short statured. Adult males average 101 pounds in weight and approximately 58.5 inches in height; the corresponding averages for adult females are 85 pounds and 54.5 inches.[6]

Although 99 per cent by weight of the food consumed is vegetable, the protein intake is high by New Guinea standards. The daily protein consumption of adult males from vegetable sources was estimated to be between 43 and 55 grams, of adult females 36 to 48 grams. Even with an adjustment for vegetable sources, these values are slightly in excess of the recently published WHO/FAO daily requirements (Food and Agriculture Organization of the United Nations 1964. The same is true of the younger age categories, although soft and discolored hair, a symptom of protein deficiency, was noted in a few children. The WHO/FAO protein requirements do not include a large "margin for safety" or allowance for stress; and, although no clinical assessments were undertaken, it may be suggested that the Tsembaga achieve nitrogen balance at a low level. In other words, their protein intake is probably marginal.

Measurements of all gardens made during 1962 and of some gardens made during 1963 indicate that, to support the human population, between .15 and .19 acres are put into cultivation per capita per year. Fallows range from 8 to 45 years. The area in secondary forest comprises approximately 1,000 acres, only 30 to 50 of which are in cultivation at any time. Assuming calories to be the limiting factor, and assuming an unchanging population structure, the territory could support—with no reduction in lengths of fallow and without cutting into the virgin forest from which the Tsembaga extract many important items—between 290 and 397 people if the pig population remained minimal. The size of the pig herd, however, fluctuates widely. Taking Maring pig husbandry procedures into consideration, I have estimated the human carrying capacity of the Tsembaga territory at between 270 and 320 people.

Because the timing of the ritual cycle is bound up with the demography of the pig herd, the place of the pig in Tsembaga adaptation must be examined.

First, being omnivorous, pigs keep residential areas free of garbage and human feces. Second, limited numbers of pigs rooting in secondary growth may help to hasten the development of that growth. The Tsembaga usually permit pigs to enter their gardens one and a half to two years after planting, by which time second-growth trees are well established there. The Tsembaga practice selective weeding; from the time the garden is planted, herbaceous species are removed, but tree species are allowed to remain. By the time cropping is discontinued and the pigs are let in, some of the trees in the garden are already ten to fifteen feet tall. These well-established trees are relatively impervious to damage by the pigs, which, in rooting for seeds and remaining tubers, eliminate many seeds and seedlings that, if allowed to develop, would provide some competition for the established trees. Moreover, in some Maring-speaking areas swiddens are planted twice, although this is not the case with the Tsembaga. After the first crop is almost exhausted, pigs are penned in the garden, where their rooting eliminates weeds and softens the ground, making the task of planting for a second time easier. The pigs, in other words, are used as cultivating machines.

Small numbers of pigs are easy to keep. They run free during the day and return home at night to receive their ration of garbage and substandard tubers, particularly sweet potatoes. Supplying the latter requires little extra work, for the substandard tubers are taken from the ground in the course of harvesting the daily ration for humans. Daily consumption records kept over a period of some months shows that the ration of tubers received by the pigs approximates in weight that consumed by adult humans, i.e., a little less than three pounds per day per pig.

If the pig herd grows large, however, the substandard tubers incidentally obtained in the course of harvesting for human needs become insufficient, and it becomes necessary to harvest especially for pigs. In other words, people must work for the pigs and perhaps even supply them with food fit for human consumption. Thus, as Vayda, Leeds, and Smith (1961: 71) have pointed out, there can be too many pigs for a given community.

This also holds true of the sanitary and cultivating services rendered by pigs. A small number of pigs is sufficient to keep residential areas clean, to suppress superfluous seedlings in abandoned gardens, and to soften the soil in gardens scheduled for second plantings. A larger herd, on the other hand, may be troublesome; the larger the number of pigs, the greater the possibility of their invasion of producing gardens, with concomitant damage not only to crops and young secondary growth but also to the relations between the pig owners and garden owners.

All male pigs are castrated at approximately three months of age, for boars, people say, are dangerous and do not grow as large as barrows. Pregnancies, therefore, are always the result of unions of domestic sows with feral males. Fecundity is thus only a fraction of its potential. During one twelve-month period only fourteen litters resulted out of a potential 99 or more pregnancies. Farrowing generally takes place in the forest, and mortality of the young is high. Only 32 of the offspring of the above-mentioned fourteen pregnancies were alive six months after birth. This number is barely sufficient to replace the number of adult animals which would have died or been killed during most years without pig festivals.

The Tsembaga almost never kill domestic pigs outside of ritual contexts. In ordinary times, when there is no pig festival in progress, these rituals are almost always associated with misfortunes or emergencies, notably warfare, illness, injury, or death. Rules state not only the contexts in which pigs are to be ritually slaughtered, but also who may partake of the flesh of the sacrificial animals. During warfare it is only the men participating in the fighting who eat the pork. In cases of illness or injury, it is only the victim and certain near relatives, particularly his co-resident agnates and spouses, who do so.

It is reasonable to assume that misfortune and emergency are likely to induce in the organisms experiencing them a complex of physiological changes known collectively as "stress." Physiological stress reactions occur not only in organisms which are infected with disease or traumatized, but also in those experiencing rage or fear (Houssay *et al.* 1955: 1096), or even prolonged anxiety (National Research Council 1963: 53). One important aspect of stress is the increased catabolization of protein (Houssay *et al.* 1955: 451; National Research Council 1963: 49), with a net loss of nitrogen from the tissues (Houssay *et al.* 1955: 450). This is a serious matter for organisms with a marginal protein intake. Antibody production is low (Berg 1948: 311), healing is slow (Large and Johnston 1948: 352), and a variety of symptoms of a serious nature are likely to develop (Lund and Levenson 1948: 349; Zintel 1964: 1943). The status of a protein-depleted animal, however, may be significantly improved in a relatively short period of time by the intake of high quality protein, and high protein diets are therefore routinely prescribed for surgical patients and those suffering from infectious diseases (Burton 1959: 231; Lund and Levenson 1948: 350; Elman 1951: 85ff; Zintel 1964: 1043ff).

It is precisely when they are undergoing physiological stress that the Tsembaga kill and consume their pigs, and it should be noted that they limit the consumption to those likely to be experiencing stress most profoundly. The Tsembaga, of course, know nothing of physiological stress. Native theories of the etiology and treatment of disease and injury implicate various categories of spirits to whom sacrifices must be made. Nevertheless, the behavior which is appropriate in terms of native understandings is also appropriate to the actual situation confronting the actors.

We may now outline in the barest of terms the Tsembaga ritual cycle. Space does not permit a description of its ideological correlates. It must suffice to note that Tsembaga do not necessarily perceive all of the empirical effects which the anthropologist sees to flow from their ritual behavior. Such empirical consequences as they may perceive, moreover, are not central to their rationalizations of the performances. The Tsembaga say that they perform the rituals in order to rearrange their relationships with the supernatural world. We may only reiterate here that behavior undertaken in reference to their "cognized environment"—an environment which includes as very important elements the spirits of ancestors—seems appropriate in their "operational environment," the material environment specified by the anthropologist through operations of observation, including measurement.

Since the rituals are arranged in a cycle, description may commence at any point. The operation of the cycle becomes clearest if we begin with the rituals performed during warfare. Opponents in all cases occupy adjacent territories, in almost all cases on the same valley wall. After hostilities have broken out, each side performs certain rituals which place the opposing side in the formal category of "enemy." A number of taboos prevail while hostilities continue. These include prohibitions on sexual intercourse and on the ingestion of certain things—food prepared by women, food grown on the lower portion of the territory, marsupials, eels, and, while actually on the fighting ground, any liquid whatsoever.

One ritual practice associated with fighting which may have some physiological consequences deserves mention. Immediately before proceeding to the fighting ground, the warriors eat heavily salted pig fat. The ingestion of salt, coupled with the taboo on drinking, has the effect of shortening the fighting day, particularly since the Maring prefer to fight only on bright sunny days. When everyone gets unbearably thirsty, according to informants, fighting is broken off.

There may formerly have been other effects if the native salt contained sodium (the production of salt was discontinued some years previous to the field work, and no samples were obtained). The Maring diet seems to be deficient in sodium. The ingestion of large amounts of sodium just prior to fighting would have permitted the warriors to sweat normally without a lowering of blood volume and consequent weakness during the course of the fighting. The pork belly ingested with the salt would have provided them with a new burst of energy two hours or so after the commencement of the engagement. After fighting was finished for the day, lean pork was consumed, offsetting, at least to some extent, the nitrogen loss associated with the stressful fighting (personal communications from F. Dunn, W. MacFarlane, and J. Sabine, 1965).

Fighting could continue sporadically for weeks. Occasionally it terminated in the rout of one of the antagonistic groups, whose survivors would take refuge with kinsmen elsewhere. In such instances, the victors would lay waste their opponents' groves and gardens, slaughter their pigs, and burn their houses. They would not, however, immediately annex the territory of the vanquished. The Maring say that they never take over the territory of an enemy for, even if it has been abandoned, the spirits of their ancestors remain to guard it against interlopers. Most fights, however, terminated in truces between the antagonists.

With the termination of hostilities a group which has not been driven off its territory performs a ritual called "planting the *rumbim.*" Every man puts his hand on the ritual plant, *rumbim (Cordyline fruticosa* (L.), A. Chev; *C. terminalis,* Kunth), as it is planted in the ground. The ancestors are addressed, in effect, as follows:

We thank you for helping us in the fight and permitting us to remain on our territory. We place our souls in this *rumbim* as we plant it on our ground. We ask you to care for this *rumbim.* We will kill pigs for you now, but they are few. In the future, when we have many pigs, we shall again give you pork and uproot the *rumbim* and stage a *kaiko* (pig festival). But until there are sufficient pigs to repay you the *rumbim* will remain in the ground.

This ritual is accompanied by the wholesale slaughter of pigs. Only juveniles remain alive. All adult and adolescent animals are killed, cooked, and dedicated to the ancestors. Some are consumed by the local group, but most are distributed to allies who assisted in the fight.

Some of the taboos which the group suffered during the time of fighting are abrogated by this ritual. Sexual intercourse is now permitted, liquids may be taken at any time, and food from any part of the territory may be eaten. But the group is still in debt to its allies and ancestors. People say it is still the time of the *bamp ku,* or "fighting stones," which are actual objects used in the rituals associated with warfare. Although the fighting ceases when *rumbim* is planted, the concomitant obligations, debts to allies and ancestors, remain outstanding; and the fighting stones may not be put away until these obligations are fulfilled. The time of the fighting stones is a time of debt and danger which lasts until the *rumbim* is uprooted and a pig festival (*kaiko*) is staged.

Certain taboos persist during the time of the fighting stones. Marsupials, regarded as the pigs of the ancestors of the high ground, may not be trapped until the debt to their masters has been repaid. Eels, the "pigs of the ancestors of the low ground," may neither be caught nor consumed. Prohibitions on all intercourse with the enemy come into force. One may not touch, talk to, or even look at a member of the enemy group, nor set foot on enemy ground. Even more important, a group may not attack another group while its ritual plant remains in the ground, for it has not yet fully rewarded its ancestors and allies for their assistance in the last fight. Until the debts to them have been paid, further assistance from them will not be forthcoming. A kind of "truce of god" thus prevails until the *rumbim* is uprooted and a *kaiko* completed.

To uproot the *rumbim* requires sufficient pigs. How many pigs are sufficient, and how long does it take to acquire them? The Tsembaga say that, if a place is "good," this can take as little as five years; but if a place is "bad," it may require ten years or longer. A bad place is one in which misfortunes are frequent and where, therefore, ritual demands for the killing of pigs arise frequently. A good place is one where such demands are infrequent. In a good place, the increase of the pig herd exceeds the ongoing ritual demands, and the herd grows rapidly. Sooner or later the substandard tubers incidentally obtained while harvesting become insufficient to feed the herd, and additional acreage must be put into production specifically for the pigs.

The work involved in caring for a large pig herd can be extremely burdensome. The Tsembaga herd just prior to the pig festival of 1962-63, when it numbered 169 animals, was receiving 54 per cent of all of the sweet potatoes and 82 per cent of all of the manioc harvested. These comprised 35.9 per cent by weight of all root crops harvested. This figure is consistent with the difference between the amount of land under cultivation just previous to the pig festival, when the herd was at maximum size, and that immediately afterwards, when the pig herd was at minimum size. The former was 36.1 per cent in excess of the latter.

I have estimated, on the basis of acreage yield and energy expenditure figures, that about 45,000 calories per year are expended in caring for one pig 120-150 pounds in size. It is upon women that most of the burden of pig keeping falls. If, from a woman's daily intake of about 2,200 calories, 950 calories are allowed for basal metabolism, a woman has only 1,250 calories a day available for all her activities, which include gardening for her family, child care, and cooking, as well as tending pigs. It is clear that no woman can feed many pigs; only a few had as many as four in their care at the commencement of the festival; and it is not surprising that agitation to uproot the *rumbim* and stage the *kaiko* starts with the wives of the owners of large numbers of pigs.

A large herd is not only burdensome as far as energy expenditure is concerned; it becomes increasingly a nuisance as it expands. The more numerous pigs become, the more frequently are gardens invaded by them. Such events result in serious disturbances of local tranquillity. The garden owner often shoots, or attempts to shoot, the offending pig; and the pig owner commonly retorts by shooting, or attempting to shoot, either the garden owner, his wife, or one of his pigs. As more and more such events occur, the settlement, nucleated when the herd was small, disperses as people try to put as much distance as possible between their pigs and other people's gardens and between their gardens and other people's pigs. Occasionally this reaches its logical conclusion, and people begin to leave the territory, taking up residence with kinsmen in other local populations.

The number of pigs sufficient to become intolerable to the Tsembaga was below the capacity of the territory to carry pigs. I have estimated that, if the size and structure of the human population remained constant at the 1962-1963 level, a pig population of 140 to 240 animals averaging 100 to 150 pounds in size could be maintained perpetually by the Tsembaga without necessarily inducing environmental degradation. Since the size of the herd fluctuates, even higher cyclical maxima could be achieved. The level of toleration, however, is likely always to be below the carrying capacity, since the destructive capacity of the pigs is dependent upon the population density of both people and pigs, rather than upon population size. The denser the human population, the fewer pigs will be required to disrupt social life. If the carrying capacity is exceeded, it is likely to be exceeded by people and not by pigs.

The *kaiko* or pig festival, which commences with the planting of stakes at the boundary and the uprooting of the *rumbim,* is thus triggered by either the additional work attendant upon feeding pigs or the destructive capacity of the pigs themselves. It may be said, then, that there are sufficient pigs to stage the *kaiko* when the relationship of pigs to people changes from one of mutualism to one of parasitism or competition.

A short time prior to the uprooting of the *rumbim,* stakes are planted at the boundary. If the enemy has continued to occupy its territory, the stakes are planted at the boundary which existed before the fight. If, on the other hand, the enemy has abandoned its territory, the victors may plant their stakes at a new boundary which encompasses areas previously occupied by the enemy. The Maring say, to be sure, that they never take land belonging to an enemy, but this land is regarded as vacant, since no *rumbim* was planted on it after the last fight. We may state here a rule of land redistribution in terms of the ritual cycle: *If one of a pair of antagonistic groups is able to uproot its rumbim before its opponents can plant their rumbim, it may occupy the latter's territory.*

Not only have the vanquished abandoned their territory; it is assumed that it has also been abandoned by their ancestors as well. The surviving members of the erstwhile enemy group have by this time resided with other groups for a number of years, and most if not all of them have already had occasion to sacrifice pigs to their ancestors at their new residences. In so doing they have invited these spirits to settle at the new locations of the living, where they will in the future receive sacrifices. Ancestors of vanquished groups thus relinquish their guardianship over the territory, making it available to victorious groups. Meanwhile, the *de facto* membership of the living in the groups with which they have taken refuge is converted eventually into *de jure* membership. Sooner or later the groups with which they have taken up residence will have occasion to plant *rumbim,* and the refugees, as co-residents, will participate, thus ritually validating their connection to the new territory and the new group. A rule of population redistribution may thus be stated in terms of ritual cycles: *A man becomes a member of a territorial group by participating with it in the planting of rumbim.*

The uprooting of the *rumbim* follows shortly after the planting of stakes at the boundary. On this particular occasion the Tsembaga killed 32 pigs out of their herd of 169. Much of the pork was distributed to allies and affines outside of the local group.

The taboo on trapping marsupials was also terminated at this time. Information is lacking concerning the population dynamics of the local marsupials, but it may well be that the taboo which had prevailed since the last fight—that against taking them in traps—had conserved a fauna which might otherwise have become extinct.

The *kaiko* continues for about a year, during which period friendly groups are entertained from time to time. The guests receive presents of vegetable foods, and the hosts and male guests dance together throughout the night.

These events may be regarded as analogous to aspects of the social behavior of many nonhuman animals. First of all, they include massed epigamic, or courtship, displays (Wynne-Edwards 1962: 17). Young women are presented with samples of the eligible males of local groups with which they may not otherwise have had the opportunity to become familiar. The context, moreover, permits the young women to discriminate amongst this sample in terms of both endurance (signaled by how vigorously and how long a man dances) and wealth (signaled by the richness of a man's shell and feather finery).

More importantly, the massed dancing at these events may be regarded as epideictic display, communicating to the participants information concerning the size or density of the group (Wynne-Edwards 1962: 16). In many species such displays take place as a prelude to actions which adjust group size or density, and such is the case among the Maring. The massed dancing of the visitors at a *kaiko* entertainment communicates to the hosts, while the *rumbim* truce is still in force, information concerning the amount of support they may expect from the visitors in the bellicose enterprises that they are likely to embark upon soon after the termination of the pig festival.

Among the Maring there are no chiefs or other political authorities capable of commanding the support of a body of followers, and the decision to assist another group in warfare rests with each individual male. Allies are not recruited by appealing for help to other local groups as such. Rather, each member of the groups primarily involved in the hostilities appeals to his cognatic and affinal kinsmen in other local groups. These men, in turn, urge other of their co-residents and kinsmen to "help them fight." The channels through which invitations to dance are extended are precisely those through which appeals for military support are issued. The invitations go not from group to group, but from kinsman to kinsman, the recipients of invitations urging their co-residents to "help them dance."

Invitations to dance do more than exercise the channels through which allies are recruited; they provide a means for judging their effectiveness. Dancing and fighting are regarded as in some sense equivalent. This equivalence is expressed in the similarity of some pre-fight and pre-dance rituals, and the Maring say that those who come to dance come to fight. The size of a visiting dancing contingent is consequently taken as a measure of the size of the contingent of warriors whose assistance may be expected in the next round of warfare.

In the morning the dancing ground turns into a trading ground. The items most frequently exchanged include axes, bird plumes, shell ornaments, an occasional baby pig, and, in former times, native salt. The *kaiko* thus facilitates trade by providing a market-like setting in which large numbers of traders can assemble. It likewise facilitates the movement of two critical items, salt and axes, by creating a demand for the bird plumes which may be exchanged for them.

The *kaiko* concludes with major pig sacrifices. On this particular occasion the Tsembaga butchered 105 adult and adolescent pigs, leaving only 60 juveniles and neonates alive. The survival of an additional fifteen adolescents and adults was only temporary, for they were scheduled as imminent victims. The pork yielded by the Tsembaga slaughter was estimated to weigh between 7,000 and 8,500 pounds, of which between 4,500 and 6,000 pounds were distributed to members of other local groups in 163 separate presentations. An estimated 2,000 to 3,000 people in seventeen local groups were the beneficiaries of the redistribution. The presentations, it should be mentioned, were not confined to pork. Sixteen Tsembaga men presented bridewealth or child-wealth, consisting largely of axes and shells, to their affines at this time.

The *kaiko* terminates on the day of the pig slaughter with the public presentation of salted pig belly to allies of the last fight. Presentations are made through the window in a high ceremonial fence built specially for the occasion at one end of the dance ground. The name of each honored man is announced to the assembled multitude as he charges to the window to receive his hero's portion. The fence is then ritually torn down, and the fighting stones are put away. The pig festival and the ritual cycle have been completed, demonstrating, it may be suggested, the ecological and economic competence of the local population. The local population would now be free, if it were not for the presence of the government, to attack its enemy again, secure in the knowledge that the assistance of allies and ancestors would be forthcoming because they have received pork and the obligations to them have been fulfilled.

Usually fighting did break out again very soon after the completion of the ritual cycle. If peace still prevailed when the ceremonial fence had rotted completely—a process said to take about three years, a little longer than the length of time required to raise a pig to maximum size— *rumbim* was planted as if there had been a fight, and all adult and adolescent pigs were killed. When the pig herd was large enough so that the *rumbim* could be uprooted, peace could be made with former enemies if they were also able to dig out their *rumbim*. To put this in formal terms: *If a pair of antagonistic groups proceeds through two ritual cycles without resumption of hostilities their enmity may be terminated.*

The relations of the Tsembaga with their environment have been analyzed as a complex system composed of two subsystems. What may be called the "local subsystem" has been derived from the relations of the Tsembaga with the nonhuman components of their immediate or territorial environment. It corresponds to the ecosystem in which the Tsembaga participate. A second subsystem, one which corresponds to the larger regional population of which the Tsembaga are one of the constituent units and which may be designated as the "regional subsystem," has been derived from the relations of the Tsembaga with neighboring local populations similar to themselves.

It has been argued that rituals, arranged in repetitive sequences, regulate relations both within each of the subsystems and within the larger complex system as a whole. The timing of the ritual cycle is largely dependent upon changes in the states of the components of the local subsystem. But the *kaiko,* which is the culmination of the ritual cycle, does more than reverse changes which have taken place within the local subsystem. Its occurrence also affects relations among the components of the regional subsystem. During its performance, obligations to other local populations are fulfilled, support for future military enterprises is rallied, and land from which enemies have earlier been driven is occupied. Its completion, furthermore, permits the local population to initiate warfare again. Conversely, warfare is terminated by rituals which preclude the reinitiation of warfare until the state of the local subsystem is again such that a *kaiko* may be staged and completed. Ritual among the Tsembaga and other Maring, in short, operates as both transducer, "translating" changes in the state of one subsystem into information which can effect changes in a second subsystem, and homeostat, maintaining a number of variables which in sum comprise the total system within ranges of viability. To repeat an earlier assertion, the operation of ritual among the Tsembaga and other Maring helps to maintain an undegraded environment, limits fighting to frequencies which do not endanger the existence of the regional population, adjusts man-land ratios, facilitates trade, distributes local surpluses of pig throughout the regional population in the form of pork, and assures people of high quality protein when they are most in need of it.

Religious rituals and the supernatural orders toward which they are directed cannot be assumed *a priori* to be mere epiphenomena. Ritual may, and doubtless frequently does, do nothing more than validate and intensify the relationships which integrate the social unit, or symbolize the relationships which bind the social unit to its environment. But the interpretation of such presumably *sapiens*-specific phenomena as religious ritual within a framework which will also accommodate the behavior of other species shows, I think, that religious ritual may do much more than symbolize, validate, and intensify relationships. Indeed, it would not be improper to refer to the Tsembaga and the other entities with which they share their territory as a "ritually regulated ecosystem," and to the Tsembaga and their human neighbors as a "ritually regulated population."

NOTES

1. The field work upon which this paper is based was supported by a grant from the National Science Foundation, under which Professor A. P. Vayda was principal investigator. Personal support was received by the author from the National Institutes of Health. Earlier versions of this paper were presented at the 1964 annual meeting of the American Anthropological Association in Detroit, and before a Columbia University seminar on Ecological Systems and Cultural Evolution. I have received valuable suggestions from Alexander Alland, Jacques Barrau, William Clarke, Paul Collins, C. Glen King, Marvin Harris, Margaret Mead, M. J. Meggitt, Ann Rappaport, John Street, Marjorie Whiting, Cherry Vayda, A. P. Vayda and many others, but I take full responsibility for the analysis presented herewith.

2. The social organization of the Tsembaga will be described in detail elsewhere.

3. Because the length of time in the field precluded the possibility of maintaining harvest records on single gardens from planting through abandonment, figures were based, in the case of both "taro-yam" and "sugar-sweet potato" gardens, on three separate gardens planted in successive years. Conversions from the gross weight to the caloric value of yields were made by reference to the literature. The sources used are listed in Rappaport (1966: Appendix VIII)

4. Rough time and motion studies of each of the tasks involved in making, maintaining, harvesting, and walking to and from gardens were undertaken. Conversion to energy expenditure values was accomplished by reference to energy expenditure tables prepared by Hipsley and Kirk (1965: 43) on the basis of gas exchange measurements made during the performance of garden tasks by the Chimbu people of the New Guinea highlands.

5. Marvin Harris, in an unpublished paper, estimates the ratio of energy return to energy input ratio on Dyak (Borneo) rice swiddens at 10:1. His estimates of energy ratios on Tepotzlan (Meso-America) swiddens range from 13:1 on poor land to 29:1 on the best land.

6. Heights may be inaccurate. Many men wear their hair in large coiffures hardened with pandanus grease, and it was necessary in some instances to estimate the location of the top of the skull.

BIBLIOGRAPHY

BERG, C. 1948. Protein Deficiency and Its Relation to Nutritional Anemia, Hypoproteinemia, Nutritional Edema, and Resistance to Infection. Protein and Amino Acids in Nutrition, ed. M. Sahyun, pp. 290-317. New York.

BURTON, B. T., ed. 1959. The Heinz Handbook of Nutrition. New York.

ELMAN, R. 1951. Surgical Care. New York.

FOOD AND AGRICULTURE ORGANIZATION OF THE UNITED NATIONS. 1964. Protein: At the Heart of the World Food Problem. World Food Problems 5. Rome.

HIPSLEY, E., and N. KIRK. 1965. Studies of the Dietary Intake and Energy Expenditure of New Guineans. South Pacific Commission, Technical Paper 147. Noumea.

HOMANS, G. C. 1941. Anxiety and Ritual: The Theories of Malinowski and Radcliffe-Brown. American Anthropologist 43: 164-172.

HOUSSAY, B. A., et al. 1955. Human Physiology. 2nd edit. New York.

LARGE, A., and C. G. JOHNSTON. 1948. Proteins as Related to Burns. Proteins and Amino Acids in Nutrition, ed. M. Sahyun, pp. 386-396. New York.

LUND, C. G., and S. M. LEVENSON. 1948. Protein Nutrition in Surgical Patients. Proteins and Amino Acids in Nutrition, ed. M. Sahyun, pp. 349-363. New York.

MOORE, O. K. 1957. Divination—a New Perspective. American Anthropologist 59: 69-74.

NATIONAL RESEARCH COUNCIL. 1963. Evaluation of Protein Quality. National Academy of Sciences—National Research Council Publication 1100. Washington.

RAPPAPORT, R. A. 1966. Ritual in the Ecology of a New Guinea People. Unpublished doctoral dissertation, Columbia University.

VAYDA, A. P., A. LEEDS, and D. B. SMITH. 1961. The Place of Pigs in Melanesian Subsistence. Proceedings of the 1961 Annual Spring Meeting of the American Ethnological Society, ed. V. E. Garfield, pp. 69-77. Seattle.

WYNNE-EDWARDS, V. C. 1962. Animal Dispersion in Relation to Social Behaviour. Edinburgh and London.

ZINTEL, HAROLD A. 1964. Nutrition in the Care of the Surgical Patient. Modern Nutrition in Health and Disease, ed. M. G. Wohl and R. S. Goodhart, pp. 1043-1064. Third edit. Philadelphia.

5

RED-FEATHER MONEY

William Davenport

One of the most exotic kinds of money in the world today is a belt two inches wide and 30 feet long made of glue, fibers and feathers, particularly the downy red feathers plucked from the breast, head and back of a tropical forest bird. The red-feather currency of the Santa Cruz Islands of the Southwest Pacific nonetheless fits the most rigorous definition of the term "money." It serves as a means of accumulating wealth and as a universal medium of exchange in the highly diversified commerce that flows among these islands. The currency itself is fully interchangeable, each belt having a precisely negotiable value in terms of other belts. Against the recent invasion of the Australian pound, moreover, the red-feather money has kept its integrity. It is still the only acceptable specie for the purchase of brides, fine pigs and certain forms of labor.

This improbable currency demonstrates that the use of money is not an economic sophistication limited to high civilizations. Many, but by no means all, primitive peoples have devised moneys of their own. Although the forms of the currencies are as diverse as any of man's inventions— running the gamut of animal, vegetable and mineral matter in the live, raw and processed states—the maintenance of these so-called primitive monetary systems requires the balancing of the same equation of supply and demand that confronts the U.S. Treasury and the Federal Reserve System.

If a currency is to serve as a common denominator of value, its value in turn must be carefully regulated. This is one of the most delicate operations in the management of a modern state. It involves adjustment of the demand for as well as supply of money, achieved by control over both the flow and the production of the currency. To a certain extent, especially for purposes of international exchange, the Western capitalist economies still refer their currencies to the value of gold on the world market. But in the main it is the scope of the modern state's authority and the extent of its jurisdiction that effectively fix the value of its currency.

Lacking the power to regulate demand (by such devices as manipula-

Reprinted with permission from *Scientific American*, 206:94-104 (1962). Copyright © 1962 by Scientific American, Inc. All rights reserved.

tion of the interest rate), primitive societies must rely on measures that control the supply of currency against the demand in their completely free markets. Frequently the supply is limited by natural or social circumstances beyond the control of its users, much as the scarcity of gold or silver once set the value of the dollar or the pound. Often, however, the nature of the currency is such that the society could "mint" it without limit. Scarcity is then maintained by some convention that, through consumption, destruction or deterioration, renders the currency valueless and withdraws it from circulation.

The red-feather currency system shows both principles in operation. The supply of new money is regulated by the availability of the red feathers and by the output of the hunters and artisans who make the money; old currency goes out of circulation because it loses value as its color fades. Produced by the natives of Santa Cruz Island itself, the red-feather currency circulates throughout most of the islands in the group. In these islands, where the indigenous political organization has never extended beyond a single village, it functions as international currency, the common medium of exchange among peoples who speak different languages and live in contrasting ecological settings.

The Santa Cruz Islands, part of the British Solomon Islands Protectorate, are scattered over some 15,000 square miles of the Pacific Ocean just north of the New Hebrides Islands. Santa Cruz, a volcanic island, is the largest in the group as well as its financial center. About 25 miles to the north is a chain of small coral islets called the Reef Islands, and midway between these and Santa Cruz is Tinakula, a volcano too spectacularly active for human settlement. The Duff Islands, 60 miles northeast of the Reefs, are remnant peaks of a narrow volcanic ridge. The only other large islands of the group are Utupua and Vanikoro, respectively some 40 and 60 miles south of Santa Cruz.

Partly as the result of a long history of inhospitality to visiting mariners and missionaries, the islands were left pretty much to themselves even through the first two decades of this century, when colonial powers were asserting dominion over other islands in the Pacific. It was not until 1923 that the British assumed direct administration of the islands, which they had claimed since 1899, and only since World War II has the Santa Cruz group actually been drawn into the current of world affairs. Today some 7,000 people inhabit the islands, most of them concentrated along the north coast of Santa Cruz and in the eastern Reef Islands. The people of the Duffs and the western Reefs speak a Polynesian language and are racially similar to the Polynesians of the central Pacific islands. The darker Melanesians of the eastern Reefs and Santa Cruz itself speak four local languages that constitute an independent language family. Melanesians also live on Utupua and Vanikoro, but their three languages belong to the large Malayo-Polynesian family. The cultures of Santa Cruz and the islands north of it are similar in spite of language and racial differences, and it is through this area that the red-feather money circulates. Utupua and Vanikoro have different cultures and do not use feather currency, although their economy is closely linked to that of the red-feather islands.

Diversity and specialization, necessitated in part by differences in geology and geography, characterize the economies of the islands. Santa Cruz, where there is plenty of arable land, exports taro root and yams, the staple vegetables of these people, to the Reef Islands, where the sandy soil will not grow good root crops. The natives of certain islands and districts with particular types of reef offshore, with lagoons or with easy access to the deep sea are exporters of fish; pigs are bred in sandy areas where coconuts for feeding are plentiful, and several kinds of arboriculture are associated with the rainfall and forest cover peculiar to other areas. But specialization goes beyond ecology. Such arts as the raising and training of hunting dogs, canoe building, weaving, the manufacturing of bark cloth, tools and ornaments—and currency making—are indigenous to one or another small island or to one village on an island. Each of these specialized industries and crafts is regarded by its practitioners as a right inherited in the family line, and only individuals in the proper line of succession may manufacture currency, go shark fishing, build canoes or follow any other trade.

This primitive division of labor requires in many instances that raw or semiprocessed materials be brought from one district or island to another, where the goods are finished for local consumption or for export. In the busy commerce of the interisland economy goods are rarely bartered. They are sold for currency: feather money or, increasingly, Australian currency. For all who participate the motivation of this trade goes beyond the exchange of necessities and native luxuries; the islanders buy and sell for the express purpose of making money. The accumulation of money is the way to prestige. But since the currency itself is perishable, prestige finds its tangible expression in spending as well as in accumulation, above all in helping to buy brides for members of one's family and friends and in giving feasts. Prestige won in these ways is the source of political power and authority.

The red-feather currency is made only on Santa Cruz Island. It is made on contract for a specific purchaser, who negotiates individually with the three different hereditary specialists whose combined skills are required for its manufacture. The first specialist snares the little jungle bird whose down supplies the red color of the money. The second makes individual platelets of pigeon feathers and decorates each with a band of the red down. The third assembles the platelets by binding them on two cords to form a belt.

The bird on which the entire system depends is a small scarlet-colored honey eater (*Myzomela cardinalis*) of the rain forest. The bird snarer makes portable perches covered with the sticky latex of a forest tree

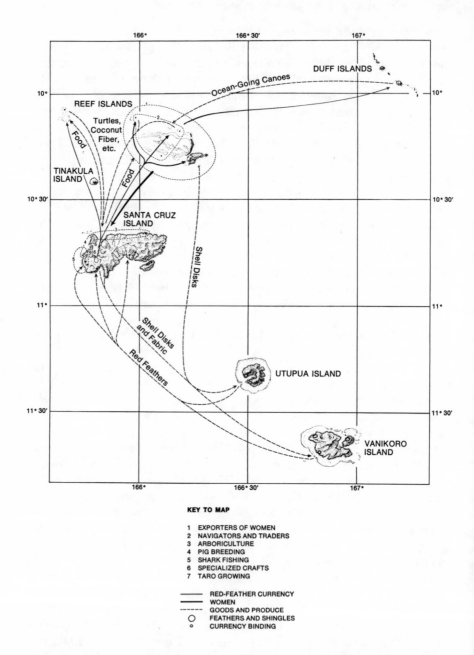

KEY TO MAP

1 EXPORTERS OF WOMEN
2 NAVIGATORS AND TRADERS
3 ARBORICULTURE
4 PIG BREEDING
5 SHARK FISHING
6 SPECIALIZED CRAFTS
7 TARO GROWING

——————— RED-FEATHER CURRENCY
————— WOMEN
- - - - - GOODS AND PRODUCE
○ FEATHERS AND SHINGLES
∘ CURRENCY BINDING

Economic map of the Santa Cruz group shows the specialized areas of origin of some of the major agricultural and manufactured products and the complex trade pattern made feasible by the red-feather monetary system. Feather money, which is made only in certain districts of Santa Cruz Island, circulates there and in the Reefs and Duffs.

86

and fastens at the top of each either a live decoy of the species or a flower that the honey eater likes. Hanging a number of these perches in adjacent trees, he shields himself behind a blind of betel palm leaves and attracts birds into the area by chirping with a whistle made from a tree bud. Investigating the flower or the decoy, the honey eaters approach the sticky perch and are caught by their wings or feet. The bird snarer plucks the red down from the birds' breasts, heads and backs; he does not deliberately kill them in the process, but they usually die as a result. In the half-shell of a coconut he packs tightly the down of 10 birds, and this is the basic unit in which he deals.

The platelet maker usually secures his own pigeon feathers, shooting the gray Pacific pigeon (*Ducula pacifica*) with bow and arrow. With a mucilage made from the sap of the paper mulberry (*Broussonetia papyrifera*), he glues the feathers together into the flexible platelet. The flat surface of a wooden platen, usually about 2¼ by 1¼ inches, serves as a gauge for fashioning each platelet in the proper size. Using the same glue, the craftsman tacks a half-inch band of red down from the honey eaters along one edge of the gray platelet. A piece of currency requires about 1,500 platelets, overlapped like shingles to expose only the band of red feathers. Since one 10-bird packet of down is enough for 50 platelets, about 300 honey eaters are required for a standard piece of new currency.

The platelets are passed on to the currency binder, who collects and prepares the other necessary materials: long-staple fibers from the bark of a rainforest tree (*Gnetum gnemon*), colored seeds for decoration and pieces of turtle shell. He stretches two three-ply fiber cords from a large stump to a springy sapling set in the ground about five feet away, and he spaces the cords about two inches apart by means of a notched spacer made from the wing bone of a fruit bat. The spacer marks the center of the belt of currency. Over it a special platelet, with a band of red in the middle instead of along one edge, is placed and bound to the cords. Working outward from the center, first toward one end and then toward the other, this craftsman proceeds to place and wrap the feather shingles one at a time. He maintains the proper distance between the cords with a sliding bat-bone spacer that he moves a quarter of an inch for each platelet [*see illustrations on pp. 88-89*]. When he has bound 750 platelets toward each end, he brings the foundation cords together, sheathes them with turtle shell and plaits them into a triangular end piece into which he works a hallmark design of his own. Finally the cords, braided together, are fastened to a bark ring. The completed belt of currency is rolled up from the ends toward the center like a scroll, the shingling of the feathered surface resembling the scales of a snake when its spine is flexed.

All three of the skills involved in the manufacturing of feather money are believed to have been given to mortals by munificent spirits who still inhabit the island, keeping a watchful eye on the work of their protégés.

None of the tasks requires exceptional skill or a lengthy apprenticeship, but the craftsman depends on secret incantations and talismans to keep in close communion with the spirits. The right to pursue a currency-making skill comes with the inheritance of these magic secrets; no unauthorized person will risk the anger of the spirits by making his own currency. Many of the islands' other specialties have their own supernatural trappings, which reinforce the restrictions imposed by heredity. No specialty is regarded as superior to any other and none, not even currency making, is likely

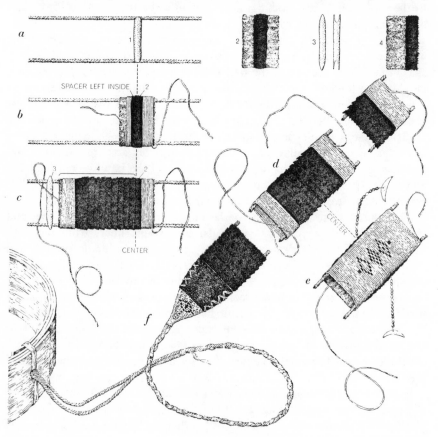

Binder's materials include (*a*) two fiber foundation cords with a bone spacer marking the center (*1*), a center platelet with red down in the middle (*2*), a movable spacer (*3*) and platelets with down along one edge (*4*). After placing the center platelet (*b*), the binder overlaps the others (*c*) one by one like shingles, maintaining the proper width with the movable spacer. He works outward from the center (*d*), which is marked with a woven design and pearl-shell pendants (*e*). At each end (*f*) he sheaths the belt with turtle shell, plaits in his hallmark, braids the two cords and attaches them to the bark cores on which the currency is wound.

to be more lucrative than another. The specialists plying each trade compete with one another, and the hereditary lines in each occupation are sufficiently numerous and dispersed so that no individual or small group can easily obtain a monopoly or control over the market.

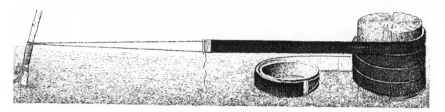

Foundation cords are stretched tightly from a tree stump to a springy sapling. The binder works on a short segment, then unties the belt and reverses it to work in the opposite direction. Each overlapping platelet covers the binding of the preceding one.

Feather currency has absolutely no other use than as a medium of exchange, a standard of value and a store of wealth. It is not worn or displayed. In other words, it has no inherent usefulness; it is a true money. Yet it is produced and circulated in a free market, controlled only by supply and demand and by the principle of devaluation over time. Inflation is avoided, in spite of the constant issuance of new money, by the depreciation and withdrawal from circulation of old money.

The size and richness of color of a new piece of currency determine its original value. These two criteria are reducible to the number of birds and the amount of labor that go into its manufacture. In addition to the down of 300 birds, the average piece embodies 500 or 600 man-hours of work by the three specialists. But the width and sometimes the length of a belt can vary. And the red hue can be more or less saturated depending on how much down was used or the extent to which the less admired orange feathers were discarded.

Depreciation comes with time from damage by vermin and molds as well as from the wear and tear of handling. Great care is taken to protect the currency. The double coils are wrapped tightly, first in a dried fan-palm leaf and then in many layers of bark cloth. Looking more like a bundle of rags than something of value, the coils are stored on a shelf under which the household fire is kept smoldering. The heat inhibits molds, the smoke keeps insects and other vermin away and the wrappings protect the money from smoke damage. In spite of these precautions, each piece of currency eventually deteriorates. When the last bit of color disappears, the belt is discarded.

The value of most currencies is referred ultimately to some standard; in the Santa Cruz Islands the standard is the unseemly combination of pigs and marriage payments. The minimum payment made to the bride's family by the groom's kin at marriage—the bride price—always consists of 10 units of currency graduated in value from a new or nearly perfect No. 1 ("bottom") piece to a No. 10 ("top") piece, which is just above the threshold of no value. The negotiation of a bride price calls for a session of formalized bargaining, involving the close examination of each coil of currency. Everyone concerned has a clear idea of the range of quality appropriate to each of the 10 units. Thus the bride price supplies not only a basic standard for the value of feather money but also a scale of ideal images in terms of which the "denomination" of any piece of currency can be expressed.

The progression is not arithmetic but geometric: each piece is worth twice as much as the one below it on the scale. If a "top" piece is given an arbitrary value of one, then a No. 6 piece is worth 16 and a "botttom" piece is worth 512. These values are not explicit. No one says that a piece is "worth 128" but all understand that an ideal No. 6 belt has a par value of two No. 7 belts. In the terminology of the pig standard, the pieces from No. 1 to No. 5 are called "porkers," because a pig suitable for a feast can be bought with currencies in this range; pieces from No. 6 to No. 10 are called "sucklings," because they will buy only pigs too small to be eaten. Except for the negotiation of bride prices, there is remarkably little haggling over the price of any purchase. The buyer of a pig or canoe or taro roots offers what he considers a fair amount of currency, and the seller accepts. If the seller feels he has been underpaid, he can seriously damage the buyer's reputation by gossiping about the transaction and refusing to deal with him again.

As in the purchase of a bride, certain other purchases must be made with specified pieces of high value. The seller has no obligation to "make change," so currency is exchanged ahead of time. This can be done by anyone, but some men who are particularly adept at money changing specialize in it and make a profit. These transactions take place before an informal gathering of witnesses in the men's clubhouse of a village, where the pieces of currency are draped over a horizontal bar for close comparison. Regardless of who has initiated the deal, the piece of greatest value (the "high piece") is hung over the center of the bar. Alongside it (and always in the direction of the Nembo River, a spring-fed stream symbolically associated with the currency spirits) is hung the "base piece," the most valuable of the belts to be exchanged for the high piece. On the other side is hung the "crown piece," the piece that makes up the difference in value between the base piece and the high piece. Values are matched in terms of the 10-point scale. For example, if the high piece is an average No. 6 and the base piece is a fine No. 7, a middling No. 7 may suffice as a crown.

In this manner the par value of the high piece is agreed on. But the price at which it now actually sells is something else again. Because high-value currency is scarcer than low-value currency, the owner of the high piece is a seller in a seller's market. The buyer (the owner of the base and crown pieces) must offer additional currency. It is not only that the high piece is newer; there are fewer new pieces in circulation. Hence market value is correlated to scarcity. The greater the par value of the high piece, the greater the spread between this value and the market price. (It is as though a $10 bill were worth a little more than two fives and a $20 bill worth more than two tens by a still larger margin.) It is the difficulty and expense of obtaining high-value pieces on the exchange market that ultimately leads a man to contract with the three currency specialists for a new piece.

Since all the feather currency originates on Santa Cruz Island, it must flow continually from its source to the Reef and Duff islands, where it is not manufactured. To maintain this one-way flow of currency the Reef Islanders have traditionally exported some of their women to Santa Cruz. Today the women go only as wives but once some went as concubines. Concubines were clearly distinguished from wives: they were shared by a group of men; they did no gardening or other domestic chores; having no dwelling of their own, they lived in the men's clubhouse. On the other hand, a concubine's possessors could purvey her services as a prostitute, sell her outright or even kill her without fear of retaliation. None of these things could be done with wives. But since the purchase price of a concubine was 10 times higher than a bride price, selling a girl into concubinage had its attractions for many Reef Island families. The British Government has forbidden the practice, but Reef Island women still go south as wives. Their bride prices are the main source of currency for their home islands. An imported wife brings extra prestige to a Santa Cruz man, and bride prices for Reef women run about twice as high as they do for domestic wives.

The Duff Islanders get their feather currency not by selling women but by building large sailing canoes that carry on interisland traffic in passengers and cargo. The men of the Duffs do not engage in that traffic themselves; they sell the canoes for feather currency to the people of a few of the western Reef Islands, who in turn specialize in voyaging and trading throughout the islands. These mariners sail even to the southern islands of Utupua and Vanikoro in search of trade. The two islands are outside the feather-currency area, but their people until recently depended on the canoes to bring them the shell disks and lengths of woven cloth they used as currency. For these precious items they traded, at fixed rates, packets of red honey eater feathers, and these were resold on Santa Cruz to the makers of feather currency. In this manner the two different money systems became interlocked and interdependent, and the economies of north and south remain so today, even though there is no longer any traffic in currency materials.

Since the end of World War II the Santa Cruz monetary system has come under pressure from the world outside. More and more Australian money has flowed into the islands; it circulates along with the feather currency and is completely interchangeable with it. Today the rate of exchange is roughly one shilling for a piece of feather money of minimum value. This makes the par value of a No. 1 piece 512 shillings, or about 25 Australian pounds. Figured in terms of labor (at the prevailing net wage rate for unskilled labor in the central Solomons, where most Santa Cruz men work at some point in their lives), the value of a new piece of currency is roughly comparable: about 20 to 24 pounds.

Plantation wages have nearly trebled since 1945. The great increase in the quantity of Australian money within the Santa Cruz group has caused a precipitate fall in its value in terms of local goods. Once a shilling bought 10 pounds of native tobacco; now it buys half a pound. During the same period, in an effort to increase copra production by channeling more islanders into plantation work, the colonial administration has taken steps that tend to depress interisland and intervillage trade in domestic products. Less feather currency is needed and less is being produced. At the moment there are only five men on Santa Cruz who bind currency, whereas a decade ago there were more than a dozen. Yet marriages go on as before, and men still refuse to marry off their daughters without receiving the traditional red-feather payment. Indeed, there is no area of the islands' economy in which confidence in the feather currency has been shaken. The craft and agricultural specialists still demand red-feather money for their best products.

With the value of feather currency rising as it becomes scarcer and that of Australian money dropping as it becomes more abundant, the market price of feather currency in Australian pounds has increased nearly 20 times in the past 15 years. Although it is recognized that 25 Australian pounds is the appropriate par value for a new piece of feather money, it takes considerably more than that to induce the currency specialists to turn one out. This is, to be sure, not true in the case of the bird snarers. As a result of the decreased production of feather money, the *Myzomela cardinalis* population has been increasing; the snarers can take birds more easily and in more accessible places and they would be willing to work for the old rates. But the labor involved in making platelets and binding new currency has not diminished. Like skilled artisans anywhere, the specialists in these processes prefer to charge more and work less. In pricing their labor they are mindful not only of today's high market but also of the fact that the value of their product in Australian money is likely to be even greater as time passes. As a result the production of feather currency has now fallen behind even the currently reduced demand. As the "bad" Australian money drives out the "good" red-feather currency in accordance with Gresham's law, a simple society in the South Seas is experiencing a monetary crisis familiar to many more sophisticated economies.

FURTHER READINGS

Extremely useful guides for the general subject area of this part are *A Pacific Bibliography*, edited by Taylor, and *An Ethnographic Bibliography of New Guinea*, compiled by the Department of Anthropology and Sociology of the Australian National University. General information and historical materials are available in *The Pacific Islands Yearbook*, published by Pacific Publications, and *The History of Melanesia*, put out by the University of Papua and New Guinea.

An introduction to the geography of Melanesia is contained in the papers by Bowman and Coulter in *Geography of the Pacific*, edited by Freeman. Useful information and accurate maps are contained in Kennedy's *A Descriptive Atlas of the Pacific Islands*. Howlett's *A Geography of Papua and New Guinea* provides an excellent description of the geography of the Australian-administered territories in New Guinea.

Additional information on ecology in the Pacific is provided in *Man's Place in the Island Ecosystem*, edited by Fosberg. Ecology in the Highlands of New Guinea is discussed by Brookfield in "The Ecology of Highland Settlement." For an ecological framework and a more comprehensive treatment of Tsembaga ritual, see Rappaport's *Pigs for the Ancestors*.

A good account of a Melanesian gardening cycle, and factors related to it, can be found in Harding's "Ecological and Technical Factors in a Melanesian Gardening Cycle." A comprehensive discussion of Melanesian horticulture is in Barrau's *Subsistence Agriculture in Melanesia*. Malinowski's *Coral Gardens and Their Magic* provides an intensive study of a single society. See also *Struggle for Land* by Brookfield and Brown.

Descriptions of currency systems in other Melanesian societies are given in Armstrong's "Shell Money from Rossel Island" and "Rossel Island Money"; Thurnwald's "Pigs and Currency in Buin"; Salisbury's "Politics and Shell-Money Finance in New Britain"; and Epstein's article in this volume.

For Malinowski's discussion of the Kula, see his "Kula: The Circulating Exchange of Valuables in the Archipelagoes of Eastern New Guinea" and *Argonauts of the Western Pacific*. For a different interpretation, see pages 562-565 of Harris' *The Rise of Anthropological Theory*. A detailed study of another New Guinea trade system is Harding's *Voyagers of the Vitiaz Strait*. For other general studies of Melanesian economics, see Salisbury's *From Stone to Steel* and Pospisil's *Kapauku Papuan Economy*.

PART II

SOCIAL
STRUCTURE

There has always been a tendency on the part of Melanesian researchers to work quite independently of one another and to pursue an almost infinite variety of topics. Perhaps this has been due to the diversity of peoples and languages and to the somewhat "exotic" flavor of life in Melanesia. A few scholars have written on religion, a few on economics, another on transvestism, still another on sexual antagonism. Others are fascinated by bird-of-paradise plumes, fertility rites, warfare, and even such genuine exotica as the preservation of children's feces and the smoking of human heads. There has never been a substantial number of investigators interested in a continuing attempt to solve a single problem or even interested in similar theoretical aspects.

The closest thing to a sustained effort has to do with the study of social structure. Even so, in Melanesia, as in Polynesia, social structure did not become a focal issue until after World War II. From approximately 1935 to 1950 the work of the great Africanists—Evans-Pritchard, Fortes, and Gluckman, among others—had its greatest impact. It is not surprising, then, as John Barnes points out in the first paper of this part, that segmentary lineage systems were reported in Melanesia when a new generation of ethnologists went in during the 1950's. But however convenient the African literature may have been for the earliest researchers in the Highlands, it soon became apparent that the societies encountered did not fit well into the "African model." Barnes' paper lists briefly the major areas of difficulty encountered and suggests several lines of inquiry that might be followed in an attempt to perceive the distinctive features of the Highlands.

Mervyn Meggitt's extensive work among the Mae Enga of the Western Highlands has resulted in the most thorough and well-documented account of a Melanesian segmentary lineage system to date. However, it has also stimulated much controversy (Barnes, 1967; McArthur, 1967) and represents what must be seen, in the light of the present situation, as an extreme position. Meggitt's short paper in this volume suggests many avenues for further investigation, virtually none of which have been adequately explored, but the article should be read only as a prelude to *The Lineage System of the Mae Enga.*

Brown's paper, written in the same year as Barnes', deals with another large Highland group and presents an interesting contrast to Meggitt. Although the Chimbu are in many ways similar to the Mae Enga, especially in terms of population density and their previous fighting for land, Brown argues that the Chimbu cannot be described simply as a lineage system. She illustrates, in detail, many of the points raised by Barnes—the openness and flexibility, the importance of nonagnates in local groups, and the difficulties inherent in trying to determine the membership in Chimbu groups. Her use of the term "quasi-unilineal" reflects the frustration of many who have worked in the New Guinea Highlands.

The problems encountered by students of social structure in the Highlands are by no means unique. Harold Scheffler's paper on Choiseul examines many of the same questions for the Solomon Islands. It also makes clear that the Melanesian materials must be seen in relation to a much broader theoretical dispute over how sociological analysis should be conducted. Scheffler argues cogently that rules or norms are not always consistent and can be interpreted only according to the situation. Likewise, he maintains that ideals, expectations, and self-interest are often opposed and do not form a coherent "system." This position allows interpretations which previously would have been ignored.

In the final selection in this part, Roger Keesing articulates a basic question which is often implied in the Melanesian literature: Does the "African model" really fit the African materials? It could be that Melanesian societies do not fit the model, not because the model is African, but because it is inadequate. Keesing attempts to demonstrate that the unilineal model, as it developed in Africa, is imperfect, and that, following Scheffler, we should attempt to see how the *same* "descent constructs" (Scheffler, 1966) are used in different societies for different purposes and in different contexts. In addition, Keesing raises many important questions having to do with process and structure, point of view, and the limitations placed on perception and description by past experience and theoretical proclivities. There is little doubt, as Keesing suggests, that the Melanesian experience will lead to a rethinking of ideas about social structure.

6

AFRICAN MODELS IN
THE NEW GUINEA HIGHLANDS

John A. Barnes

INTRODUCTION

The peoples of the New Guinea Highlands[1] first became accessible for study at a time when anthropological discussion was dominated by the analyses of political and kinship systems that had recently been made in Africa. Ethnographers working in New Guinea were able to present interim accounts of the poly-segmentary stateless systems of the Highlands with less effort and greater speed by making use of the advances in understanding already achieved by their colleagues who had studied similar social systems in Africa. Yet it has become clear that Highland societies fit awkwardly into African moulds. When first tackling the New Guinea societies it was a decided advantage to be able to refer to the analytical work available on Nuer, Tallensi, Tiv and other peoples, but it may be disadvantageous if this African orientation now prevents us from seeing the distinctively non-African characteristics of the Highlands.

The central highland valleys of New Guinea have become accessible to travellers only during the last 15 years and early ethnographical research was necessarily undertaken on the coast and in the coastal mountains. These inquiries were made before the work of Evans-Pritchard and Fortes on the Nuer and Tallensi had made its full impact on social anthropology and were carried out among peoples living mainly in politically independent villages whose social organization appeared not to offer any striking parallels with Africa. After 1945 the New Guinea Highlands were opened to a new generation of ethnographers strongly influenced by structural thinking who found here larger societies, apparently patrilineal and lacking hereditary leadership, whose structures invited comparison with Africa. When in several respects these societies were discovered not to operate as an Africanist might have expected, these deviations from the African model were often regarded as anomalies requiring special explanation. Yet in the last year or so a closer examination of the ethnographical facts, the

Reproduced by permission of the Royal Anthropological Institute of Great Britain and Ireland from *Man*, 62:5-9 (1962).

presentation of data from a wider range of Highland societies and, more recently, the discussions about non-unilineal systems in Malayo-Polynesia have considerably weakened what we might call the African mirage in New Guinea.

The Tiv, Nuer, Tallensi and others differ considerably from one another but in making inter-continental comparisons the substantial differences between them have often been overlooked. The possible existence of lineage systems in New Guinea has even been discussed without stating precisely which African lineage systems have been used as type specimens. Comparisons have often been drawn with the more abstract accounts of African societies, as for example Evans-Pritchard's essay in *African Political Systems,* rather than with the detailed descriptions of actual African situations given, for instance, in his paper *Marriage and the Family among the Nuer.* It has been easy to make the mistake of comparing the *de facto* situation in a Highland community, as shown by an ethnographical census, with a non-existent and idealized set of conditions among the Nuer, wrongly inferred from Evans-Pritchard's discussion of the principles of Nuer social structure. The New Guinea hamlet is found to be full of matrilateral kin, affines, refugees and casual visitors, quite unlike the hypothetical entirely virilocal and agnatic Nuer village (though similar to real Nuer villages). This procedure gives an exaggerated picture of the differences between the Highlands and Africa, and although most ethnographers have avoided this error in print, it persists in many oral discussions.

Yet, despite this caveat, major differences in social structure remain between, say, Nuer, Tiv, Tallensi, Dinka and Bedouin on the one hand and, on the other, Chimbu, Enga, Fore, Huli, Kuma, Kyaka, Mbowamb, Mendi and Siane. This is not the place to compare all these systems but rather to suggest topics that should form part of any detailed comprehensive comparison.

DESCENT

In the Highlands usually a majority, though rarely all, of the adult males in any local community are agnatically related to one another. Most married men live patrivirilocally. Many a large social group is divided into segments each associated with a son of its founder. It is argued that these groups are patrilineal descent groups. Yet several other characteristics of Highland societies make this categorization less certain. These may be summarized as follows:

(*a*) In many instances non-agnates are numerous in the local community and some of them are powerful.

(*b*) It is often hard to detect any difference in status between agnates and non-agnates. If a distinction is drawn it may be made in such a way that the patrilineal descendants of non-agnates after one or two generations are assimilated to the local agnatic group.

(*c*) An adolescent boy, and even an adult man, has some choice in deciding whether he will adhere to the local group in which his father is an agnate or to some other group to which he can trace non-agnatic connexion. He may be able to maintain multiple allegiance or to shift his affiliation.

(*d*) A married woman neither remains fully affiliated to her natal group nor is completely transferred to her husband's group but rather sustains an interest in both. Yet the division of rights in and responsibilities towards her is not exclusive.

(*e*) Many individuals who assert a mutual agnatic relationship are unable to trace out their connexions step by step and are uninterested in trying to do so.

(*f*) The names of remoter patrilineal ancestors are forgottten; or alternatively the genealogical structure of the group is stated to be a single (or sometimes a double) descending line of males with no remembered siblings leading to a large band of brothers about three generations above living adults; or else there is a gap of unspecified magnitude between the putative remote ancestors who give their names to contemporary segments and the father's fathers or father's father's fathers of the living.

(*g*) Even if the agnates form a recognizable core to the local community there may be no context in which all potential members of this core, including non-residents, act as a unity distinguished from their non-agnatic neighbours.

(*h*) An agnatic ancestor cult either does not exist or else does not provide contexts in which non-resident agnates, or agnates from co-ordinate segments, are brought together.

Hence it seems prudent to think twice before cataloguing the New Guinea Highlands as characterized by patrilineal descent. Clearly, genealogical connexion of some sort is one criterion for membership of many social groups. But it may not be the only criterion; birth, or residence, or a parent's former residence, or utilization of garden land, or participation in exchange and feasting activities, or in house-building or raiding, may be other relevant criteria for group membership. If, as Fortes advocates, we continue to restrict the category 'descent group' to groups in which descent is the only criterion for membership, then in many Highland societies it is hard to discover descent groups. Furthermore the genealogical connexion required for membership may not necessarily be agnatic. Other connexions can be invoked, and this appeal to other cognatic, and sometimes to affinal, ties does not have to be justified by some elaboration of, or dispensation from, an agnatic dogma. In the Highlands the patrilineal ancestors do not act as guardians of the agnatic principle.

These remarks apply unequally to different Highland societies. In some, long lines of agnatic ancestors are remembered while in others genealogical knowledge is poor and not agnatically biased; in some the local incidence of agnates is high, in others it is low; in some there is strong pressure on a man to affiliate himself exclusively with his agnates while in others he can divide his allegiance between two or more kin groups; and there are other dimensions of variation. The Mae Enga, for instance, fit well into an agnatic model whereas the Chimbu and some other peoples can be treated as agnatic societies only with increasing difficulty as we come to know more about them.

Thus although some Highland societies are appropriately classified as agnatic, the area as a whole appears to be characterized by cumulative patrifiliation rather than by agnatic descent. Here I am making a distinction between filiation as a mechanism of recruitment to social groups and to ascribed relationships and descent as a sanctioned and morally evaluated principle of belief. The Tallensi, for example, have both these characteristics. But in most, though not in all, Highland societies the dogma of descent is absent or is held only weakly; the principle of recruitment to a man's father's group operates, but only concurrently with other principles, and is sanctioned not by an appeal to the notion of descent as such but by reference to the obligations of kinsfolk, differentiated according to relationship and encompassed within a span of only two or three generations. In each generation a substantial majority of men affiliate themselves with their father's group and in this way it acquires some agnatic continuity over the generations. It may be similar in demographic appearance and *de facto* kinship ties to a patrilineal group in which accessory segments are continually being assimilated to the authentic core, but its structure and ideology are quite different.

A genealogy in a pre-literate society is in general a charter, in Malinowski's sense, for a given configuration of contemporary social relations. Where there is a dogma of descent, and in particular a dogma of agnatic solidarity, the genealogy must reflect the contemporary situation, or some desired modification of it, in terms of the dogma. But if the dogma is absent, appeal to a genealogy to validate present action is of no avail. Hence it is not surprising that several Highland societies, though again not all of them, neglect their genealogies, either by not revising them or by simply forgetting them. Where revision does take place, it may be simplification rather than the manipulation characteristic of Tiv and Nuer.

BOUNDED AND UNBOUNDED AFFILIATION

In a poly-segmentary society like Tallensi the many affiliations that govern an individual's status and activities are determined by birth. He has a specified and unique position in the lineage system and cannot escape from it though within the minimal lineage he can exercise some initiative, as well as in the affinal ties which he chooses to establish, and in the relationships which he enters into outside the lineage system. In Firth's terminology there is little or no optation in the descent system itself. New Guinea societies, on the other hand, seem to be characterized by a considerable degree of optation. The absence or weakness of a dogma of agnatic descent is one aspect of this and the possibility of affiliation with some local group other than one's father's follows from it. In some societies, Mae Enga for example, sooner or later a man must declare his allegiance one way or the other but in other societies he can, and indeed, if he is ambitious, he will, keep open until late in life the possibility of shifting from one group to another. In the southern Highlands, and possibly elsewhere, a man can successfully continue as a member of two or more groups at the same time.

In a unilineal descent system multiple membership or affiliation of this kind is obviously impossible; one of the arguments used against the alleged feasibility of non-unilineal descent systems is precisely this potential or actual plurality of membership. There are three separate issues involved: the distinction between membership of a group and residence on its territory; the feasibility of multiple affiliation in a system of competing groups; and the notion that a man must have a single home with which he is principally identified. Co-residence implies the possibility, but not the necessity, of continual day-to-day face-to-face interaction and in a non-literate society, however clearly their rights are recognized, absent members cannot play as full a part in the activities of the group as do those who are present. But just as co-residence does not necessarily imply co-activity, so some form of co-activity is possible without continuous co-residence. This is particularly relevant to those Highland societies where there is no nuclear family residence and where a man sleeps with his fellows while his wives sleep with their young children and pigs in their own houses. Under these conditions, where a man spends the night is only one indication among many of where his principal allegiances and interests lie. His gardens may be scattered, not only in the sense of being located on various ridges and in various valleys but also by being on land under the control of several local groups. In effect, even in those societies where a man's main allegiance is always to one and only one local group, he may have substantial interests in a number of others. There is no great difference between unilocal residence in these circumstances and the manifest poly-local residence reported from some of the southern Highland societies.

Multiple affiliation may give individuals greater security and room to manœuvre but may be detrimental to group solidarity. A group can either be jealous of its resources and discourage immigrants or it can seek to build up its strength by recruiting new members. The choice it makes will depend at least in part on the availability of garden land and other natural assets under its control and on its strength as a fighting unit *vis-à-vis* its likely or actual enemies. Either it can restrict membership by insisting on agnatic purity or in some other way or it can build up its numbers by recruiting non-agnates and by bringing back agnates who have strayed. Highland societies vary in the choice made; probably enough has been published to make a preliminary comparative survey worth while. No simple answer is likely, for it should be remembered that restrictive policies act both ways. A man whose agnatic group is short of land may support a policy restricting use of the land to agnates, but if he is short of land himself he may be relying on exercising his claims as a non-agnate in the territories of neighbouring groups.

In the Highlands an individual often has allegiances, of the same kind if varying in degree, to several groups which may be either at enmity or amity with one another. This multiple allegiance is quite distinct from the allegiances of different kinds to different groups which occur in even the most determinate unilineal societies. This multiplicity in New Guinea is largely a result of individual initiative and is not due to the automatic operation of rules. A 'rubbish man' is typically a man who is a member of one local group but who has no ties that lead him outside it, whereas a 'big man' is likely to have a great variety of individual and group ties, along with a clear primary identification with one specific group.

Moreover it is proliferation of ties at the individual rather than at the group level that seems to distinguish New Guinea from Africa. As we would expect, both kinds of bond occur in both areas. In most parts of the Highlands there are fairly stable alliances between large groups such as clans and phratries, and sometimes enduring relationships of hostility as well, and these are often expressed in an affinal or fraternal idiom. It is also true that in all the poly-segmentary African societies that we are considering, explicit recognition is given to the rights and obligations which a man has with respect to the groups to which he or his agnates are linked matrilaterally. Yet the relative importance of what we might call high-level and low-level non-agnatic (and also pseudo-agnatic) ties seems to differ in the two areas. Complementary filiation plays a greater part in the lives of New Guinea Highlanders and traditional inter-group ties seem less important. It may be argued that this is due to the imposition of colonial peace, for when warfare was endemic inter-group affiliation was presumably more significant than it is now. But the accounts of pre-contact fighting, of the military alliances arranged and the refuges sought after defeat, do not bear this out. In any case pre-colonial fighting is at least as close to the present in New Guinea as it is in the relevant regions of Africa.

The emphasis on low-level rather than high-level affiliation is clearly associated with the greater range of choice in the New Guinea systems, and in particular with the widespread cultural emphasis on ceremonial exchange. Although exchanges and prestations may be spoken of as arranged by the clan or sub-clan and may even be timed on a regional basis, the great majority of these ceremonial transactions are undisguisedly transactions between individuals. In establishing a position of dominance in these trans-actions a man is seriously handicapped if he lacks the support of his agnates, but he cannot hope to succeed without utilizing in addition a wide range of other connexions, some matrilateral, others affinal and yet others lacking a genealogical basis. If he is successful it is his local group, usually but not invariably consisting of his close agnates, which more than others enjoy his reflected glory. Among Tiv and Tallensi, and less certainly among Nuer, it seems that a man acquires dominance primarily because he belongs to the dominant local group, whereas in the New Guinea Highlands it might be said that a local group becomes dominant because of the big men who belong to it. The contrast is greatest between the Highlands and those African societies where leadership within lineage segments is determined more by rules of seniority than by individual effort.

Two aspects of this contrast require special mention. Fortes, in his discussion of what he calls the 'field principle,' draws attention to the fact that Tallensi matrimonial alliances are established not at random but in accordance with social interests. The pattern of marriages is determined partly by the choices made by individuals within the range of potential spouses permitted by the rules, and partly by the configuration of rules themselves. Prohibition of marriage within one's own clan, or mother's sub-clan, or preference for marriage with a specified kind of cousin, indicate the variety of interest involved. Two alternative trends can be seen. Either marriages are restricted to a certain group, so that enduring connubial alliances, either symmetrical or one-way, are maintained and renewed down the generations, or else every marriage between two groups is an impediment to further marriages between them. In other words, matrimonial alliances are either concentrated or deliberately dispersed. The latter alternative is more common in the Highlands and accords well with the emphasis on a multiplicity of freshly established inter-personal connexions rather than on group and inter-group solidarity.

The other aspect that should be mentioned is the availability of natural resources. Some of the differences between New Guinea and Africa may be due simply to the differences between pigs and cattle, but obviously this is only part of the story. In the African societies which we are considering a man is largely dependent on his agnatic kin for economic support, but this is less true of the New Guinea Highlands. Inheritance and the provision and distribution of bridewealth play a major part in African societies in determining the structure of small lineage segments and in establishing their corporate qualities. In New Guinea a man depends less on what he can hope to inherit from his father and pays less attention to the ill defined reversionary rights which he may perhaps have in the property of his agnatic cousins. In both areas a man looks first to his agnatic group for garden land, but it seems that in New Guinea he can turn with greater confidence to other groups as well. Before the coming of commercial crops there were in the

Highlands, apart from groves of nut pandanus, comparatively few long-lived tree crops or sites of particularly high fertility such as in Africa often form a substantial part of the collective capital of a lineage segment. In New Guinea a man's capital resources consist largely in the obligations which he has imposed on his exchange partners and on his death these resources may be dissipated or disappear entirely. Hence to a greater extent than in Africa every man in the New Guinea Highlands starts from scratch and has to build up his own social position. Once again, we must not carry the contrast too far. Clearly even in New Guinea it is generally an advantage to be the son of a big man, just as in Africa the eldest son of an eldest son does not attain leadership without some personal ability; but the contrast remains.

In general terms this contrast might be phrased as between bounded affiliation in Africa and unbounded affiliation in the Highlands; or between African group solidarity and New Guinea network cohesion.

SOCIAL DIVISION AS CONDITION OR PROCESS

Concentration on the network of alliances between individuals and between small groups may perhaps explain why comparatively little attention has been paid in New Guinea studies to the processes whereby groups such as clan and sub-clan segment and divide.

In the analysis of segmentary societies there are always two points of view. On the one hand poly-segmentation is seen as an enduring condition whereby there are in existence, and perhaps have been for a long time, a fixed hierarchy of segments, each segment of higher order containing several segments of lower order. Evans-Pritchard and Fortes's earlier work discusses how in different contexts segments variously oppose and support one another without changing their status in the segmentary hierarchy. The terms 'fission' and 'fusion' were applied to these shifts of opposition and alliance in different contexts. On the other hand we may turn our attention to the ways in which new segments are formed and how existing segments are upgraded, downgraded and eliminated. Many recent writers have followed Forde in using 'fission,' 'fusion' and other terms to refer to these processes of status alteration of segments rather than to the contextual shifts with which Evans-Pritchard and Fortes were initially concerned.

In New Guinea the contemporary pattern of poly-segmentation has been documented for many societies. There has been some discussion of how the fortunes of war have led in the past to changes in this pattern, and a little has been said about contextual shifts of opposition and alliance. There has been less analysis of how, for example, increasing population over the years may result in a segment of one order converting itself, gradually or suddenly, to one of higher order. Meggitt's study of the dynamics of segmentation among the Mae Enga, dealing with this process at length, has not yet been published.[2]

This omission arises partly because it is hard to get any reliable time depth from the field material; Highlanders are poor oral historians. But it is due also, I suggest, to a basic difference between New Guinea and Africa in the way in which over-large groups split up. In Nuer, Tiv and Tallensi we have a clear picture of how, given adequate fertility, two brothers from their childhood gradually grow apart until, after several generations, their agnatic descendants come to form two distinct co-ordinate segments within a major segment. Even if some analytical queries remain, the process over at least the first three generations is well understood. This kind of segmentation we may well call chronic, for in a sense the division of the lineage into two branches is already present when the brothers are still lying in the cradle. The details of the process may be unpredictable but the line of cleavage is already determined. Segmentation or fission in New Guinea appears not to take this inexorable form; one cannot predict two generations in advance how a group will split. Instead it seems that within the group of agnates and others there is a multiplicity of cleavages or potential cleavages. In a crisis these are polarized, two men emerge as obvious rivals and each with his followers forms either a new unit or a distinct segment of the existing unit. Segmentation, as it were, is not chronic but catastrophic. The regularities, if any, in catastrophic segmentation are obviously harder to determine than in chronic segmentation. In Africa the dogma of descent acts as a continuously operating principle, providing each individual with an ordered set of affiliations, so that in any crisis he knows his rightful place, even if he is not always there. In New Guinea affiliations are not automatically arranged in order in this way; what might be called the principle of social mitosis, whereby potential recruits to rival co-ordinate segments sort themselves before an impending crisis, is absent; the break, when it comes, appears to come arbitrarily. In addition, changes in the polysegmentary pattern in New Guinea seem to come about more often than in Africa as the result of defeat in war. The causes of war may be predictable but who is killed and who lives, which group wins and which loses, is in New Guinea as much as anywhere else a matter of luck. Here again we have to deal with an apparently arbitrary process.

This lack of predictability or regularity in changes in the segmentary pattern is, of course, another aspect of the basic contrast between group solidarity and individual enterprise. The sanctions that maintain the segmentary *status quo,* whether derived from economic or physical pressures, or from cult or dogma, are weaker in the Highlands than in Africa and the incentives for change are stronger.

A characteristic of Highland cultures, and perhaps of Melanesia as a whole, is the high value placed on violence. The primitive states of Africa, and even the African stateless societies which we have been considering, are readily likened to the kingdoms and princedoms of mediæval Europe, valuing peace but ready to go to war to defend their interests or to achieve likely economic rewards. Prowess in battle is highly rewarded but warfare is usually not undertaken lightly and most of the people most of the time want peace. In New Guinea a greater emphasis appears to be placed on killing for its own sake rather than as a continuation of group policy aimed at material ends. In these circumstances we might expect to find a less developed system of alliances and countervailing forces, and less developed arrangements for maintaining peace, than we would have in a polity directed to peace and prosperity. Secondly, we would expect that leaders, whatever their other qualities, were moved to violence at least as much as their fellows and possibly more. The Highlands of New Guinea cannot have been the scene of a war of all against all, for the pre-contact population was large and often densely settled; indigenous social institutions preventing excess violence and destruction must necessarily have been effective, for otherwise the population would not have survived. Likewise other qualities than prowess in violence were required for leadership, in particular the ability to engage and co-ordinate the efforts of others in ceremonial exchanges. Yet despite these qualifications I think that it may still be hypothesized that the disorder and irregularity of social life in the Highlands, as compared with, say, Tiv, is due in part to the high value placed on killing.

CONCLUSION

I have sketched some of the difficulties that follow from assuming that the societies of the New Guinea Highlands can be regarded as variants on a pattern established by the Nuer, Tallensi, Tiv and similar African societies, and I have tried to indicate ways out of these difficulties. There are major ecological differences between the two groups of societies and any full commentary would have to take account of these, in particular the lack of storable food in New Guinea. Despite the great difference in structure, culture and environment, one route to a better understanding of the Highlands lies, I think, through a closer examination of the detailed information available on the stateless societies of Africa. Perhaps this examination may lead incidentally to a clearer formulation of the salient characteristics of these African systems.

It so happens that stateless societies were studied and described in Africa before ethnographical research really got under way in the Highlands. It would be interesting to work out how, say, the Nuer might have been described if the only analytical models available had been those developed to describe, say, Chimbu and Mbowamb. At the same time, if the differences between the patrilineal poly-segmentary stateless societies of Africa and the societies of the New Guinea Highlands are as great as I have suggested, it might be worth while looking for other societies in Africa that could provide closer parallels.

NOTES

1. This paper was presented to Section VII, 10th Pacific Science Congress, in Honolulu on 31 August, 1961. It was written at sea, away from books, and I cannot cite sources. I hope to publish later a fuller discussion substantiating and certainly qualifying the many generalizations in this paper.

2. Mervyn Meggitt published an article on this in the same year as this paper (1962) and subsequently a book, *The Lineage System of the Mae Enga* (1965).—*Editor's note.*

7

GROWTH AND DECLINE OF AGNATIC DESCENT GROUPS AMONG THE MAE ENGA OF THE NEW GUINEA HIGHLANDS[1]

Mervyn Meggitt

The Enga live in the Western Highlands District of the Territory of New Guinea, among mountains that rise from about 6,000 to more than 11,000 feet above sea level. Most of the population is concentrated in river valleys at altitudes ranging from about 4,000 to 7,500 feet.

The culture of the western Enga (generally called the Mae) differs from that of the eastern Enga (the Laiapu). The Mae are further divided into the Yandapu and the Mae proper (who together include some 30,000 natives), and the Laiapu into the Syaka and the Laiapu proper (who number together about 25,000). These four peoples comprise the central Enga, whose population density averages about 110 to 120 per square mile and in places exceeds 250. Population density of the surrounding fringe Enga is much lower—averaging perhaps 30 to 50 per square mile.

The central Enga are primarily gardeners, but they also keep pigs. Hunting is unimportant. The staple crop is sweet potatoes, grown under a system of long fallowing. To feed its members, each domestic gardening unit needs access to about five times as much arable land as it currently cultivates. Since many of the ridge tops and upper slopes are horticulturally useless, cultivation of the valley floors and lower slopes is intensive. In the central valleys, clans have occupied all the usable land, and land disputes are common. In the past these were a direct cause of much of the constant inter-clan warfare; nowadays they are the subject of bitter litigation.

The central Enga belong to named and localized patriclans, which form elements of segmentary lineage systems. The clan territory, which has sharply defined boundaries, may cover from half a square mile to six or seven square miles; the mean is between one and two square miles. The Mae Enga clan-parish, i.e., the local group of clansmen, their wives, children,

Reproduced by permission of the publisher and Mervyn Meggitt from *Ethnology*, 1:158-165 (1962).

and certain attached non-agnates, usually comprises about 350 members, although the range is from about 100 to 1,100. The people live, not in compact villages, but in homesteads scattered about the clan territory. As a rule, each wife has her own house, which she shares with her unmarried daughters, infant sons, and the family pigs, whereas the husband and older sons reside with other male agnates in a small clubhouse.

Ideally, the clans are exogamous, and 92 per cent of marriages conform to this norm. Land and other important property is normally inherited patrilineally within the clan. On the average, 86 per cent of the men of a Mae Enga clan-parish are putative agnates, who trace patrilineal descent through about seven generations from the eponymous clan founder. The clan-parish is a relatively autonomous group, which organizes its own rituals, ceremonial exchange relationships, payments of homicide compensation, and, until recently, military operations. There are no hereditary or formally elected chiefs or headmen; in each clan the initiation and direction of political and administrative activities are in the hands of wealthy and energetic men who, largely through their own efforts, have acquired "big names."

A cluster of contiguous clans makes up a named, nonexogamous phratry, whose founder is thought to have been the father of the clan founders. A phratry (of which there are about twenty) generally includes about eight clans, with a range of from four to twenty. Although the men of a phratry regard themselves as "brothers" and have the right to witness each other's clan rituals, they rarely act together as a group. Sometimes one phratry engaged in formalized warfare with another, but ordinary interclan fights seldom mobilized whole phratries. Moreover, although intra-phratry warfare was deplored, it often occurred.

Each clan comprises from two to about seven or eight named subclans, whose founders are taken to have been the sons of the clan founder. Subclan domains exist within the clan territory, and subclansmen tend to live on their own lands. The subclan as a corporate group is mainly concerned in the payments of death (as distinct from homicide) compensations to maternal kin and in the regular performance of purificatory rituals for bachelors. Occasionally large-scale gardening operations involve all the men of the subclan.

The subclan is in turn divided into from two to four named patrilineages, whose founders were the putative sons of the subclan founders. Patrilineage lands are dispersed through the subclan holdings, but men of the patrilineage commonly live together in one or two clubhouses. Patrilineages generally mobilize for the exchanges of wealth that accompany marriage, for the payments of compensation following injury, for the building of houses for their members, and, less often, for the provision of gardening aid.

Each lineage-parish, or ward, is composed of a number of families, most of whose heads are the grandsons or great-grandsons of the patrilineage founder. About 85 per cent of the families are elementary, i.e., generated by a monogamous husband, and the rest composite, i.e., generated by polygynists. The mean number of family members is five; the range is from two to fourteen. Eight per cent of the families include only one generation, 80 per cent two generations, and the rest three.

The cultivated and fallow land belonging to the patrilineage is divided among its component families, so that the head of each administers an estate in trust for his male heirs. He portions off each son from the estate to enable the latter to marry and found his own family. The elementary family constitutes the basic gardening and pig-raising unit in Mae Enga society.[2]

Having set the ethnographic scene, I want now to define certain processes of change that operate in the Mae Enga lineage system. The definitions have emerged from analysis of an array of field material which, for lack of space, cannot be presented here. In brief, it includes census figures, genealogical responses, observations, and in some cases quantifications of runs of behavior, biographical accounts, and putative histories of particular descent groups. Within this congeries of data I have sought evidence of empirical regularities and predictability in the changes that occur in and among the localized agnatic hierarchies.[3]

Segmentation, which may proceed at all levels in a local hierarchy of Mae Enga agnatic groups, is a process whereby one group generates from its own members subordinate units that may later become coordinate with it. It does so without necessarily losing its own identity, although its position in the hierarchy may change as a result. Segmentation is to some extent stimulated and directed by a *de facto* popular recognition that group status is at least partly determined by the size and activities of the group.

In *fission,* two independent groups of coordinate status arise simultaneously from the parent clan and quickly replace it. It ceases to be a functioning group, and its identity is soon forgotten. In *splitting,* part of a clan separates to form a new group, but both the offshoot and rump sections retain for an indefinite period the identity of the original clan of which they are now coordinate branches. The Mae Enga themselves realize that the two situations differ. Of clans that have arisen by fission, they say that these have different names and founders and are therefore different groups. The sections of a split clan, on the other hand, have one name and are therefore to be regarded as one clan, although they actually function as discrete, independent clans.

Fusion is a process whereby an autonomous agnatic group merges with another of coordinate status to form a new group of the same or of a higher order. In *accretion,* a group which is a unit of one lineage hierarchy joins a higher-order group of another hierarchy to become part of the latter. That is to say, outsiders are attached to a group and form a subordinate body within it, additional to those arising from segmentations.

In the violent interclan struggles for land that have occurred through the years, many Mae Enga clans have been destroyed by invaders and their fleeing members killed or attached to related groups. Unless the investigator actually encounters the survivors themselves, however, he is not likely to learn the details of such events. I was nevertheless able to acquire some evidence from which inferences could be made about the decline and disappearance of agnatic groups. The main difference to be recognized, I have found, is that between sudden and violent *destruction* and gradual decline leading to *extinction*. This difference in turn parallels a distinction between extra-phratry and intra-phratry relationships among neighboring groups.

Absorption of groups is a peaceful, long-term process which may be regarded as the opposite of segmentation. Segmentation occurs within a local lineage hierarchy; subordinate groups emerge, increase in size, and assume new functions, and in doing so they achieve higher status by becoming coordinate with units that previously included them. In absorption, groups that are declining in numbers have to relinquish particular activities and descend in the hierarchy. At each stage in their descent they are absorbed as subgroups of units with which they were previously coordinate. Absorption may occur at all levels from family to clan within a local lineage hierarchy.

This completes an enumeration of the kinds of changes that Mae Enga agnatic groups may undergo. At each level of the local lineage hierarchy, segmentation generates new groups that may in time ascend to higher positions in that hierarchy. Fission creates new groups at the clan level and above, whereas splitting and subsequent migration of offshoot groups involve only clans. The process of accretion transfers groups from one hierarchy to another. In absorption, the reverse of segmentation, groups descend to lower levels in the local hierarchy, whereas extinction involves their total disappearance. Fusion, a process that would lead to a reduction in the number of groups in a hierarchy, apparently occurs rarely, if at all.

The formal religious ideology in terms of which the people express their theory of the origin and nature of agnatic groups denies that the hierarchical positions of the groups may alter. Yet in other contexts change is admitted, and the group genealogies that provide part of the content of the ideology are reformulated to meet the new situations. For a group to attain or to maintain a particular status in a local hierarchy, it must be able to perform the tasks appropriate to that status; and to achieve this, it must exceed a certain minimal membership. Although the formal ideology states that the generation depth of a group determines its span and population size, the people in fact assume that the size of the group membership in some measure determines the generational status currently given to the group and hence the span of the group.

Another significant point emerging from a discussion of group changes concerns the importance of the demand for arable land as a factor impelling many of these changes. In terms of the Mae Enga dependence on indigenous crops and techniques of cultivation, the people as a whole appear to have barely enough land suitable for gardens. The situation is further exacerbated by the differential availability of this land. In the central valleys, where the population is densest, there is no unclaimed arable land left for exploitation; in the peripheral valleys, where the population is sparser, the land is correspondingly poorer in quality and less productive. Moreover, in the central area in particular, the arable land is not evenly distributed among the clans. As the membership of groups changes in consequence of natural increase, disease, and warfare, some clans have land to spare while others become short. Consequently, groups rising in hierarchical position are constantly exerting pressure on static and declining groups in order to acquire the extra land they need to support their increasing numbers and so validate their new statuses.

Peripheral clans can to some extent meet the land shortage by sending offshoot groups to colonize uninhabited parts of outer valleys, but the land in these localities is generally too swampy or too elevated to support many settlers. Central clans, however, have nowhere to send their extra members. In the recent past they solved the problem by destroying weaker neighbors. Thus a continual redistribution of arable land accompanied the changes that occurred in the size and political strength of groups. Often this took the form of a chain reaction. As one clan expanded at the expense of another, this pressure was transmitted like a shock wave along the valley until it was absorbed by a clan of more than average strength and resilience. A clan experiencing pressure simultaneously from two directions apparently had little hope of surviving, and its neighbors expanded to fill the empty space left by its destruction. Then, as the reverberations of this conflict subsided, new pressures were set up as clans began to expand elsewhere in the valley, and the whole process was repeated.

These redistributive mechanisms can no longer operate, in the central valleys at least, following the Administration's prohibition of interclan warfare. But the establishment of peace and the improved medical facilities are slowly raising the net reproduction rate of all Mae Enga clans, so that a general increase in the pressure on land resources must follow.

CONCLUSIONS

This account has indicated that there is some degree of regularity and predictability about the processes of change within the Mae Enga agnatic groups. If we know that certain factors are present in a given situation, we can at least make informed guesses about the nature and outcome of the group transformations likely to follow. As a recapitulation I present a series of propositions about Mae Enga changes—propositions which appear to be plausible in the light of the evidence I have gathered. I might point out that these statements are not all of the same analytical order.

Segmentation and Fission

(1) When the membership of an assemblage of closely related males within a patrilineage exceeds the male membership of the rest of the patrilineage, that assemblage will become a new patrilineage.

(2) When the membership of an assemblage of closely related males within a patrilineage equals or exceeds the average male membership of all patrilineages in that clan, the assemblage will become a new patrilineage.

(3) When the male membership of a subclan exceeds that of the rest of the clan, the largest patrilineage in that subclan will form a new subclan.

(4) When a clan includes only two subclans, each of which approaches the average size of Mae Enga clans (namely, 350 members), they will form by fission two new clans that will replace the parent clan.

(5) The degree of physical contiguity of new clans emerging by fission will affect the rate at which they assume separate identities.

(6) When a clan contains more than two subclans and one of those exceeds the average size of Mae Enga clans, it may form a new clan without necessarily replacing the parent clan.

(7) The more groups there are in a larger unit involved in the process of segmentation, the more uneven are their rates of growth likely to be, and the more likely are they at a given time to occupy different hierarchical positions.

(8) When phratry membership exceeds eight clans, the phratry in a region of dense population is likely to segment into two additional subphratries, whereas, in a region of sparser population, it is likely to form two new phratries by fission.

Splitting

(9) The migration of an offshoot group during clan splitting tends to reduce the causes of conflict and thus helps to maintain the common clan identity of the branches.

(10) The maintenance of active relations between the branches of a split clan depends not only on the physical distance between them but also on their proximity to a common trade route.

Accretion

(11) The direction of accretion of subgroups is from overpopulated toward underpopulated clans.

(12) The direction of accretion is toward the clans of the migrants' mothers' agnates and wives' agnates.

Absorption and Extinction

(13) Declining clans with powerful neighbors belonging to other phratries tend to be destroyed violently, whereas those with powerful neighbors of the same phratry tend to be absorbed peacefully.

(14) Declining groups within a static clan tend to be absorbed peacefully by larger coordinate groups.

(15) Declining or static subclans within an expanding clan tend to be evicted by stronger coordinate groups.

I may cite an example of the kind of prediction that is possible on the basis of such knowledge. Given a declining clan in a densely populated central valley whose neighbor is an expanding clan of a different phratry, we should expect before long to find the weaker clan destroyed and some of the survivors living as an accreted group with the nearest declining clan that includes many of the refugees' maternal kinsmen and affines. If the same situation, however, arises in a sparsely populated peripheral valley, we should expect to find the refugees living as an independent clan elsewhere in the valley or as a subclan accreted to any other clan with which cognatic or affinal relations exist.

Two questions arise. What constitutes acceptable evidence with which to test such predictions? And have they in fact been verified?

Adequate confirmation might simply be taken as the anthropologist's subsequent discovery of historical or quasi-historical data that accord with particular propositions but that were unknown to him when he formulated his hypotheses. For instance, now that the Australian Administration has suppressed warfare among the Enga, this kind of historical evidence has become the most significant for testing propositions about the violent destruction or military expansion of the local descent groups, although it is true that nowadays certain patterns of interclan litigation also provide valuable evidence. On the other hand, there is the confirmation of predictions by the later occurrence of the expected events. Evidence of this kind continues to become available for the testing of predictions about the peaceful growth, decline, or extinction of given descent groups. It should be recognized, moreover, that, although the empirical features of these two categories of evidence differ, the categories are of the same analytical or logical status.

In answering the second of the two questions asked above, I can only assert that, when I returned to the Mae Enga in 1960, I undertook to test various of the propositions and predictions I had formulated. While it was not easy to discover a great deal of new, directly relevant, and unequivocal evidence, what was available, in both empirical categories, confirmed the relevant propositions. No obviously negative instances were encountered.

One may also ask: Where does this kind of analysis lead? In the present case its prime virtue is that it enables the anthropologist to go beyond a synchronic, albeit quantified, description of the structure of the Mae Enga lineage system and to pursue a diachronic, organizational analysis both of repetitive and of irreversible changes that occur in the system. That is to say, he can try to state—in sharply defined, quantitative terms—not only to what extent the Mae Enga lineage system is agnatic and segmentary, and how it maintains certain crucial features, but also how these and other significant characteristics vary regularly or irregularly in response to changes in demographic, environmental, or ideological factors.

Corresponding analyses can be made of other descent systems, e.g., elsewhere in the New Guinea highlands at first, then through wider areas of New Guinea and Melanesia, and so on. On the basis of these we can undertake meaningful, multivariate, and temporally extended comparisons among regions and among systems; and we can achieve valid and reliable measures of change and covariation. Then—and, I believe, only then—can we talk intelligibly of causal analysis.

NOTES

1. The data on which this paper is based were collected during field work carried out in the Western Highlands District of the Territory of New Guinea in 1955-57 and 1960. I thank the Research Committee of the University of Sydney for its financial assistance. The paper, read at the Tenth Pacific Science Congress in Honolulu in August, 1961, is a highly condensed version of a chapter from a longer manuscript on "The Lineage System of the Mae Enga of New Guinea," which includes a more detailed treatment of the evidence supporting my propositions. I am grateful to Nancy Bowers, Roy Rappaport, and Peter Vayda for their criticisms of the draft of the paper.

2. References to other ethnographic and analytical materials on the several groups of Enga are assembled in the Bibliography.

3. The term "hierarchy," as here used, has no connotation of graded social statuses or ranks. It refers simply to a structural arrangement of superordinate, coordinate, and subordinate positions.

BIBLIOGRAPHY

BULMER, R. 1960. Political Aspects of the Moka Ceremonial Exchange System Among the Kyaka. Oceania 31: 1-13.

BUS, G. A. M. 1951. The *Te* Festival or Gift Exchange in Enga. Anthropos 46: 813-824.

ELKIN, A. P. 1953. Delayed Exchange in Wabag Subdistrict. Oceania 3: 161-201.

GOODENOUGH, W. H. 1953. Ethnographic Notes on the Mae People. Southwestern Journal of Anthropology. 9: 29-44.

MEGGITT, M. J. 1956. The Valleys of the Upper Wage and Lai Rivers. Oceania 27: 90-135.

——— 1957. Housebuilding Among the Mae Enga. Oceania 27: 161-176.

——— 1957. Mae Enga Political Organization. Mankind 5: 133-137.

——— 1957. Ipili of the Porgera Valley. Oceania 28: 31-55.

——— 1958. Mae-Enga Time Reckoning and Calendar. Man 58, No. 87.

——— 1958. Salt Manufacture and Trading in the Western Highlands. Australian Museum Magazine 12: 309-313.

——— 1958. The Enga of the New Guinea Highlands. Oceania 28: 253-330.

8

NON-AGNATES AMONG
THE PATRILINEAL CHIMBU[1]

Paula Brown

Melanesian social structure has not been found easy to describe in traditional social anthropological categories. Not only are the forms of social
structure diverse—the complex terminology and classification of Hogbin
and Wedgwood[2] failed when new societies were studied—but the structure
itself is flexible, and we may be hard put to decide, for example, whether
descent groups are mainly agnatic with numerous accretions, or cognatic
with a patrilineal bias. We find that people are more mobile than any
rules of descent and residence should warrant, that genealogies are too short
to be helpful, that we don't know what 'corporate' means when applied to
some groups, that local and descent groups are fragmented and change
their alignments. Most of the societies have no formal offices, no positions
of seniority, no hierarchy of any sort. These negative features make structural analysis difficult.

Anthropologists working in Melanesia have been entranced by such
bizarre matters as the transvestite rite of *naven*,[3] the *kula* ring,[4] cargo cults,[5]
pig fertility ceremonies, penis gourds, and bird of paradise headdresses.
These have captured our attention and seem much more worth writing
about than the elusive social structure. The structure of Chimbu society,
which has been my main research interest, does not, at first glance, seem
elusive at all, but I feel that study of the readily observable political and
descent groups does not lead to an adequate description of the social structure. Before turning to the Chimbu, I mention some of the approaches
which have been made to Melanesian social structure.

Most social anthropologists working in Africa have easily discovered something which can be called social structure in Evans-Pritchard's sense of
enduring groups and constant relations;[6] African societies have a lineage
system, associations, age-grades, centralized states, or some combination of
these. The corporate unilineal descent group seems to be present in some
Melanesian societies, and analysis along similar lines has been attempted in

Reproduced by permission of the publisher and Paula Brown from the *Journal of
the Polynesian Society,* 71:57-69 (1962).

the New Guinea highlands by Meggitt[7] and Salisbury.[8] There is one important difference—most of the New Guinea highland groups have short and adaptable genealogies, and descent is 'stipulated' rather than 'demonstrated' in Fried's terminology.[9] Although the phratries and clans are segmented, there is no continuous genealogy from living men to founding ancestors. Genealogical ties are not stressed in the subdivision, opposition or solidarity of groups.[10]

Fortes uses the term 'complementary filiation' to point to the individuation of members of a unilineal descent group by their cognatic ties to persons outside it, to the mechanism of segmentation, to ties with other unilineal groups of the same sort, and to the possibility of double unilineal descent.[11] Leach suggests that affinal ties must be separately considered.[12] By using 'non-agnatic ties,' I intend to refer to a person's ties with a large field of recognized kin and affines outside the patrilineal exogamous clan. A man's non-agnates include: his mother and her agnates, his mother's mother and her agnates, his father's mother and her agnates, his wife and her agnates, his sister's husband and his agnates, his father's sister's husband and his agnates. In the patrilineal African societies for which non-agnatic relations have been described, each of these is a clearly definable unit, rights and duties respecting them are prescribed, and on some occasions they must be represented.

Descent determines membership in a lineage.[13] In contrast, affiliation in Chimbu and many other Melanesian societies is not always definitive; men who join other groups than their natal ones become indistinguishable from natal members, and membership may be achieved. African lineage systems have longer genealogies, and where non-agnates have become members, the genealogy often shows the link generations later; in Chimbu either genealogies are too short to show such incorporation, or a non-agnate becomes an agnate in the genealogy as known to succeeding generations.

The ramage, alternatively called an ambilateral, cognatic or non-unilineal descent group,[14] has been described in Oceania, and in Melanesia seems to be present in parts of coastal New Guinea and the eastern island groups, certainly in the Solomons. At least one highlands society—Huli—seems also to have this character. Discussions of non-unilineal groups have been most concerned with recruitment, exclusiveness or non-exclusiveness of membership, choices, and other problems of group composition.

Curiously, there are several alternative explanations for the presence of these groups, or, if you like, the failure of descent groups to become unilineal. Radcliffe-Brown felt that unilineal institutions are almost a necessity in any ordered social system,[15] but these societies with non-unilineal descent groups had not been adequately described in 1935, and we still lack a thorough account of them. Forde[16] suggests that the proliferation of unilineal kin and the formation of large and segmented clans requires physical mobility and territorial expansion; further, local exclusiveness and barriers to expansion inhibit this proliferation of unilineal groups. In Melanesia, this has not been substantiated by studies showing that non-unilineal or small unilineal groups are found in certain ecological situations and large unilineal groups in others. Terrain, bordering groups and potential density would be relevant factors.

Goodenough[17] takes up a different point—that non-unilineal structure is adaptable: it reallocates land, a scarce resource, most efficiently when the population fluctuates and expands irregularly. There is still another view of the relation between group structure and environment—Pouwer's. He sees non-unilineal groups as adapted to a hostile environment. These statements are not necessarily contradictory, but all require further research.

I find the most recent discussions of Pouwer and van der Leeden[18] concerning 'loose structure' in New Guinea closer to my own approach than the earlier ones which despaired of finding an ordered social system where the cultural alternatives, local variations and individualism seemed to permit a vast range of social relations.[19] I shall, then, consider such features as interpersonal relations, exchange and reciprocity, and the variable composition of local groups. Pouwer's argument relates these features to the small size of groups in the inhospitable environment of coastal New Guinea, while I shall show them in an area where population density is highest, and where large quasi-unilineal groups are found.

In my analysis, I shall try to show that Chimbu groups are open; membership in them is ordinarily ascribed by birth but may be achieved, and there are what Firth calls 'optative' features in group composition.[20] But the uncertainty of group membership is only one aspect of a more pervasive characteristic of the system. Ties with non-agnatic cognates and with affines permeate nearly all activities and are of dominant interest to the people. They are especially prominent in exchange, prestige, wealth and ceremonial; the changes in group composition which occur are a result of some types of mutual aid between kin and affines.

In trying to understand Chimbu social structure, I have combined and modified several modes of analysis. There are both resemblances and differences between Chimbu enduring groups and African lineages; extra-agnatic ties are important in social relations and also affect group composition. The enduring groups in Chimbu are neither lineages nor non-unilineal descent groups, but quasi-unilineal groups which are open to new members. The ties with non-agnates are not formalized relations between a man and a descent group, but interpersonal relations of exchange, aid and often close affection. Although I will not be able to substantiate this here, I shall assert that this is a common Melanesian type of social system, found in varying forms in many societies of the area.

The social anthropologist working in the New Guinea highlands finds a system of segmentary patrilineal groups which has many features in common with African segmentary systems. Chimbu clans are exogamous, marriage is patri-virilocal, descent group membership and inheritance are patrilineal; clans and their segments are localized (although segment territories are not compact blocks); the hierarchic and contrapuntal features of segmentary unilineal descent groups are present. These characteristics are common to most of the New Guinea highland societies so far known.

Each Chimbu tribe, a political and territorial unit with a population of several thousand people, is composed of two or more exogamous clans. It is a different sort of group from the clan-territorial-political group found in many highland societies. Almost half of Chimbu marriages are between clans of the same tribe. Tribal solidarity is a consequence of common defence, common pride in ceremonies, and the thick mesh of cognatic and affinal ties between clans. Intertribal relations are compounded of mutual hostility, competition, and a mesh of kin and affinal ties less dense than those within the tribe. While forty-four per cent of marriages are between neighbouring tribes, less than seven per cent of them are between any two tribes.[21]

Clan activities, where the clan forms a unit for some purpose, are not frequent. Some of them are connected with marriage and exogamy—the girls of a clan collectively invite the boys of another clan to a courting party. Exchanges are held between clans, and the clan is the usual unit in ceremonial dancing at the pig feast. Marriage and death payments are mainly the concern of clan segments—the subclan or clan section. In practical activities and donations to the payments made by members, co-operation is within the subclan.

Necessary co-operation in subsistence activities is limited: a man can build his own houses and prepare his own gardens; the family can provide its own food, shelter and clothing. But a minority of men live and work alone; most men join with others in their subclan to build and reside in a men's house; they co-operate in fencing garden blocks which enclose the land of a number of men, within the subclan and in others; and they co-operate occasionally in parties to clear land and prepare gardens for other men in the subclan. Men depend upon others of the subclan for donations to the gifts they are obliged to make, for support in disputes, and in other aspects of their external relations.

But there are no occasions on which all subclan members (a group of about 125 people) collaborate in a single enterprise. Furthermore, at every subclan enterprise there are some persons present who are not natal agnatic members. Nominally, activities are carried out by a clan or segment of some order; in fact the group of actors is never completely or exclusively a segment. There are also cross-cutting groupings based on locality. Subclan sections of ten to fifteen men are usually broken up among small men's house units which are composed of members of more than one subclan section.

Although about eighty per cent of the men, at any time, live on the territory of their natal subclan, garden patrilineally inherited land, and participate in the activities organized by the leaders of their natal subclan and clan, we found very few men who had not at some time in youth or adulthood resided with non-agnatic kin or affines. Every man has several alternative choices of kin and affines whose activities he may join, and where a home can be made for him. While a man remains with his agnatic group, his interests and activities are by no means limited to his agnates. He often visits and helps cognates and affines in neighbouring clans. When a clan or tribe plans a ceremonial distribution, each member is concerned with his outside exchange relationships, his obligations and ability to repay, the sources he can call upon for assistance. Of the occasions on which clans and tribes combine, ceremonial distributions are the most common, and the aim of these is the restoration of balance, new payment, and repayment of obligations to outside kin and affines. One of the main joint activities of unilineal descent groups is the mass display and prestation to others.

Chimbu have no formalized behaviour requirements between certain categories of kin and affines—no strict respect, avoidance or joking behaviour. Kinship terms are somewhat adaptable to relative age, and an adoptee uses and extends parental and sibling terms in his adoptive group. Relations between agnates are not markedly different from those between non-agnatic cognates and affines; residence, participation and co-operation are more significant in interpersonal relations than are the particular cognatic or affinal connections.

In Chimbu no compulsive sanctions exist; there are no automatic supernatural sanctions, no formal leaders, and no legal machinery to settle internal disputes. A gathering may be called for any kind of work, to discuss a dispute, plan, perform a ceremony, or for any activity requiring collaboration of the subclan, clan or tribe. From early morning the air is rent with shouts by all the leading men telling everyone to come. This is followed by a period, usually lasting for hours, in which men straggle to the meeting place, there is much more shouting, and those present complain that everyone has not come. Some meetings never take place, others carry on with a partial assembly. Now, the Australian administration has established effective control and a system of native officials with limited power. In the past no authority could control an angry Chimbu or force all men to support a single cause.

Chimbu are quarrelsome, grasping people. They place a high value on possessions and strongly resent appropriation by others. They take insult easily. And they are exhilarated in battle. The solemn duel or private debate has no appeal for them; they kill in a sneak attack, but the public recognition of this daring act is its aim. Although they put down their rather feeble arms in a few years after Europeans entered the area, this was done because punishment for outbreaks of violence was consistently applied by zealous government officers, and the former territorial gains in warfare were not attainable. Litigation has supplanted boundary fights.

In a free-for-all atmosphere, Chimbu developed large groups—the tribe includes hundreds of active adult men. Quarrels and raids often sparked large-scale fights. The opposition between segments of a group was the first stage of mobilization in disputes, and quarrels between sections of a clan might be restricted to a single clan. However, each side sought allies, first their own kin and affines, and then whoever could be drawn in by these outsiders. Any small dispute between members of different tribes could lead to intertribal fighting, bringing out most men of both tribes in battle. Beyond this, allies were temporary and unpredictable. A small slight would send them away, or to the opposing side. We can only account for the very large size, by New Guinea standards, of Chimbu tribes by the special features of density, distribution of territory, and alliance. Tribes or, occasionally, subtribes have a large land block within which segments have scattered parcels; any attack on a part of a tribe threatens the land of members of many segments, and they join together in defence. Within the tribe there is some accommodation of members from surplus land, and by this means the land is filled up by people with an interest in protecting their holdings. This sort of interdependence among fellow-tribesmen in defending territory is a prime factor in tribal solidarity.

The enduring groups in Chimbu play little part in subsistence production, but rather more in providing basic resources in land and in protecting the individual from outside attack and supporting him in disputes with outsiders. The tribal territorial unit contains groups which may intermarry; thus land loans and assistance from kin and affines within the tribe redistribute land holdings and interests in different parts of the territory.

When we turn to other concerns of the Chimbu, the things which bring wealth, prestige and pleasure, we see the great part played by non-agnatic ties. The gifts and exchanges of food, pigs and valuables are not required by economic necessity. There is little regional variation in access to goods and resources, and no seasonal shortage of any important type of food. Pigs are reared and fattened for distribution at large ceremonies, but a more regular supply of pork would better serve nutritional needs. Several types of goods are sought after. Before the Europeans came in 1933, only fragments of shells reached the highlands, but now whole goldlip and bailer shells are common. Traditional valuables included the ceremonial 'Hagen' axe and a wide range of feathers and plumes, of which the bird of paradise species were most highly regarded. The valued articles are not found or made in Chimbu. They come into the area by trade and in gifts, and then circulate mainly in prestations. Feathers and plumes are worn at ceremonies by dancers, and a few shells are also worn. The axe is carried by dancers. Salt is consumed mainly on ceremonial occasions with pork.

Chimbu produce pigs to exchange for these goods. Pigs are not raised for domestic consumption; they are distributed ceremonially and exchanged for valuables. While nutritional research may show that the small quantity of pork consumed by Chimbu in feasts is vital to health, the Chimbu only know that they like to eat pork—they often steal to get it—and that pork fat rubbed on the skin makes one attractive to the opposite sex.

Valued objects in Chimbu are bound together in an exchange complex involving transactions with non-agnatic kin and affines outside the clan. At the foundation of the system is land, individually held and cultivated but associated with patrilineal groups. The exchange system rests upon the products of the land—vegetable food and the pigs and people it feeds. The feather and shell valuables which come from outside Chimbu can only be obtained by exporting food, pigs and women. After they enter the area, the valuables circulate between clans linked by intermarriage.

Marriage, birth and death are occasions for the presentation of valuables between intermarrying groups. Marriage initiates an exchange relationship between two groups, especially between the husband and the bride's close male agnates. An interest in valuables for personal adornment begins in adolescence, when girls begin to wear some shells and feathers, especially when entertaining boys, and boys decorate themselves when visiting girls. As courtship proceeds, a girl may go to the boy's locality for a few days, staying with one of his female relatives. If no marriage arrangements proceed, she is decorated by the boy's agnates with feathers and shells, washed in pig grease, and sent home. Girls are always married in their middle teens, by choice or arrangement.

As a boy reaches marriageable age, about 20, his agnates make up a payment for him, getting contributions from other men of the subclan and clan, and from their exchange partners (affines and kin) outside the clan. The assembled payment is shown to the agnates of a marriageable girl, who may already be the boy's choice. Leading men of the subclan, and sometimes cognates of the boy and girl bargain and compare the pigs which will be cooked and exchanged. Some marriages are preceded by months of unsuccessful attempts with the agnates of various marriageable girls. Finally, a day is appointed on which the boy's party takes a large display board covered with feathers and shells, a load of axes, a quantity of money and about five cooked pigs to the bride's home. Just as the groom's party includes non-agnatic relatives, so does the girl's. Aside from the formal prestation of the groom's payment, there is an exchange of equivalent articles between the two parties. The bride is richly decorated in feathers by her agnates before being given to her husband, and at the same time a man of the groom's party who has a close affinal or kinship connection to the bride's group is also decorated. He is expected to help her and mediate in any quarrels. After the bride is taken to her husband's group, her agnates divide the payment among themselves and her mother's agnates. A few days later there is another gathering of the two parties, this time at the groom's home. The bride's party brings a large quantity of vegetable food to exchange with the groom's party, and the women married into the groom's group present the new bride with a quantity of household goods and personal articles.

Chimbu marriage is viewed as bringing groups together. The speeches emphasize the cementing role of marriage and the mutual hospitality of the intermarrying groups. Sometimes it is stressed that this is a rare, distant tie to another tribe; at other times, that here has been regular and friendly exchange with the neighbours within the tribe, and visiting should continue. After this mutual expression of good will and the dispersion of the payments, the bride's group will try to send her back if she runs away from her husband, and the husband's group will try to see that he treats her well. Still, many women have several short-lived marriages before they settle down, and many men can recount a number of temporary marriages, some of which fail because the first wife drives newcomers away, or the man sends a lazy woman home. Only a few men fail to keep any wife.

A successful marriage is followed by exchanges, visits, and gifts between the agnates of the bride and the agnates of the groom. A formal gift to the infant's matrilateral kin is made after each birth, and older children often visit matrilateral kin. The bride is visited by her siblings and parents, who often remain for years at their kinswoman's husband's home. Such close ties are often a prelude to further marriages between the two groups. I found no case of marriage within the clan, and the breach of the rule prohibiting marriage with the mother's subclan is rare, but brothers and sisters may marry into the same subclan or clan, and affinal ties can multiply between pairs of subclans. Many children are raised by kin outside their clan when one or both of their parents have died, and they are quite likely to marry into a clan to which they have kinship ties. The ties of kinship within the clan which result are an additional factor in intraclan solidarity and mutual aid. We found several instances of land gifts to fellow-clansmen linked to the donors by non-agnatic ties. Distance, the death of close kin, and other interests often sever kinship ties. A married woman may rarely be able to visit her matrilateral kin and female agnates who have married at a distance from her husband's home, yet she may co-operate closely with a clanswoman who has married into her husband's subclan. In contrast, the ties of men are more easily maintained: male agnates remain together, their sisters return to visit them, and they visit their kin in other clans. It is the removal of a woman from her natal group which begins to break her kinship bonds.

The exchange pattern between affines may be carried into the next generation, but it is not perpetuated long: there is no special relationship with the mother's father's or father's mother's or mother's mother's group. Payments at death, to a married woman's agnates and to a man's, boy's or unmarried girl's mother's agnates serve to settle debts, although some exchange relationships may continue among the survivors.

The apparent one-way traffic in valuables, whereby the group giving a woman is repeatedly paid by the wife-receiving group, only occurs in life cycle gifts. In the wider exchange system, the group which has given a wife donates goods and gives pigs to the woman's husband on many occasions. The actual relations between affines and kin are characterized by mutual aid, reciprocal gifts, sharing, fond attention to children, and genuine grief at death. While the Chimbu dream of women, pigs and valuables, true affection and generosity prompt them to redistribute their receipts widely, to take in a wife's younger brother, wife's sister's child or sister's child as permanent dependants with only a remote expectation of a return from them some day. In bringing up a young man, the adoptor has an obligation to provide for his marriage, and gains the dubious asset of the young man with numerous other obligations as an eventual supporter to his old age. Visiting kin and affines is a welcome change from the monotonous daily routine and demands for aid within the subclan. Aside from the personal reward of a share in the payment, a man takes pleasure in negotiating the marriage of a girl in a group where he has few connections, and in extending his range of visiting-places as a result. There is another pleasure in having many kin nearby who will share interests and help in enterprises.

Ceremonially, the reciprocity between kin and affines is expressed more in large displays and distributions than in the life cycle gifts. Prestations of pandanus nuts are made periodically between tribes and also between clans. The ceremonial prelude to the distribution is a dance-mime attack upon the donor tribe. The decorated display of nut parcels and other foods may cover a circle over fifty yards in diameter. Each prestation is an element in an exchange cycle between two tribes, but the actual gifts are between individuals who are kin and affines, exchange partners in continuous interaction.

Relationships are similar in the more complex pig ceremony and prestation. Here also an entire tribe is the donating unit; but in this case the recipients are from all other tribes. The celebrating tribe musters forces: its manpower builds a village, sings and dances; its wives and daughters grow additional food and fatten the pigs; pig herds are increased to the maximum possible. The tribal wealth in feathers, and all they can borrow from kin and affines, is accumulated. Some special decorations are made and painted, for the tribe displays its valuables and artistry in the dances. Each man is concerned with his own personal non-agnatic relations—the people he can borrow feathers from, those who have cared for his pigs, and those to whom he owes pork. Throughout, there is a double goal of tribal display and the repayment of personal debts. Marriages are arranged to coincide with the mass pig killing. The ritual purpose of the ceremony— fertility of pigs and gardens—takes little time, but it is the climax of the activities. Hundreds of pigs are slaughtered and then displayed around the central spirit-house; later the jaws are hung there, and sweet potato vines are blessed while the massed dance and mime occupy the ceremonial ground. Although the Chimbu have discarded male initiation, some ancestral decorations, and pig killing in cemeteries—those elements concerned with the ancestors and male cult—the emphases upon display and distribution remain.

There is no tribal co-operation after the pigs are killed. Each donor calls his non-agnates to help butcher and cook the meat. The next day pork is distributed to these helpers and other exchange partners. Our sample reveals a wide range of non-agnatic kinship and affinal ties honoured by gifts of a half-side of pork, in which the sister's husband and son—people who have received wives from the donor—are given pork as often as the wife's brother and mother's brother—those who have given wives. Many recipients are exchange partners more distantly connected to the donors by such ties as mother's sister's son. The recipients carry away the meat, further share it among their own agnates and non-agnatic kin and affines. As the pork is widely distributed, the reputation of the donating tribe spreads to distant and unconnected tribes; the source of their reputation is their non-agnatic kin and affines who have loaned them finery to display, admired their dancing, received their pork and passed it on.

Chimbu group membership, recruitment and participation can now be viewed against this pattern of exchange and aid between non-agnates. Life is short in the New Guinea highlands, and children must often be reared by kin other than their parents, within or outside their agnatic group. The adoptive father may be the child's father's agnate, but he may also be the mother's second husband in the same or another clan, the mother's brother, the father's sister's husband, mother's sister's husband, or older sister's husband. This person may act as a sponsor, helping a lad with his marriage payment, giving him land and asking him to remain. The boy will be asked by his father's agnates to join them, and promised aid, but he suffers no serious disadvantages if he remains with non-agnates. In time, he will be accepted as a member of the adoptive group, dissociated from his own agnates. He may even marry a girl of his father's clan, although I discovered only one such case.

By becoming a member of a group with which he would normally have an exchange relationship, he cannot have the benefits of that relationship, although he can still exchange with other kin and affines. If his sponsor is an important man, he will be given adequate land and join his entourage of followers. A few adoptees attain positions of leadership in their adoptive group. The situation is different for a man who resides with his wife's agnates: he usually remains a fringe member of the group in which he lives, and is expected to participate in his natal group. He is never recognized as a full member of the wife's group, for he remains an affine of his sponsor.

There are many reasons why a man might leave his agnates: formerly, in flight after defeat, many people went to other groups for shelter and received land; widows often take their children to become dependants of another man; men leave after a quarrel, or just for a change. Visits last for days or years, and with the passage of years the non-agnate becomes indistinguishable from agnates in the part he takes in group activities. Those who reside with, and garden with non-agnates for years are the minority. A few carry their ties with a group of kin or affines into full participation and identification with non-agnates. No sharp classification of members is made. Only the anthropologist asks about genealogies, to be told that a certain young man is the sister's son of a subclan member; his father died, and his mother brought him to live with her brother; then the brother helped him, negotiated his marriage and gave him land, so he has joined his mother's group. Chimbu often add: they are glad to have him; his father's agnates did not look after him. When the anthropologist asks why certain people receive a nurturing payment at a funeral, it comes out that the dead woman's father died when she was a child, and she lived first with her mother's brother and then with her mother's sister, so survivors of her three childhood protectors receive gifts.

Recruitment into Chimbu clans is not restricted to agnatic descent or 'serial filiation' (as Fortes[22] terms it). Boys who are reared by non-agnates are, in time, fully participating members of their sponsors' group; only some of their agnates may recall their origin and press them to return. Their sons are indistinguishable from the sons of agnatic members of the group. Men who join kin or affines have a less certain status—their origin is remembered by their contemporaries and elders, even if they disregard their obligations to their agnates and support their adoptive group in all activities.

Nevertheless, the Chimbu ideology is agnatic; relations between subclans, and between clans in a phratry are conceived as relations between descendants of brothers. The absence of extended genealogies obviates the need for genealogical revision, and the descendants of an adoptee do not form a sister's son's branch of a lineage as occurs in Tiv[23] and Tallensi.[24] Chimbu clans and their segments would seem to be patrilineal, in ordinary usage, but not lineages.

The Chimbu groups do not conform to Firth's definition of a 'ramage' or an 'optative' system.[25] In a ramage, the individual can choose to join his father's or mother's group; the group is a lineage, but non-unilineal. Nor are the Chimbu groups closed. Chimbu groups incorporate non-agnatic members from a wide range of kin, and only in the case of those who remain in the group they joined at birth or in childhood is membership definitive; every group includes some people as participating members who have natal ties elsewhere. The criteria for unilineal and non-unilineal descent groups advanced by Davenport[26] do not seem to apply to Chimbu, because the single alternative principle of affiliation is not present.

Chimbu activities are nominally undertaken by named groups, but participants do not include all members nor exclude non-members. Nevertheless, we can identify enduring groups with a stable core of natal agnatic members who regularly participate in activities. This core is composed of men who, by ties of kinship and affinity have a network of interests outside their patrilineal group. These interests may divert them from support of their group—each man avoids fighting his own kin and affines, uses his wealth to help non-agnates, works for and gives land to outsiders, and visits them. These outside interests of the members reduce the group's resources, but the group gains from help given by its outside kin and affines. The group can only exist as part of a system of groups stitched together by cognatic and affinal ties. Exogamy and the exchange system require the interdependence of groups. The valued objects, pigs and women circulate through these ties. Sometimes, these ties remove men from their agnatic groups and change the composition of groups. But this is only an occasional result of the social relations between kin and affines.

Finally, I want to suggest that this context for the study of social relations and group composition may give us a wider perspective on Melanesian social structure. Many societies besides Chimbu have enduring quasi-unilineal groups and set great store by kin and affines outside the group, for mutual aid and exchange. The forms of residential mobility and participation vary, and so does the strength of the unilineal ideology. Where the clans are small and communities composed of several, permitting local endogamy, the unilineal group may be difficult to discern as an activity group. Co-operation with local kin and affines dilutes the strength of the unilineal group.

In examining descriptions of other New Guinea societies, I found that most of them are said to have a unilineal descent group of some sort, often small, and frequently localized. It is usually the unit within which land, goods, and incorporeal property are inherited. Running through these societies, in varying forms, is a close tie of some sort with cognatic kin and affines. The forms include feasts, exchanges, services, division of marriage payments, land gifts, inheritance, ceremonial sponsorship, instruction in magic. While the core (father-son or mother's brother-sister's son) is coresidential, it is frequently noted that some affines and non-unilineal kin reside with the core group and use its land. Brother-sister exchange marriage is approved in a number of these societies, creating a reinforced affinal tie between families.

Of course, some sort of tie between cognatic kin outside the unilineal group is well documented in other parts of the world. But in Africa, where especially the mother's brother-sister's son tie has been described,[27] the relationship is frequently formalized and ritualized. These New Guinea societies are not usually so formal; rather, a man may get land from his father or mother's brother or sister's husband or wife's brother, marriage may be virilocal or uxorilocal, co-operation is with the brother or the brother-in-law. Where avunculocal residence is the rule, some men stay with their fathers, and both sons and daughters may inherit. These practices have not the rigidity and formality of respect or joking relations, and do not produce clear-cut localized units. There is a flexibility in New Guinea which seems to be the product of quasi-unilineal descent groups and close friendly ties with kin and affines. As a result, the enduring groups are open, and recruitment is not exclusively by descent.

NOTES

1. The field-work upon which this paper is based was supported by the Australian National University.
2. Hogbin and Wedgwood 1953.
3. Bateson 1958.
4. Malinowski 1922.
5. For example, Worsley 1957; Burridge 1960.
6. Evans-Pritchard 1940:262-263.
7. Meggitt 1959.
8. Salisbury 1956.
9. Fried 1957:23.
10. Some differences between African lineages and the social groups of the New Guinea highlands were discussed by J. A. Barnes in a paper entitled "African Models in the New Guinea Highlands" presented to the Tenth Pacific Science Congress in the symposium "Recent Research in the New Guinea Highlands".
11. Fortes 1953:33-34.
12. Leach 1957:53-55.
13. Fortes 1959.
14. Goodenough 1955; Firth 1957; Davenport 1959.
15. Radcliffe-Brown 1952: 48.
16. Forde 1948.
17. Goodenough 1955.
18. Pouwer 1960, 1961; van der Leeden 1960.
19. Held 1951:51-55; van Baal 1954.
20. Firth 1957.
21. Brown and Brookfield 1959: 52.
22. Fortes 1959.
23. Bohannan 1954.
24. Fortes 1945.
25. Firth 1957.
26. Davenport 1959.
27. Radcliffe-Brown's famous paper (1924) was followed by many accounts.

REFERENCES

Baal, J. van, 1954. "Volken." In *Nieuw Guinea.* Ed. W. C. Klein. 's-Gravenhage, Govt. Printer, Vol. II; 438-461.
Barnes, J. A., 1962. "African Models in the New Guinea Highlands." *Man,* forthcoming.
Bateson, G., 1958. *Naven.* Stanford, Cal., Stanford University.
Bohannan, P., 1954. *Tiv Farm and Settlement.* Colonial Research Studies No. 15. London, HMSO.

BROWN, PAULA and BROOKFIELD, H. C. 1959. "Chimbu Land and Society." *Oceania*, 30: 1-75.

BURRIDGE, K. O. L., 1960. *Mambu.* London, Methuen.

DAVENPORT, WILLIAM, 1959. "Nonunilinear Descent and Descent Groups." *Amer. Anthrop.*, 61: 557-572.

EVANS-PRITCHARD, E. E., 1940. *The Nuer.* Oxford, Clarendon.

FIRTH, RAYMOND, 1957. "A Note on Descent Groups in Polynesia." *Man*, LVII, art. 2.

FORDE, DARYLL, 1948. "The Integration of Anthropological Studies." *J. R. Anthrop. Inst.*, 78: 1-10.

FORTES, MEYER, 1945. *The Dynamics of Clanship among the Tallensi.* London, Oxford.

———— 1953. "The Structure of Unilineal Descent Groups." *Amer. Anthrop.*, 55: 17-41.

———— 1959. "Descent, Filiation, and Affinity: a Rejoinder to Dr. Leach." *Man*, 59, arts. 309, 331.

FRIED, MORTON H., 1957. "The Classification of Corporate Unilineal Descent Groups." *J. R. Anthrop. Inst.*, 87: 1-30.

GOODENOUGH, WARD H., 1955. "A Problem in Malayo-Polynesian Social Organization." *Amer. Anthrop.*, 57: 71-83.

HELD, G. J., 1951. *De Papoea Cultuurimprovisator.* 's-Gravenhage/Bandung, van Hoeve.

HOGBIN, H. I. and WEDGWOOD, C. H., 1953. "Local Grouping in Melanesia." *Oceania*, 23: 241-276; 24: 58-76.

LEACH, E. R., 1957. "Aspects of Bridewealth and Marriage Stability among the Kachin and Lakher." *Man*, 57, art. 59.

LEEDEN, A. C. VAN DER, 1960. "Social Structure in New Guinea." *Bijdr. Taal-, Land-, Volkenk.*, 116: 119-149.

MALINOWSKI, B., 1922. *Argonauts of the Western Pacific.* London, Routledge & Kegan Paul.

MEGGITT, M. J., 1959. The lineage system of the Mae Enga of New Guinea. Ph.D. thesis in anthropology, University of Sydney.

POUWER, J., 1960. " 'Loosely Structured Societies' in Netherlands New Guinea." *Bijdr. Taal-, Land-, Volkenk.*, 116: 109-118.

———— 1961. "New Guinea as a Field for Ethnological Study," *Bijdr. Taal-, Land-, Volkenk.*, 117: 1-24.

RADCLIFFE-BROWN, A. R. 1924. "The Mother's Brother in South Africa." *South African Journal of Science*, 21: 542-555.

———— 1952. "Patrilineal and Matrilineal Succession." In *Structure and Function in Primitive Society*, 32-48.

SALISBURY, R. F., 1956. "Unilineal Descent Groups in the New Guinea Highlands." *Man*, 56, art. 2.

WORSLEY, PETER, 1957. *The Trumpet Shall Sound.* London, Macgibbon & Kee.

9

CHOISEFUL ISLAND
DESCENT GROUPS[1]

Harold W. Scheffler

Choiseul Island descent groups are similar in type to those which are found so often, though perhaps not exclusively, in the Malayo-Polynesian area and which Firth[2] terms ramages. I retain this term but prefer to rephrase his definition of it as "the kind of group constituted by using both/ either parents as links in membership" to read, "a localized and corporate kin group in respect of which entitlement to membership is (nominally at least) by cognatic descent." Such groups are commonly described as being "recruited" through "ambilateral" or "ambilineal" principles, but I prefer to speak of "entitlement to membership" and "cognatic descent" because it is commonly said that anyone who can trace a descending genealogical connection from the founder or who has had an ancestor regarded as a member of the group is entitled to membership in it or is reckoned as a member of it in some sense and, furthermore, because the genealogical criterion itself would appear to be only one of several, perhaps many, factors involved in the actual formation and maintenance of such groups. It is apparent that affiliation with ramages is neither wholly ascribed nor wholly a matter of free and open choice.

In brief, the argument defended here in relation to Choiseulese society is that cognatic descent acts to place persons in kin categories from which operative groups are recruited by "filiation" operating in conjunction with a number of other less clearly specified criteria. To demonstrate this argument, which I suggest is of a more general applicability, I present a brief analysis of some aspects of descent group affiliation in Choiseulese society. I am concerned here with how individuals become attached to and identified with particular groups, which is of course only a part of the larger problems of group formation, maintenance, and integration into a larger society. To the latter problems I refer only in passing.[3]

Choiseul consists of approximately 1,100 square miles of forest-clad ridges and valleys located in the northwestern corner of the British Solomon

Reproduced by permission of the publisher and Harold W. Scheffler from the *Journal of the Polynesian Society*, 72:177-187 (1963).

Islands Protectorate. It is about eighty miles long and twenty miles across at its widest. Its aboriginal population of perhaps eight to ten thousand (now 5,700 and growing) was widely dispersed in small hamlets, though from time to time villages of several hundred persons formed for purposes of defence or to carry out public gift-exchange obligations with other groups. The climatic and general environmental conditions are typically insular Melanesian and in the past permitted only a subsistence economy based primarily upon taro supplemented by yams and bananas. The people now live in some eighty or so hamlets and villages (with maximum populations of 150 or so) scattered along the coasts but concentrated in the few relatively flat areas. In the past they lived exclusively inland for protection from head-hunting raids from New Georgia and other islands to the south, but the area has been missionized and thoroughly pacified for some thirty or forty years, and the Choiseulese are now a quiet Oceanic peasantry thoroughly involved in the copra trade and dependent upon it to maintain their style of life. Horticulture is still the main source of staples, but the sweet potato is now the principal cultigen. A blight struck taro a few years ago, and the potatoes require less attention in any event, leaving more time for copra making. The island contains six major dialect areas, and while this analysis pertains particularly to the Varisi-speaking area, it is probably equally valid for the others, for the island is culturally uniform.

The most general term for kin group or category in Varisi is *sinangge*. The exact reference of the term varies according to the context, but it may be clarified (though it seldom is) by the addition of descriptive terms.

One usage of *sinangge* is egocentric, referring to all of those persons with whom one can trace cognatic connection and to whom he may, at least nominally, turn for support. This is his *sinangge lavata,* "big *sinangge*".

Another reference is to named "cognatic descent categories" which consist, again nominally, of all of the descendants, through both males and females, of an apical ancestor known to have founded that *sinangge*. From the individual's point of view all of the cognatic descent categories to which he belongs converge upon him to form his *sinangge lavata* or what may be termed his "kinship circle". But *sinangge* most commonly refers to a unilocal group recruited in large part from a particular cognatic descent category. This is the group I call a ramage; the Choiseulese some times refer to it as a *sinangge sukasuka,* "small *sinangge*". *Kapakapa* is also used in relation to the local group but refers specifically to coresident descendants of the apical ancestor while *sinangge* in this context may include the whole of the local group, including for instance, inmarrying spouses, which is what I mean by ramage. *Kapakapa* may be translated as "ramage core".

Finally, *sinangge* may refer simply to any collection of kinsmen, such as a task group for gardening, fishing, or warfare. In this context even affinal kin are included, but in general *sinangge* signifies that the persons referred to trace common cognatic connection of some sort and they co-operate on the basis of a cognatic kinship sentiment which enjoins them to *vari tavisi,* "help one another".

Kinship, aside from that imposed by affinal bonds, stems from common membership in cognatic descent categories. These categories also link ramages to one another, for the members of one ramage belong to various and sometimes numerous cognatic descent categories. But the ramages themselves are the most significant structural units, for it is around them and through them that most social activities are organized. Task groups are recruited initially from them, although a task group may not involve all of the members of any one or any several ramages.

Sinangge, regardless of their nature, are neither exogamous nor endogamous by cultural prescription. Everyone agrees that first cousins are not marriageable, but some feel this proscription should apply to second cousins as well. Otherwise it is considered best to marry a kinsman.

The ramage is the primary residential and proprietary segment.[4] Its most important properties are its land, upon which it is domiciled, and its *kesa* or shell valuables. (*Kesa* consists of cylinders of fossilized clam shell which are bound together into sets and used in important transactions such as brideprice and warfare alliance payments.)

The whole of the island is divided into a large number (certainly well over 100) of tracts of land of varying size and irregular shape; each is the principal corporate property of a *sinangge* and bears its name. It is this tract from which the group often derives its name. Most, but not all, tracts are further subdivided into units belonging to segments of the *sinangge.* Such segments, named and known as "branch" *sinangge,* may form discrete ramages which remain linked genealogically to the originating or "truncal" ramage. The truncal ramage or segment is variously known as the "straight part", "trunk", or "base" of the *sinangge.* Independent branches arose through the fission of a group or alternatively grew up, as it were, outside of the truncal ramage through the accretion of cognates and affines to an influential man or *batu,* here called a manager, who had been a member of the truncal ramage. Branches achieved their distinctiveness from the original unit as well as other ramages through participation in such activities as revenge, warfare, and gift-exchanges which were accompanied by feasts. Only some segments developed their independence through this essentially political process while many remained thoroughly identified with the truncal segment and constitute today only separate interest groups within the ramage. The larger *sinangge,* including branches, are here called major *sinangge,* and the segments, which may or may not have attained independent political status, minor *sinangge.* Major and minor refer only to genealogical status and imply nothing about political or residential status. The fissioning process came to an end with pacification and the termination of competitive gift-exchanges, a process which cannot be described here.

In attempting to explain the *sinangge* to me and, what is more important, in talking about such things among themselves, the Choiseulese often asserted: "The important side is that of the father; we follow our fathers." But it was almost always added, "We keep two sides because it is not good to lose the mother's side." The reference here is not simply to matrikin in general but to the mother's *sinangge* of premarital origin in particular. It is recognized that, by logical extension, one could then be said to "keep" or "look after" many *sinangge*. Thus one may claim membership in any *sinangge* with which one can trace a cognatic connection regardless of how far one may be removed spatially or genealogically from the ramage of that *sinangge*.

The meaning of such statements lies in *how* the father's "side" is "important" and what is meant by "keeps" in relation to *sinangge*. *Miasoka*, "to keep" or to "care for", may be used in the sense of ownership, but it seems also to refer more generally to having an interest in something. Furthermore, the Choiseulese have no word which is the simple equivalent of "belongs to"; when one wishes to say that one is in some sense a "member" of a particular *sinangge* one says, "I am *sinangge* Gambili," or whatever. Now since they say this about many *sinangge*, including those with which they are not immediately resident, but in which they have kinsmen, it is clear that "keeps" does not necessarily refer to one's domicile or ramage membership. What the speaker means is that he appears, or should appear according to his understanding, in the genealogy of the unit to which he refers. Consequently, when it is said, "We belong to the same *sinangge*," no more may be meant than "We are kinsmen." "Belonging" seems to be an idiom of kinship relations, a way of stating kinship. But why choose this idiom in particular and how is the father's *sinangge* the most important? An answer to these questions requires an examination of the ideology of ramage organization.

Assuming the existence of a particular ramage, it is said: "Upon marriage, men do not go out or leave the ramage, but women usually do," or "Men abide while women marry and then go out." This is to say, through patrivirilocal residence the men of a *sinangge* come to form the nucleus of a ramage, its *kapakapa*. Those who trace their descent from the apical ancestor of the *sinangge* solely through males are said to be *popondo valeke*, "born of men" or of agnatic status. These men are said to have primary rights and interests in the property and affairs of the group; they are "strong" within it. Primogeniture is said to determine precedence in the agnatic line and, thereby, who will be *batu* or manager of the people and their estate.

It is realized, however, that a ramage can never be composed solely of persons of agnatic status if only because many, if not most, men will marry "outsiders" and bring in "alien" women. There is also the presence of "illegitimate" children to be considered. If a girl has a child out of wedlock, the genitor, who is usually known, has no claim to the child because he did not pay a brideprice. The child thus belongs solely to its mother's *sinangge,* for socially speaking it has no father. There is also an alternative form of marriage, *tamazira,* in which no brideprice is paid to the bride's father (or his representative) and uxorilocal residence is then required. The children of such marriages also belong primarily to the *sinangge* of their mother; it is their "strong" side. The father's *sinangge* still retains an interest in them, just as does the mother's *sinangge* in brideprice marriages, and they are always welcome within either group. To put this another way, a person's domicile is assumed to follow from that of his father, but in certain circumstances it may legitimately follow that of his mother. As will become apparent, his residence—where he actually has his dwelling at any particular time—may not be the same place.

So far, this might be taken to be a system of "patrilineal descent" with "bilateral reckoning of kinship" expressed in a special idiom and with provision for "emergency" recruitment to "lineages". Yet even at this point one wonders if such terms are appropriate, and additional elements of the ideology strengthen this impression. For instance, it is said that persons may permanently change their *sinangge* (ramage) affiliations. Anyone is said to be always welcome in any ramage of any *sinangge* in which he is reputed to have a "linking ancestor". In several ways, then, persons who are not of agnatic status may come to reside with a ramage and claim membership in its *sinangge.* As cognatic, but not agnatic, descendants of its founder they are referred to as *popondo nggole,* "born of women", regardless of how far back in their personal genealogies the female connection lies. They form a class of "secondary" members in that they may exercise only limited rights and interests in the ramage and its estate, and these are said to be subservient to those of persons of agnatic status. The rights of those "born of women" are "weak" and not "strong" or "active" like those of agnatic affiliants. The former "dwell under" the latter. They are "guests" who live on and utilize the *sinangge* estate, but they do so only so long as they "keep their peace", live quietly and cause no trouble. Nevertheless, they do "belong" to that *sinangge* for they do, after all, trace cognatic connection with its founder. They are also members in the very pragmatic sense that they are, or were, obliged to participate in and contribute to ramage activities such as gardening, vengeance, and gift-exchanges. They may voice an opinion and even take the initiative on certain occasions, but they must do so always with the understanding that it is on sufferance of the agnatic affiliants. Otherwise they may be asked to leave.

Members of the cognatic descent category who do not reside with its ramage are its *sasanggi,* those "born of" that *sinangge.* At least one of their ancestors was recognized as a ramage member, and they have certain rights of usage over the *sinangge* estate, rights which, it is said, cannot be refused; but their primary interests and rights lie elsewhere with the ramage in which they have agnatic status. However, it is said that they may become resident with the ramage to which they are only *sasanggi* and do so simply by option or choice (*vine*), and again, according to the ideology, they are not to be refused this right. However, it is admitted that known trouble-makers are seldom welcome. So long as they remain non-resident they are not obliged to do so but they may participate in ramage activities. They are, however, expected to refrain from conflict (as in warfare in the past) against ramage members or, for that matter, any kinsman. The *sasanggi* are said to belong to or "keep" the *sinangge* but the reference is clearly to the cognatic descent category. To ramage members the *sasanggi* are all kinsmen, and they may be close kinsmen. They are persons upon whom one may call for all sorts of assistance, and as kinsmen they should not refuse. When it is said that one belongs to many *sinangge* it is meant, then, that one has interests in the personnel and estates of many *sinangge* and, furthermore, the right, or perhaps more accurately the privilege, of domicile upon those estates. Some people assert that one's rights are "all the same" regardless of the nature of one's association with various ramages, but I think few people take this idea very seriously.

The realities of social life are seldom so simple, for social life is much more complex than the dogmas people espouse about it. The dogmas are, nonetheless, *more* than merely statements of how things work out or how people "should" behave, something people try perhaps unsuccessfully to "live up to". They are not merely "guideposts to action", but they are forms of social action in themselves, statements of values that may be, but are not necessarily, personally held and acted upon; and this is, at least in part, simply because the values expressed in the dogmas are only a single element in the total system of motives influencing Choiseulese conduct. The "organization"—in Firth's sense—of Choiseulese society is at the same time and in some ways, both more and less fluid than the dogmas would seem to indicate. Categories of right, for instance, are not rigid and there is mobility into and out of them. Primary rights conferred, according to the dogma, by agnatic status, may be acquired by secondary members and those who were *sasanggi* may become secondary or perhaps even primary members, and such rights as they acquire may be held by their offspring too.

Every person has, in some sense, at least several *sinangge* allegiances, but as might be expected his primary allegiance is to the group with which he is most closely identified, and his ties with other groups, which confer upon him at least nominal interests in their property and personnel, are of varying quality and utility depending largely upon his proximity to those groups but ultimately upon many other factors as well. Recruitment to ramages is initially by filiation, that is, by virtue of one's birth (or adoption) and with reference to one of his (or her) parents;[5] *but filiation here refers to a process and not a principle.* Persons are *born into* operating groups and become identified with them by virtue of parental connection and, later, the establishment of vested interests in the group's personnel and property develops through protracted residence and the relatively exclusive interaction with one's ramage mates which follows from that residence. Filiation in this society is most frequently through one's father though not infrequently, and quite legitimately, through one's mother. There are no "rules" of postmarital residence, but there are considerations which make patrivirilocality most desirable, such as the presumed importance of agnatic status within the ramage.

Changes of local group and/or ramage affiliation are permissible on the basis of rights conferred by cognatic descent, and there is no "rule" concerning the genealogical range over which this privilege extends. Operationally, however, the privilege may be revoked, but in the past the need for manpower encouraged its recognition. Today there is little change of affiliation, but this is in part because the Christian missions and Protectorate government discourage changes of residence. It is also due in part to the fact that there are relatively few areas which are economically attractive, and those persons and groups with consolidated interests in them are reluctant to recognize the more tenuous claims of others. Even in the past persons did not change ramage affiliation arbitrarily nor even very freely, and only those who have established and/or maintained vested interests in the property of the ramage or its personnel may be relatively sure of being able to exercise fully the privileges of membership. Changes of affiliation require the consent of those who have already established vested interests in the group through domicile or proximate residence and all the activities implied therein, and, moreover, protection of one's own property interests requires that one establish and maintain a clear-cut allegiance to one ramage in particular. The cognatic descent idiom is not generally taken literally, and it is often no more than a way of talking about kinship and its duties and obligations. The dispersion of persons who have at least nominal rights in relation to various ramages has important consequences for the larger social order, especially in relation to the maintenance of a modicum of peace in aboriginal times (see Scheffler 1963b). What is most obvious at this point, however, is that changing ramage affiliation is necessarily a cooptative process and not a simple matter of choice. It should be noted here that not every change of residence is a change of affiliation, for there is, or was, much "visiting" between the groups in which one has an interest. Avowedly temporary moves are sometimes converted to permanent changes of allegiance, however. "Visitors" sometimes stay on to become identified with the host groups. When parents take children with them, the latter change affiliation too.

A ramage is composed, then, of descendants of its founder and their guests who are living together on the *sinangge* estate. They need not be agnatic descendants of the founder except, presumably, for certain limited purposes, particularly leadership status. However, even this much significance of agnatic status is undermined by the fact that the common Melanesian pattern of the acquisition of prestige through competition and public gift-exchange prevailed here too, and no man could be a manager in the fullest sense unless he were markedly successful in competition with other men, even those of his own ramage. He had to earn renown in the political sphere with which to back up the presumed powers acquired by primogeniture and agnatic status. All other ramage members, regardless of their genealogical status, were only his "hands". It is patently obvious, however, that the manager was as much dependent upon their continued allegiance as they were upon his political talents. The position of the ramage within the larger society and its own internal operations demanded, therefore, that dogmatic distinctions be glossed over except in certain crisis situations having to do only with the internal affairs of the group itself. In external relations, such differences faded into insignificance. Nevertheless, such distinctions did and still do generate factions and schisms within the group, and sometimes men are led to consider whether they might find life more satisfying elsewhere.

In the past the ramages were not stable units. The residential and political status of "branches", for instance, was not a direct function of their order of segmentation but rather of the status of their managers. Relative status and consequently relative attractiveness, was worked out in competition and often violent conflict with other managers and their groups. Mortality in warfare was apparently quite high, and there was a corresponding high rate of mobility to avoid these conflicts. Consequently, the composition of local groups was varied and fluid, cognatic and affinal ties being utilized to obtain shelter and protection among close or distant kin and with a powerful manager. Periods of peace allowed the ramages some degree of stability and, unless nearly annihilated in warfare, a ramage maintained at least a core of its membership resident on its estate. This general situation encouraged the recruitment of kin to ramages if for no other reason than to increase military potential and ability to perform gift-exchanges resulting from revenge and warfare alliances.

High mortality occasionally left a ramage without an agnatic line, and in such cases non-agnates were left with the primary rights, but extensive participation in and help with ramage affairs were the more usual effective basis of one's claim to an active interest in a group and its resources. A non-agnate might be able to point to several generations of continuous affiliation by his ancestors and cite their significant activities in support of the group when requesting support (such as in brideprice, revenge, rights to land usage, etc.). Ideally, this support could not be refused. But if a man were a trouble-maker his non-agnatic status would be thrown up at him at every opportunity and his privileges refused on genealogical grounds. If he were hard working, helpful to his kinsmen, and did not alienate the ramage through lack of co-operation or by attempting to extend his interests in its estate at the expense of others, the fact that he was not an agnate would not arise, and if it did would be minimized by his supporters. Non-resident members of the cognatic descent category were in a similar position. The property of ex-members, such as land and groves, remained the property of their descendants who were reputed to be able to resume them at any time, and this was a common basis of a choice to affiliate elsewhere. Alternatively, a person might go on using such property without residing with the larger group holding custodial rights over the segment in which he had more particular interests. This often happens since there is a preference for marriage between proximate groups and a person may come to have interests in and to be called a member of two or more relatively contiguous groups at the same time.

It should not be forgotten that non-residents may become active members of the ramage only by fiat of the group itself. Where the claim is contested, as it doubtlessly seldom was in the past but may well be today, the onus of proof of the worthiness of it is upon the claimant. Almost any incident in the past and present relations between the claimant and his ancestors and the established members of the ramage may be deemed relevant or irrelevant to his claims. The relevance is not absolute but is dependent upon the total quality of his relations with the ramage (that is, his desirability as a member) or other considerations such as the availability of primary resources, today, coconut land. The principal rationalizations for refusing the privilege of residence include the group being "too full", that is, the area cannot support additional persons, and also that "the tie has been covered by the passage of too many generations". Population pressure may have been something of a factor in the past, for enduring large groups were not possible given the aboriginal ecology. Yet one suspects that room could always be made for a desirable member.

Threat of withdrawal of one's co-operation, sorcery, or, if one were a "big man", actual violence were the sanctions available to those refused what they took to be their rights. Property disputes have always been the most common grounds for sorcery accusations. Fear of sorcery or accusations of it were common reasons for opting to change affiliation, while such factors as persistent quarrelling, consistently poor gardens, or personal health, and fear of violent conflict also led persons to make temporary or permanent changes of affiliation.

Today much of this is changed. The ramages are no longer the solidary units they once were, there is no intergroup conflict and they do not have the political and economic significance they once had. The modern economic situation has also been detrimental to group solidarity for it tolerates nuclear or small extended family production which the Choiseulese prefer for various reasons. Modern ramages are more stable in composition than their earlier counterparts, but this is partly artificially imposed. Interest in a stable crop like coconuts seems likely to have a stabilizing influence too. However, many ramages have become entirely defunct or exist only as cognatic descent categories merged with one or more other local groups and off their own lands. Between 1910 and 1925 the missions and government, for purposes of their own convenience, persuaded and pressured the people to leave the interior hills and settle on the coasts. A desire to enter the copra trade also stimulated this movement. One consequence has been that the genealogical qualifications for managerial status are now stressed and practical qualifications are no longer important —the former are the only means of validating claims to such status. Ramage membership today means little for other than land tenure interests; few groups perform any activities as corporate solidary units. There seems also to be a tendency for fragmentation of land interests in a more definitive manner than in the past. Men attempt to establish separate and exclusive rights over what was once corporate property and to deprive others of their rights of usage. Partly this is a consequence of the fact that control over land has traditionally been one of the ways of validating claims to managerial status, and thus many men may become managers (*batu*), at least in their own eyes. The problem is particularly crucial in relation to good coconut land.

When pressing claims today only the subtle sanction of sorcery or its threat remains to force others to one's will, for violence has been outlawed and threat of withdrawal of co-operation, though still said to be important, means little in the present economic situation. But Choiseulese society has always been one without "law" in our naive sense of the term, and it seems to me that in order to comprehend the sense of their social order we must be constantly aware of the fact that it was, and still is though to a lesser extent, a society in which one could attain and maintain one's interests only through other men and only on terms either of force or agreement. It is true that today there are native courts instituted by the Protectorate government, but to the extent that the government does little to back them up they lack "teeth" and Choiseulese society remains "lawless". An important corollary of this situation is that everyone's rights are contingent rights. The Choiseulese, or at least some of them, clearly recognize the difficulties generated by the lack of clear definition of one's rights; but they recognize the advantages too. One perceptive informant remarked, "Our customs are not firm. We look only for that which will help us to live well, and the rest is just talk." To call it "just talk", however, is not to demean the significance of the ideology. It is to say that ideals, expectations, and self-interest are often opposed to one another and taken together they do not form a coherent "system". Nor are the rules or norms of conduct in themselves mutually consistent, and, furthermore, in the absence of specifically juridical institutions there are no relatively objective means available to test the "true" meaning of any norm nor to test whether any segment of conduct is in conformity with the norms or dogma, nor, for that matter, which norms are "really" relevant to any particular situation.

The rules or norms must be interpreted according to the needs of the situation. Their social significance is necessarily contingent upon who perceives the situation and how he perceives his needs within it. On the other hand, their sociological significance is not to be seen as typological criteria but as elements in the rhetoric of social life. I am not trying to say that the ideology of Choiseulese society is "all things to all men" but simply that it is precisely ". . . the manipulative, bargaining, transactional approach to life which is the system" in Choiseulese social life.[6]

Implied in the above discussion is a specific conception of sociological analysis, in particular that it is necessarily more than an analysis of ideology or culture and that it cannot be limited to concepts of social structure as statistically modal forms of conduct. My thesis here is the simple one that any social system consists in interaction and the task of sociological analysis is to determine what is systematic in coexistent classes of social relation. It is only those relations that give meaning to the ideology or culture shared by parties to them, and it is only in transactions occurring between those parties that the ideology has any sociological significance for it is only there that it has any social significance. We therefore grossly distort the ideology and foreshorten our understanding of it by giving it a label or purporting to analyze it out of that context. Any approach which separates "theory" from "practice" is fallacious since both are part and parcel of any social system. The anthropologist's task is not to separate "ideal" from "actual" but to show how a social system works, again not despite deviations, so-called, from the ideology, but *through* the ideology.

NOTES

1. This paper is a revised and expanded version of one presented at the Australian National University, July 1961, and at the Annual Meeting of the American Anthropological Association, Philadelphia, November 1961. Stimulation and criticism have been provided by J. A. Barnes, F. Eggan, J. D. Freeman, M. Groves, D. Schneider, and W. E. H. Stanner, for which I am grateful, but they are of course in no way responsible for the data or interpretations presented here.
2. Firth 1957:6.
3. For detailed treatment see Scheffler 1963a.
4. Cf. Sahlins 1961:325.
5. Cf. Freeman 1958:51. This usage of filiation differs from that of Freeman and Fortes (1959), and it is recognized that confusion may result. This is regrettable, but it seems to me unavoidable at the moment. Barnes (1962:6) has also used filiation in a sense similar to my own. He makes a distinction, in relation to New Guinea Highland societies, "between filiation as a *mechanism* of recruitment to social groups and to ascribed relationships and descent as a sanctioned and morally evaluated principle of belief". Thus Barnes speaks of "cumulative patrifiliation" rather than

agnatic descent. In accordance with this, it might be argued that if any ramage did prove to be agnatically composed, as some Choiseulese ramages are, at least inasmuch as all of the adult male household heads are agnatically related, then that would be due to cumulative patrifiliation and not agnatic descent.

6. Cf. Stanner 1959:216.

REFERENCES

BARNES, J. A., 1962. "African Models in the New Guinea Highlands." *Man*, 62: 5-9.

FIRTH, R., 1957. "A Note on Descent Groups in Polynesia." *Man*, 57: 4-8.

FORTES, M., 1959. "Descent, Filiation and Affinity: A Rejoinder to Dr. Leach." *Man*, 59: 193-97, 206-12.

FREEMAN, J. D., 1958. "The Family System of the Iban of Borneo." In *Cambridge Papers in Social Anthropology*, 1: 15-52.

SAHLINS, M. D., 1961. "The Segmentary Lineage: A Mechanism of Predatory Expansion." *American Anthropologist*, 63: 322-45.

SCHEFFLER, H. W., 1963a. *Kindred and Kin Groups in Choiseul Island Social Structure*. Unpublished Ph.D. dissertation, University of Chicago.

———— 1963b. "The Genesis and Repression of Conflict; Choiseul Island." *American Anthropologist* (forthcoming).

STANNER, W. E. H., 1959. "Continuity and Schism in an African Tribe." *Oceania*, 29: 208-17.

10

SHRINES, ANCESTORS, AND COGNATIC DESCENT: THE KWAIO AND TALLENSI[1]

Roger M. Keesing

INTRODUCTION

We cannot meaningfully describe the descent system of the Kwaio of the Solomon Islands as either agnatic or cognatic. As in many Oceanic societies, it is in some sense both. If it is worth trying to unscramble these senses of descent, it is not because a typology of descent systems is a useful goal. Rather than reducing complexity to simplicity, we hope to sort out component elements, and use them to build models—models that replicate formally the complexities of social relations, and enable us to deal with them analytically.

The Kwaio have a complex system of "ancestor worship," still intact despite almost a century of contact with Europeans. By focusing on Kwaio relations with their ancestors, and the articulation of this system into the social order, I hope to show some essential features of the Kwaio descent system. Kwaio ancestor worship and its relation to the social structure show many parallels to corresponding systems in Africa. With their hierarchies of shrines marking segmentary ritual groupings, the Kwaio particularly invite comparison with the Tallensi. By exploring parallels and contrasts with the Tallensi, I will seek to isolate crucial elements of the Kwaio descent system. In the process, I will argue that the classic Tallensi system requires some rethinking in the light of Kwaio evidence.

THE KWAIO OF MALAITA

Some 3,000 Kwaio-speaking pagans still live scattered through the mountainous interior of central Malaita Island, in the British Solomons. Though steel tools, plantation labor, and the Pax Britannica have profoundly affected Kwaio life, Kwaio social organization remains surprisingly unchanged (Keesing 1966a, 1966b, 1967a, 1967b, 1968b, 1970b, 1970c).

Reproduced by permission of the American Anthropological Association and Roger M. Keesing from the *American Anthropologist*, 72:755-775 (August, 1970).

Kwaio settlements are tiny (usually one to three households), scattered, and frequently moved. The continuities in this shifting scene are provided by a matrix of territories and shrines. The landscape is divided into small territories or *fanua,* each composed of a patchwork of land tracts. Each *fanua* is, or once was, the spatial locus and principal estate of a "descent group." Such a group is mainly agnatic in composition and ideological character, but many contain nonagnatic affiliants as well. These descent groups are small in scale, and their male members often are scattered. As we shall see, the primary expression of their unity is in ritual. Although a descent group is not explicitly exogamous, it tends to be derivatively so—because the bilateral category within which marriage is normatively prohibited[2] is usually extended to include more distant agnates and coresidents. A descent group has no formal political leader, but it often has a "big man" (Sahlins 1963) active in feasting. Mortuary feasting and bridewealth transactions provide focal points for inter-descent-group competition.

Along with an emphasis on agnation is a strong ideology of cognation, expressed in terms of cognatic descent and cognatic kinship. It is insisted that a person has similar interests in paternal and maternal kin and property. Descent linkages are traced cognatically to numerous *fanua,* through grandparents and beyond, entailing secondary rights to live and garden in these territories. Many men live in a number of these territories in the course of their lives. Long residence with mother's or father's mother's kin may lead to affiliation with them, or to various forms of multiple membership (Keesing 1968b). A person's rights and kinship relationships can be usefully viewed as a composite bundle that combines patrilateral and matrilateral elements (which themselves represent the cumulative bilateral synthesis of such bundles in preceding generations).

The Kwaio Descent System

To penetrate analytically below these generalizations, we must examine first some Kwaio cultural categories and principles that underlie social relations. We can begin by examining a set of relationships conceptually crystallized in Kwaio culture:

Cognatic descent—The relationship between a person and his 'ancestor' (*wala-fu-na*) whereby the former 'descends from' (*oliolita-na*) the latter.

Agnatic descent—The person is 'born of men' (*futa ani wane*) from the ancestor.

Nonagnatic descent—The person is 'born of women' (*futa ani geni*) from the ancestor (note that this requires only one female link, not a continuum of them).

Cognatic kinship—One person is 'born with' (*futa fe'enia*) another (see Keesing 1968a for the outer limits of this category).

Laterality—A person is related to persons or place through 'father's side' (*gula na ma'a ana*) or 'mother's side' (*gula na ga'ia;* alternatively, *gula na ini ana* 'mother's brother's side').

In different contexts, or in litigation, Kwaio may express ideologies that emphasize either agnatic or cognatic principles in the social order (1970c). However, when we seek to account for decisions and the allocation of rights in these domains of social structure, it is possible to construct a fairly simple model that reflects the synthesis, and salience, of both agnatic and cognatic elements:

(1) Agnatic descendants of the founding ancestor of a *fanua* are entitled to exercise primary rights in the corporation and to be primary members of the associated descent group. The *fanua* to which a person is agnatically related is *fulina* 'his true estate' and his rights there are primary whether or not he has activated or maintained them. Primary rights entitle him to garden there for profit, to participate in certain first fruit rituals, to have a say in alienation, and to receive a share of the profits.

(2) The sons and grandsons of female members have a right to *assume* primary rights, but they can secure them only through prolonged residence and use of the estate (which implies at least partial deactivation of rights over the paternal estate). When this happens, the female link is treated as if it were a male link for most but not all purposes (not, for example, ritual succession). This can, though rarely does, happen through two successive female links.

(3) The descendants of other women, who have not strengthened their matrilateral rights, fall into a category of *nonagnates* who hold secondary interests in the estate. They are entitled by virtue of *nonagnatic descent* from the founder to live and garden on the estate.

(4) When priority rankings of rights must be made among nonagnates, they are determined by the number of descent links to the closest past primary owner. The closer the genealogical linkage to a person with primary rights (mother or grandmother), the stronger the secondary rights (other things being equal). If agnates die out or cease to exercise primary rights, those nonagnates with the strongest descent entitlement legitimately assume them.

Ancestors, Shrines, and Sacrifice

Membership in, and relations to and between, descent groups are conceptualized and expressed largely in terms of relations with ancestors. Ancestral spirits or *adalo* constantly interact with the living—conferring *mana* (Kwaio *nanama*) when they are pleased, visiting sickness, misfortune, and death when they are displeased. Relations with *adalo* are mediated by 'priests' and maintained by raising propitiatory pigs (*fo'ota*) and sacrificing expiatory pigs when taboos are violated.

All adult men and women become *adalo*. Most, however, are revered only by their children and grandchildren. They then pass into a sort of limbo, with only a few being accorded great powers and singled out for special sacrifice (see Keesing 1970a for an analysis of this process). Any Kwaio adult thus maintains ritual relations with deceased parents and grandparents ("minor" *adalo* for which "minor" *fo'ota* pigs are raised); and with a cluster of distant and powerful ancestors ("major" *adalo* for which "major" *fo'ota* pigs are raised).

We can now see how the system of ancestor worship is articulated with *fanua* and their associated descent groups. The founding of a *fanua*, which traditionally occurred some nine to twelve generations ago, was ritually expressed by the founding of a "shrine." At this shrine, the founder sacrificed to his ancestors, particularly those of the *fanua* from which he came. The shrine is the place where the founder and his descendants are buried and where they receive sacrifices. The *fanua* and associated descent group generally bear the name of this shrine.

A descent group is in fact primarily conceptualized as a ritual community (Keesing 1970b). The Kwaio term is *tau*, which more commonly denotes the sacred men's house maintained by the descent group priest. This demarcation as a ritual community is clearly expressed in *libaŋa*, a sacrament men and women of the group undergo separately prior to close contact with the "sacred." More rarely, especially after the priest's death or after the performance of a "high sacrifice," the group keeps extremely rigid taboos. Involvement and commitment of descent group members at such times must be total; as a result the contrast between membership and descent relatedness (which entails lesser taboos and temporary and partial involvement) is ritually dramatized.

Kwaio conceive of the relationship between descent groups largely in terms of the relationship between shrines. When a new shrine is founded, especially in a newly founded territory, it is viewed as a branch of an existing one. The process whereby the Kwaio landscape was cleared and populated is conceived in terms of hierarchies of shrines: X is the first shrine, Y is the first offshoot from it, and Z is the second offshoot. Such relationships are ritually expressed in the status of the priests of such linked shrines, according to rules that symbolize the hierarchic order of the shrines.[3]

To understand these traditional linkages, we need to know that the most powerful ancestors appear on genealogies several generations above the founding ancestors of most territories. The founding of territories is viewed partly as the dispersion of the immediate descendants of these powerful ancestors, who are thus propitiated by a number of priests at a number of shrines.

Within some descent group territories, segmentation has taken place. That is, two territories have been carved out of one, with members acting as two descent groups in most contexts but acting as a single group in others. Such a split, usually precipitated by internal feuding, is symbolized by one of the segments founding a separate shrine with a separate priest. Here again the relation of segments is ritually expressed through priest-hoods, shrines, and sacrifice.

Each descent group has one or sometimes two principal ancestors through whom sacrifice is made to lesser ancestral members of the descent group. This results in what I have elsewhere called an "ancestral kin group" (1966b) with a most powerful "leader"—a "group" that reflects in many ways the structure of Kwaio descent groups with their "big men." One can also reasonably view this in Kwaio terms as a single perpetual corporation, clustered around territory and shrine, comprising both living and dead.

COGNATIC ELEMENTS OF KWAIO RITUAL AND SOCIAL ORGANIZATION

All of these relationships with ancestors can, I think, be conceptualized and comprehended in terms of an agnatic lineage system—without explicit segmentation on a scale comparable with classic African systems, but seemingly of the same genre. However, we can find in Kwaio relationships with ancestors a number of apparent expressions of cognation, not agnation:

(1) Any individual raises propitiatory pigs (*fo'ota*) to a cluster of ancestors, only some of whom are agnatic. Table 1 shows the distribution of these ancestors according to laterality. Table 2 shows the frequency of

TABLE 1. LATERALITY OF ANCESTORS

	Frequency	*Percent*
Patrilateral	841	72.0
Matrilateral	327	28.0
Total	1168	100.0

different categories of propitiated ancestors.

We can see in the cluster of powerful ancestors, patrilateral and matri-lateral, for whom an individual raises propitiatory pigs a direct reflection of the bundles of rights and kinship relationships he receives through each parent. The sacred pigs in his pen are, as it were, the embodiment of these networks of kinship ties, and as they mix with the sacred pigs his wife raises for her own ancestors, they symbolize the bundles the two parents combine to pass to their children.

(2) Ancestors are propitiated not on genealogical grounds, but on the basis of, first, their recognized powers and dangers; and second, the

TABLE 2. LINEALITY OF ANCESTORS (PATRILATERAL)

	Frequency	Percent
Agnatic*	369	31.6
Patrilateral Nonagnatic	472	40.4
Matrilateral	327	28.0
Total	1168	100.0

* Up to the founding ancestor of the descent group.

closeness of contact with their sacredness entailed by residence and social relations. Figure 1, showing a typical set of relationships between a man

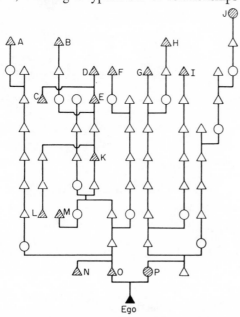

FIGURE 1. Ancestors propitiated by a Kwaio man.

and the ancestors he propitiates, illustrates the wide diversity and bilaterality of the genealogical ties involved.

(3) As can be seen from Figure 1, these relations are not only to lineal ancestors, but also to collaterals and even spouses of collaterals; in short, to deceased cognatic kin as Kwaio define them (Keesing 1968a). It is crucial to the argument that follows that Ego in Figure 1 is *related to* ancestors L and M (by cognatic kinship) but not *descended from* them. He derives no property rights from these relationships.

(4) Many of the ancestors to whom sacrifice is made within a territory are not former members of the descent group associated with it. They are ancestors associated with other descent groups, and relationship to them is traced through in-marrying women. The local shrine is, as it were,

a branch office at which a local officiant acts in lieu of the regular priest. Figure 2 illustrates this relationship. This officiant is usually not the priest of the descent group's principal shrine. Alternatively, members of descent group *A* related to group *B*'s ancestor through an in-marrying woman may send pigs to group *B*'s priest for sacrifice. Founding of a "branch" shrine expresses partial separation of the ritual category, a sort of lateral independence, while using the original shrine of the other descent group expresses secondary participation in that corporation, and interest in its land.

(5) Although common ties to descent group ancestors symbolize the unity of group members, divergent ties to other ancestors through mothers,

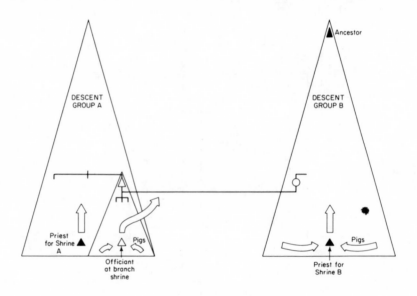

FIGURE 2. Sacrifice at branch shrine.

grandmothers, and great-grandmothers symbolize members' separation from one another. Genealogical segments of a descent group sacrifice together to the ancestors outside the descent group they share in common—whether at their local shrine or an outside shrine.

(6) Such a nonagnatic, outside ancestor can with the passage of time become increasingly incorporated into the local ancestral group. As the ancestor becomes common to all or most descent group members (through the passage of generations), he (or she) receives sacrifice at the descent group's principal shrine, through its own priest. Such an "outside" ancestor, related through an in-marrying woman, can even come to be the most powerful ancestor of a descent group.

(7) Many of the linkages between shrines and descent groups above the genealogical level of the founder are nonagnatic. One set of linkages

uniting many descent groups to a common powerful ancestor is diagrammed in Figure 3. Table 3 examines the most powerful one or two ancestors propitiated by each descent group and shows the frequency with which

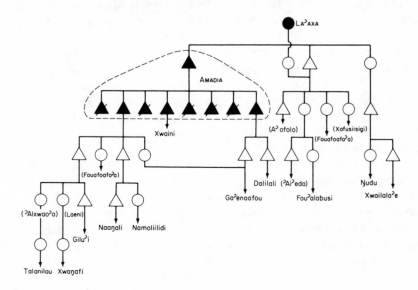

FIGURE 3. Descent groups tracing descent from Amadia. Those in parentheses trace descent tie but do not sacrifice to Amadia, in some cases due to a competing ancestor, i.e., La'axa. Sacrifices to Amadia are for the father and his eight sons.

TABLE 3. PRINCIPAL DESCENT GROUP ANCESTORS

	Frequency
Type I	19
Type II	13 (3)
Type III	27 (11)
Type IV	8

Type I: Principal ancestor is agnatic ex-member of descent group.

Type II: Principal ancestor is agnatically linked above the level of the founder (number in parentheses indicates frequency with which this is an *ancestress* from whom descent is agnatically traced).

Type III: Principal ancestor is related through a cognatic link, i.e., an in-marrying woman, below the level of the founding ancestor (number in parentheses indicates frequency with which this linkage is through the *wife* of the founding ancestor (cf. Tallensi).

Type IV: Principal ancestor is nonagnatically linked above the level of the founding ancestor.

they are (a) agnatic former members, (b) agnates above the founding level, (c) nonagnates joined below the founding level, and (d) nonagnates joined above the founding level.

(8) When a nonagnatically related segment of secondary owners assumes primary ownership of a *fanua* because its agnates have died out, this succession is symbolized by one of its members assuming the priesthood. By establishing residence in this *fanua* and allowing rights in their own estate to weaken or lapse, they can assume the structural position of agnates (without emendation of genealogies). We can call them "quasi-agnatic" descent groups and view them as new descent groups emerging out of old ones. They do so by establishing a new ritual community, linked to the one they replace and to the one from which they came, and sacrificing to the ancestors of both.

(9) At propitiatory sacrifices to an ancestor, *all* adult male descendants who recognize their cognatic descent from this ancestor[4] partake of the sacrifice. Those who cannot come are sent portions. Thus the ritual commensal group is broadly cognatic, not agnatic. This means that sacrifice by descent group members to a descent group ancestor entails participation by many nonmembers; a descent group sacrifice is not solely a descent group affair.

(10) Owing to the sorts of networks shown in Figure 3, a single powerful ancestor may be common to as many as seventy-eight percent of adult men (in my sample). At mortuary feasts where hundreds of people from different groups gather, all the men related to such an ancestor ritually partake of portions, thus expressing their common cognatic descent. In contrast, sacrifice to such a distant ancestor at a local descent group shrine normally involves participation only by those members and nonmembers who raise pigs for sacrifice at that shrine.

(11) Of the ten most commonly propitiated ancestors in my sample area, three were women. While ancestresses frequently are recognized in more strictly agnatic descent systems, their elevation here to the highest degrees of power I take to be in part a reflection of cognatic emphasis.

(12) Nonagnatic affiliants to a descent group are included among its ancestors when they die and receive sacrifice along with agnatic ancestors. Just as in life ideally they do not succeed to the priesthood or secular primacy ahead of agnates (though they often do in fact), so they would not assume primacy in the "ancestral kin group." An ancestor who had a dual descent group membership in life can receive sacrifice both from those with whose descent group he affiliated as a nonagnate and from those in whose group he was an agnate. This reflects, on an eschatological plane, the possibility of dual membership. Among the living, such a possibility is expressed in ritual when the same person, at the same event, undergoes the *libaŋa* sacrament twice, once as a member of each group.

In examining "cognatic" elements of Kwaio descent and ritual, it is important to distinguish a fine line between cognatic descent and cognatic kinship. It will prove crucial in the argument to follow.

If we view Kwaio constructs involving descent and kinship on purely formal grounds, we find cognatic kinship and cognatic descent merging. That is, Ego's cognatic kin (except those who are spouses of collaterals in ascending generations, like *M* in Figure 1) share with him at least one (usually two) ancestor in common. Hence, it would seem that Ego and Alter share *common descent* from the same ancestor and/or ancestress by virtue of their cognatic kinship.

But when we note that only a few founding ancestors are relevant for Kwaio *descent* reckoning (the founders of *fanua* or *fanua* segments), while any ancestor can serve as the apical link in kinship reckoning, the divergence between cognatic descent and cognatic kinship begins to come into view.

Relatedness to the founder of a *fanua* (and hence *descent* reckoning) is relevant in only certain contexts: contexts involving that *fanua,* as with the exercise of land rights; contexts where the descent group centered on that *fanua* is acting collectively, whether in feasting, ritual, etc. The higher-level, distant ancestors like Amadia (Figure 3) do not in most contexts function as the apical ancestors of descent categories, as do the founders of *fanua*. Amadia is propitiated by a number of priests at a number of shrines. By tracing a relationship to Amadia through one of these descent groups, for example, Naaŋali because a girl from Naaŋali married his great-great-grandfather, a man establishes cognatic descent rights in Naaŋali, but not in any other descent group territory shown on Figure 3.

These higher links that unite Kwaio descent groups to a common distant ancestor are thus treated for most purposes as though they were filial linkages. Some clusters of groups—those whose priests partake of each other's sacrifices—are treated in those contexts as related by descent at a higher segmentary level. Finally, when all those men present at a mortuary feast partake ritually of a sacrifice to Amadia or some other commonly shared ancestor, they are acting *as if* their relationship were one of descent, not merely cognatic kinship, and therein lies the significance of the sacrament.

Cognatic kinship between individuals, in contrast, is relevant in a much wider range of contexts, not necessarily having anything to do with a particular *fanua,* its ancestors, or its descent group. Given this perspective, the divergence between cognatic descent and cognatic kinship now comes more clearly into focus.

In Figure 4, a girl from *fanua B* married a man from *fanua A* some generations ago. An interesting asymmetry now emerges. The members of descent group *A* are members of cognatic descent category *B*. They have secondary rights to use land in *fanua B,* ritual interests in its ancestors,

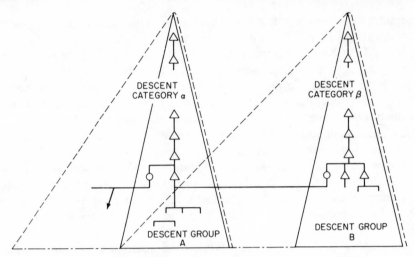

Figure 4. Descent group relationships through out-marriage.

a right to partake of sacrifices by descent group *B,* and so on. This relation-ship of the *A*'s to the *B*'s is one of *cognatic descent* vis-à-vis *fanua B.*

But the mirror-image relationships do not obtain. The *B*'s have no rights of land use in *fanua A,* they are not related to its ancestors, they have no interest in sacrifices by the *A*'s to their descent group ancestors. Their relationship to the *A*'s is one of *cognatic kinship,* traced through the out-marrying *B* girl, with her parents as apical ancestors.

It is interesting to note that if we looked at a man in descent group *C,* whose great-grandmother was a *B,* we are likely to find that he and a member of group *A* regard their relationship as one of *common cognatic descent* from the founder of *B.* It is not their business to know how the two *B* women were related, and hence through what precise genealogical links they could trace connections. The common *fanua* and its ancestors serve as a simplifying device for tracing relationship. The *A*'s and the *C*'s, as groups, can use this as a model of their relationship to one another, because their common descent from the ancestors of *B,* expressed in sac-rifice, symbolizes their connection.

There are thus four principal forms of relatedness between Kwaio descent groups. The first is agnatic and segmentary, as where Dalilali and Ga'enaafou (Figure 3) act as coordinate descent groups in many contexts but act as a single group (Dalilali) in others. The second is that of cognatic descent (the relation of the *A*'s to the *B*'s) or common cog-natic descent (the *A*'s to the *C*'s). The third is cognatic kinship (the *B*'s to the *A*'s or *C*'s). The fourth is one of affinity. It is important that in Kwaio culture the affinal relationship turns into the asymmetrical cog-natic one after one generation, rather than remaining one of "perpetual affinity" (Schneider 1965).

Given the agnatic-symmetrical and cognatic-asymmetrical linkages between Kwaio descent groups, expressed on social and ritual planes and mirrored as well at the highest levels of genealogies (Figure 3), we might well ask about another formally possible relationship: reciprocal cognatic descent-inclusion through symmetrical ("exchange") marriage. Such marriages are recognized and vaguely approved ideologically, but they turn up quite rarely in descent group genealogies (Keesing 1965). But in some areas where descent groups are closely allied and have probably maintained close relations for many decades, they express such symmetrical linkage at the level of distant ancestors, not through a model of reciprocal affinal alliance, but by each tracing cognatic descent from the distant agnatic ancestors of neighboring descent groups, and hence exchanging sacrifices (Figure 5).

Finally, it is worth noting an intriguing mirror-image relationship between the ancestors and the descent system of the living. If we look at a living person and trace out his property rights and descent interests, we see how his major interests are agnatic and how through in-marrying women —his mother, father's mother, father's father's mother, father's mother's mother, and so on—he traces relationship upward and outward bilaterally to a score of places and to ancestors to whom he sacrifices (Figure 1). If we turn this upside down and look from the perspective of a powerful ancestor, we see a mirror-image. His closest relationships are with his agnatic descendants, but he also traces descent *down*ward and outward through the *out*-marriage of his daughters, sons' daughters, daughters' daughters, and so on—to descendants in many places who sacrifice to him at different shrines (Figures 2 and 3).

ANCESTOR WORSHIP, KWAIO AND AFRICAN

Fortes (1965) has recently summarized the body of theory about the relationships between ancestor worship and social structure in Africa developed in the course of thirty years of intensive social anthropology research. The basic hypothesis is that ancestors represent a protection of the jural authority components in a social system. Since authority in African systems with ancestor worship is manifest principally through lineages, the most elaborated ancestral schemes are associated with segmentary lineage systems. In these, authority is vested at different levels and, correspondingly, spans of relatedness are defined in terms of apical ancestors with whom relations are maintained.

There are, of course, many variant forms. It has been argued, particularly by Goody (1962), that these reflect variations in patterns of inheritance and succession, the structure of property owning corporations, and rules of descent. The permutations of agnatic, uterine, and double descent—plus the effects of complementary filiation and divergent maternal filiation in polygynous agnatic systems—provide a framework for the structural analysis of variation in ancestor worship.

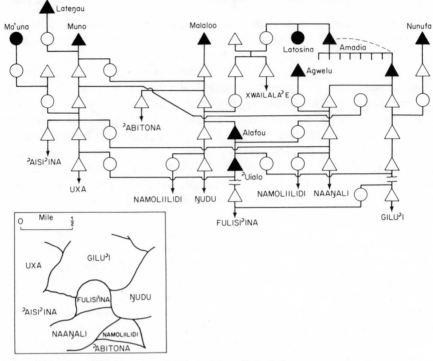

FIGURE 5. Descent ties of interlinked descent groups.

KEY TO FIGURE 5

Descent Group Abbreviations

'AISI'INA	A	NAMOLIILIDI	Na	UXA	U
GILU'I	G	NAANALI	N	'ABITONA	Ab
FULISI'INA	F	NUDU	Ng		

Patterns of Sacrifice

By Gilu'i Priest
  G to Amadia
  G to Nunufa
  G to Latosina
  G to Agwelu
  F to Amadia
  F to Nunufa
  N to Latosina
  U to Amadia
  Ng to Latosina
  Ab to Amadia
  U to Agwelu

By Fulisi'ina Priest
  F to Agwelu
  F to Alafou
  F to 'Uialo
  F to Malalou

  U to Agwelu
  A to Agwelu
  Ng to 'Uialo

By Nudu Priest
  Ng to Malaloo
  Ng to Amadia
  Ng to Muno
  Ng to Alafou
  G to Malaloo
  Na to Malaloo

By Uxa Priest
  U to Lateŋau
  U to Ma'una
  U to Muno
  F to Lateŋau
  F to Ma'una

By Naaŋali Priest
  N to Amadia
  N to Nunufa
  N to Agwelu

By 'Abitona Priest
  Ab to Muno
  Ab to Malaloo

By 'Aisi'ina Priest
  A to Ma'una
  A to Lateŋau
  A to Muno
  N to Ma'una

By Namoliilidi Priest
  Na to Amadia
  Na to Agwelu

154

That ancestor worship can occur in the absence of strictly unilineal descent is recognized:

One also finds practices consistent with our definition of ancestor worship in "bilateral" societies, that is, societies in which unilineal groups are absent. In Polynesia they appear in association with . . . a ramage; and they are found in societies like that of the Gonja of Northern Ghana that lack any boundary-maintaining kin groups, at least in the domestic domain. . . . Nevertheless, it is the lineage group organized around a unilineal genealogy that provides the typical congregation in the worship of the ancestors [Goody 1962:381].

Comparison of the Kwaio system of ancestor worship with that of the LoWiili or LoDagaba (Goody 1962), the Lugbara (Middleton 1960), or a number of less intensively documented systems generally confirms the following expectations:

(1) They are most similar in those respects where the Kwaio system emphasizes agnatic descent.

(2) The Kwaio system differs from these African systems principally in those respects where it emphasizes or reflects cognatic descent or cognatic kinship.

(3) A second set of differences derives from the lesser degree of hierarchical lineage segmentation in Kwaio.

(4) Another set of differences derives from the less-clearly defined secular authority in Kwaio descent groups.

A great range of ethnographic facts could be adduced in support of these generalizations: they will be obvious to those who know the African ethnographies. But this, the point I set out to emphasize, has been over-shadowed in the course of my comparative research by another. And it is this more surprising and more significant point to which I now turn.

The gulf between the way Kwaio (and I as their ethnographer) conceptualize their system and the way Fortes and Goody conceptualize the African systems seems far wider than the gulf between what the Kwaio and Africans *do*. And if the gulf is generated more by the models than by the facts, we had better look very carefully at the models.

Let me illustrate the problem, and explore a way out, by examining the ancestor worship of the Tallensi—those classic believers in agnation. Fortes' analysis introduced sharply the distinction between *descent,* the agnatic lineage principle that operates in the jural sphere, and *kinship,* that web of individuating bilateral ties built out of filiation and operating in the nonjural spheres of domestic and interpersonal relations. Complementary filiation then became the means of dealing with the close relations with the maternal lineage and other nonagnatically related lineages and kin.

The importance of agnation in Tale thought and action clearly is profound. Fortes's model equips him well to deal with the complicated segmentary orderings of Tale society, mirrored by corresponding ritual hierarchies and shrines. The hierarchies of the Kwaio system are less deep and less ramified, but if I introduced all of the complexities of ritual relations I could produce a book almost as intricate as *The Dynamics of Clanship among the Tallensi* (1945). Fortes is less well equipped to deal with cognation, particularly when it entails rights, property, and ancestors rather than mere bilateral kinship. The concept of "complementary filiation" has troubled some because it compounds (1) interpersonal relations with mother's brother, (2) widespread ties of bilateral kinship (emphasizing *laterality* rather than lineality), and (3) secondary rights and interests in the *mother's agnatic lineage*. Furthermore, it fails to deal successfully with the relationships, often important in such systems, to father's mother's kin and lineage, father's father's mother's kin and lineage, mother's mother's kin and lineage, and so on.

Some clues to the sources of these difficulties emerge if we examine ancestor worship among the Tallensi and note a number of elements that resemble structurally those elements of the Kwaio system we have identified as "cognatic."

(1) Just as a Kwaio individual's ritual status is defined by the cluster of bilateral ancestors he raises *fo'ota* pigs for, so, according to Fortes, the *yin* ancestors of a Tale man—those who play a special part in his destiny—are a unique bilateral cluster:

They form a particular combination . . . . They may be patrilateral or matrilateral ancestors or a combination of both lines. . . . Of [a] pair of brothers, one's *yin* ancestors may be their mother's father, maternal grandfather, and maternal great-grandfather; and the other's might be their mother's mother, her father, and his father [1949:229].

The spirits of maternal ancestors and ancestresses play as big a place in a person's life as his paternal ancestor spirits [1950:27].

(2) A Tale man, like a Kwaio man, does not sacrifice only to the *lineage* ancestors (as opposed to parents and grandparents) of his own lineage:

An ahəŋ ("sister's son") may attend domestic sacrifices to any of his matrilateral ancestors and sacrifices to the founding ancestor's shrine . . . of the lineage of his true or classificatory mother's brother [1949:321].

He sacrifices to these nonagnatic ancestors on many occasions. Furthermore, the relationship of a man to these lineages is conceptualized in terms of such sacrifice:

The chief criterion by which a native identifies his mother's brother or a lineage standing in the relationship of a 'mother's brother' to his lineage is that 'he sacrifices on my behalf' or 'they sacrifice on our behalf.' This implies a specific ritual duty and privilege vested in a particular person or lineage, not a vague general relationship with a certain class of relatives [1949:283].

Elsewhere, it is clear that "mother's brothers" and their lineages are not confined to the mother's agnatic kin. They include the lineage of father's mother and apparently the lineage of mother's mother and father's father's mother (which are *yaab yiri* "grandparent lineages"; the latter include as well "any lineage with which a person has matrilateral connexions" (1949:240):

The distinguishing attribute of an ahɔb ('mother's brother') in Tale thought is that he sacrifices on behalf of his ahɔŋ ('sister's son') and ahɔŋ in this context includes all sororal kin, both those who are strictly ahɔŋ ('sister's sons') and those who are strictly *yaas* ('grandchildren') [1949:321].

Fortes's frequent references to kin and lineages to which a Tale is related through either his father or mother (i.e., any nonagnatic relationships) as "matrilateral" lead to repeated ambiguity.

(3) Furthermore, just as some sacrifices to a Kwaio man's ancestors from other descent groups are performed by a local officiant at a local "branch" shrine, a similar relationship occurs among the Tallensi:

As every man has shrines consecrated to those of his matrilateral ancestors who have revealed themselves as directly concerned with his own life, in his own home, he generally attends sacrifices at their lineage home only on special occasions [1949:322].

Fortes is troubled by this seeming departure from agnatic primacy in relations with ancestors:

We are here touching on one of the most complex features of Tale religious custom. The shrines consecrated to a man's matrilateral ancestors in his own homestead provide him with an indirect route to them. When he sacrifices to them on these shrines, he is, as it were, approaching them through an inter-mediary spirit or group of spirits. He is never able to approach them directly. Only their agnatic descendants can do that. Generally, a matrilateral ancestor spirit (male or female) who has a shrine consecrated to him or her by a daughter's son or descendant demands sacrifices on that shrine. But there are many occasions on which the spirit demands that the sacrifice be offered to him or her directly on the shrine consecrated to him or her at a son's or agnatic descendant's house. It is on such occasions that the 'sister's son' or 'grandson' has to take the animal he has been commanded to offer to the homestead of his 'mother's brother' or 'grandfather' [1949:322].

(4) Just as the group that gathers for a Kwaio sacrifice comprises the cognatic descendants of the ancestor receiving the sacrifice—not merely agnatic descendants—the Tale congregation is similarly bilateral: "When a man sacrifices to an ancestor spirit, any descendant of that ancestor has the right to be present and to share in the sacrament" (1949:321). And just as Kwaio are obligated to include nonagnatic descendants in sacrificial meat distribution, so Tallensi are obligated to invite "sister's sons" to par-

take of sacramental food; and at some events the participation of a much larger range of nonagnates ("sister's sons" in the widest sense) is appropriate (1949:323).

Extra-clan kinsfolk from far and wide are present. I have counted as many as thirty, ranging from the full sister's son of the new lineage head to a distant 'sister's son,' whose matrilateral ties with the clan went back to the founding ancestor of his maximal lineage [1949:324].

The occasion is a sacrament in which all the descendants of the lineage ancestors, through both men and women, participate [1945:150].

(5) Just as segments within a Kwaio descent group are ritually differentiated according to the ties with the nonagnatic ancestors they do not share, a formally similar process occurs among the Tallensi. This is particularly manifest with the bɔɣar shrines so central in structural definition of the lineage system. Each bɔɣar is "consecrated to the founding ancestor of a lineage and his mother" (1949:328). Since the half-brothers of polygynous marriages are often defined as the founders of segments, there are some contrasts with the Kwaio system, in which the in-marrying women through which ritually differentiating ties are traced are below the apical agnatic ancestors (founders' wives and the wives of their descendants). But structurally the result is the same. Fortes notes how pervasive is the principle that "social differentiation within the lineage framework springs from maternal origin" (1949:330). The resemblance to the Kwaio system at the higher ranges (Figure 3) is discernible as well, since the new shrine founded to the progenitrix and son is conceived as a link to her ancestors, "an offshoot of her lineage bɔɣar" (1949:330).

(6) A Tale man, like his Kwaio counterpart, recognizes secondary relationships to a wide range of places and descent groups, and his attachments to them are remembered, expressed, and legitimized by shrines and sacrifice:

When he [a Tale man] was explaining his various ancestor shrines to me he accounted for his possession of one on the grounds of . . . his patrilineal great-great grandfather's mother's mother having been a daughter of SɔK; and for another . . . since his mother's mother's mother came from Arogo [1949: 298–299].

What, then, are we to make of these apparent parallels to the Kwaio ritual system? What Fortes in general takes to be manifestations of complementary filiation, Kwaio treat in two ways: as cognatic kinship, and as cognatic descent, which they treat as conceptually distinct. Several possibilities emerge from this—e.g., the Kwaio and Tallensi are more different than they look; the Kwaio misunderstand their own system and talk about complementary filiation in two different ways; I misunderstand the Kwaio system; I misunderstand the Tallensi system, etc.

With the misgivings appropriate to one who questions a tribal elder, I will explore instead another possibility: that Fortes partially misunderstood the Tallensi. The evidence suggests to me that on theoretical grounds Fortes was not prepared to recognize cognatic descent when he found it and that he thus subsumed under the notion of complementary filiation both a culturally secondary descent principle and relationships of cognatic kinship.

For reasons recently analyzed cogently by Scheffler (1966), most British anthropologists have considered descent to be:

(1) unilineal (whether agnatic or uterine), and
(2) a rule defining membership in a *social group*.

The tendency has been to restrict further what *type* of group this could be —a legal corporation (Goody 1961).

With this set of assumptions, Fortes perceived not only the agnatic principle but also an almost "submerged" line of uterine descent. But if such a thing as cognatic descent is conceptualized by the Tallensi, Fortes did not find it.

First, let me make clear what I mean by descent (and filiation), and why. Then I will examine more closely what Fortes means and why, and we will consider what difference it all makes. Finally, we will look carefully at the Tallensi and Kwaio evidence.

My position is generally similar to Scheffler's (1966). I begin with the premise that cultural principles (sets of ideas) must be distinguished from their expression in social events and interactions. Any analytical usage that cannot treat separately a cultural rule or definition and its manifestation in behavioral events or transactions cannot comprehend the way these can vary independently. The same cultural principle can be expressed in a wide range of contexts and several cultural principles can apply to a single context or event.

I take "descent" to refer to a culturally recognized *continuum of filial* (parent-child) *links* between a person and his ancestors. The basic types of continua known to be recognized in some cultures are (1) agnatic, where all links in the continuum must be male; (2) uterine, where all must be female; and (3) cognatic, where as long as a continuum exists the sex of intervening links is unspecified. Other continua are logically possible, but exemplars are doubtful (e.g., alternating descent). Moreover, the nesting of a unilineal continuum inside a cognatic one produces the category of nonunilineal descent, where at least one link must be of opposite sex from the rest (i.e., nonagnatic descent, nonuterine descent).

Filiation, in contrast, is the relationship between a person and his *parents*. As has commonly been recognized, a descent continuum is the cumulative result of filial links of specified type, but definition is in terms of the continuum, not the serial links (Scheffler 1966).

A particular descent continuum or, as Scheffler calls it, a "descent construct" may be relevant in a range of social contexts: in defining the membership of corporate groups, determining membership in a named category, determining principles of succession to office, determining the distribution or inheritance of various sorts of rights or properties, and so on. Often two or more descent constructs are relevant in the same or different contexts in the same society.

Cognatic *kinship,* in contrast, is a relationship of a person to his bilateral consanguineal kin, living or dead, lineal and collateral, and those non-consanguineals (e.g., stepkin, Keesing 1968a) categorically equated with them. What kin are defined as cognates will vary according to cultural rules, but the network is universally bilateral and basically genealogical.

In his 1959 clarification of his earlier positions (e.g., 1953), Fortes adopted what could have turned out to be a similar stance: "Descent can be defined as a genealogical connection recognized between a person and any of his ancestors or ancestresses" (1959: 206). Filiation is "the relationship created by the fact of being the legitimate child of one's parents" (1959:206).

But he went on to clarify and narrow these definitions on the basis of what "domain"—"domestic" or "politico-jural"—the principles of descent and filiation "emanate from." In this, he moved from the cultural to the social plane and ended in a restriction of descent to a unilineal rule of membership in a social group.

Having separated the jural from the domestic or nonjural, he attempted to show again that the rights and relationships a woman in an agnatic lineage system exercises and can transmit to her children are nonjural and, being nonunilineal and in the "domestic domain," hence *filial.* Again, this confuses the nature of a cultural construct with the contexts and forms of its social application.

Scheffler's conceptual reorientation seems to me a logical advance over the British usage. It begins with a distinction between "ideational order" and "phenomenal order" that is proving crucial in a rethinking of social anthropology (Goodenough 1964:11–12). Moreover, it equips us to make the kinds of separations that the data we have on descent systems show to be necessary. Our ability to comprehend Kwaio conceptualizations in this domain is a case in point. In contrast, "complementary filiation" strikes me as a residual category generated by a clumsy and rigid theoretical apparatus to fill its own gaps.

I will argue that *it is possible*—albeit not certain—that Tallensi recognize three descent constructs: an agnatic construct, a uterine construct (*soog*), and a cognatic construct. The latter, in combination with the agnatic, creates a nonagnatic construct. I will further argue that this is not a trivial and scholastic point. It is not solely a matter of which definitions are better but rather raises fundamental questions of comparative sociology. If it is realized that cognatic *descent* principles are often operative in societies with marked emphasis on unilineality in the structure of corporate groups, it leads us to think not in terms of *typological contrasts in descent systems*—with "cognatic societies" as an analytical waste-basket—but rather in terms of variations in the ways and contexts in which the same descent constructs are utilized.

The model of Tale society this would suggest is of a hierarchy of agnatic lineages, each defined in terms of an apical ancestor. There is a further category comprising all of the *cognatic* descendants of the apical ancestor at each level. The superimposition of the two descent categories creates a class of *nonagnatic descendants* of the ancestors of a lineage, who define their relatedness to one another, to the agnatic lineage, to its property and territory, and to its ancestors *in terms of this descent continuum* (Figure 6).

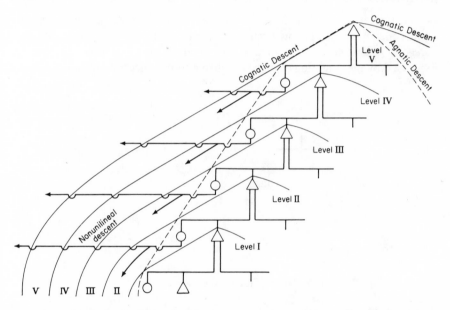

FIGURE 6. A possible paradigm of the Tallensi descent system.

One reason descendants of lineage women at higher levels of its genealogy seldom take part in lineage affairs can be seen in Figure 6. They are members of the cognatic descent category containing a maximal lineage, but they are not members of lower level cognatic descent categories containing lineage segments. In activities involving lineage segments, they do not appropriately take part; in activities (such as the succession of a new lineage head) that involve the whole lineage, they may appropriately participate:

The . . . sacrifices made by a new lineage head . . . when he formally takes over the custody of the bɔɣar . . . are occasions of special solemnity marking the re-establishment of the proper structural form of the lineage around a new lineage head. Not only do all the adult members of the lineage attend . . . but representatives of other branches of the clan and very many extra-clan kin, descendants of daughters of the lineage, also attend [1945:227–228; cf. 1949: 323–324].

The members of a segment of a maximal lineage gather at the homestead of the head of the segment to sacrifice to their immediate founding ancestor. 'Sisters' sons' of the segment have the right to be present [1949:caption to plate 16a, facing p. 289].

There are a number of ritual ceremonies at which all the segments of a clan or maximal lineage must be present. *Ahɔs* ["sisters' sons," in the context any descendants of lineage women] of every branch of the clan usually attend such ceremonies. Then they are divided into two groups: *dugni ahɔs*, those who are linked through their mother or other ancestors to the inner lineage responsible for the ceremony; and *yɛŋha ahɔs*, outside *ahɔs*, whose mothers or ancestresses came from other segments of the clan [1949:296].

Furthermore, any agnatic lineage at a particular level is distinguished from coordinate lineages in terms of its *inclusion in the cognatic descent category of another lineage at a higher level* (Figure 7). It is this that is expressed by the founding of its bɔɣar shrine to the ancestors of that lineage.

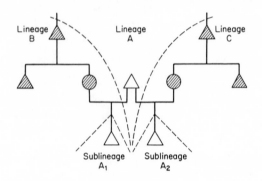

Figure 7. Nonagnatic ties of agnatic segments.

Any Tale individual thus belongs not only to an agnatic descent group (at various levels), but to a multiplicity of cognatic descent categories. Some (those to which he is related through his own mother) he shares only with his full-brothers (and members of other lineages). Others he shares with segments of his own lineage, with these providing a ritual symbol of the segments' separate existence.

The degree to which he can participate in each of these categories is limited by his resources and by situational rules. We have seen that he has the right to be present and share in the sacrament at a sacrifice to any of his ancestors, agnatic or cognatic (Fortes 1949:321). The range of non-agnatic descendants who participate in a sacrifice depends in part on the occasion and in part on the segmentary level that the shrine represents and the apical ancestor defines.

It is quite possible, as in Kwaio, for nonagnatic descendants to be ranked according to the closeness of their linkage to a full member—hence the greater participation of a sister's child than of a sister's son's son's child. This is no less compatible with a cognatic descent construct than is a rule defining relative seniority of segments or individuals with an agnatic descent construct. Furthermore, the rights and interests of a nonagnate attenuate more quickly with each female link than with male links—as they do in Kwaio society. The Tallensi distinguish as two subtypes of nonagnatic connection a relationship through a single female link (which "is assimilated to the *ahəb-abəŋ* mother's brother–sister's [child] tie" 1949:298); and a relationship through two or more women, a "secondary matrilateral tie" modeled on the *Yaab-Yaaŋ* [MF-DC] tie (1949:298). Fortes notes the attenuation of entailments when relationships are traced through mother's mother (1949:298).

However, this distinction between "mother's brother" and "grandparent" nonagnatic descent is made only in certain contexts. As contrasting categories *Yaab* is clearly marked (in the linguistic sense) in opposition to *ahəb;* with that opposition neutralized when reference is made to the whole category of nonagnatic descendants of a lineage founder or to all those lineages to which a person is nonagnatically related:

In the early stages of my field work . . . the natives seemed to label any extra-clan kinsman a 'mother's brother (*ahəb*)' or 'sister's child (*ahəŋ*)' quite indiscriminately. . . . A person was apparently labelled a 'sister's son' if he was related to the speaker through any ancestress who was a member of the latter's clan, and . . . as a 'mother's brother' if the woman forming the link was the speaker's mother or ancestress and a member of the other person's clan [1949: 295].

ahəŋ in this context includes all sororal kin, both those who are strictly *ahəŋ* and those who are strictly *yaas* [1949:321] .

It is worth noting the distantness of such nonagnatic descent linkages remembered and invoked for ritual or other purposes:

Thus Lɔyani called himself, in various contexts, an ahəŋ of Tɔŋ-Puhug, because his own mother came from there; an ahəŋ of Gorogo because his father's mother came from that place; and also an ahəŋ of Sie and of TɔŋKuorəg because other patrilineal ancestors of his were ahəŋs of those clans. But when he was explaining his various ancestor shrines to me he accounted for his possession of one on the grounds of his being a *Yaaŋ* of Sɔk—his patrilineal great-great-grandfather's mother's mother having been a daughter of SɔK; and for another on the ground of his being an Arogo *Yaaŋ*, since his mother's mother's mother came from Arogo [1949:298–299].

The similarity to Kwaio conceptualizations and genealogical networks is striking. Such long chains of connection make most dubious a notion that filial linkages, rather than descent continua, are used—particularly since shrines, ancestors, and participation in sacrifice provide the structural definition of the categories.

Note for instance the way the gift of land from a man to a close or distant "sister's son," however it may depend on interpersonal relationships between giver and recipient, is legitimized with reference to the ancestral cult:

They secure the blessing of his matrilateral ancestors for the recipient of the land . . . for . . . the land really belongs to the ancestors who first cultivated it [1949:310].

[In subsequent years] . . . he may bring a fowl to offer at the ancestral *bɔɣar* of his *ahɔb* lineage in gratitude for the beneficence of the ancestors whose land he is working [1949:311].

A model of Tallensi society in terms of overlapping nonagnatic descent categories gives a greater intelligibility to a host of other details of custom. A striking example is the formal definition of leviratic succession to marriage.

There are circumstances in which descent through a woman is partially assimilated to the true agnatic line. . . . A sororal nephew (*ahɔŋ*) of any degree whatsoever, that is, any member of another clan who has a cognatic link with the clan in question through an ancestress however remote, is formally equated with the sons of the clan in the matter of leviratic rights. An *ahɔŋ* has the right to seek the hand of a widow of his maternal uncle's clan (*ahɔb yiri*) on the same terms as a true member of that clan. . . . In practice sororal nephews are rarely allowed to assert this right, and then only if their cognatic link with their maternal uncle's clan is not more than about four generations back [1945:150–151].

Tallensi go to some pains to recognize and preserve the asymmetry in the "mother's brother"–"sister's son" relationship. That is, *ahɔŋ* have secondary interests in the lineage and ancestral cult of *ahɔb,* but the reverse is not true: "A man has no interest in or bonds with any of his sister's children's agnates except her children" (1949:297). This asymmetry is preserved by prohibiting a man from marrying a girl in an *ahɔŋ* inner lineage, which would in the following generation reverse the relationship and lead to ambiguity. This preservation of asymmetry, when combined with the complex patterns of intermarriage Fortes describes (1949:286 ff.) between nearby lineages, entails a web of ritual interlinkage and overlap in cognatic descent categories very similar to the Kwaio system illustrated in Figure 5.

Such a model of Tallensi society, even in barest outline as we have presented it, would account more powerfully for a great range of ethnographic detail than does the concept of "complementary filiation." Fortes's contention that the relationships, rights, and duties transmitted through female links are different in kind from the relationships transmitted by agnatic descent and apply in different "domains" may be quite true. But if we follow the analytical path charted by Scheffler, this is not a matter of what type of construct is being used—in each case a descent construct—but of what it is being used for.

But here we encounter precisely the difficulty that led Fortes to the position he has taken. Are not all ties of bilateral cognatic kinship relationships of *descent* by this definition? Tallensi, like Kwaio, are quite clear that what they mean by cognatic kinship is being "born with" someone, and that entails being able to trace back to find an ancestor or ancestress they share in common. By viewing such relationships as descent—as our and Fortes's definitions seem to imply—are we not taking two distinct analytical concepts that have proven useful and lumping them into one?

I do not believe so. Even though Tallensi and Kwaio establish kinship by finding a common ancestor, they are doing so by tracing *consecutive filial links*. The emphasis is on the pair of persons (one or even both of whom might be deceased) who trace their connectedness by successive links, not on the apical ancestor who joins them. This is one reason why stepkin (e.g., FBW, MBW, FZH) are so often structurally and hence terminologically equated with consanguineals (Lounsbury 1964, 1965).

Cognatic *descent,* in contrast, places emphasis on the focal ancestor and the continuum of relatedness to that ancestor. *Common descent,* as opposed to cognatic kinship, is expressed in terms of the relationship to the ancestor, characteristically in contexts involving the corporation, territory, or shrine founded by that ancestor. Hence, in Figure 4 the relationship between *A*'s and *B*'s is asymmetrical. Vis-à-vis the territory of the *B*'s and its founding ancestor, the *A*'s and *B*'s are united by common cognatic *descent*. Vis-à-vis the territory of the *A*'s, the *A*'s and *B*'s are related by links of cognatic kinship through the parents of the *B* woman who married into *A*. Cognatic descent in such systems is defined with reference to the apical ancestors that demarcate territorial or political units, or property-owning corporations, at various levels.

The repeated definition of categories and individual status in terms of ancestors and sacrifice would seem to imply a Tale conception of cognatic descent, as well as of cognatic kinship. But since we have defined "descent" in terms of the conceptualizations of the people under study, not the analytical operations of the observer, we would ideally need some direct evidence of Tallensi recognition of cognatic descent.

It is scarcely necessary to show that Tallensi recognize cognatic kinship, relatedness between individuals based on successive filial links. Fortes's evidence clearly establishes such models. Some aspects of Tallensi relationships to their ancestors I infer to be based on such cognatic kinship reckoning. Just as a Kwaio man's *fo'ota,* the ancestors he propitiates, are related to him by cognatic kinship rather than cognatic descent (and are, in fact, addressed by kinship terms), so the *yin* ancestors of a Tale man—his deceased parents and grandparents who play a special part in his destiny—are related by kinship, not descent. Note that these ties to *yin* ancestors are individual and personal, not collective and public: and it is in this interpersonal realm (whether both "persons" are alive or not) that cognatic kinship prevails.

However, we need more direct evidence of a conceptual recognition of cognatic descent continua. There is, to be sure, much indirect evidence. Simply to define the rule that when an ancestor receives a sacrifice all of his cognatic descendants are entitled to attend and partake of the sacrament (1949:321) would seem to require such a conceptual construct, whether it is lexically labeled or not. Recall here that there is no Tale term for "agnatic descent"; we infer its conceptual prominence from the way it is used.

It is worth noting that cognatic descent also seems to turn up in reference to uterine constructs. Two people related by a continuum of uterine links are *saarǝt,* and have a special and close relationship. Yet this relationship carries through to their descendants through male links, suggesting a class of nonuterine descendants recognized in certain special contexts.

Strong suggestive evidence comes from the pervasive asymmetry in the *ahǝb-ahǝŋ* relationship. We noted how in Kwaio society the line between cognatic descent and cognatic kinship emerges most sharply in the asymmetry between *A*'s and *B*'s in Figure 4; where the *A*'s and *B*'s share common descent from the ancestors of *B* and all it entails and where the *B*'s are related by cognatic kinship to the descendants of the out-marrying *B* girl.

One of many apparent contradictions or needless complexities in Fortes's description is his emphasis in *The Dynamics of Clanship* on clan exogamy and his disclosure in *The Web of Kinship* that any persons who are genealogically related are forbidden to marry.

They draw a sharp distinction between *dɔɣam,* kinship, and *deen,* in-lawship. The crux of the rule of clan exogamy and of the collateral prohibition of marriage with consanguineous kin of any degree (and the natives do not distinguish these two classes of restrictions) is the principle that *dɔɣam* and *deen* are irreconcilably contradictory. They must not be 'mixed' [1949:16].

One way to account for this is to say that clanship has nothing to do with exogamy, which is defined in terms of cognatic kinship. But why, then, the apparent Tallensi references to exogamy in contexts involving lineages? There is another possibility. If the rule of exogamy were phrased in terms of *cognatic descent,* so that no two persons could marry if they shared common descent (agnatic or cognatic) from some clan's founder and ancestors, then the two "kinds" of exogamy "the natives do not distinguish" would be manifestations of the same simple principle. That is, any two people cognatically descended from the same ancestors, hence in the same ritual descent category, could not marry. Agnatic codescendants would be the canonical "nonmarriageables" because of their more direct relation to these ancestors. But is this what *dɔɣam,* which Fortes glosses as "kinship," means to Tallensi?

If people say 'we are *dɔɣam*', the basic analogy they have in mind is that of siblings. Two men who are cognatically related to the same lineage . . . describe themselves thus. They visualize their relationship primarily as one of common though independent religious allegiance to a particular line of common ancestors, in sacrifice to whom they may both partake [1949:18].

In Fortes's analysis of Tallensi conceptualization of kinship, in fact, we find further strong evidence of a distinction between cognatic descent and cognatic kinship, corresponding to the Kwaio one illustrated with Figure 4. That is, the asymmetry of the *ahəb–ahəŋ* relationship (where *ahəŋ* is related by descent to *ahəb's* lineage and its ancestors, but *ahəb* lineage members are related by kinship but not common descent to the descendants of the out-marrying girl) is explicit in Tallensi folk models. Let us place the previous quote in its wider context:

Any relation of kinship belongs to one of two classes. If people say 'we are *dɔɣam,*' the basic analogy they have in mind is that of siblings. Two men who are cognatically related to the same lineage—e.g. two men who have a common maternal uncle's lineage (*ahəb yir*) or whose fathers or grandfathers had a common maternal uncle's lineage—describe themselves thus. They visualize their relationship primarily as one of common though independent religious allegiance to a particular line of common ancestors, in sacrifice to whom they may both partake [1949:18].

The other and more important class of kinship ties pre-supposes the analogy of the parent-child relationship. When a person says of another . . . 'I have begotten . . . him,' or, speaking of lineages, 'we (my lineage),' have begotten . . . them (their lineage),' what is meant is that the latter can trace a line of descent to the former or to the former's lineage [1949:19].

This has taken me far beyond the original intended scope of my paper. To go further in reanalyzing the Tallensi data would require another, longer paper (cf. Worsley 1956); and if one went beyond this to other African systems—such as the Lugbara, who explicitly conceive such nonagnatic linkages in terms of descent (Middleton 1960:9, 1965:29)—it would require a book.

If a reinterpretation of the Tallensi and much other African material supported such a hypothesis, it would have serious implications for our thinking about social structure. We would be led not to sort tribal societies into unilineal (and double) descent systems and a negatively defined cognatic class. Rather, we would be forced to study the differential implications and usages of the same descent constructs in different societies. We would not say that the Tallensi have an agnatic system and the Maori have an "ambilineal" system, but rather, that agnatic and cognatic descent constructs are used in each in different ways to determine the distribution and transmission of different rights. We would be led to ask what rights accrue to agnates and what rights to other cognatic descendants; how impenetrable the boundaries of these categories are (e.g., can a nonagnate who grows up with maternal kin be defined as an agnate in terms of rights?); how rankings or priorities for status succession within each category are defined; and how cross-cutting and multiple relationships of cognatic descent, with the shifting and contextually defined allegiances they imply (Keesing 1966b), bind descent groups into a wider system. Fortes's concepts of "complementary filiation" and "the web of kinship" have enriched our understanding of the latter. But by forcing the cognatic descent elements of "unilineal" systems into a conceptual mold that hides their relationship with societies where cognatic descent principles are more central, he has, I think, obscured our comparative understanding of social structure.

Scheffler has observed that Fortes departs from his initial "simple and sound usage [of 'descent'] to a concept of descent as it is manifest among the Tallensi, and it is the Tallensi model that becomes the preferred analytical model" (1966:545). Perhaps the time has come to rethink whether this *is* the Tallensi model.

NOTES

1. A preliminary version of this paper was read at the annual meeting of the American Anthropological Association in Washington, D.C., December 1, 1967. For helpful suggestions, discussion and comments, I am indebted to James Baltaxe, Paul Bohannan, Paula Brown, William Davenport, Raymond Firth, Meyer Fortes, Ward Goodenough, Harold Scheffler, David Schneider, and Nur Yalman. Geoffrey Shuey has assisted me in analysis of the Tallensi data. Field research on which this study was based was carried out from November 1962 to November 1964 and in July and August 1966, supported by the U.S. Public Health Service. Support from the National Science Foundation and Social Science Research Council has contributed to analysis of Kwaio data.
2. Which includes fourth cousins, bilaterally defined; however, many marriages in modern times are to closer kin (cf. Keesing, 1965).
3. The priest of the senior shrine can eat the sacred head of a pig sacrificed by the priest of a junior shrine. The latter can eat other sacred parts of pigs sacrificed by a senior priest, but not the head. Such linkages obtain between shrines sharing a single complex of sacrificial magic, not all the shrines shown on Figure 3.
4. Or in some cases cognatic kinship *with* the ancestor.

REFERENCES CITED

FORTES, M. 1945, The dynamics of clanship among the Tallensi. New York: Oxford University Press.
   1949, The web of kinship among the Tallensi. New York: Oxford University Press.
   1950, Oedipus and Job in West African religion. Cambridge: Cambridge University Press.
   1953, The structure of unilineal descent groups. American Anthropologist 55: 17-41.
   1959, Descent, filiation and affinity: a rejoinder to Dr. Leach. Man 59: 193-197, 206-212.
   1965, Some reflections on ancestor worship in Africa. *In* African systems of thought. M. Fortes and G. Dieterlen, eds. New York: Oxford University Press, pp. 122-142.
GOODENOUGH, W., 1964, Introduction. *In* Explorations in cultural anthropology. W. Goodenough, ed. New York: McGraw-Hill, pp. 1-24.
GOODY, J. R., 1961, The classification of double descent systems. Current Anthropology 2: 3-12.
   1962, Death, property, and the ancestors. Stanford: Stanford University Press.
KEESING, R. M., 1965, Kwaio marriage and society. Unpublished Ph.D. dissertation. Harvard University.

1966a, Kwaio kindreds. Southwestern Journal of Anthropology 22: 346-353.

1966b, Kwaio descent groups. Offset monograph. Center for South Pacific Studies, University of California, Santa Cruz.

1967a, Statistical models and decision models of social structure: a Kwaio case. Ethnology 6: 1-16.

1967b, Christians and pagans in Kwaio, Malaita. Journal of the Polynesian Society 76: 82-100.

1968a, Step kin, in-laws, and ethnoscience. Ethnology 7: 59-70.

1968b, Non-unilineal descent and contextual definition of status: the Kwaio evidence. American Anthropologist 70: 82-84.

1970a, Kwaio word tabooing in its cultural context. *In* Journal of the Polynesian Society (in press).

1970b, Descent, residence, and cultural codes. *In* Essays in Oceanic anthropology. L. Hiatt and C. Jayarwardena, eds. (in press).

1970c, Kwaio fosterage. American Anthropologist 72 (in press).

LOUNSBURY, F., 1964, The formal analysis of the Crow- and Omaha-type kinship terminologies. *In* Explorations in cultural anthropology. W. Goodenough, ed. New York: McGraw-Hill, pp. 351-394.

1965, Another view of the Trobriand kinship categories. *In* Formal semantic analysis. E. Hammel, ed. American Anthropologist 67 (5, pt. 2): 142-185.

MIDDLETON, J., 1960, Lugbara religion. New York: Oxford University Press.

1965, The Lugbara of Uganda. New York: Holt, Rinehart and Winston.

SAHLINS, M., 1963, Poor man, rich man, big man, chief: political types in Melanesia and Polynesia. Comparative Studies in Society and History 5: 285-303.

SCHEFFLER, H. W., 1966, Ancestor worship in anthropology: or observations on descent and descent groups, Current Anthropology 7: 541-551.

SCHNEIDER, D., 1965, Some muddles in the models: or how the system really works. *In* The relevance of models in social anthropology. M. Banton, ed. New York: Praeger.

WORSLEY, P., 1956, The kinship system of the Tallensi: a reevaluation. Journal of the Royal Anthropological Institute 86: 37-75.

FURTHER READINGS

For further reading on the New Guinea social-structure controversy in addition to Meggitt's *The Lineage System of the Mae Enga* and "The Pattern of Leadership Among the Mae Enga of New Guinea"—the reader should see Barnes' "Agnation Among the Enga" and McArthur's "Analysis of the Genealogy of a Mae Enga Clan." See also Langness' "Some Problems in the Conceptualization of Highlands Social Structures" and "Bena Bena Political Organization." Ryan's two early papers, "Clan Organization in the Mendi Valley" and "Clan Formation in the Mendi Valley," are of relevance, as are a paper by Glasse on "The Huli Descent System" and a paper by Watson on "Society as Organized Flow: The Tairora Case." Salisbury has written on "Unilineal Descent Groups in the New Guinea Highlands." Wagner's *The Curse of Souw* deals with some of the same issues in a group on the periphery of the Highlands. "Social Structure in New Guinea" by van der Leeden and three articles by Pouwer—" 'Loosely Structured Societies' in Netherlands New Guinea," "A Social System in the Star Mountains," and "Structure and Flexibility in a New Guinea Society"—should be examined for the western half of the island of New Guinea. Two articles review the literature dealing with the general question of flexibility and looseness of structure: "Descent, Residence, and Leadership in the New Guinea Highlands" by deLeprevanche and "The Plasticity of New Guinea Kinship" by Kaberry.

For the more general area of Melanesia and the broader issues, Scheffler's *Choiseul Island Social Structure* and "Ancestor Worship in Anthropology" are suggested, as are two earlier papers delineating many of the problems: Goodenough's "A Problem in Malayo-Polynesian Social Organization" and Davenport's "Nonunilinear Descent and Descent Groups." The reader should also see Goodenough's paper on "Kindred and Hamlet in Lakalai, New Britain" and Davenport's "Social Structure of Santa Cruz Island." Also for New Britain, see Epstein's "Variation and Social Structure." Firth's analysis in *We, the Tikopia*, although dealing with a Polynesian outlier, is an extensive treatment of social structure that must be read by any student of the Pacific. His article "A Note on Descent Groups in Polynesia" is also of relevance. Hogbin and Wedgwood's paper "Local Grouping in Melanesia" was an early attempt to cover the diversity of Melanesian social structures and the inability of the traditional anthropological language to come to grips with that diversity. Hogbin's *Kinship and Marriage in a New Guinea Village* can be read with profit also. There are, finally, other papers by Keesing that should be consulted: "Kwaio Kindreds," "Statistical Models and Decision Models of Social Structure," and "Non-unilineal Descent and Contextual Definition of Status."

PART III

SOCIAL PROCESS

However rigorously anthropologists may attempt to analyze the structural principles of different societies, it is obvious that in all of them life goes on as part of a continuous, seemingly unending process. This process involves much variation perhaps, but always concerns the common facts of birth and growth, maturity and marriage, war and peace, success and failure, illness and death. The goal of this part is to describe the process as it occurs in Melanesia.

Although culture and personality research has been under way for a long time in Melanesia (Langness & Gladwin, n.d.), there is an amazing lack of studies dealing with child training and the socialization process. Ian Hogbin's paper, the first in this part, is an early and remarkably thorough account of the first eight years of life on the island of Wogeo, which is off the north coast of New Guinea. It discusses indigenous beliefs about conception, birth, the relationship between husbands and wives, and the way children learn and become members of their social group. It indicates well the overwhelming power of cultural tradition.

K. E. Read's account of the sacred *nama* flutes of the Highlands, in addition to setting forth some general features of religion, picks up where Hogbin leaves off and briefly describes male initiation rites among the Gahuku-Gama. Read also gives us many clues to understanding New Guinea societies in his discussion of male superiority, generational continuity, and the fertility aspects of the great *idza nama* festivals. For his longer, more personal account, see *The High Valley*.

Ralph Bulmer pursues, in greater detail, one of the themes introduced by Read—the political functions (or consequences) of Highlands ceremonial exchanges. After months of preparation, thousands of pearlshells and pigs are moved across the valleys in the Moka, an exceedingly large-scale exchange ceremony in the Western Highlands. Bulmer concentrates on the nature of the social ties binding the participants and attempts to show how the Moka ritual may have been linked to leadership and warfare. He shows how the process of periodic exchange coordinated the whole of Kyaka society and helped its continuity by limiting the violence which was so much a part of Melanesian life.

Warfare in many parts of Melanesia was linked to headhunting and cannibalism. The Reverend Zegwaard has given us a valuable account of one instance among the Asmat, a group in West Irian, formerly Dutch New Guinea. Here

171

what seems to us a truly bizarre form of human behavior is shown to be integrated with mythology, initiation, marriage, personal prestige, kinship, fertility, magic, religion, territoriality, and politics. And, as is common in Melanesia, the people themselves have no other explanation for this behavior except "It is the way of our ancestors." While warfare appears to have been ritualized in this manner in parts of Melanesia, it was not universally so ritualized. Nor were cannibalism and headhunting universal, although they were widespread.

Marriage is not dealt with as a special topic in this collection but has importance in the papers by Hogbin, Read, and Zegwaard. In most of Melanesia, marriage is so intimately linked with such matters as warfare, male superiority, initiation and fertility rituals that it virtually cannot be described independently of them.

Death always seems to be an occasion for ritual, but the Nakanai of New Britain have carried it well beyond the usual. Here mortuary feasts bring prestige to those who can successfully organize and carry them out. Elaborately rehearsed dances are privately owned, and performances involve complicated theatrical tricks such as snakes protruding from the performer's mouth, a fire burning in his lap, or some other dramatic effect. There are many taboos and a long period of mourning, exhumation, ritual killing, and—as so well described by Professor Goodenough in the concluding article of this part—true pageantry.

11

A NEW GUINEA CHILDHOOD FROM CONCEPTION TO THE EIGHTH YEAR

Ian Hogbin

Wogeo, the largest of the Schouten islands, lies thirty miles off the north coast of New Guinea between the mouth of the Sepik River and Wewak, the principal government station in the East Sepik Administrative District. The people, numbering about nine hundred, live in a series of small villages located on the coast. Every village is made up of two separate units composed mainly of agnates each with its own headman, and, in addition, there is a division of the whole society into matrilineal moieties. The latter groupings, however, are of little importance except in regulating marriage and ceremonies.

My intention is to present a discussion of the way infants are customarily treated until the end of the eighth year. This is prefaced by an account of the theories of conception, the pregnancy taboos, and the procedure at birth.[1]

The native calendar is so crude that a record of birthdays is out of the question. Unaware, therefore, except in a general way, of the age of any child born before my arrival, I was forced to rely upon estimates, and the figures quoted in the following pages are to be understood as such.

Although always more of a spectator than an actual participant in native life, I was accepted by the residents of Dap, where I lived for the greater part of my stay, as to some extent a member of the village. Close personal relationships were established with a number of householders, and, as many of them appear in the following pages, it will be convenient to begin with a list of their names. They include:

The headman, Marigum.
Marigum's three wives—Yam, Nyem, and Matiti.
Marigum's three children by Yam—the baby girl Jauon and the two boys Sabwakai and Dal.

Reproduced by permission of A. P. Elkin, Editor of *Oceania,* and Ian Hogbin from *Oceania,* 13:285-309 (1942-43) and 16:275-296 (1945-46). Edited by permission of the author.

Marigum's son by another wife, now dead, a man named Tafalti.[2]

Marigum's "classificatory" brother, Waru.

Waru's wife, Mujewa.

Their adopted baby daughter, Kamara.

Wiawia.

Wiawia's wife, Yakena.

Their two children—Gwa, a little boy, and the baby girl Jaga (Yakena gave birth to another daughter during my visit).

Yakena's mother, who lives with them, Gabwe.

Sabuk.

Sabuk's two wives, Uj and Bagim (Uj had an adopted son and Bagim three children, the youngest of whom was born during my visit).

PREGNANCY

Pregnancy is considered to be as much the father's concern as the mother's, and his future rôle is continually emphasized throughout the whole nine months. The Wogeo natives are aware that sexual intercourse is necessary before conception can take place, and, although their theories about the processes are in most respects wide of the mark, they insist that the element contributed by the man is as important as that which comes from the woman. Gestation is also supposed to have as marked an effect on the father as on the mother, and both are equally bound to regulate their behaviour, though in different ways, in order to promote the child's welfare. Practical training in parenthood may be lacking, but the heavy responsibilities are made perfectly clear.

Most primitive peoples have a generally-accepted conception belief that is more or less in accord with a few of the known facts. Wogeo is something of an exception, for, although all the natives agree that both the father and the mother play a part and that repeated intercourse is necessary, they frankly admit that they do not know exactly what takes place. Three suggestions were put forward by intelligent informants—that the conjunction of semen (*jabejabe*) and the female secretion (also called *jabejabe*) results in the formation of the embryo, which is nourished until birth by the menstrual blood; that the blood contains the seed and that the semen and secretion, "like the white of an egg," provide the food; and that the semen and secretion coagulate the blood and then seal it in the womb. The fact that maternal and paternal kin are sometimes distinguished as "blood" (*dara*) and "water" (*dan*), a euphemism, as is admitted, for "semen," seems to indicate that the first suggestion is to be regarded perhaps as the orthodox point of view.[3]

That contributions from the father and the mother are believed to enter into the child's physical make-up is proved by the explanation given for the transmission of hereditary characteristics. Tafalti, it was pointed out, is pigeon-toed like his father "because of the semen" and has his mother's dark skin "on account of the blood." But as the natives are so firmly convinced that intercourse must take place several times, they believe that the child of a promiscuous woman may have several physiological fathers, every one of whom will have left some mark. A bastard living in Job village, near Dap, was said by the inhabitants, including one of the men concerned, to have "Kumun's mouth, Wakalu's forehead, Kakamari's ears, and Sawang's hair." The population is small, and, as inbreeding has been going on for generations, such resemblances may be more real than fancied.

The man is said to be as liable to suffer from morning sickness as his wife, and I knew of three or four, all apparently in perfect health, who often vomited after meals for the first two or three months. Expectant fathers, moreover, are subject to a feeling of "heaviness," with the result that they tire easily and have to avoid strenuous or dangerous activities, like hunting and fighting. I was warned not to send Sabuk shooting pigeons while his wife was pregnant—"The cartridges would be wasted;" said my friends, "no one in that condition could hope to shoot straight."

Taboos fall more heavily at first on the woman—she has to give up sexual intercourse, though her husband is still allowed to cohabit with his other wives, and she refrains from eating more foods than he. She avoids intercourse partly because the excitement may be injurious to the child and partly because an addition to the semen already in the womb would later on seriously impair the quality of her milk. All kinds of nuts except coconuts and many kinds of fish are also forbidden "on account of the milk," though many queer cravings are freely indulged. Several women insisted on eating raw breadfruit, and I knew two who chewed charcoal and a third who consumed her husband's supply of red ochre. Yams are avoided by both husband and wife for fear that the child might have the same rough skin, and many parents even refuse to walk under yam vines trained to climb up the trunks of trees. Finally, the man does not eat shark meat lest the child should be born with an over-large mouth. Such restrictions are felt to be burdensome but seem to be willingly accepted in the early years of married life, when both husband and wife are anxious to reach the status of parenthood.

There is no special ceremony to secure easy delivery, but, during the last couple of months, the woman rubs herself when bathing with the leaves of two trees that have particularly greasy sap. As soon as she begins to do this the husband, who hitherto, on account of his "heaviness," has gone fishing only on rare occasions, sets out to catch a *matame*. I am unaware of the scientific name of this fish, but it is light-coloured, fat, and has no scales. The theory is that by catching it he ensures that the child will also have a light, clear, healthy-looking skin.

Pregnancy is a busy time as preparations have to be made for a period of three or four months when the woman will be too occupied with the baby to attend to much of her other work. The provision of an adequate supply of taro is the couple's chief concern, and a much larger area than usual is put into cultivation. Extra skirts have also to be made, for until the child has learnt sphincter control it is bound to dirty its mother at least once or twice every day. (Sago- and pandanus-fibre skirts can be washed but are not particularly durable at the best of times.) The supply is augmented by presents from relatives and friends.

These activities take up most of the woman's leisure, but, in any case, as soon as her abdomen begins to be noticeably enlarged, she seems to lose all desire to go visiting. Long journeys over narrow paths which alternately cross muddy swamps and rocky headlands would certainly be burdensome, but the chief reason for her reluctance to mix with persons to whom she is not closely related is said to be "the sniffs of the men." They do not consider her to be in any way dangerous to them, nor is her condition regarded as funny or indecent, as it might be in some circles amongst ourselves— the only occasion when I heard the announcement of a pregnancy greeted with salacious guffaws was when the woman's husband had been dead for three years—but it is a fact that the menfolk are in general inclined to look upon her as anything but beautiful.

Many husbands, especially in the early years of married life, are keenly solicitous of their wife's welfare, nevertheless, and try to spare her by doing the odd jobs, often to the amusement of the rest of the villagers. Labim, for example, not in the least put out by the sniggers of his associates, used to chop the firewood. Sabuk's affection for his favourite wife went still further, and, when he contracted malaria during the fourth month of the pregnancy, he told me that he was pleased to think that, by suffering now, he might be sparing her the worst of her labour pains later.

Couples make no plans for their offspring's future before its arrival, however, never so much as choosing a name for it in advance, as this is regarded as unlucky.

Birth

The man even plays a part in birth itself, for while his wife is in labour he remains indoors, taking care to see that every knot in the house has been untied and all the boxes opened. Female relatives are permitted to attend the woman until the child makes its appearance, but, as from that moment she is considered to be ritually unclean, they have to retire and leave her to look after herself as best she can. She continues to be a danger to all who approach until the next full moon and keeps herself secluded in a little hut, the *bwaruka,* which has been specially built for the purpose. During her absence the man is expected to regulate his behaviour and refrain from violent exercise and the use of axes and knives.

Shortly before the birth is expected, the hut is erected by the husband, or the brother if the woman is unmarried. Old timber lying close to the village is generally used, but, although the workmanship is crude, a raised floor is always put in and great care taken to see that the thatch is proof against the rain. The interior dimensions of two of the huts built when I was on the island were six feet by five by six high, and within this space there was a hearth, a pile of firewood, and a wild-palm spathe to serve as a bed. One, owing to the husband's procrastination, had to be erected in a great hurry with the assistance of a few men while the woman was in labour.

The precise location of the hut largely depends on whether the woman already has a young child who is likely to seek her out, a danger that must at all costs be avoided. If she has, the building is hidden deep in the forest at some distance from the village, and the child is informed that she has gone to see relatives on the other side of the island. On her return she explains that, while away, she found the infant in a cave nestling amongst a flock of bats.

The first birth is often difficult, and the mother or mother-in-law, or one or two older persons of experience, are in constant attendance for several days beforehand. Some women, probably on account of anatomical abnormalities, continue to have trouble with later infants, but the majority seem to come through the ordeal well, and several informed me that their labour was seldom protracted. If relatives are not already at hand, a message is sent immediately the pains begin either to them or to the neighbours, and the woman retires to a secluded portion of the beach. A bundle of leaves is spread out to make a rough couch, and the attendants busy themselves in assisting her in every way possible. Until the child arrives they support her back, press on her shoulders, and hold up palm spathes to provide shelter from the sun or rain. The delivery is announced with yells to the menfolk waiting in the village, short sharp calls for a male and a long-drawn-out halloo for a female.[4]

After resting for a few minutes to regain her strength the woman cuts the cord with a bamboo knife—even to-day steel is not used—and gathers up the afterbirth and bloody leaves and throws them into the sea. She then washes both herself and the infant and staggers with it to the hut, where one of her kinsfolk has in the meantime kindled a fire and arranged the bed. The other women, having watched her from a safe distance, then prepare her a dish of stewed figs, which she has to eat while they are still steaming hot.

The father, surrounded with unfastened bundles and open boxes, does not as a rule appear to be unduly worried, though a certain strain is sometimes apparent, and one man with whom I sat was unable to carry on a coherent conversation. On another occasion, too, when a woman had been in labour for several hours, her husband found that he could not eat a platter of food sent along by kindly neighbours. "I cannot swallow," he explained, "it sticks in my throat." Again, I twice saw people leave their work to sit with the husband and distract his attention when news was brought that his wife was having difficulty.

The natives do not attempt to correct malpresentations by manipulation, and, if the labour is prolonged—forty-eight hours is by no means unusual—they have to fall back on magic. The husband is first informed so that he can make certain that no knot or box has been missed, and, if this fails to bring relief, a specialist is summoned to perform the rite known as "the spate" (*dan-sauasaua,* literally, water strongly flowing). He recites a spell over a bowl of water which is then carried to the beach and allowed to trickle on the woman's abdomen. A second specialist may be tried later, and sometimes even a third, and the rite is repeated over and over until she either gives birth or dies. I heard of one instance in which the delivery was supposed to have been delayed by the woman's refusal to confess to an intrigue with a man of the same moiety, but this affair was both flagrant and notorious, and further enquiry failed to bring to light any general belief in supernatural punishment for moiety or clan incest.

Should the infant be premature or stillborn, as often happens, it is disposed of with the afterbirth, but if it dies in the hut the mother puts the body into a basket and gives it to the husband, who carries it into the remote jungle away from any habitation. He is careful not to touch it with his hands and thus avoids having to perform a ceremony of purification afterwards. Unwanted children and those with obvious deformities are buried alive at birth, though the woman is not relieved of the obligation to spend the full period in seclusion. Those who become crippled in later life through injury or disease, on the other hand, are looked after with loving care, and one youth who had lost the use of his legs by a fall in early boyhood was his father's constant companion. Two pairs of wooden "shoes" had been made, one for his hands and another for his knees, to enable him to crawl about without hurting himself, and, through his father's encouragement, he was already an expert fisherman and carver.

The woman almost always manages to reach the hut by herself but is occasionally so weak that someone has to come to her aid. The wife of one of my informants was so ill that she had to be carried in a mat, though the bearers took the precaution of covering their hands with rags to prevent contact with her flesh. I was told that if they had touched her they would have been equally unclean and have had to remain outside the community for the same period. Several cases were quoted, and it appeared that, if the need arises, someone—either the mother, or the mother-in-law, or a sister, or a husband's sister—is always prepared to submit to the necessary inconvenience.

If the woman dies in childbirth, or shortly afterwards while she is still in the hut, the traditional mourning is omitted and the body buried as quickly as possible without decorations or ornaments. Contact with the dead is always regarded as hazardous, but, since the danger is in this case greater than usual, the husband and the brother make the funeral arrangements by themselves without asking for outside help.

There can be no doubt that the interval spent in the hut is highly beneficial. Instead of being forced to work at once, as is the custom in some communities, she has time to rest and renew her strength, and, since she is not bothered with household cares, she can devote herself fully to the baby's welfare. She gives herself up, in fact, to its enjoyment, and, sleeping and waking, it lies cuddled in her arms close to her breasts.

While she is in the hut she is fed by relatives and neighbours, who also keep her water-bottles full and supply her with firewood for warmth. Only one type of food is permitted, the special vegetable curry known as *sur,* a delicacy always given to persons in a ritually dangerous condition. Owing to her special state she has to be careful not to use her fingers when eating, and for at least a week each morsel has to be conveyed to the mouth with a fork made from the wing of a bird. Water for drinking has also to be poured into half a coconut-shell first, and she uses a bone or a piece of wood instead of her nails when scratching herself.

The infant may be temporarily removed from its mother after about a week, when the grandmothers are permitted to hold it for a few minutes at a time. The father does not take it yet but usually displays the greatest interest, and one often sees him examining its tiny body with glances full of affection. He still remains idle for a few more days—if he were to use an axe he might break the baby's sinews—and then resumes his normal activities one by one. His meals, and those of the older children, may be prepared by his sisters, but in most instances the neighbours ask him to join them. Male relatives come along to see him and express satisfaction, and those with the necessary skill prepare potions (*karag*) which are supposed to assist the woman's recovery.

The child's name can now be openly discussed, and various suggestions are made regarding which of the ancestors ought to be commemorated. The father's and the mother's kinsfolk have the right of choosing one each, but the final selection rests with the grandfathers or the father's and the mother's eldest brother. The mother's relatives generally exercise their privilege only in the case of the firstborn son and daughter, however, and even then their choice is seldom heard in use. Thus Dal, the favourite son of the headman Marigum, was called "Kaneg," the name given him by his maternal grandfather, only when he was actually in the latter's village, and not invariably there.[5]

The naming of the firstborn requires a ceremony, which is attended by all the relatives. The father's father or the senior uncle, or the father himself if these are both dead, repeats the names of the ancestors, and, when the one chosen is reached the assembled people call out loudly, "Yes, the child shall be called such-and-such." The man in charge of the arrangements then breaks a young coconut open and takes a mouthful of the fluid, which he spits out in a fine spray over those present. A stalk of wild ginger is also split in two and hung on the front of the birth hut.

If the infant is the firstborn son or daughter of a headman's wife the crowd is still larger, and a distribution of food takes place afterwards. For a boy the names of every famous past headman from the neighbouring islands are repeated, but for a girl those of the wives of headmen from the districts to which the parents belong suffice. The natives could offer no satisfactory explanation for this custom, but it probably has its foundation in the desire to emphasize the continuity of tradition.[6]

At last, on the morning after the night of the next new moon, the woman pulls down her hut, throws the timber away, and returns to her family. Her first tasks, symbolizing her re-entry into ordinary life, are the preparation of a dish of hermit crabs for the women of the village and the presentation of a cooked taro to each of the men. She is now free to go about her affairs in the normal way, though two ceremonies have still to be carried out. At the first new moon she takes the baby to one of the older men, usually the headman of her husband's clan, for the performance of magic to make it healthy and strong, and some time later she gives its dried umbilical cord, which she has carefully saved, to someone who is going far out to sea. If this is not thrown overboard in deep water the child is believed to have little chance of growing tall and strong.

PROTECTING THE CHILD'S HEALTH

The infant mortality rate is high, and, as disease and death are always attributed to supernatural intervention of one sort or another, the native baby is surrounded with special precautions over and above the more ordinary care. Gastric disturbances are in Wogeo regarded as one of the major risks, and taboos are imposed upon the nursing mother to keep her milk wholesome and pure. In the early months of the child's life, too, she is not permitted to let anyone else nurse it above a few minutes, for contact with other women is thought to be dangerous. Again, she has to make every effort to prevent its crying. The theory is that its vital spirit, if offended by unkindly treatment, may return to the other world, leaving a now lifeless husk of body behind.

The milk of a woman who has recently indulged in sexual intercourse is supposed to have been rendered too "heavy" for easy digestion, an effect produced also by the consumption of certain foods, notably pork, nuts, and a number of different kinds of fish. Mothers are therefore expected to refrain from cohabiting with their husbands—and other men—for the space of two years or so and for from half to three-quarters of this period to take the utmost care over what they eat. The diet restrictions seem for the most part to be faithfully kept, but about the sexual prohibition I am unable to speak with certainty. Everyone interrogated replied that she was herself far too concerned with her child's welfare to be lax, but, when pressed, several expressed doubt about the conduct of other women. One or two, including Yakena, the wife of my neighbour Wiawia, became pregnant a second time with suspicious rapidity, but the guilt of the others remains unproven, for the men assured me—and I could not seek futher confirmation—that only a few unfortunates begin to menstruate while still suckling a small infant.

Weaning is usually delayed, as was stated above, till the end of the third year, and, perhaps for this reason, few women are without milk except during the final months of their pregnancies. The fact that a person's breasts are full, however, usually means that she is looked upon as potentially harmful to the young offspring of her neighbours. Unless she is keeping the taboos in the interests of a member of her own family, her milk, according to the Wogeo view, is rank poison to the infants under about two years old, and giving one of them suck, even unintentionally, would be looked upon, I have little doubt, as almost murder. To avoid all possibility of criticism most women accordingly refrain from touching very young babies belonging to other people, and even an aunt picking up a small nephew is careful to keep him at arm's length, frustrating his attempts to nuzzle towards her either by a quick turn of her body or else by giving him back without delay to his mother.

Aged grandmothers and the unmarried girls of the community are the only exceptions to the general rule. As there is no milk in their breasts, they are thought to be incapable of doing much harm and are allowed to hold the child closely and press it to their bosom. As one might have expected, it is noticeably far happier when in their keeping than in the care of women who handle it with more consideration for its health than its comfort.

Young girls from the age of seven or eight onwards are all immensely interested and often beg to be allowed to nurse the baby, but the mother, afraid that they may drop it, never entrusts it to them for long. Mujewa told me that, glad as she was sometimes to have a small girl available to mind Kamara, she always felt uneasy if they went to the other side of the village and was not satisfied till they had returned. Keke, a girl of about nine who made herself useful to several of the Dap mothers, was by two of them permitted actually to carry their infants only when they were themselves watching, and at other times when her help was required she had to sit down before the babe was placed in her arms. So eager was she to have them that she did not seem to mind, and, hailing me if I was in sight, would call out, "Hogbin, come here quickly and look at this baby of mine."

Further proof of the implicit acceptance of the doctrine about pure and impure milk is provided by the fact that women whose supply is for some reason inadequate never seem to think of asking anyone else to supplement it. I was also informed that, should the mother die and no one come forward with an offer to keep the taboos, the infant would be buried with her even if perfectly healthy. Feeding it with the milk of a person living a normal existence, the villagers stated, would be futile. One of the more important culture heroes was interred for this reason; but as his constitution was stronger than that of ordinary humans he managed to survive by sucking the sticky fluid from the root of a breadfruit tree growing close by. The desire for a reasonably large family is intense, and there is almost always someone ready to adopt an extra child. If she wins the widower's promise that she may claim the babe as her own, she willingly submits on its behalf to some, at least, of the restrictions. The amount of nourishment to be obtained from the breasts of a person whose own offspring is now more than two or three years old is probably small, but on this point the only evidence I have to offer is the high percentage of orphans who die—thereby, incidentally, giving the natives confirmation of their belief.

Motherless babes are never entrusted to the temporary care of a woman with a young infant of her own. One at a time is considered to be all that any person can manage. The invariable comment of those to whom I showed the photograph, subsequently reproduced as Plate V in my *Experiments in Civilization,* of a Malaita woman holding her baby at one breast and the orphan whom she had agreed to foster at the other was "Foolish: by suckling the two she'll kill them both. She ought to have looked after her child and let the other be." (Twin births are rare, and it is apparently very uncommon for even one of the children to live.)

The child's continued good health is thought to be bound up also with its vital spirit (*vanunu*). The natives maintain that, until the talking stage is reached, this spirit is free to return whence it came and that great care is necessary to prevent it taking umbrage and doing so. The only hope of pleasing it, they say, is to treat the child with indulgence, and infants are accordingly fed even before they are hungry, comforted before they are hurt, and reassured before they are frightened. During the time when the mother looks after her baby almost unaided she may be said to be practically its slave, a status to which other relatives who later take an interest are also at first reduced, at least while in its presence.

All Wogeo children who cannot as yet talk properly are thus to our way of thinking sadly spoiled. Never in any circumstances slapped or beaten no matter how naughty they may have been, they accept the granting of their most outrageous demands as a matter of course. Parents keep the household knives concealed in order to avoid having to refuse requests that these be handed over, but fragile ornaments like ear-rings are presented at once. Although such objects, never intended for rough treatment, are often broken within a few minutes, I never remember hearing a single expression of annoyance or irritation. I was impressed, too, with the readiness with which persons who were normally most reluctant to ask me for anything for their own use would cast their scruples aside if one of the children wanted something.

Anxiety for the child's welfare ensures it an audience for its smallest woes, and if at a slightly later stage it falls down, everyone in sight rushes to pick it up. As all try to persuade it that no harm has been done, it invariably insists, with piercing shrieks, that the injury is serious. The grown-up who raises it to its feet passes a stone three times round its head to recall the frightened spirit, and the rest hit the ground and pretend that a wicked frog has hopped into the village "on purpose to trip up our little son."

Temper tantrums at this age frighten the whole village, and everyone hurries with a gift of food to distract the child's attention. Should their efforts be unsuccessful, the father continually repeats the child's name loudly, begging the spirit to remain. The whole of Dap became a hubbub on one occasion when Jauon discovered that her mother proposed to leave her behind with an elderly relative and go off alone for a day's gardening. Although still only a tiny tot, she threw herself on the ground screaming and, every time one of the women tried to pick her up, fought, kicked, and bit. Her father, Marigum, ran up and down wringing his hands, calling out, "Spirit, stop; Jauon, Jauon, Jauon; your mother will look after you. She will not go to the garden." After the passion had subsided the mother sat nursing the child for the whole day and when leaving the village on later occasions always took care to slip away unobserved.

I noticed that a few women also, when they had taken their infants to the gardens or a strange village, made a practice before returning of saying the name over several times. The object, they explained, was to inform the spirit of their intention to go back home in case it had wandered away to do a little exploring on its own account. A further precaution against the loss of the vital spirit is the refusal to comment on the child's healthy appearance, though in this case the envy of the ghosts of the dead is given as the reason —they might steal the spirit for one of their ghostly feasts.

MOTHER AND CHILD

The father has little to do with his offspring for the first eighteen months or two years. Till then, unless a widowed grandmother is a member of the establishment, the mother often has to look after it without regular outside assistance. Relatives and friends, to spare her the journey to and from the garden, do their best to keep her supplied with vegetables for three or four months, but she may have to cook by herself, keep the place tidy, watch the other children, and carry out a hundred and one other household tasks. If possible, however, one of her unmarried sisters, or an unmarried sister of her husband, comes to stay. The object is not so much to act as a nurse-maid as to relieve the woman of some of her responsibilities. When Bagim had a baby, for example, her young sister undertook the task of cooking for the rest of the family but was seen with the infant in her arms only on the rarest occasions. Resident grandmothers also spend more of their time at housework than in looking after infant grandchildren.

The mother puts her nipple into the child's mouth whenever it cries, even if she is busy, in which case she sits down and, to keep her hands free, supports its weight on her thigh. But if she has nothing to do she gives herself up to it just as she did in the birth hut and watches its every movement with intense absorption. Holding it firmly with one hand under its back, she either fondles it with the other or else gently massages her breast "to help it by making the milk flow more freely." She rarely, if ever, plays any sort of games with it, but one sees her crooning to it, caressing the fleshy parts of its body with gentle fingers, and implanting breathy kisses over and over again in the region of its genital organs.

The diet consists for several months of mothers' milk alone. Even water is forbidden at the beginning, though after about the ninth week coconut fluid is allowed. The first additional food, which is given in about the fifth month, is the variety of banana known on account of its softness by the same word as that for "water," *dan*. The mother bites a morsel of the fruit, chews it, and inserts it in the infant's mouth with the tip of her tongue. This banana is particularly sweet and hence is relished by most children. They smack their lips and look around for more. Not until the upper and lower incisors have been cut are they given any of the staple food, taro, and at first this also is thoroughly chewed for them beforehand. Perhaps because of the coarse flavour taro is disliked by some, who do their best to spit it out. The mother does not scold but perseveres with great patience till the wet pellets are swallowed with resignation if not relish. The soft pappy flesh of immature coconuts is given at much the same stage, and some time afterwards, when the first molars have been cut, still other foods. No child is ever forced to eat against its will, and one who insists till a later age than usual that its mother shall masticate its meal is always humoured. "By and by he will eat properly," says the woman without the slightest annoyance or shame at its backwardness. Fish is considered to be harmful until well into the third year, and pork, which, in any case, is available only on rare occasions, is withheld until after weaning.

At night the baby sleeps enfolded in its mother's arms on the floor, but in the daytime, when not actually nursing it, she puts it into a basket, which then hangs on a convenient rafter near where she is working. This receptacle, though generally new and always lined carefully with soft clean leaves, is of the ordinary type for carrying vegetables from the garden, and, as it is fully fifteen inches deep and no effort is made to keep the top open, the inside must be both dark and stuffy. The child rarely makes any objection, nevertheless, and usually lies quiet even when awake. Voices are not lowered to avoid disturbing it, and it learns to tolerate all but the loudest noises. It is always removed and carried about when really irritable, but an attempt is usually made to still its cries first by rocking the basket gently to and fro, or by scratching the outside. The adults' habit of curling up in a corner when troubled or depressed, trying, in their own words, "to shut things out with sleep," is possibly to be accounted for in part by such treatment during their infancy, as is their detestation of cold rainy weather. On wet days they sometimes do not get up at all, refusing to be bothered even with preparing meals. Early conditioning also enables them to sleep anywhere, in practically any position, no matter what is going on around them. Indeed, they are rarely in full possession of their faculties early in the morning, and for at least half an hour the men either wander about looking thoroughly miserable or else crouch over fires as though half drugged.

As soon as the baby appears to be really at home in its basket, generally by about the second month, some women prefer to be independent of their neighbours and begin gathering food for themselves. I knew one, for example, who was visiting her garden regularly three months after her baby's birth. The women who had been helping her had their own families to attend to, and, while they would probably have been willing to assist for some weeks longer, she had no wish to be under any further obligation to them. Yakena, Wiawia's wife, on the other hand, remained at home for a much longer period. She was by no means energetic at the best of times, but, as she explained, why should she neglect her baby when her widowed mother had no responsibilities and no one else to gather food for?

The woman sets off for the cultivations in the morning carrying the basket suspended from her forehead and, on the return journey, if no one is available to give her assistance, puts the vegetables on her back and slings the baby in front from her neck. Few children have any objection to her vigorous movements, and most of them crow quietly while she imitates such noises as best she can. The basket hangs on the bough of a tree swinging in the breeze, though from time to time she leaves her digging and goes across to see how the occupant is progressing, taking care to remain unobserved lest it should cry to be taken out. Only when it becomes fractious does she leave her work and sit with it in the shade.

The basket is used as a cradle for about three or four months, when further confinement is thought to be harmful. One woman explained that if she had continued to put her small son inside he would have cried at not being able to kick his legs. As it was, she sat him in a corner and he crowed contentedly and played with his fingers and toes. A further difficulty, of course, is the child's increasing size.

The baby has still to be taken to the garden in order to be fed and comforted when it cries. The mother at first carries it in her arms, but as soon as possible it is trained to ride on her back. She swings it up by one arm, and it rests with its feet on her buttocks, clinging either to her hair or a necklace. European mothers would probably feel sick with apprehension at the sight of a tiny mite perched so precariously, but I never heard of any accidents, and the children must feel safe, for, when frightened or hurt, instead of running to the comfort of friendly arms, as I have seen them doing in other communities, they more frequently seek the shelter of a friendly back.

Not until the infant has learned to eat a small amount of solid food, at the end of the first year, is it considered to be old enough to be left at home, but, as many women have no mother, mother-in-law, or younger sister with whom they can leave it, they may even then of necessity have to continue taking it to the garden. If a nurse is available they remain away during the mornings only for a few weeks, but, as soon as it seems to be accepting their absence with equanimity and they no longer have to be sent for in a hurry to comfort it, they take the opportunity of working unencumbered and delay their return until the early afternoon. Their first task on entering the house is to allow the child to suck its fill, and, while it does so, caresses are usually lavished upon it to make up for those that it has missed during the day.

PERSONAL HYGIENE

The natives are sensitive regarding personal cleanliness, and even tiny babies have to submit to a daily bath. A coconut full of fresh water is poured over them, and they are then vigorously rubbed with the palms of the hands. But as the water is not heated and towels are lacking, objections are often expressed in no uncertain terms. The mother takes little heed, however, and proceeds with an indifference which is the more remarkable since at other times she is so sympathetic. This lapse is excused on the grounds that the vital spirit is even readier to leave a dirty baby than one who is allowed to cry. "There, now you are clean again," I used to hear Mujewa saying as she brushed the drops off Kamara's shivering body. "Your skin is fresh, and you don't smell any more. When you grow up you must always be clean like this."

Towards the end of the second year a sea-water bathe is substituted, but the child is always protected from the biggest waves and gently soothed if frightened. The nurse gradually entices it into deeper and deeper water, reassuring it with comforting words that she is at hand to give support if it swallows a mouthful or loses confidence. No instructions are given in swimming, but it seems to watch her movements and eventually to imitate them. So fond of the water does it become that it often clamours to be taken to the beach, and the parents rarely have to insist that washing is desirable after playing in the mud.

Sphincter control, on the other hand, is not expected during infancy, and nobody is embarrassed if a baby makes a mess. If it defecates while in its basket the mother takes it out, washes it, and prepares a lining of fresh leaves before putting it back. From the age of six months onwards the excrement is thrown into the bush, but until then the soiled leaves are hurled into the sea, for if ants were to go near them there is some fear that the child might be taken ill. When it has a bowel or bladder movement while she is nursing it she does not twitch it away from her, though after about a year she tries to recognize the signs beforehand and, if possible, place it on a few leaves left in readiness in a corner. I occasionally heard women express annoyance with themselves for not having been on the watch, but even these refrained from blaming the baby.

Some time later, in the third year, the mother begins to make grunting noises while the child defecates and a loud hissing sound as it passes water, and, instead of sitting it on a pile of leaves, she holds it over the edge of the veranda, lifting its legs to prevent them from being soiled. Some women also try to anticipate its needs and take it outside when it wakes up after a nap and when it has finished its meals. The noises, like everything else it hears, are soon imitated, and explanations are then offered of the disadvantages of remaining in the house. The Wogeo attitude in such matters is characterized by disgust at the excreta but little or no shame regarding the physiological processes, which are referred to freely in all types of company without euphemisms. The adults accordingly endeavour to make the children share their distaste. "You must tell me, and I'll take you outside," said Salome to her daughter Kuma. "The smell of fæces vanishes in the open air, but here inside it is disgusting: it makes everything nasty." Backward children may have to be slapped once or twice—by this time the vital spirit is too firmly attached to run away of its own accord—but no one ever suggests that their behaviour is immodest, nor do the parents appear to feel humiliated. "Learn from your nose, girl, learn from your nose," Salome remarked at a later date. "Leave her alone: she'll learn soon enough when she's bigger," remonstrated the father. Yet within a week he was boxing the child's ears for easing herself in front of him while he was eating his dinner.

Few children need further reminders by the time that they have been weaned, though some of them require assistance to cleanse themselves. The mother still has the duty of getting rid of the fæces, but once a youngster begins to play with older boys and girls it learns to ask one of them to take it to the patches of thick brush which serve as latrines, one for the men and one for the women. An older companion is always necessary, for the village pigs, which consume the excreta, have to be kept at a distance with stones. Even the elders withdraw only a few paces for urination, turning their backs on those present, with whom they often continue their conversation without interruption.

LEARNING TO WALK AND TALK

The Wogeo baby is not allowed to crawl and is discouraged from walking until it is nearly two years old. The natives feel that it ought to be capable of taking care of itself before it begins to move about freely, and, when at last permitted to make the attempt, it is usually strong enough to acquire a mastery over its legs within a few days. The precaution is explained by anxiety lest it should wander away unobserved and come to some harm— it might perhaps fall off the edge of the veranda or make its way into the fireplace. As soon as it shows the slightest wish to go down on all fours it is therefore either picked up or else put firmly in a corner.

Most babies appear to learn their lesson early and sit still contentedly for an hour at a time. Sometimes a handful of pebbles serves them as a toy, but their chief amusement always seems to be making queer noises. A few of the more strong-willed give a certain amount of trouble, however, and I have occasionally been in houses where the mother, too busy to hold her infant, had to haul it into its corner at intervals of five minutes or less. Yet only one or two gave any indication of resenting such treatment, and the rest obviously thought that they were having a pleasant game.

Towards the close of the second year—many, perhaps most, parents wait until the canine teeth are being cut—the child's knees are rubbed with bespelled leaves to ensure that its legs will soon be strong enough to bear its weight. Shortly afterwards, if it is normal and healthy, it rises to its feet, and within two or three days it is almost as far advanced, though as yet perhaps not quite as confident, as a European child who has progressed by slow and painful stages.

If the attempt is unduly delayed the magical rite may be repeated, but no one seems to think that active encouragement of any kind is necessary. When I told the natives how we coax our babies to stand at a much earlier age, they admitted that such methods might be suitable where there was no fireplace or veranda from which to tumble, but they openly laughed at me for speaking of "teaching" children to walk. A child walks of its own accord, they said, once it has reached the appropriate stage of growth; I would be saying next that trees had to be instructed in how to bear fruit.

Further magic is carried out soon afterwards to make the infant hurry up and talk. Soft pliable leaves are bespelled and rubbed on its lips so that the tongue can readily be twisted into the appropriate positions. At the same time, training is considered to be essential, and the early shouting of queer noises is encouraged with this object in view. The infant bubbles, pouts, and says, *"gu-gu-gu,"* to which the mother replies, imitating the sounds as best she can. Later, as she feeds it, she endlessly repeats the words for "mummy" (*ne*—the childish form of *mem,* "my mother"), "milk" (sus), and "breast" (*nyon*). *Ne* is usually the first recognizable expression uttered, though the child can as yet have no notion of the meaning, for "*ne-ne-ne,*" "*gu-gu-gu,*" and other syllables are babbled indiscriminately. Then suddenly it seems to realize that *ne* has application to persons, though both Kamara and Jauon shrieked the word to everyone they saw before narrowing down the use to their own mother. The grandmother repeats *bum,* "my grandchild" and also "my grandparent," and, if she is in the habit of nursing the child constantly and it is really familiar with her, this expression is learnt quite early also. *Mam,* "my father," *wawam,* "my mother's brother," and the second meaning of *nyon,* "mother's or father's sister," are mastered at a slightly later stage, for it is not as yet so well acquainted with these persons. Other people are called by their names, though the child's first efforts in this direction are usually much abbreviated. Thus

Jauon used to call her half-sister Magar "Ka," and Matiti, one of her step-mothers, "Titi."

Names of objects are learnt through repetition. The mother or some other relative points something out and says the word over and over till the child has repeated it to her satisfaction. As she prepares the meal, for example, she may say, "This is a pot (*bwara*), pot, pot. I am putting food into a pot, pot, pot. You say it: 'pot, pot, pot.' Now, what is this?—a pot, pot, pot." Other persons present take up the lesson in their turn, remarking, "Yes, a pot, pot, pot. Your mother puts food into the pot, pot, pot." "Pot, pot, pot," replies the child. "Yes, pot, pot, pot," echo the adults. A chorus of this kind may go on for ten minutes or longer, particularly if other children are present to join in. Not infrequently, too, each important word in a speech to a small child is said over three times. I once heard someone say to Kamara, "Tell your mother, mother, mother, to fetch the coconuts, coco-nuts, coconuts, for me to break open, break open, break open, for the pigs, pigs, pigs." It is scarcely surprising that many words in the Wogeo dialect have reduplicated syllables.

Real baby talk of the type indulged in sometimes by ourselves, full of such expressions as "bow-wow" and "puff-puff," is unknown. *Ne,* "mummy" (short for *mem,* mother), is the rare exception. The child's own attempt at a difficult word, however, or its misuse of a term, may be adopted by the household and become a sort of family expression. Thus all Marigum's wives followed Jauon in calling me "Batete" when I happened to be their guest, and three brothers of my acquaintance called their mother *mam,* "my father," thus perpetuating a mistake made by the youngest in his in-fancy thirty years before.

Father and Child

The father does not begin to come into his own until the toddling stage is reached. Association with infants is thought to be weakening to members of the male sex, and few men will consent to handle a baby for even a few seconds until it is at least a year old. If one of them does take it, he holds it well away from his body, often at arm's length, and, as is only to be expected, it begins screaming at once at the lack of adequate support and has to be returned to its mother. I caused considerable surprise by nursing little Jauon and open amazement when I let her remain in my arms after she had gone to sleep. Her father would wish to devote himself to her, it was admitted, and even be prepared to risk his health to some extent in doing so, but no one else would undertake the responsibility.

Remarks of this kind made me realize that the prohibition is felt to be a hardship, and, at a later date, after the birth of his third child, Wiawia stated definitely that he would like to have imitated me but feared lest he might become ill. "I want to nurse my baby as you nurse Jauon," he remarked, "but infants are bad for me. I don't want to die; and, besides, if I did, who would look after the child properly while it was growing up?"

In the meantime several other men had pointed out that the fact that they did not handle their infants implied no lack of interest. The father's regard, they maintained, is almost as deep as the mother's, a view amply confirmed by my own observations. Thus I repeatedly watched men glue their eyes on the baby for upwards of a quarter of an hour while it was being suckled, and not infrequently they imitated the mother's actions, pretending that they were caressing it and stroking its body. Waru often scolded Mujewa if, by some sudden movement, she dislodged her nipple from Kamara's mouth, and I once or twice saw him strike her when the child cried. Fathers also encourage their young offspring in its gurgling and chuckling and do not seem to feel that they are in the least ridiculous when sitting for half an hour making the most absurd noises. Their anxiety, moreover, is just as marked as that of the women if the child is ill, and their sorrow equally genuine if it dies. The only case of suicide within recent years occurred when a man killed himself on the day following his young son's funeral, and during my own visit Wiawia threatened to hang himself when a neighbour, as a thoughtless joke, told him that his eldest child Gwa had been drowned. One of the village youths had taken the boy out fishing, but a storm had come up, and, after the canoe had foundered, he had had to swim with his young charge to the shore, where they arrived frightened but unhurt. The neighbour, who was on the beach at the time, carried Gwa into his home and then sent a message to Wiawia to come and claim the body.

So keen is the affection of the father that women sometimes play upon it to secure better treatment for themselves; and the recognized method by which a wife punishes her husband for beating her is to take the children for a prolonged visit to her kinsfolk. Labim was an interesting example. He often cuffed the senior of his two wives, who was barren, but rarely touched the second, for, according to the neighbours, every time he did so she took the baby to see her parents. Gabwe, Wiawia's mother-in-law, who shared his dwelling, one day tried these tactics and, to pay him out, so she said, for being disrespectful to her, took the children to a village on the other side of the island. On discovering their absence, however, he flew into such tantrums of rage that his wife immediately fetched them back, advising her mother to remain away until his anger had subsided.

By the time the canine teeth are being cut, round about the end of the second year, though the child and its affairs are still felt to be primarily the women's concern, the fear of weakening influences is so much reduced that the father is able to take his baby and look after it for short periods himself. Young men, who may not have had much experience, are sometimes almost unbelievably clumsy at first and have to receive instructions. "Hold him tighter and put your hand behind his back," the women advise—only to add shortly afterwards, "Not so tight," or "Don't squeeze him so." The baby, although it may object to being handled unskilfully, soon accepts its father's attentions, especially if, as usually happens, he takes over the job of feeding it at meal times. The mother, far from being jealous, is glad to be relieved of some of her responsibilities.

The father continually refers to himself as *mam*, "my father," a word in consequence soon picked up. "*Mam, mam, mam,* come here to me," he calls from one end of the village to the other. "*Mam, mam, mam,*" it answers him. One or two men boasted that their children had been using this expression long before they could say even "mummy," but their wives laughed such assertions to scorn. "*Ne* is always uttered first," they insisted. "The child knows its mother's face from the beginning—does she not suckle it?—and it calls her *ne* when it can say nothing else."

OTHER RELATIVES

In polygynous households the attitude of the father's other wives depends to a great extent on the feelings of the child's mother. The headman Marigum's three spouses, Nyem, Matiti, and Yam, for example, are past their first youth and have for the most part put jealousy behind them. The first two were accordingly eager to help Jauon's mother, Yam, who was grateful for their assistance, especially as the child was headstrong and troublesome. Nyem, already middle-aged and thus less fitted for energetic work in the garden, practically adopted the rôle of grandmother. Yam used to leave the child with her, at first during the mornings only but later for the whole day, when planting had to be done or when Marigum asked her to accompany him in visits to other places. The term *ne* was reserved for the mother, however, and the older woman was addressed by a nickname of Jauon's own invention. She usually appeared to be satisfied with the company of either and if mildly frightened ran to whoever happened to be near. When ill, however, she invariably expressed dissatisfaction with Nyem and refused to allow Yam to leave her, and Yam alone was able to soothe her after a severe temper tantrum.

In houses where the women are continually quarrelling, on the other hand, they show little interest in one another's children. Sabuk's two wives never shared their offspring, not even at meal times, when the work would have been lightened for them both if they had taken turns at nursing and preparing the food. Each preferred to keep to her own fireside and ignore the other, and, on one occasion, Bagim, the younger woman, actually refused to allow her son to eat some food given to him by his stepmother on the plea that it might be poisoned. Sabuk was angry when informed of what had taken place and beat her severely for making such stupid charges. "You two silly creatures can quarrel one with the other," he told her, "but these are all my children, and you must both be mothers to them "

Wakalu's two wives, Buruka and Yar, were also on a footing of mutual mistrust. I ventured to ask Buruka in private why she never entrusted her family to her co-consort. What reason had she, I asked, for keeping the children to herself? "Give my babies to that gaping vagina? Never," she replied, using the coarsest expression in the language. "She thinks of nothing but copulation, and the children would starve while she went off to meet some man—one who probably wouldn't even be her husband."

Although little boys and little girls whose ages do not differ by much play together freely, the attitude of the older boys to babies is in marked contrast to that of the older girls: boys more or less ignore them, whereas the girls enjoy acting as nurse and are always begging to be allowed to do so. The influences liable to be weakening to males are supposed to be especially dangerous to the immature, and the parents in consequence warn the lads to keep their distance. Sabwakai, Jauon's second brother, aged about ten, took practically no notice of her till she could run about, and Dal, the eldest, appeared to observe her only at odd intervals. Even afterwards, though they taught her new words and saved delicacies for her to eat, they never picked her up unless actually requested to do so by their father or mother. Yet she never showed alarm at their presence and learnt to lisp "Thabi" and "Da" at a very early age.

The average child seems to have a keener appreciation of its sisters, for it has been accustomed to lying in their arms occasionally before it could walk. Once it can fend to a certain extent for itself it is entrusted to them for an hour or two at a time, and by the third year it plays with their mud pies and toddles about the village in their company. The other little girls welcome it, giving it food and playthings, and, though it sometimes cries at first if left alone with them, it soon learns their names and joins in their games.

Other relatives of importance include the sisters of the father and the mother. These women, it is thought, have a definite obligation to make the child look upon them with affection and trust. Unless they are unmarried they are not allowed to fondle it while the milk taboos are in operation, but once it can walk they cuddle it closely and do their best to suckle it. *Nyon,* the kinship term they themselves use and try to make it apply in turn to them, is in fact the word meaning "breast." "My little *nyon,*" I have heard them saying. "*Nyon*—you know *nyon* already—the same as mother's milk. We two are *nyon.* I am the same as your mother's milk. Come, *nyon,* suck; my milk is sweet; suck." "Suck, little one," adds the mother. "She is your *nyon.* Call her *nyon* and take her milk."

Women who do not live up to their obligations—a small minority—are much criticized by the rest. Bauo, one of Wiawia's sisters, a shrewish creature of uncertain temper with a sharp bitter tongue, who had no time for anyone save her own sickly offspring, was once publicly reproved by him for her lack of interest in his family. At the same time, the children's idiosyncracies sometimes render the establishment of amicable relations difficult. Jaga, for example, was usually shy and consistently rejected the breasts of all her aunts. On one occasion, when she could already speak about twenty or thirty words, I watched Lakia, a half-sister of her father, making overtures to her. "Come and sit on my knee," said the woman, patting her lap. "I think I have something for you here in my basket—something you'll like. Let's both have a look together." "Go along with you," the grandmother gently chided, as the child hung back and clung to her skirts. "Go along. You don't want Hogbin to think that you're a silly girl who is afraid of her aunt, do you? Lakia won't hurt you. See what she has in her basket. I expect it's a red banana—I told her you liked them —or perhaps it's a ripe mango." Greed at last overcame Jaga's reluctance, and, although she would not sit on Lakia's lap, she consented to accept several mouthfuls of fruit. This performance had to be repeated many times before she began running spontaneously to meet her aunt with a greeting.

Once the child's confidence has been won, occasional offers to look after it are expected. Thus Jauon used to spend about one day in ten in the care of her father's sister, a near neighbour, and one every two or three weeks with her mother's eldest sister, who lived at some distance. These invitations, said the natives, enabled her to learn who her kinsfolk were.

The wives of neighbours also display a friendly interest, especially if bound to one or other of the parents by close blood ties. In that case they not only pick the child up, pet it, and give it food, but make a point also of trying to comfort it if for some reason it is in distress. A number of the women, too, seem to be of a particularly affectionate disposition and, as the natives point out, are always going out of the way to be kind. Their houses are often full of children to whom they may not be closely related, and they frequently give away small baskets full of cooked food.

Apart from the grandfathers and the brothers of the father and of the mother, who consistently try to win the child's affection, the male relatives take little notice of it as yet. Its place, they maintain, is in the house with the women, and they have no wish to have their discussions disturbed until it can understand what they are talking about. The grandfather and the uncles, like the father, often nurse it within the family circle, however, and also play games and tell it simple stories. Grandfathers and grandchildren use the reciprocal term *bum,* and mother's brother and sister's children the word *wawam;* the father's brothers are addressed by their personal names.

WEANING

So long as the infant is at ease only with its mother, her breasts are considered to be indispensable for the sake both of nourishment and of comfort. But by about the end of the third year, when other relatives, through their warm friendliness, have succeeded in winning its confidence, weaning is considered to be advisable. If a child were suckled much longer it would be dependent on its mother for life, I was informed, and grow up weak and sickly.

A definite technique is seldom necessary, and most women succeed in inculcating a preference for solid foods by gentle persuasion. "Come, come, my child, you have grown too big now for my nipple," I used to hear them chiding. "The breast is for little babies, not for a big boy like you. Look at your father: nobody suckles him. He eats taro, sweet potatoes, and fish. You've tasted them, too, and you know you like them. Why don't you ask him to give you some? Don't be afraid. Go along and say, 'Father, I want some taro. I'm tired of mother's milk.' " Judicious praise followed if the child made the proper response—"That's a good fellow; you know what is good for you—what will make you grow fast and be a big man." If such methods fail, as they occasionally do, the women fall back on joking and sometimes ask the bystanders to join them in good-natured banter. I one day saw a woman pick up an earth worm, too, and conceal it in her basket. "I'll pretend that it came out of my breast next time my son wants me to suckle him," she explained. "Nothing I say has any effect, but he won't like seeing a worm alongside his mouth."

Emotional upsets seem to result only on the rare occasions when the mother has become pregnant too soon and is forced to wean the child before its interest in the kinsfolk has fully developed. The process, instead of being gradual, is then as rapid as possible, for further suckling is supposed to be injurious to the embryo. She smears her nipples either with bitter herbs or with mud, which she declares, with great disgust, to be fæces. This rude severing of ties distresses the child considerably, and the relationship between the two is often shaken to its foundations. Jaga, for example, after Yakena had conceived once more, at first spent several days weeping in a dark corner and then concentrated all her affections on her grandmother. "Go away, go away; bad mother," she screamed in babyish accents as she threw herself into the old woman's arms at her mother's approach. The villagers disapproved of Yakena for having been so indifferent to her daughter's health and happiness as to have had sexual intercourse so soon and stated that the little girl would probably feel resentment for a long time. "It's always the same when this sort of thing happens," my friend Jaua told me. "The child leaves its mother for the father or one of its grandparents, and sometimes never listens to her again afterwards." The number of inadequately spaced births was too small to enable me to state definitely that he was right.

PLAY

Children continue with their play even when infancy is at an end and, until the eighth year is reached, are usually left to amuse themselves at home on about four days in every five.

For a year or two boys and girls run about together, but the villages are small, and one seldom sees a gathering of more than half a dozen. Swimming is probably the most popular pastime, though such games as cat's cradles, wrestling, hide and seek, and football, using a round fruit instead of a ball, are also played. Imitating the activities of the elders is another favourite sport, but play marriages, common elsewhere in Melanesia, do not take place. Competitiveness is almost never in evidence, and if planning is necessary one or other of the elder boys, usually he who thought of the game first, makes the arrangements and gives the orders.

Grandmothers and unmarried girls are the usual guardians, but, if two or three women, all neighbours, have no convenient relative in their households, they sometimes accept this responsibility in rotation. They seldom take part in the game but remain close at hand with one eye on what is happening, ready to rebuke horseplay or murmur comfort if someone is hurt. Both the father and the mother, on their return from work in the evening, display a mild interest in how the day has been spent, and not infrequently their suggestions for new activities are accepted for the next day.

The Dap children generally played on the beach not far from my house, and the following account of what took place on three different occasions is taken practically *verbatim* from my notebooks.

One day when I was watching them the old woman Gabwe had been entrusted with Gwa and Jaga, her grandson and granddaughter respectively; Kalasika and Niabula, the young sons of two neighbours; and Wanai, the daughter of a third. As I came on the scene all five were splashing in the water and laughing gaily. Suddenly Gwa called out, "I am a shark!" and began biting Kalasika's toes. This led to a wrestling match, though after about ten minutes they were so exhausted that they had to lie down on the beach to recover breath. The rest at first sat watching, but Jaga soon became bored and climbed into Gabwe's arms where she went to sleep. After a time Wanai, too, walked away, but, in searching in the village for something to eat, she unearthed a piece of string and on her return persuaded Niabula to make cat's cradles with her. The other two boys had in the meantime gone back to the water, where they once more pretended to be sharks. Niabula joined them after an interval, but when they both chased him and gave him a ducking, he fled in terror to Gabwe, who scolded Gwa and told him that he would be punished if he did not moderate his boisterous behaviour. Wanai was now busily making mud pies and at this point begged Kalasika to build her an oven where these might be cooked. Gwa joined in the game, and, although no fire was kindled, the grubby mess was wrapped in leaves and put into the middle of a pile of stones. Wanai next made out that her water bottles were empty and told Niabula to fill them. "No, that's women's work," said Gwa. "We men don't touch such things. You go yourself." An argument would have developed had not Gabwe interposed and persuaded them all to sit down and play a hand game with little white stones.

On another occasion when Gabwe was minding Gwa and Jaga they were joined first by ten-year-old Keke, from the next house, and then by Nyem, one of the headman Marigum's wives, who was at home looking after her co-wife's daughter Jauon. The women seated themselves under a tree and, wanting an uninterrupted chat, told Keke to see that the two small children did not get into mischief. She played hide and seek with them for a time but was then persuaded by Gwa to teach him some new cat's cradles, at which she was particularly expert. Jaga and Jauon were much too energetic to sit still for long, however, and within a quarter of an hour they had walked off to a pile of wet charcoal and ashes. After covering themselves from head to foot, they pranced up to their nurses and danced around them, uttering blood-curdling yells. Shocked at the filth, the women told them to go down to the sea at once and wash. Keke followed guiltily and gave them a good scrubbing but later returned to Gwa and went on with her cat's cradles. That evening he proudly showed his father the two new figures he had learnt, thereby earning congratulations on his skill.

An instance of the children's fascination with the doings of their elders occurred at a later date when young Tabulbul organized a food distribution in imitation of one that had taken place the previous day. He and his sister, Mwago, were spending the morning with their aunt, and Gabwe, as usual, was looking after Gwa, Niabula, and Wanai (Jaga had been taken on a visit to relatives in Mwarok village). The two groups soon joined forces, and Tabulbul, as the eldest, began telling the others what to do. He first set them collecting round pebbles, which, he stated, were coconuts. When sufficient had been accumulated, he declared that he, Mwago, and Gwa were the Dap folk, and that Wanai and Niabula were the inhabitants of Kinaba and Job respectively, the two neighbouring villages. "Now let us fetch mats for the display of our coconuts," he ordered, and forthwith began to lay out a row of leaves and set the pebbles on top. Niabula brought his pile along next, and Wanai added her quota at the end. "The Kinaba villagers bring short measure, as we expected," Gwa muttered, repeating word for word what he had heard his father saying. Then, seeing a butterfly, he ran off after it, crying out that here was a pig to add to the other food. Tabulbul tried to recall him with the reminder that pigs and coconuts are not given away together, but he refused to listen and, having at last caught it, proudly brought it along. "Let us carve it properly," he said, and for the next quarter of an hour the pebbles were forgotten while the butterfly was solemnly disembowelled and cut into joints. Mwago became so fascinated, in fact, that she ignored the distribution entirely and spent the rest of the morning making an oven and cooking her share of the "meat." The other four divided the pebbles, and then Wanai went away to sit with Gabwe, leaving the boys to have a swim by themselves.

Play continues to be of importance during late childhood, but, as most children have by now developed a sense of responsibility, an increasing amount of time is spent in learning the different kinds of work traditionally associated with their sex.

The boys attach themselves to the father and do their best to help him at garden work, fishing, and other tasks. As they cannot yet be trusted to look after themselves properly, however, he is still forced to leave them at home if he expects the job in hand to occupy his full attention. On such occasions they wander off looking for entertainment with other lads who have also been left behind. Sporting with the girls is forbidden, since association with females is considered at this stage to be likely to stunt their growth, but, to judge from the complete indifference of those I knew best, the prohibition is probably unnecessary.

There are no regular gangs, for few villages can assemble more than six small boys—Dap had only four—and even these are seldom all at home together. The neighbouring settlements may provide a couple more, but the average group seems to number about four or five. Swimming, wrestling, football, and hide and seek still hold out attractions, but there are now a number of new amusements, including fishing, sailing model canoes, shooting at birds with arrows, and fighting with spears from reeds. Headmen's sons now act as leaders, and, although others make suggestions, theirs is the final decision about what shall be done.

As in earlier years, a keen interest is taken in food distributions and similar ceremonial, and fish are often divided with great formality. Once the boys pass their eighth year, however, warnings are issued against imitating religious ritual, and one of the more familiar myths relates of how Wofa and his playmates were killed for this offence. Yet Sabwakai, the headman Marigum's youngest boy aged about ten, one day persuaded a number of his contemporaries to hold a series of mock initiation ceremonies deep in the bush where no woman was likely to see. The men, on hearing what had occurred, were appalled at the sacrilege and gave them all a sound thrashing.

Youths in their early teens are usually too much caught up in adult concerns to have much time to spare for games with the children during the day, but one occasionally sees them hurling a ball about or racing model canoes. The evenings are devoted to recreation, nevertheless, and they either sit singing songs and playing the flute and hand-drum or else, on moonlit nights, join the smaller boys for a romp in the centre of the village.

The girls become conscious of their social liabilities at about the same time as the boys, in the eighth year, and from then onwards the majority make determined efforts to assist their mothers in every way possible. Their absorption into the life of the grown-ups is more rapid than is the case with their brothers, and during late childhood and early youth their play is confined almost entirely to the occasions when they are helping an older woman to mind the little ones. Small groups sometimes sit together over a cat's cradle, but one or other is soon called away to look after the baby, fill the water bottles, or fetch stones for the oven. Far from being a nuisance in the house or garden, where the women's work is mainly done, even the smallest girl is useful, and instead of being left to wander about with a playmate, she trails behind the mother almost everywhere.

THE COMMUNITY AND THE CHILD

In spite of their provision for its amusement, the adults consider that, once the child is weaned, it can be regarded as already in some degree a responsible being worthy of admission to a place in their own world. While this opinion is hasty, no doubt, when its backwardness is taken into consideration, one must bear in mind that infants have far more experience of everyday life than is customary for older children in our own society. The more important activities are carried out in their presence practically from birth and thus have few closed secrets even when the details of the different techniques, and the reasons for their employment, are as yet unknown. Many matters relating to sex, although not all of them, are freely discussed in front of the children, and by the third year they will almost certainly have been in the presence of death. Care is indeed taken to bring everyone, including the babies, to the bedside of dying relatives, who are induced, if possible, to speak a word or two in farewell.

The child's change in status after weaning is illustrated by the new arrangements in the gardens, where special allotments are now set aside and referred to as its property. Wiawia, when showing me a patch of bush that he had just finished fencing, pointed out the two sections allocated to Gwa and Jaga. "This is the little girl's first garden," he explained. "She's just been weaned, you see, and now has her own plot. Yes, you're quite right: she's far too small to do any of the work. But her mother and I will say to her, 'This ground is yours,' and she'll soon understand. We shall put the seedlings aside and plant them next time we make a garden in a similar area. Then, when she and Gwa grow up, they'll be able to cultivate the descendants of these very plants."

The child also has a couple of young pigs assigned to it and, in the evenings, at feeding time, is encouraged to call them by name. Some parents even make pretence of consulting a youthful "owner" and asking permission before a beast is killed, and I have once or twice known men apologise for failure to contribute to a feast on the grounds that the only pig available belonged to a young son who had made it a special pet. Such explanations were criticized afterwards as flimsy or frivolous, but the fact that they were offered at all argues some recognition of the child's property rights.

Again, the presence of the children at dances is taken for granted, and on such occasions their decorations are almost as carefully arranged as those of their elders. The youngsters stand alongside the principal performers, imitating them as best they can, often, as is freely admitted, to the detriment of the general effect. No one ever seems to think of sending them away, unless, as I once saw happen, somebody trips over them and falls.

But perhaps the most striking proof of the grown-ups' acceptance of the child as already one of themselves is provided by their frequent long-winded explanations. Few orders are given without the wisdom of the course suggested being pointed out, and force is only applied after persuasion fails. Thus a small boy who picks up a knife is cautioned of the danger he is running before being ordered to put it down, and the slap following an unheeded warning is administered not so much to punish disobedience as to discourage foolishness.

Similar explanations accompany moral training, and, when Gwa displayed some unwillingness to hand half a biscuit to a playmate, his grandmother gave him a long lecture in which she went into a multitude of details of what might happen *if* he became notorious for his meanness. His friend would talk about him behind his back, she averred, and he would have such a bad name that when he married and had a family—he was then between four and five!—no one would help him to make his gardens.

Finally, every child old enough to be trusted is expected to help its elders according to its capacity. Such assistance is taken for granted, and the grown-ups rely upon it to such an extent that I have twice known parents refuse permission when a daughter only seven years of age had been invited to visit another village at a time when they were engaged in some heavy undertaking. Boys and girls are always being sent on errands—to fetch fire from a neighbour, to find a forgotten handbag, to borrow tobacco, or to carry messages—and I often heard the adults, when making plans for the morrow, allocating light, but nevertheless essential, tasks to them.

As is to be expected, the youngsters in turn give every indication of regarding themselves as an integral part of the social organization. In their relations with me, for example, they identified themselves with their culture, and, on my asking them the reason for a particular line of behaviour, generally replied, with a sniff at my ignorance, "That is our custom, the custom of us people of Wogeo." A remarkable instance of a child identifying himself with the grown-ups took place when a number of us were discussing the habits of the natives on the mainland. At one stage a man who had just returned from spending a number of years on a plantation informed us that the people of the village nearby were accustomed to seeking intercourse at all times, even when the women were menstruating. "Disgusting!" exclaimed a lad of seven. "Why, our imbecile knows better than that." He was unlikely to have any sexual experience for the next decade, but no one smiled or seemed to think him precocious.

Another boy, Tabulbul, already referred to, was so well aware of his claim to the land his father had cultivated that he left his widowed mother when only seven years old in order to be near it. On her husband's death three years before she had brought her young family from his village to Dap, where her brother lived. "I am tired of walking between the two places," Tabulbul told me, "and have left Dap to stay with my father's kinsmen. I can't look after my land properly if I live with my mother."

EDUCATION

Yet, for all their ready adoption of the elders' point of view, the upbringing of the young is not allowed to become a mere haphazard process. The natives have a definite concept of education, for which they use the word *singara,* the primary meaning of which is "steering." Children, they maintain, have to be guided in order to achieve technical knowledge and a proper sense of right and wrong. One of the chief disadvantages orphans have to overcome is lack of deliberate instruction—they are forced to pick up what they can from this house and that, to learn without being taught.

The guiding hand of the grown-ups is particularly in evidence when the boys decide to have a game with model canoes. Each lad makes a vessel for himself, and the party then adjourns to the shallow water off the beach. The men as a rule sit watching and afterwards give a detailed commentary on the different craft taking part. This one, they point out, was unwieldy because the outrigger booms were too long, that one went crab-fashion because the float was crooked, the sail of a third was too small to take full advantage of the wind, and a fourth would have been more stable with a few stones in the hull. The patience of one man when his little son, too unskilled as yet to carve a model out of wood, had fashioned a rough craft from half a coconut shell, was most touching. He treated the boy's efforts with the utmost seriousness, and his criticism could hardly have been more carefully phrased if the canoe had been a masterpiece of ingenuity. Suggestions are usually put to the proof at once and additional information sought if a prediction fails to come true.

Children are also encouraged to work side by side with their parents even when their efforts are likely to be a hindrance. Thus when Marigum was making a new canoe he allowed his youngest son, Sabwakai, to take an adze and chip at the dugout. On my enquiring whether the boy did not impede his progress, the father agreed that he would be able to work faster alone. "But if I send the child away," he added, "how can I expect him to know anything? This time he was in the way, but I'm showing him, and when we have to make another canoe he'll be really useful."

The children are in most cases even more eager to learn than the elders are to teach. Sabwakai took up the adze on his own initiative and on another occasion asked permission to come along with his father to one of our conferences at my house. "By listening to what I tell you," the father explained to me with a smile, "he thinks he'll find out about the things he'll have to do when he's a man."

Moral training is also considered to be necessary, and, although I doubt whether parents are as disinterested as the statement would imply, they usually remark, when forced to administer a slap, "I beat you, but only that you may learn."

A distinction is drawn, however, between naughtiness that is the result of bad upbringing and naughtiness that grows out of inherited temperamental defects. Faults arising from improper teaching are generally supposed to correct themselves when the child grows older and mixes with people outside the immediate family circle—though in practice I found that offences committed by grown-ups are not infrequently attributed to their early home environment. When his eldest son Tafalti quarrelled with him, Marigum insisted, for example, that he had never been able to train him properly in childhood as a grandfather was always interfering and taking the boy's part.

Fundamental vices, on the other hand, are accepted as incurable, and children who are sufficiently unfortunate to be cursed with them are considered certain to remain a problem for life. An anatomical abnormality is thought to be the cause of this misfortune: the duct believed to lead from the outer ear to the lungs, the seat of understanding, is said to be so narrow that, although the superficial indications of perfect hearing may be present, few statements are fully comprehended. "I thought you were a boy like the rest but now begin to believe that you are one of those without ears," I used to hear the parents chide. "My jaw aches from talking, and my hand pains me from beating you, yet still you do not listen. Is it because you cannot? Were you born disobedient and mischievous?"

Sympathy is always expressed for the parents of children of this sort, but strong exception is taken to one whose offspring are unruly for the want of training and discipline. "He's a foolish fellow, the sort who makes us angry," said Waru of Gubale. "It isn't as though his son hadn't any ears, for I know he's a good lad. But he can't learn without help. If someone doesn't act as a father to him soon, he'll turn out a ne'er-do-well."

Leaving aside its practical significance, education is looked upon, quite literally, as a sacred duty. The natives consider that their way of life, having been taken over direct from the heroes of old, the *nanarang,* is the perfect ideal, and just as these beings gave the early ancestors the true refinements of behaviour and the latter in turn taught the inheritance to their children, so each generation is under the obligation of handing it intact to the next.

Such is the respect shown for the work of the culture heroes that I do not exaggerate in saying that the local opinion is that the culture owns the people rather than the reverse. In the course of centuries many changes must have occurred—steel axes and knives, for instance, are now regarded as vital necessities—but a premium is put upon conservatism, and I was frequently informed that innovations cannot be tolerated because the heroes had forestalled all possible improvements. The elders are as much horrified as pained by the new things of the present day, and even the wearing of European clothing calls forth strong criticism. I knew several men of the old school who, with shrill denunciations, refused to allow their daughters to wear dresses, and one who burnt a frock his sister had received as a gift. Considerable moral disapprobation is also felt for such a comparatively minor matter as a breach of the rule that persons of different moieties must not strike one another. No troubles have arisen, however, from infringements of the sexual code, a serious cause of dispute in other Pacific communities, for the natives were promiscuous long before anyone went away to learn different habits on European plantations—indeed, so also were the culture heroes.

The reason most frequently advanced for the practice of adoption gives another illustration of the reverence for the cultural traditions.[7] A man must have someone to watch over his lands and perform the magic the heroes gave to his forebears, and, if unable to beget an heir, he must take over someone else's child and rear the boy as his own. Real distress is often expressed at the decline in population recently noticeable in one or two villages, such as Mwarok. "Who will look after the land?" people ask. "Who will carry out the magic of the Mwarok heroes? We must let the people take some of our children."

Again, a man fearing that he may die before his sons reach maturity teaches his spells to relatives, sometimes even to women, who could not possibly use them, "so that the magic may not perish." "Our fathers gave the magic of the heroes to us," said Jaua, "and we must make certain that our sons receive it also." That this practice is inspired in part by genuine love for the children and a desire to make adequate provision for their future is proved by the promise extracted that the relatives will in due course give the necessary instruction to the true heirs, but this aspect of the question seldom receives explicit recognition.

The culture is so highly valued, and its mastery by the members of the younger generation considered to be so urgent, that the adults take great care to play as prominent a part as possible in its transmission. Association with playmates of the same age has a considerable effect on the child's mental growth, but it is never entrusted to the care of youngsters only a little older than itself for long periods, as has been recorded, for example, in Samoa.[8] Further, if an adolescent girl has to look after a small relative for an odd half hour, as sometimes happens, she does not attempt to bully it into subservience but reasons and argues with it as an adult would do. I one day watched Keke when she was minding a neighbour's little boy, and, although he caused her a great deal of trouble by running into the sun, I noticed that she did not once lose her temper or try to restrain him by force. "See, it is pleasant to sit here in the cool," she kept saying. "The sun is hot, and your head is not yet strong like your father's. The heat doesn't hurt him, but he'd be sitting under this tree here if he wasn't working." At last, finding that she was making no progress, she asked him to be good for her sake, pleading that she would be the one to be whipped if his parents returned and found him playing in the open. On other occasions children begged me to intervene and use my powers of persuasion.

Most of the child's relatives play a part in training it, but the parents are normally the chief instructors. The father is mainly responsible for the son and the mother for the daughter. This association results in a good deal of copying, and I often heard children repeating their parent's pet phrases and characteristic intonations with remarkable accuracy. Adoption is common, and the natives have a saying, "Use your eyes to find out who begot a strange child and your ears to discover who is rearing it"—the implication being that it will resemble its real parents in appearance and its foster parents in speech and behaviour. The similarity is in a number of instances so striking that the child appears to have been invested with the personality of the adult.

TECHNICAL TRAINING

A child acquires the various skills mainly through direct participation in everyday tasks. It may watch the adults for a time and then, without any encouragement imitate them as best it can, but more usually the parents give a demonstration as soon as it displays a marked willingness to assist. The explanations are so detailed that the need for seeking additional information seldom arises, and "why" questions, the everlasting bane of parents in our own community, are rarely heard.

The initial impulse to engage in the activities of the elders arises spontaneously from play motives, and helping with gardening, fishing, and the rest seems for several years to be looked upon as a form of recreation. The child gives its services for the most part willingly enough, however, even after the deeper significance of its efforts have impinged upon its consciousness.

Praise is probably the most effective spur to industry, and I was constantly hearing zeal rewarded with approval. Yet the adults are seldom more than half serious in their tributes, and, although lazy children are sometimes compared to their disadvantage with those who have worked hard, a precocious youngster is never consciously set up as a model to the rest of the village. Everyone is so firmly convinced that physical disaster would result from an immature person working really hard that attempts to create rivalry and competition so early are regarded as out of place. At the same time, the children always welcome commendation, and they often boast loudly of their attainments. The parents only interfere if playmates are openly sneered at or slighted for their lack of ability.

Karui, aged not quite eight, was already taking his labours seriously, and I one day heard him asking his step-father to allow him to plant some banana trees. The man stood behind him the whole time, telling him when the holes were deep enough and how far apart they ought to be, but did not handle either the trees or the digging stick himself. At last, when the job was completed, he asked whether the boy could manage in future by himself. "Yes indeed; I know already," was the reply. "Good! You have done well," the step-father returned. "But you aren't a man yet and you'd better go now and sit down." That evening, when the party returned to the village, Karui began telling his friends of what he had done. "I planted the bananas alone, like a man," he said. "You fellows are still babies, but I now have an orchard of my own." "Enough!" his mother interposed. "You did well, but these boys will soon be planting bananas, too. Your tongue wags too much. Come and feed the pigs."

Clearing the bush seems to excite the children most, and they often ask how long it will be before a new cultivation has to be prepared. Games of hide and seek in the brushwood are admitted to account in part for their enthusiasm, but, in addition, it is said that they love handling knives and axes "as the men do." Worn-out blunted implements are given to them in early childhood, but as soon as they become proficient these are replaced by small tomahawks, and saplings are then set aside for them to cut down.

Instruction in climbing the tall almond trees is unnecessary, for, like European children, these boys go scrambling about in the branches when they are only four or five years old. At seven or eight they begin to accompany their fathers to the nut groves, though for a time they are dissuaded from attempting to reach too great a height. Some children, however, are as expert as their elders, and I often saw Sabwakai picking nuts on a limb over fifty feet above the ground. Once he lost his nerve when out on a branch and began screaming for his father, who was in another tree not far away. Marigum called to him reassuringly—though he told me afterwards that "his belly turned over in anxiety"—and told him how to worm his way backwards to the trunk. A rescue was then effected with the aid of a rope. The old man sat comforting the boy for about an hour but finally suggested that they both go up together. "If you don't climb the tree now you may be frightened to-morrow," he added. "I'll follow close behind and tell you where to put your feet."

The walks to and from the cultivations give an excellent opportunity for indicating the different allotments into which the country is divided. "This piece of ground on the right here, from the stream to the big ficus tree yonder, is called Suaua," the parents explained. "Jaua makes his gardens there. Then on the left the ground is called Maeva all the way to the three heaps of rock by the side of the path. It belongs to Marigum." The child soon absorbs the information and when still quite small is able to answer the enquiries of visitors who sometimes pretend ignorance to test its knowledge.

Participation in fishing expeditions begins at about the age of four or five, when the father takes the boy out with him in a canoe. If he cries or is for some reason restless and troublesome—as Gwa was—a second trip may be postponed for several months, but this is on the whole unusual. At first the father only remains at sea about an hour, carefully choosing either a dull day or late afternoon to avoid all risk of sunburn or headaches. The boy sits at the bow and is allowed to splash with a paddle until the fishing grounds are reached, but when the line is baited one end is fastened to the outrigger boom in case a fish should bite while he is not paying attention. As he becomes more experienced the elders explain the methods of catching the different species, and within a few years his haul is a valuable addition to the larder. They also point out dangerous currents, tide rips, and hidden rocks and give lessons in steering and handling the canoe in a choppy sea.

A boy in his teens sometimes tries a younger brother out by persuading him to come for a short voyage and then leaping into the sea and swimming ashore from a distance of two or three hundred yards. As a rule both enjoy the sport thoroughly, though young Niabula was stricken with terror and made no effort to prevent himself from drifting away from the island. His brother in desperation at last put out in another craft and fetched him back.

The girls play at work just like the boys. Jaga had her little garden basket almost before she could carry herself properly, and I often saw her in the evenings marching off with the women to the spring with a small coconut water bottle slung over her shoulder. The procession also included Mwago, aged five, who was able to carry two bottles, and Keke, who, at ten, took nearly a full load. Keke was already of great assistance, too, in carrying home vegetables; her basket often held five or six pounds, and on one occasion she staggered in with nearly twelve. A relative informed me that she had wanted to fill it to the brim and had had to be restrained lest she should injure her back.

The first serious task entrusted to the little girls in the garden is scraping the earth from the tubers, but long before this I used to see them playing round with a digging stick. Mwago one day planted twenty new shoots, under her mother's supervision, an accomplishment of which she boasted several times to her companions. By the time they are ten or eleven many of them can safely be entrusted with their own small allotments. "This taro is from Keke's garden," her mother anounced one evening as the food was handed round to a group of guests. "She dug it up this morning all by herself." On the conclusion of the meal, when the party moved outside, one of the visitors began telling a neighbour about the child's proficiency. "If she continues to be as busy as this," he concluded, "some man will soon be wanting her to marry him."

Housework begins with various odd jobs, such as putting the sliced food into the cooking pot, throwing away the rubbish, and sweeping the floor. The child's efforts are sometimes more bother than help, but the mother does not complain unless she is in a hurry. "I'll send her away presently and do it again myself," whispered Mwago's aunt to me as the child struggled valiantly with a broom as big as herself. But on the following afternoon the little girl sat weeping in a corner, because, as the aunt explained, she had been prevented from cracking any of the nuts for the evening meal. "She doesn't yet understand how to tap the shell properly, and when she works with us the kernels are all smashed," said the woman. "That doesn't matter if we are alone, but to-night we have visitors."

The earlier efforts at cooking have to be closely watched, but girls of about ten or twelve can usually, if necessary, prepare certain dishes unaided. Keke was so pleased when her first vegetable stew was pronounced satisfactory that she told the whole village and the next night insisted on making another pot for presentation to various relatives. A cousin of much the same age thereupon begged to be allowed to try her hand, and for the next week the two of them exchanged platters nearly every evening. Yet, though they both basked in the compliments showered on them, neither sought to prove that her own dishes were superior.

Now successful in this sphere, the two of them decided that they were old enough to make their own petticoats. Their mothers accordingly showed them how to prepare the fibre, attach it to the belt, and cut it evenly into a series of fringes, and within a few weeks the two of them were running from house to house showing off their workmanship. The same friendly spirit was still in evidence, and Keke actually waited till the cousin's garment was completed before donning her own.

Morals

In moral training the practical issues are stressed, and the elders quote the maxim that friends are more helpful than enemies if behaviour seems likely to give offence. Any ethical reasons for exercising restraint are ignored, and the fact that honesty is the best policy is the most cogent argument by far in its favour. Thus the stock admonition if children begin meddling with other people's belongings is simply, "That's his; he'll be cross if you break it; better not touch it."

Again, no one ever tries to shame a child into conducting himself properly; the emphasis is laid rather on the injunction that he should not cause embarrassment to others. When he engages in a wordy argument, for example, and seems to be about to insult his companions, he is told that if his remarks are going to be unpalatable he had better keep them to himself. Warnings are also issued against further humiliating a playmate who has been reproved. "Continue with your game," the parents of the other children whisper. "Don't let him see that you heard. He will be angry with you for making him feel ashamed."

It is worth drawing attention to the contrast between this type of educational practice and that of Malaita, one of the Solomon Islands. There the parents consciously strive to inculcate feelings of personal responsiblity; a child who interferes with someone else's property is told not, "That's his; he'll be cross if you break it; better not touch it," but "That isn't yours; put it down," and one who has made fun of companions after a rebuke has the enormity of his offence brought home to him by some such remark as that he ought to go and hide his head for having said such things. It is no accident that in Malaita there is a word closely corresponding with our term "conscience," a concept conspicuously absent from the Wogeo tongue. Wogeo behaviour is ruled not by a still small voice but by the notion of what other people's reactions may be. If they are unlikely to be annoyed or there is a reasonable chance of them not being able to pin the guilt on a particular person, almost anything is permitted.

Inside the household a good deal of easy freedom obtains, and, although technically every single object is individually owned, husband and wife share their tools and all other possessions save clothing with the greatest goodwill. The child is allowed the same latitude, and, as most things for which it asks are handed over, without demur, it speaks of them as "our" rather than as "father's or "mother's." Axes and knives, which until weaning are kept hidden, are withheld for a few months afterwards, but the parents are more occupied with the dangers of careless handling than with any notions of property.

The neighbour's property, on the other hand, is respected, and a person wishing to borrow from another, unless the two are closely related or great friends, always asks permission and apologizes for his intrusion. The children are accordingly cautioned not to touch things when paying calls for fear of arousing the host's resentment. Gwa, on being reproved for playing with the platter in the house of a neighbour, replied that he would be careful. "What about the oil that Karui upset in our fireplace yesterday," his father reminded him in a whisper, "Karui is a big boy, bigger than you, yet he let the bottle fall, and you know how cross we all felt. You wouldn't like the people here to say the same things about you that we said about him, would you? That's right. Put it down and sit still."

Visiting houses and gardens in the absence of the owners is also deprecated, because, if afterwards something is found to be missing, suspicion inevitably rests upon those seen in the vicinity.

About meanness, however, the people have somewhat stronger feelings: they stress that it is unwise but indicate that it is also disgraceful. The parents are accordingly at great pains to make the child generous, coaxing him at first but not hesitating, if necessary, to use blows. Liberality, they point out, ensures both a return of hospitality and an abundance of helpers, but the sweetness of charity for its own sake is never quite lost sight of. Kasule's advice to her seven-year-old son Tabulbul, with the moral aspect touched upon as a sort of afterthought, is characteristic. "Always take care to see that those who enter this house leave it with full bellies," she told him. "Learn to give away food now and continue giving after I am dead. If you do this people will never let you be hungry no matter how far you have to go. Besides, giving away food is good." At this point, an uncle interposed and reminded the boy that he must also think about enlisting aid in his cultivations. "If you're mean," he said, "no one—no, not one—will help you in your gardens." The anticipation of such difficulties by fifteen years or so did not strike him, or anyone else, as being funny.

The parents always hand gifts to the children for presentation to relatives and also expect them to help in the entertainment of guests. The mother, when serving the meal, calls the younger member of the family to her side and sets a woven platter in its arms. "Take this to our kinsman over there and set it neatly at his feet," she whispers. "He is of our blood, and we must be careful to have something ready for him to eat." The father meantime smiles encouragement and grows expansive about the child's lofty motives. "See, our little daughter is sorry for those who travel far," he exclaims in a loud voice. "She says to herself, 'Let me care for this man's aching limbs by filling his belly.' No one is permitted to leave this house hungry if she is at hand." Bwa turned to me on one occasion as her little girl re-entered the house after taking a dish of food to her grandfather next door and remarked in a loud aside, "There, wasn't I telling you that Gaus is already a good grand-daughter? She is sorry for the old man and always makes me give him a meal even if we have to go short ourselves." "Nonsense," I replied—I knew Bwa and her husband well—"she's much too small; and besides, you know you always have plenty to spare." "That's true," Bwa answered; "but when Gaus has grown only a little bigger she'll be thinking of her grandfather first."

The lesson is at times learned only too well, and more of the family supplies given away than can actually be spared. Gwa, for example, was most puzzled at being reprimanded for handing a bundle of tobacco leaves intended for household consumption to a group of men who were passing through the village on the way to a funeral—as he said, he was merely following instructions. His father told him that in future he had better confine his giving to his own property and wait and see what other people had to say before making free with theirs.

The attitude to emotional outbursts is equally practical; personal dignity is felt to be of infinitely less importance than the amity of the village, and parents are much concerned with directing the child's anger along harmless channels. Cooperation, which benefits everyone, would be impossible, they explain, without the appearance of goodwill, and free outlet for every minor grievance is therefore unwise. Yet no demand is made for the complete suppression of feelings, for the people believe that a permanent state of tension might then develop. The relevant maxim that is almost always quoted runs, "If you are angry, smash a pot; otherwise you'll be angry for a month."

Quarrelling is strictly forbidden, and the most easy-going parent always interferes at the first sign of violence. "What, you would strike a kinsman! That is wrong," he scolds as he drags the delinquents apart. "Kinsmen help one another: they never fight. Do you think that the boy you've hit will like you afterwards? And if he doesn't like you, what will he say when you ask for his help?" If really angry the children express their resentment with unrestrained passion and roll on the ground screaming and frothing at the mouth. Usually, however, the elders lead them away in opposite directions, present them with an axe, and tell them to take out their rage on a tree. Most of the big timber close to the villages is as a result deeply scarred.

The elders do their best to comfort a child who is out of temper, but abandonment to the emotions is normally accepted with complacency; the culprit is hurting no one but himself. The treatment seems to be successful, for even when children sulk with one another for a week, they seldom attempt to renew the fight.

Such tantrums and weeping fits are liable to take place even in the boy's early teens if he is temporarily deserted, on account of some important undertaking, by a relative with whom he is particularly intimate, usually the father or grandfather. So intense may his misery be that hasty efforts are sometimes made at great inconvenience to bring the missing parent or grandparent back.

The female nature is supposed to be less violent than the male, and little girls are, in fact, more self-controlled. "Tears from a girl!" the mother exclaims in mock astonishment if they weep or fly into a rage. "Why, perhaps she's a boy after all. She'll be growing a penis next." The reason for the rarity of such outbursts is clear: the girl's life of freedom ends so much earlier than that of their brothers, and after about the eighth year, instead of associating with playmates, they accompany the women.

MORALS AND MYTHOLOGY

Myths provide an ultimate standard for judging—and justifying—conduct. The ancient culture heroes did not, however, in their divine wisdom, present men with a Decalogue for guidance; instead, some of them stole and were punished, others suffered for being mean, and others, again, brought misfortune upon themselves by bad temper, disobedience and unkindness.

Knowledge of the stories forms a part of everyone's equipment, and in the course of a few years the children hear dozens. Indeed, they often repeat them for their own entertainment, not infrequently developing remarkable dramatic talents in the process. Different voices are assumed for the various heroes and their actions cleverly imitated. (A favourite cycle gives the doings of Wonka and his two foolish brothers, Yabuk, who roared like a volcano when he spoke, and Magaj, who squeaked like a mouse.)

The more important myths are told with a good deal of solemnity, but the moral content is not specifically indicated, and recitals are never preceded by any such remark as, "Disobedience is wrong; listen to what happened to the hero who disobeyed his parents." Yet the point of an argument is sometimes underlined by a reference to the appropriate culture hero, and, in addition, oblique references, not unlike our own to such biblical characters as the Good Samaritan and the Painted Jezebel, are not infrequently used with the implication that a certain line of conduct is worthy either of praise or blame.

Myths are approached, nevertheless, in a realistic spirit. When they are told formally, it is true, the accent is on the moral content—a certain hero stole and was punished for it; thieving is therefore unwise. But after listening to fireside conversations I came to the conclusion that the actions of these beings may also be used as sanctions for behaviour that is in fact anti-social. Thus a person who covets something belonging to a member of another village is as likely as not to ignore the hero's fate and to argue that, as stealing was apparently common in the past, there is no reason why he should not help himself.

A detailed account of the mythology would be out of place here, and I shall content myself with summarizing one or two of the tales.

The first relates of how two children were punished for thieving. Kanak-Bokeboken ("crooked betel-pepper") and Bua-Bokeboken ("crooked areca nut"), when left in the village to play, entered every house and took all the food, with which they stuffed their bellies to bursting point. After sleeping for a short space they decided to express their pleasure by decorating themselves and dancing. But towards evening they grew frightened and hid in a tree. As they had feared, the grown-ups were indignant, and the probable consequences of return appeared to be so unpleasant that they re-mained where they were. Days passed, and one boy, who had put on a tail of coconut leaves, turned into a bird-of-paradise, while the other, who was wearing a coronet of pandanus, became a cockatoo. They flew away to the mainland, never to return (birds-of-paradise and cockatoos are not found on Wogeo).

Another story tells of how a woman, distressed by her son's constant disobedience, made him kill her. In her despair she had run away weeping into the forest, but when he at last found her she lied and told him that her tears were merely the result of a painful boil on her left breast. Taking his dagger, the boy proceeded to lance what looked like a small tumour. "Deeper, deeper," said his mother, and the weapon finally pierced her heart.

A number of folk tales teach similar lessons. A typical example gives an account of how a tree-climbing kangaroo paid his guests out for eating all his food. He discovered that he could catch crabs easily by putting his tail into their holes and flicking it to the surface as soon as he felt a nip at the end, and he decided to invite all his kangaroo friends to let them into the secret. They were so greedy, however, that nothing was left for the host, who accordingly followed them home and, after they had climbed into the branches for the night, scratched the trunks of all the trees. The natives of the neighbouring village, seeing the marks, set traps, and the kangaroos were all killed.

PUNISHMENT

Continued misbehaviour is met first by sarcasm or intimidation. The parents suggest that the child is, after all, not human but a ghost or that it must surely belong to another district; or they say that it will receive no pork when the next pig is killed, that they will banish it to the forest, or that they will report its naughtiness to the headman. In practice, however, they never even put it supperless to bed, and they are much too afraid of sorcerers to send it away from the village. The headman, if he hears his name mentioned, may deliver a short lecture, but discipline is felt to be a family affair, and he takes no steps to administer punishment. The children soon learn that they have little to fear, though the disapproving tone in which the elders speak generally has the effect of making them mend their ways. "He knows quite well that he'll have his share of pork," Wiawia told me after he had been scolding Gwa. "But he's also aware that I only threaten him when I'm vexed. As soon as I've let him see that I'm really cross he obeys me."

The spirits are supposed to take almost no interest in the doing of mortals, and the children are in consequence never terrorized by talk of supernatural intervention. Parents sometimes tell them half playfully that the forest spirits will take them away, and I heard references on several occasions to the bogey-man Karibua, who steals children when they refuse to go to sleep, but the lack of conviction is so very apparent that nobody takes much notice. I knew of only one child, Niabula, who was seriously frightened, and it is significant that his mother at once began to reassure him that there was no truth in what she had been saying. She and her husband later agreed that, as the boy was more than usually nervous, they had better refrain in future from letting the names of the spirits pass their lips.

Illness and death are supposed to follow if adequate precautions are neglected when a person has come into contact with the world of the sacred, but young children are carefully excluded from the religious life of the community and removed to a distance during the performance of important ceremonies. The men's house, where various sacred objects are stored, remains a potential danger, nevertheless, and they are repeatedly warned that entry is forbidden. "Come away, come away," the adults call urgently if they venture too close. "The men's house is for grown men only; to you it is death." The height of the building from the ground presents an obstacle to very small children, and I was acquainted with but one lad who followed his father inside. "Cover the masks," the man exclaimed in great agitation when he noticed the child at his heels. Then, carrying him quickly outside, he patiently explained the terrible risk and probable consequences of future disobedience. No one could have doubted his real concern, and the boy was certainly aware that he was not being fobbed off with excuses.

Food cooked by women who are menstruating has also to be avoided,

though not until after about the eighth year. Children are from this age onwards cautioned, too, against touching their mother during her periods.

The adults' fear of black magic becomes so apparent after a death has
occurred in suspicious circumstances that the children are inevitably impressed, and even the tiny tots are apprehensive. A wave of alarm sweeps
through the village, and for the space of several days little else is discussed.
Plans for visiting distant places are temporarily abandoned, and no one
now stirs more than a few yards from the village without a companion for
fear that he should come face to face with the sorcerer.

If the child's naughtiness continues unabated after it has been warned to
stop, the parents next threaten it with violence. "I'll cut you into little pieces
if you don't cease making that noise at once," Karui's step-father shouted
when the boy banged an empty tin a few yards from the house and pretended to sing. "Fetch that firestick from Waru immediately or I'll smash
your head in as if it were a coconut," Sabuk yelled to Manoua on another
occasion. Gwa's father told him, too, that he would whip him till the blood
flowed down like rain. Yet when driven at last to action the elders are
usually satisfied with boxing the child's ears, cuffing it on the back of the
head, or belabouring it once or twice round the shoulders—never on the
buttocks—with a stick. They strike only when, tried beyond endurance, they
momentarily lose control of themselves, but everyone maintains the fiction
of being inspired by the loftiest motives. "We hit the children only to teach
them," they insist, and I have actually heard a man say, as he banged his
son on the head, "Alas, I don't want to hit you, but you won't learn otherwise." The bystanders preserve the illusion by reiterating, "Teach him,
teach him," or "Good; slap him to make him do as you say in future."[9]

Punishment is usually inflicted by the parents, but uncles, aunts, and
other relatives have few scruples if the child is particularly troublesome.
The fact that they help to feed it is held to give them the right of correction,
and objections are only raised if the blows are unduly hard.

Wogeo women are almost as heavy-handed as the men and would certainly not subscribe to the theory that discipline is the prerogative of the
father. Children in consequence are never subjected to the torture of awaiting a thrashing in the evening after his return. Execution is, indeed, immediate, and, if no steps are taken to implement a threat at the moment of its
utterance, it is invariably forgotten.

The injury to personal dignity is resented most, and the lighter taps are
followed by floods of tears, even after teen age has been reached, when
force is very rarely resorted to. The child's hands are held if it attempts to
hit back, and after a time it usually retires by itself to some quiet corner
or else visits a relative. Those of especially violent disposition may hurl
stones, however, and Sabwakai once made a cut at least two inches long
in his mother's cheek. Frightened by what he had done, he made no attempt
to escape when his father gave him a good hiding. When on another occa-

sion a little girl snatched a knife and attacked her mother, the father quickly seized her arm and urged her to cut down a tree if she felt angry.

After the lapse of an hour or two the parent makes an attempt to regain the child's confidence. He puts an arm lovingly around its shoulders and either offers it a delicacy or invites it to accompany him to the beach or to the cultivations. The child at first resists the overtures, but he perseveres with further acts of kindness, until in the end relations are back on the old footing.

NOTES

1. It includes, for boys, the first stage of initiation, when the lobe of the ear is pierced, and is brought to a close by the second stage of initiation, when they are seized and carried to a sacred place, to be fed, so it is said, to the spirit monsters, from whose bodies they subsequently emerge wearing clothing for the first time.

2. My paper "The Father Chooses his Heir," *Oceania,* Vol. XI, 1940-1, pp. 1-40, is largely devoted to a consideration of the relationships of Marigum and the members of his family.

3. On occasions when this distinction is of no importance or irrelevant the word *dan* may be used in a general way for all kinsfolk.

4. This portion of my account may be inaccurate in some of its details, for it is in the main based on information supplied by men, who would never on any account have approached while a birth was in progress. I have no doubt that, had I made the request, I would have been permitted to be present; but I came to the conclusion that, identified, as I was, with the male half of the population, I stood to lose more than I would have gained by doing so. I refrained from questioning the women closely on the subject for the same reason, though several were excellent informants.

5. A man is sometimes embarrassed when asked the name of his father, who is always addressed by the kinship term *mam,* but otherwise there are no restrictions, and even relatives by marriage speak of one another without hesitation. Dal's mother calls him by that name unless they are together in her father's village, when she addresses him as "*mam*". Acknowledgment is thus given to the fact that he is called after her father, whose name, Kaneg, however, she is reluctant to utter.

6. The same procedure is followed when a new ceremonial house is named and when certain spirits are summoned from overseas to preside at initiation and other ceremonies.

7. *Vide* I. Hogbin, "Adoption in Wogeo," *Journal of the Polynesian Society,* Vols. XLIV and XLV, 1935-6.

8. *Vide* M. Mead, *Coming of Age in Samoa.*

9. The contrast with Malaita is again interesting: there the adults frankly admit that they whip the child only when angered. As the blow is administered, moreover, instead of pretending an interest in education, they usually made some reference to "payment for disobedience."

12

NAMA CULT OF THE CENTRAL HIGHLANDS, NEW GUINEA

K. E. Read

In this paper I propose to examine a cult of the Gahuku-Gama, a complex of religious and social activities, of beliefs and sentiments, which surrounds the sacred *nama* flutes.[1] I am primarily concerned with the sociological functions of the cult, with the manner in which these inter-related beliefs and activities assist in the regulation, maintenance and transmission of sentiments on which the constitution of Gahuku-Gama society depends. This is the hypothesis formulated by Durkheim, Radcliffe-Brown and others, and while there are many other problems associated with religious belief, I choose to exclude the rest from the present examination.

The Gahuku-Gama are a congeries of tribes numbering about eight thousand people, situated in the vicinity of Goroka in the Central Highlands. They have been known to Europeans for only eighteen years, and though in that time considerable changes have taken place in the groups nearest the Administrative centre, acculturation has not proceeded at a uniform rate throughout the area, and a large proportion of the population still follow the ways of their forefathers, little affected by either Government or Mission agencies. My studies of these people in 1950-51 were the first undertaken by an anthropologist in the Goroka Valley.[2] The Rev. Helbig of the Lutheran Mission had previously studied the local language for a period extending over twelve years, but to date the results of his work have not been published.[3]

The tribes to which I have given the name Gahuku-Gama are a group of people with uniform language and culture. They have no inclusive name for themselves, nor have they a name for the common language.[4] Nevertheless, they are aware of these uniformities, contrasting them with differences from the surrounding peoples, the Bena-Bena to the east, and the Asaro to the west. Extensive trading relationships link them to groups as far away as the Ramu Valley; but, as a whole, the members of the group are more closely related than they are with any peoples beyond their territorial boundaries.

Reproduced by permission of A. P. Elkin, Editor of *Oceania,* and K. E. Read from *Oceania,* 23:1-25 (1952-53).

Sociologically, we may term the Gahuku-Gama a "people," implying by that a group possessing an idea of their common cultural heritage and between whose members there is significant interaction of various kinds which traces out a network of social relationships coincidental with definable territorial limits. The criteria for this definition cannot be discussed here, but warfare may be mentioned since it is both crucial for the definition and is also an element within the *nama* cult.

Component tribes within the Gahuku-Gama people—up to a short time ago—regularly fought with one another. They are linked together on the basis of traditional friendships and corresponding enmities, and warfare (*rova*) between enemy tribes is conceived of as something which is never concluded. It was—and to a certain extent still is—expected as a normal condition of group life; the accepted leaders are pre-eminently the renowned successful warriors, and the formal instruction given to boys and young men emphasizes the importance of this institution. Warfare, however, took place only within the territorial boundaries of the group. It occurred only as a regular expected activity between "known" groups; that is, it did not occur to any great extent between Gahuku-Gama tribes and the outsiders surrounding them, although, in point of fact, the majority of such people were easily accessible.[5] While on the one hand, therefore, warfare is responsible for a complicated pattern of cleavages, it is also a form of co-ordinated activity which, through its aspects of expectation and regulation, characterizes the "in" group as opposed to those known outsiders with whom it did not occur.

Gahuku-Gama culture is characteristically Melanesian in respect of certain salient features. I mention here only the absence of chieftainship and of any *sui generis* political machinery or offices. The political system is essentially similar to that which I have described for the Ngarawapum of the Markham Valley, but with a marked difference in scale.[6] The group, indeed, is numerically much larger than we are accustomed to find in New Guinea, though by no means as large as other Central Highland groups.[7] With the exception of the Kuman and the Mbowamb, segmentation and the inter-relationships between segments are also more complicated than anything to be found in the published literature.[8] I give, therefore, only the barest outline of the social structure.

The tribe is the widest political unit, the largest group within which warfare did not as a rule take place. Fighting was a recognized means of redress between tribal segments, but it was always expected to be concluded, probably with the payment of compensation by the transgressors. The tribe numbers between 500 and 1,000 people, and its members recognize a common inclusive name. They combined for offence against their traditional enemies, and, as far as possible, co-operated in the defence of their settlements. The tribe has no common rights as a whole to the tribal territory, which is vested primarily in the sub-tribe and its component segments. But members of the tribe are united by bonds of sentiment, by a long tradition of friendship which is part of the enduring order felt to exist behind all things, and which, like most emotional ties, possesses a value which transcends specific relationships based on co-operation and common interests. Nevertheless, the sphere of co-ordinated activity belonging to the tribe is not negligible. Co-operation in offence and defence have been cited, and the great *idza nama* festivals are primarily an expression of tribal unity.

Each tribe normally comprises two named sub-tribes numbering from 200 to 500 people.[9] Members of the sub-tribe refer to themselves as "one people," *ha'makoko ve none.* A common interest in defence and offence is, once again, the principal index of sub-tribe unity; but members of the sub-tribe also hold their initiation ceremonies together, and in many cases— though not invariably—the *idza nama* festivals are regarded as a corporate undertaking.

Beyond the level of segmentation represented by the sub-tribe, the structural pattern is subject to considerable variations and to exceptions which can mostly be explained in terms of the conditions of social life which exist for specific groups. I am not, however, concerned to delineate these complications.

The sub-tribe invariably comprises a number of named patrilineal clans. These clans are mostly grouped in twos or in multiples of two. This recurring combination evidently expresses an important structural principle which bears on the nature of group formation; it is related to the way the people regard social and natural phenomena as wholes made up of equal parts.

The patrilineal, and predominantly local, clan comprises men and women who regard themselves as being of common origin and descent. There is no named forbear for the group as a whole, but an original ancestor is believed to have existed. Ideally, the clan is exogamous; its members of the same generation call one another "brother" and "sister"; they acknowledge an inclusive name; and the group has certain joint rights to the clan territory. The members of the clan may or may not reside in the same settlement. It is highly probable that once they always did. The villages were then palisaded as a protection from attack. Nowadays, however, there may be two or more settlements per clan, though it is a common practice for males to have houses in each residential unit.

Each clan is further divided into a number of unnamed sub-clans or *dzuha.* Members regard themselves as directly descended through males from a common male ancestor and thus as related. This man's name is seldom remembered, but the group believes implicitly in his existence in the past. Members refer to themselves as "one *dzuha*" (*ha'makoko dzuha none*) and the group is conceived of as a unit which, in the course of time, has grown from one man.[10]

The *dzuha* is a strictly exogamous, land-holding, and predominantly local group. The members characteristically reside together, either in a specific portion of the village or in a separate settlement. In a number of cases, however, the vicissitudes of warfare or exile consequent on repeated enemy attacks have resulted in a dispersal of segments amongst different tribal and sub-tribal groups. This naturally affects internal solidarity, but the scattered segments retain their common identity for a considerable time.

The *dzuha*, finally, is made up of a number of related patrilineages, genealogical units whose members trace a known descent through males from a known male ancestor. Genealogical knowledge is not extensive, and the people cannot as a rule remember farther back than the generation of their great-grandparents. The patrilineage thus normally has a depth of between four and five generations. The genealogical inter-connections of patrilineages within the *dzuha* cannot be stated exactly; but the common descent of members of the inclusive unit is maintained by the assertion that the founding ancestors of each component lineage were brothers, themselves descended patrilineally from an unnamed male ancestor common to the *dzuha* as a whole. While the patrilineage is, again, mostly a local residential group, the very strong bonds which exist between age-mates may operate to modify the internal structure. Thus some men prefer to set up house and identify themselves in everyday affairs with the members of other lineages with whom they passed through the initiation rites and spent a long apprenticeship in the men's house (*zagusave*). Being a corporate group, members of the patrilineage have common rights to a portion of the *dzuha* land; they have a common interest in the initiation and marriage of the younger members, and they recognize a collective responsibility for political action.

Nama Flutes

The sacred *nama* flutes appear within the context of three activities: male initiation ceremonies, the great pig-killing festivals (*idza nama*), and a fertility rite known variously as *asijo teho* ("our ancestor") or *nama ge'isa* (*nama* "fence").

The first two of these are ideally elements within a single ceremonial complex, the long period covered by initiation culminating in the *idza nama* and concluding with the dance which takes place on the day the pigs are distributed. The special conditions required by initiation and festivals do not always coincide, however, and either may be held without the other. The fertility rite occurs irregularly, probably at from three to five year intervals, performance depending on the natural decay of a wooden structure which is erected during the rite. Under abnormal conditions, as in times of severe drought or famine, it may take place more frequently.

Both initiation ceremonies and the *idza nama* festivals are held during the latter months of the year, from July to November, the dry season, and it is at this time that the *nama* flutes make their dramatic appearance, carried in procession from the men's house where the decision to institute the ceremonies has been taken by the elders. Food has previously been cooked there, and at the conclusion of the meal the company proceeds along the garden paths, sounding the flutes as they go. As the party approaches a settlement branches of crotalaria and other shrubs are broken off and held in front of the flutes to conceal them. An advance guard goes ahead to warn the waiting women of what is coming, and, as the procession passes, these men stand guard, bow in hand, to make sure that no female or uninitiated male looks at them. The smaller boys and girls scatter in all directions. Women either turn their backs or lower their heads where they sit, those with babies or infants hiding them against their breasts. Old women, however, are permitted to stand up and face the men, emitting a shrill stylized shout which is returned in deep-throated voice by the males as they run forward and leap up and down, brandishing their weapons. From this time onwards no night passes without the flutes being heard near the settlements. Indeed, the after-dark and before-dawn procession of men and flutes through the surrounding gardens becomes a characteristic male activity in succeeding months, while at irregular intervals, as particular stages are reached, the *nama* are accorded specific ritual treatment. Finally, they are returned to the men's house at the conclusion of the ceremonies which occasioned their appearance.

The *nama* flutes are made of a single piece of bamboo approximately two feet six inches long and four to five inches in diameter with a hole three to four inches from one end.[11] When they are played, the open end near the mouthpiece is closed with a handful of mud. The flute is then held in the left hand with the mouthpiece against the player's lips while the palm of his right hand is used to produce the tune by alternately opening and closing the farther end. Flutes are always played in pairs, which are referred to as age-mates, *aharu.* Women and children are not permitted to see them. The penalty in former days was immediate death at the hands of the men-folk. The *nama,* when not in use, are wrapped in bark cloth and carefully concealed in the roof of the men's house.[12]

Each pair of flutes has its own distinctive tune which by tradition has been handed down in the *dzuha.* The group may possess from one to three of these tunes. There is no rule as to the number, but new ones can only be acquired by the gift of a friendly group who wish to signify a particularly close tie with the recipients. It follows that a *dzuha* seldom owns more than two. They are regarded as the common property of the male members and, in most cases, are said to have been handed down from remotest ancestral times.

The *nama* flutes are also named, the name of each pair invariably repeating—though sometimes in a shortened form—the sound of the tune which is played on them.[13] Thus a person, on hearing a particular tune, immediately knows to which group it belongs and, within the limit of his local knowledge, is able to refer to it by name.

Women and children are led to believe that the tunes are produced by large birds, *nama,* which appear in the *zagusave* and are tended by the men throughout the period covered by initiation and the pig festivals.[14] The flutes, as material objects, are not in themselves sacred. Some are probably of a fair age, but, being fragile, they do not retain their usefulness for long; indeed, a large number of them are manufactured for specific ceremonies. This does not involve any ritual, though it would seem that a certain amount of technical knowledge is required in order to produce instruments of the desired tone and pitch.[15] The completed flutes may be decorated with some simple poker-work designs, but many of them have no adornment of any kind.

The material flute is neither sacred nor possessed of supernatural qualities. Men explain that human agents produce the tunes and that the sound originates with the expulsion of human breath into the hollow tube. They also agree that the *nama* bird does not exist and was invented for the express purpose of misleading the women and children. The secrecy surrounding the flutes, even the penalty of death exacted in the past, are thus designed to prevent women learning the truth. "Should they know," the men explain, "they would laugh at us." This statement implies more than male embarrassment at the discovery of deception, for it is felt that the whole structure of male superiority would be threatened by the ridicule.

But to conclude that the flutes are merely the central objects of a charade designed for the glorification of a particular sex is to be very wide of the mark. Such a conclusion, moreover, does not accord with the emotion with which they are regarded and the manner in which they are treated.

BELIEFS AND RITES

Some of the *nama* tunes are attractive but to European ears become wearisome from excessive repetition. For the natives, however, they possess aesthetic qualities capable of arousing strong feelings, and both players and listeners derive emotional satisfaction from a virtuoso performance. Only thus can we explain the pleasure men express throughout the months when the instruments are carried nightly through the gardens—the eagerness with which they tend a new pair of flutes and discard one after another until a successful combination is made—the way they criticize unskilled players and give instructions to the tyro. Their appreciation is derived partly from the fact that two flutes are needed, each of a slightly different pitch, to produce a satisfying tune. One man said while I was watching the manufacture of a particular pair: "By itself it is nothing," and he held up one of the finished flutes. "But with its age-mate, then there is something one cannot understand; here is something at which to shake the head and wonder." Particular tunes are said to be more satisfying than others, and the group to which these belong take pride in their possession. Such tunes are said to excite the sexual desires of women, and I have heard players addressed by other men with the words: "Oh, your *nama* turns my belly: if I were a woman I would want to come to you now."

The manner in which the flutes are treated also contradicts the casualness of their manufacture. Throughout the ceremonies when not in use they are kept in the men's house, resting side by side in their pairs on a bed of leaves and crotons. From time to time they are decorated with flowers, perfumed grasses and coloured leaves, particularly when they are brought forth during the day at the larger gatherings. Special food is given to them too, on those occasions which mark the completion of different stages in the long sequence of activities. A small oven is made at this time in addition to that which contains the food for the assembled company. One or two sucking pigs, some bananas, sweet-potatoes and greens are prepared in it and later distributed amongst the elders. Some of the pig, however, is sprinkled with salt and set aside for the *nama*. This is taken inside the men's house, where it is divided into small pieces, a portion being placed inside the mouthpiece of each flute. The ceremony is described as "giving salt to the *nama*," and by killing a medium sized pig any individual may perform the rite on behalf of his group at any time during the festival period. The men eat the pig—as they also consume the small portions placed in the mouths of the flutes—and the rite may be viewed as an excuse for eating pork. Indeed, the people admit that the mythical *nama* do not eat. But the offering is an act of faith, nevertheless, and a manifestation of religious belief.

These beliefs are not formulated precisely, but native statements and the manner in which the flutes are treated lead one to conclude that the tune is the important sacred element. It is handed down from generation to generation in the *dzuha*. Men alone are permitted to play the flutes, and women therefore cannot inherit a tune and take it outside the group when they marry. It remains the common and traditional heritage of the males, and though men may play the flutes belonging to related groups at the ceremonies, it would be a serious offence for them to do so without permission at any other time.[16]

The *nama* tune, then, is in the first place a symbol of unity. But it also links the members of the *dzuha* with their ancestral past. It symbolizes, on the one hand, the solidarity of males, and, on the other, the common origin and continuity of a particular group of men.

The *nama* are also regarded as the spiritual manifestation of a benevolent power to which the fortunes of the *dzuha* are linked. The nature of the power is difficult to discover, but its reality is attested both by the ritual treatment which the people accord the flutes and by the general concern for their preservation, a concern which goes far beyond that required to maintain an elaborate deception. Most men nowadays agreed, indeed, that women know the secret of the flutes; but they still carry on the rites. I think that it is unlikely that the women were deceived even in the past, for, although the men make a great show of protecting the flutes' identity when females are actually present, they make no attempt to conceal them when they take them through the gardens (the procession of men, silhouetted on some hilltop, is frequently visible from a considerable distance). Again, bamboo is also used to make the musical instruments which are played at all times by young people of both sexes, and there is not a great deal of difference between the sounds produced by these small flutes and the sacred *nama*. In short, women know that the explanation devised by the men is designed to mislead them; yet they respect the secret, even in groups where the traditional relationships of superiority and subordination between the sexes have undergone modifications. The element of deceit has a functional significance, as will be shown, in a culture which places an extreme emphasis on the differential importance of men. But when it is so obvious that deception is being practised, we must seek an additional explanation. The conclusion which is supported by the available evidence is that the conscious falsification is the least important element within the cult, and that it in no way affects the essential belief as to the nature of the *nama*.

The events which took place in the area in late 1950, following a baptismal ceremony carried out by the local branch of the Lutheran Mission, support this interpretation. Certain converts, on returning to their village afterwards, were evidently fired with an excess of religious zeal and in order to demonstrate their Christian faith publicly burned the sacred flutes belonging to their group. This action had widespread and probably unforeseen consequences. Some of the flutes destroyed had been given by a neighbouring group, and these people were so incensed that they were only with difficulty restrained from attacking their erstwhile friends. Other adjoining groups also expressed deep concern, indeed horror, at the action, and a deputation was despatched to the Government Station to seek the support of the Administration for the punishment of the resident native evangelist, who was considered to be primarily responsible. The administrative officer was not able to accede to this request, but he pointed out that there was no law compelling the people to accept a Mission teacher, and the episode ended with the man's expulsion by his pupils.

The people directly involved were deeply moved, and even remotely situated groups expressed concern. The public burning of the flutes in the presence of both sexes was considered to be a threat to male superiority; moreover, everyone was afraid of possible supernatural consequences. The deputation of men who sought Government support pointed out that the *nama* "belonged to their ancestors" and that the well-being of their group would suffer if they were prevented from according them traditional respect. They implied that they were being deprived of security and cut off from a supernatural source of assistance, a power which watched over their interests and ensured the continuity of their existence.

The whole episode was remarkable in that it brought forth one of the few reasonably articulate statements which I heard concerning the religious significance of the flutes. Beliefs which at other times have mostly to be inferred from observed behaviour were given a clear expression in an atmosphere of violent emotion.

The supernatural force which is felt to reside in the *nama* is related conceptually to that possessed by the spirits of the dead. Ancestor worship plays a conspicuous part in the religion, but underlying it is a generalized belief in an ancestral quality within a more inclusive supernatural power concept rather than the allocation of specific functions to the spirits of the dead. The spirits of the recently dead are felt to concern themselves in certain situations which confront their living descendants. Thus they are thought to punish those who have transgressed accepted norms of conduct with illnesses and other misfortunes. Their favour must then be sought by means of prayer and sacrifice. But only a very limited range of events is attributed to the intervention of specific spirits, and, generally speaking, the nature of ancestral power is more diffuse. The dead do not have to be invoked by name in any of the ceremonies designed to secure their assistance, and the great fertility rite is referred to simply as *asijo teho,* "our ancestor."

This is carried out to ensure the welfare of the group through the succeeding years and to provide protection against the attacks of enemies, to secure the fertility of crops and pigs, and to prevent the animals from breaking into the gardens and destroying the fruits of human labour. It is a major religious ceremony, embracing the foundations of a stable and continuing social life. It is essentially an appeal to a higher power which lies behind the continuity of existence and at the same time a collective expression of belief in it.

The rite is also known as *nama ge'isa,* and as the two names are interchangeable, it may be assumed that they designate a unitary concept rather than specific elements within a ritual complex. The *nama* flutes are certainly not symbols of the supernatural power of the dead, but there is a close association between them. This is implied when the people couple them in designating the fertility ritual, and it is also manifest in the disposal of the flutes in the cemetery. Destroying the old flutes is said to be necessary to preserve the secret from the women, but they could easily be burned or thrown into the long kunai grass. Offerings are sometimes made to the dead in the cemetery also, and I therefore infer a close association between the *nama* and ancestral spirits. The two are not the same, and no one ascribes a common identity to flutes and spirits; yet, a conceptual linkage is implied within the more diffuse belief in a transcendental ancestral power which operates in nature and in social life. Both flutes and spirits are manifestations of this more generalized supernatural force which the people feel to lie behind the continuing order of all things. This is the essential core of religious belief, though it is to be inferred rather and is not given dogmatic statement. The power is also unnamed, but it links the past with present and future and provides that if men behave in accepted ways and fulfil their obligations and preserve the established forms of relationships, then they may obtain the benefits of collective existence.

The force in essence is simply the spiritual content of society, a translation to the supernatural plane of the traditions, aims and aspirations of a group, of those collective sentiments which activate its members in their daily intercourse. It is the spiritual content which exists in all established relationships, a force which is recognized by the Gahuku-Gama not only as their institutionalized ways of behaving bring material satisfactions, but also as these forms of collective expression, indeed the very structure of their social groups are conceived to be part of an enduring order transcending time and space. In their different ways, both flutes and spirits are the agencies through which the living meet this force and re-affirm their faith in it. Both symbolize the power behind the enduring order which, deriving from the past, is manifest in the present and which, by proper observances, can be expected to take care of the future.

NAMA AND THE MEN'S ORGANIZATION

The sociological functions of the cult can only be assessed by returning to the ceremonial complex in which it appears and by delineating the relationships of these activities with other aspects of the culture.

The flutes make their most dramatic appearance at the men's initiation rites, a highly elaborated sequence of events which may be spread over the best part of four months, culminating, when conditions permit, in the *idza nama* festivals. Space does not allow me to give a full account of the initiation ceremonies here, but they conform to the generally established pattern of *rites de passage* despite the incorporation of features somewhat unusual for New Guinea. The chief of these is the complex elaboration which is accorded to age as a principle of association and the resulting structure of successive age groups with clearly defined functions and strong internal solidarity.[17]

The initiation rites serve primarily to introduce the younger members of the community into the men's organization and to admit them to the institution of the *zagusave*. They express unmistakeably the rigid sex dichotomy of the culture, the community of male interests and their essential opposition to the sphere of women, and also designate successive stages of physiological and social growth, both of which are conceived as a continuing inter-linked sequence beginning in the womb and gradually progressing to old age.

Boys aged from five to seven years are removed from the care of their mothers during the course of the ceremonies. They are not officially acquainted with the secret of the *nama* yet, but the men compel them to bathe at dawn in a stream near the village and afterwards greet them with mock-triumphant shouts. They probably find the experience a shock, for they go to the stream in company with older boys and are surrounded by a throng of armed and decorated warriors whose continuous vigorous chanting is accompanied by the mass shrilling of the *nama* flutes. The children "go back to their mothers" at the end of the day, but their eventual separation from the women and their membership in the men's organization has been ceremonially foreshadowed.

The older boys, from ten to fifteen, are simultaneously admitted to their novitiate in the *zagusave*. They are taken away from the settlements in the early morning, carried in the same procession to a stream nearby, and there compelled to undergo extremely painful rites designed to rid them of the contaminating influence of women, thus ensuring their manly vigour and physical maturity and fitting them for their future role as warriors. On their return they are confined for a time in the men's house, where the secret of the *nama* is revealed. Their principal duty henceforward is to serve the older youths and men in the *zagusave*. They are allowed only the minimum of contact with women and race about in small bands practising vomiting and blood letting and, in general, preparing themselves for wider participation in the affairs of men.

Finally, the initiation ceremonies mark the removal of youths of fifteen to nineteen years of age from the status of novices to that of betrothed warriors. This group has already undergone the rites on a previous occasion, but they now pass through them again and are thereafter secluded in the *zagusave* for a period varying from a few weeks to two months. They are not permitted outside during the day and have to observe certain dietary prohibitions, the chief being abstention from drinking water. The elders meanwhile set out to obtain wives for them. Formal instruction in their future duties, rights and obligations is given to them, and they learn to become proficient on the *nama* flutes. Their distinctive bachelor headdresses (*ge'ne*) are removed and sumptuous new decorations prepared. They are reintroduced to the group in the early hours of the day on which the *idza nama* dance takes place.

Acceptance into the *zagusave* marks a formal break with the life of the women and is thus a major stage in the boy's progress from childhood to full male status. It begins an important period of education, wherein, through formal instruction and close association with those of his own age, the sentiments which underlie the solidarity of the male community and the common interests of its members are forged and cemented. The universal virtues of respect of one's elders and the inter-dependence of alternate generations are expressed in terms of service to the senior members of the group and the reciprocal right to expect from them assistance through the various stages which mark one's progress to social maturity. The youth is in the *zagusave* isolated from the women of the group for a number of years. He does not eat food which they have cooked and spends the greater part of his time as a member of a band of boys of approximately the same age. The elders instruct him in the traditions and history of his tribe and in the type of conduct considered fitting for a man, and he learns that the greatest esteem he can hope for is to be considered a powerful warrior.

Few social relationships outside the family are as important as the bonds established by age. A boy and his age mates share a wider range of common interests and activities than close kinsmen. They have mutual interests, share the same experiences, submit to the same moral teachings and are therefore supposed to be friends for life. The typical features of the relationship can be seen in children of five years of age, in the groups of small boys who walk about with their arms round each other's shoulders, talking and whispering confidentially, and in the little girls who run screaming through the kunai, their long hair dresses clutched in the hand of some boy while his friends menace them with toy bows and arrows. Later, this same group of boys pass through the rites of initiation together, and through all stages of their novitiate in the *zagusave* their common interests and dependence on those who are senior to them are emphasized. Their principal duty is to serve the senior members, performing the domestic chores about the men's house, fetching firewood and water and doing the everyday cooking. They should be betrothed at the same time, and their elder kinsmen ought to procure the brides as the period for the *idza nama* festivals approaches. Finally, after a lengthy period of waiting during which the elders continually criticize their conduct, they are permitted to cohabit with these women. The young men shoot an arrow into the thighs of their future wives, and in a ceremony afterwards share a formal meal with them. It sometimes happens, however, that a girl has not been procured for a particular youth, and when his age-mates perform these rites he may feel his position so keenly that he runs away to an enemy group, seeking death rather than remain in his own community.

For the senior members of the group, no less than for the initiates themselves, the ceremonies described are the supreme expression of the community of interests between men. The whole sub-tribe is concerned and the boys of the required age from each component segment initiated on the same day. The procession to the stream comprises men drawn from every clan and *dzuha*, brilliantly decorated and strung to a high pitch of emotion. Chanting, and accompanied by their *nama*, they carry the boys away at a brisk pace, leaving the paths and striking through the kunai, where they trample down saplings and any other small obstacles in symbolic representation of their strength and invincibility. The boys are compelled to watch and assist the older men as they demonstrate the rites of vomiting and blood-letting. They are forced to hold the ends of the u-shaped lengths of cane which their seniors have thrust down their own throats, and to move these up and down while the latter retch in the water. Later, when their own turn comes, the men exhort them with the words: "You have done this to us; now we do it to you." The women, armed with a variety of weapons, from bows and arrows to stones and heavy pieces of wood, set upon the company when they return to the settlements. Heads are frequently broken and minor injuries sustained by almost all concerned in the fight, and occasionally more serious harm is done. The elders constantly watch over the new members thereafter and chastise them when necessary.

As age group follows age group the collective sentiments, common interests and values of the men's organization are transmitted from generation to generation. The *nama* must be given due prominence in the process as a focus and abiding symbol of unity. The secret of the flutes is the most important revelation given to the boys. The rites of vomiting and blood letting may serve a useful psychological purpose in conditioning the aggressiveness expected as the male ideal; but the *nama* are a more permanent symbol of the community of men. The boy is probably well aware of the nature of the secret long before it is explained to him, but the official revelation means that he may now be present on all occasions when the flutes are played. As he takes part in the ceremonies he is continually impressed with the common purpose which unites his sex. The *nama*, moreover, are a symbol of the corporate identity of his *dzuha* and of the common heritage and continuity of the group to whom he is related by ties of consanguinity and the strongest social bonds. These ties have an obvious material utility. At the same time, belief in the supernatural power of the *nama* gives them a spiritual backing, a personal and group significance which transcends mere sentiment and material considerations; and confirms, as it were, the universal validity of the relationships, aims and aspirations of men. Through the *nama*, successive generations are brought into contact with the ancestral past of their culture and are united in a spiritual bond which is renewed at each performance of the rites. The cult is pre-eminently both an affirmation and expression of the enduring order of established forms of male relationships and the absolute nature of the social values which underlie them.

The organization which each youth enters on initiation must also be viewed in relation to a wider framework of social life, and, in particular, to the rigid distinction between the spheres, and relative importance, of men and women. This sex dichotomy, male superiority and solidarity on the one hand, and the subordinate dependence of women on the other, finds its highest formalized expression in the activities of the *zagusave*. The separation of men and women, as we have seen, is clearly marked in the initiation ceremonies; indeed, it is even foreshadowed when a boy is not much over five years of age. Segregation is thereafter almost complete for a number of years, and in later life relationships between the sexes are fraught with prohibitions designed to preserve an essential distance. The dominance of male values, however, is not maintained by simple considerations of practical merit. Buttressed by its religious association with the *nama*, it is lifted out of the context of a particular time and place and transposed to a supernatural plane, where it is seen as an aspect of the universal order.

The cultural differentiation of male and female is more than the simple assignment of complementary roles based on observable or imputed physiological differences. Men are conceived to be the more important members of society. They are, ideally, aggressive, flamboyant, given to quick outburst of anger—the warriors, guardians of custom, and repositories of knowledge on whom the continued welfare and security of the group depend. Women's role is seen to be one of submission. A disproportionate share of both the drudgery and heavy work entailed in daily life falls to them, while men are free to gossip, indulge in speech making, and put on their brilliant decorations and seek diversion elsewhere. Even in procreation, the woman is assigned a secondary part. She is merely a receptacle for the man's semen. Without a man, it is said, a woman is nothing; but the converse does not apply, for a man, as a member of the male sex, always, as it were, carries around with him the potentiality of fatherhood, requiring only the submissiveness of a woman to achieve expression. A closer spiritual tie is in consequence felt to exist between a father and his child than between a mother and her child. In childless marriages, too, the woman is always blamed.

Men, however, feel that women are not content with their role. They feel, indeed, that they need to maintain a constant vigilance to preserve their superiority, and that women, given the opportunity, are prepared to challenge it. Women are supposed to be unwilling to bear children and to take steps to prevent or terminate pregnancy, thereby withholding from men their right, as males, to beget children. Women do, in fact, dislike bearing children. Having a baby "hurts the vulva," they say. "It is like dying, for how do we know we shall get up again?" They also admit practising manual abortion and claim a knowledge of pharmacological specifics to induce sterility. Men therefore have to know how to cause pregnancy, and the resulting struggle for expression is typical of the underlying tension of sex relationships. In this, and in a multitude of other ways—from the high rate of divorce consequent on the desertion of women down to beliefs in sorcery—the male sees an essential opposition between his own aims and those of the opposite sex. The female principle is in itself considered to be inimical to men, and care has to be exercised to see that the youths have as little contact with it as possible, at least until they reach physical maturity. A wife is not permitted to touch her husband's hair or his decorations, to hold his head or his nose, and after she has borne a child he undergoes a special rite to cleanse him of contamination from the fluids she has discharged. These derive some of their dangerous qualities from fluid residues absorbed at the wife's own birth and released with her children. Antagonism is never far below the surface in the relationships of men and women, and the solidarity of men is in consequence elevated in the scale of values to a position where it transcends even the recognized wrong committed in adultery.

The superiority of the male, however, has largely to be achieved and continually demonstrated in acceptable terms. It is the result of conscious striving as well as differential rights which automatically distinguish a superior status; and in the final analysis, the idea which men hold of themselves is based primarily on what men do rather than on what they have at birth. They recognize, indeed, that in physiological endowment men are inferior to women, and, characteristically, they have recourse to elaborate artificial means to redress the contradiction and to demonstrate its opposite. A girl's growing breasts and her first menstruation are signs of a maturing process which is without obvious parallel in the boy, a fact that the men resent. Betrothals are often broken off because the girl has outstripped the boy in physical growth. She sometimes runs away to a more mature man, but just as frequently he refuses to consider her as his future wife, and points out that she is obviously "too old" for him and that were he to remain bound to her he would run the risk of hearing her comment on his immaturity. Numerous instances are to hand of girls who have thus slighted a youth and later, "when he grew big," desired to come back to him and been killed to avenge the former insult.

The challenge of the physiological processes of growth and sexual maturity in women is met by men's initiation rites and, thereafter, by the practice of regular self-induced bleeding and magical acts. Informants unfailingly connect menstruation with a girl's physical growth. They point to its inevitable but unexplained advent and the concomitant signs of nubility, the increasing stature, the rounding and development of the bodily frame. It is a certain sign of her progress on the path to womanhood. But for the boy manhood and physical superiority are more a matter of chance and have therefore to be guarded, even engineered, in order to redress the balance of physiological inferiority. Initiation rites, in consequence, serve the same purpose for the male as menstruation for women. The one has been explained to me in terms of the other, and the same idea—the cyclical expulsion of blood—undoubtedly lies behind the men's ritual of nose bleeding. Even after his admittance to the *zagusave,* however, the welfare of the boy is guarded by prohibitions and ceremonies without parallel in the life of a girl. His manhood is never the certain result of a natural process, nor is it established by his sexual maturity alone, for its supreme expression is cultural, the result of demonstrated ability in those activities which are designated male.

On the one hand, therefore, men are considered to be superior to women; but, on the other, they labour under an initial physiological inferiority and are also continually compelled to assert their dominance in cultural terms and to affirm it in the face of threats which may or may not constitute a conscious challenge. The situation is fraught with psychological and social consequences which could well impair the efficiency of Gahuku-Gama social organization. Any generally accepted system of belief or institutionalized activities which can be shown to serve the dual purpose of confirming male dominance and simultaneously justifying the dependent status of women must accordingly be granted due significance in the processes which provide for the maintenance and persistence of established forms. The *nama* cult does not stand alone in this respect but that it has this functional significance is incontestable.

The cult quite openly incorporates certain practices designed to keep women in ignorance of its secret; and to the extent that these are recognized as false, it is permissible to regard the *nama* as an artificial and consciously contrived mechanism through which men hope to demonstrate and preserve their superior status. But this does not affect the importance of the flutes as a symbol of male dominance and solidarity. What is important to the members of the cult, and for the preservation of the established forms of sex relationships, is that the possession of the *nama* serves as a practical means of confirming and attesting the community of men. The *nama* symbolize those interests which are common to the sex. The flutes are a focus of sentiments and attitudes ascribed to the sex as a whole, a symbolic expression of male superiority, of the differential importance of male activities and male values. Disregarding any underlying belief, the *nama* cult is both an index of male dominance and an institution serving to maintain the *status quo* of male hegemony.

But we have seen that the cult of the flutes is more than this, for the *nama* are capable of arousing strong emotions in both sexes and are accorded ritual treatment even in the privacy of the *zagusave*. There is an element of conscious deception, which, however, need not detract from any psychological or social functions, for underlying it is the firm belief in the *nama* as both a manifestation and channel of access to that supernatural force on which the welfare of the group depends. The flutes not only symbolize the power behind the continuing order but also link each group with its ancestral past; and thus they bring an unimpeachable validity to the existing relationships of men and women. Through these religious associations male dominance is shed of the material trappings of a vested interest and becomes a part of the spiritual content of society never formulated precisely but existing in the minds of the members and ultimately no less a force behind the continuity of established forms than the material satisfactions people expect therefrom. The ascendancy of men becomes something more than a physical or social superiority; and the submissiveness of women is itself justified to them as a spiritual dependence which transcends the context of a particular relationship.

IDZA NAMA FESTIVALS

No assessment of the functions of the *nama* cult is complete without some consideration of the *idza nama* festivals, the highly complex sequence of activities which forms the ideal climax of initiation rites. Festivals similar to the *idza nama* occur throughout those Central Highland cultures on which we at present have information. They take place at five to seven year intervals, but that of the Gahuku-Gama may occur annually or at longer periods depending on available resources. When held in conjunction with initiation, they serve incidentally to introduce a new group of young warriors to the community and are thereby an attestation of male values and of pride in the men's organization. But they also have the more immediate object of discharging group obligations. The blood of allies which has been spilled in battle is wiped out on this occasion by giving them most of the pigs which are killed. Traditional ties between groups are renewed, and opposition to other groups is given a collective ceremonial expression.

The festivals are also competitive. They are related to individual and group prestige and are reciprocal. They are initiated in the first instance to discharge a community debt incurred in warfare, but the recipients of the pigs are also bound to return the gift at a future date. And such are the ramifications of alliances that, at any one time, a particular tribal segment may be receiving from a number of others while simultaneously acknowledging the assistance rendered by a different combination of neighbours. Each sub-tribe, indeed, is the central link in a mesh of these reciprocal duties.

The integrative importance of the *idza nama* can hardly be over-estimated, for not only do they confirm the ties between political groups but also embody those constant values and common ends which exist for the members of any group throughout the whole society. To a differential extent in the sub-tribe and its segments, the festivals are the ultimate heights of collective and individual achievement. Personal wealth—itself the end result of values operative in family, lineage, *dzuha* and clan; the universals of kinship, its binding force and the compulsive sentiments which underlie it; group prestige, with all that it implies in terms of social inter-dependence; political leadership and the ties and corresponding cleavages on which, to a large extent, well-being and continued security depend—to all these the *idza nama* gives support and expression.

Throughout the festival period of several months the celebrating community is brought into daily contact with that supernatural force which watches over and guards human welfare and destiny. Purely secular activities at times overshadow and conceal important religious elements; but the latter are always present, manifest in the focal position occupied by the *nama*, in the ceaseless sounding of the flutes, which continues night after night, and in the specific ritual which surrounds them. So closely inter-related are the secular and the supernatural that each expression of

a social tie or value is at the same time a recognition of spiritual dependence. Seen in this context, the *nama* become a symbol of sentiments and
aspirations which are the foundation of a stable continuing existence. They
are a projection to the supernatural plane of society itself, of its fundamental
interests and major values; in short, the symbolic expression of the spiritual
element in group existence.

As the dry season of the year, the recognized "time for killing pigs,"
approaches, people begin to speculate on the possibility of holding a festival.
They may be already committed to return a gift; on the other hand, there
are also outstanding debts incurred in former battles which have yet to be
repaid. Almost everyone has therefore attempted to make some provision
for the time when these obligations must be honoured, farming out his pigs
to relatives or friends as far away as the Chimbu border, migrating with
livestock and moveable possessions to areas where conditions are said to
favour a more rapid growth in the animals, and, later, setting out with
gold-lip shell and other valuables to augment his stock through traditional
channels of trade.

A man who has many pigs of the required size may initiate the festival.
He first of all sounds out the heads of other households in his *dzuha* and
clan; for the *idza nama*, from the outset, are a corporate undertaking, neces-
sitating the maximum participation of the adult members of every segment
of the group which finally decides to celebrate. Many discussions in consequence take place throughout the weeks preceding a formal decision.
Numerous meals are made at the men's house, where the matter is talked
over by the clan elders; and, since pigs are their special charge and care,
women are acquainted with the prevailing tenor of opinion. Inter-clan
gatherings serve to sound out the views of other segments of the sub-tribe,
and if there is a generally favourable reception, the way is cleared for the
formal commencement of the sequence of activities.

The festivals normally involve the whole sub-tribe, and they may even
extend beyond it. The contributions made are of three principal kinds:
pigs of the most highly valued size and quality which are given whole to
the guests; smaller animals which are divided centrally and partly consumed
by the hosts, and young sucking pigs which are cooked with quantities of
sweet-potatoes and distributed on the day of the concluding dance. Before
a decision is reached the group has to be certain of obtaining from its members sufficient of all these resources to discharge its debt to its ally, and,
at a later stage, the recipients may demand more than has been promised.

The festival is inaugurated by the men of the sub-tribe at a meal in the
men's house. At this stage, individual members of the component segments
have intimated their willingness to supply sufficient pigs to ensure the
success of the festival, though final arrangements are as yet far from complete. The *nama* make their first appearance at the close of this day. The
men bring them out and parade them through the settlements and neigh-

bouring gardens and thereafter sound them continually through all the weeks of preparation.

The first shrilling of the flutes occasions great excitement and heralds a period in which the tenor of everyday life gradually mounts. The chain of events which distinguish the festivals has now been set in motion. Normal daily procedure is gradually forgotten. Gardens are neglected (through they require little attention at this time of the year). Formal meals at the men's house are held almost weekly, and people are preoccupied with making new clothing and decorations, assembling firewood and stones for the ovens, refurbishing houses or constructing new dwellings. The health of the pigs is subjected to magical safeguards, and as they are brought in from relatives, from friends, and from outlying areas, the stench in the village becomes almost unbearable.

Neighbouring communities know that an *idza nama* will be held as soon as the flutes are sounded, and throughout the following weeks there is considerable speculation, augmented by diplomatic enquiries, as to which group will be asked to dance. The group holding the festival do not, however, make known their intention; indeed, their reticence, though ostensibly due to a lack of final decision, seems designed to keep people guessing and to accentuate a sense of their own importance. Their prestige at this time stands particularly high. Everyone knows the enormous outlay required to hold the *idza nama,* and the sounding of the flutes is tantamount to an assertion that a particular group is able to attain the height of cultural achievement. It is evidence of their prosperity and of their ability to discharge whatever obligations they may have incurred. Incidentally, it is also an affirmation of those constant values on which prosperity depends, an assertion of knowledge and of careful husbandry, of individual achievement, of familial and group responsibilities.

From the first day the *nama* sound for the group as a whole, but their symbolic significance is differentially attested by principles of internal alignment. Thus only the flutes of those segments whose members have contracted to supply the largest pigs are brought out and played for the festival. These are the pigs which are handed whole to the guests, the most important and valuable item in the contribution. Their possession is itself a sign of wealth, and it is unlikely that all men, at a particular time, will possess animals of this quality. It follows that the group is principally dependent on a few individuals among its component *dzuha,* though in actual quantities killed, pigs of the remaining categories outnumber the prime specimens. At the same time, the owners of such animals can only employ their wealth to its best advantage in the context of a group activity. Custom and sentiment prevent a man killing his pigs and eating them: he may employ them to discharge a personal obligation—such as a mortuary gift—but the highest prestige, as well as an eventual return in kind, attaches to employment in the *idza nama.* While the sub-tribe must therefore rely on the contribution of certain of its members in order to achieve the culminating form of cultural expression, these individuals are no less dependent on the larger organization to reap the esteem to which their wealth entitles them. The festival thus maintains its corporate character while simultaneously according social recognition to important individuals.

This recognition is granted in several ways but principally, as I have indicated, by means of the sacred flutes. The gift of a large pig entitles its owner to bring out the *nama* belonging to his *dzuha*. A *dzuha* whose members supply only the smaller animals cannot bring out its flutes, though in all other respects it participates on a basis of equality with the remaining segments. The gift of a large pig from any one man is, however, sufficient for all the members of his *dzuha* to be represented by their *nama* at the festival, for although the contribution of a single individual may be initially responsible, the *nama* remain a corporate possession. Again, therefore, prestige is achieved within a group context. The members of a particular segment, no less than the community at large, are dependent on the resources of a particular man or men for the peculiar emotional satisfaction and the social recognition derived from the sounding of their flutes; but the man of wealth is also dependent not only on the adult males of his own *dzuha* but also on members of related segments in sub-clan, clan, and sub-tribe. According to the structural position from which we view this system of relationships, the *nama* thus express and symbolize a personal achievement—itself the result of accepted social values—the unity and corporate identity of those of common descent, the inter-dependence, indeed, the collective responsibility, the common aims and ends of related parts within the larger organization.

A few weeks probably pass from the first sounding of the flutes until the next important stage in the festival sequence. This occurs when the prospective guests are officially invited to participate, and it takes place again at one of the several *zagusave* belonging to the hosts. Men of the sub-tribe gather there in the morning to prepare ovens and food for the feast. They are decorated with feathers and paint, and there is a note of high excitement in the gathering. A bundle of sticks, *nakahuni*, has previously been assembled, and it is the handing of these to the visitors which constitutes the formal invitation. Each stick, varying between four and six inches in length, represents a pig which will be given away at the festival. The longest *nakahuni*—occasionally decorated with cassowary feathers—signify pigs of the best quality and size; a stick which is split down the centre represents a half pig. The whole bundle has been put together in the course of repeated discussions and semi-formal gatherings throughout the preceding period, and, subject to certain basic principles, the donor of each stick has indicated a specific individual to whom he wishes to give it.

Since the *idza nama* serve pre-eminently to acknowledge political alliances and obligations incurred through the death of friends in battle, the group selected as the recipients is normally a traditional ally, a sub-tribe of the same tribe or some other group which has given assistance or made common cause with the donors. It is necessary, moreover, that a specific, historic occasion should be so acknowledged. The event celebrated may have been of recent occurrence or may have taken place almost a generation beforehand—owing to the extremely warlike patterning of Gahuku-Gama culture the history of each sub-tribe includes many such occasions which require formal recognition. A choice is thus made within a fairly wide range of possibilities, and the *nakahuni* are then assembled on the basis of obligation to the surviving relatives of allies who were killed. The largest pigs are marked for their sons or brothers of these men, then, in order of importance, the remainder for the heads of other households in their *dzuha*, for a sister's or a daughter's husband, or maternal relatives of an individual donor. The number of *nakahuni*—and therefore the number of pigs of all categories—is governed broadly by the necessity of ensuring that when the distribution is made each *dzuha* and lineage, indeed, each individual who could rightly claim recognition (and who is willing to accept the obligation of repayment), will have received a stick. It will be noted also that, in addition to honouring a group obligation, the festival also affords an opportunity of expressing personal bonds of kinship and affinity between specific individuals.

Acquainted of the intention to give them the *nakahuni* a day or so before this feast is held, the visitors now arrive at the *zagusave* as the donors are ready to open the ovens. They approach in a slow, dignified procession, careful not to appear over-anxious, though all of them are eager for the time when they will eat the pig. As they enter, their hosts give them a ceremonial greeting, rushing to meet them with upraised weapons, leaping around them and emitting the traditional deep-throated shouts. They halt some distance from the ovens and are then told to sit down while the food is removed. In the meantime they are given bundles of sugarcane to quench their thirst.

When the food is taken from the ovens, sweet-potatoes and joints of pigs are set aside for the guests. The names of particular individuals are called out, and they come forward to accept the food, retiring again to divide and eat it with their own group. Meanwhile, the hosts discuss the final allocation of the *nakahuni*. Several medium sized pigs are arranged on the ground, together with baskets of cooked vegetables, sugarcane and raw bananas. The *nakahuni* are handed over to the spokesman of the group, and he stands up to address the gathering.

His speech invariably draws attention to the long association of friendship between his people and the visitors. He points out the way in which they fought together to resist and subdue their common enemies, proceeding then to remark on the specific occasion which it is proposed to honour. He recalls those who were killed in battle and signifies that it is the intention of his group to assuage the grief and anger of the relatives of the dead by giving them pigs and asking them to dance.

The spokesman of the visitors then signifies his formal acceptance of the invitation. Standing up, he addresses his hosts in similar terms, acknowledging the ties between them and confirming that the death of some members of his group in this battle has been the cause of great sorrow and anger. He concludes by asserting: "We are not enemies; we are not another people; we can eat your pigs."

The spokesman of the hosts than hands over the *nakahuni*. He calls out the name of a principal recipient amongst the visitors, and the latter comes forward, supported by one or two younger men who carry away on their outstretched arms a gift of pig and vegetables. The *nakahuni* are placed inside each carcase in small bundles which are later untied and distributed by the recipients.

Each gift of *nakahuni* is acknowledged by the visitors with a frenzy of shouting and leaping, with cries of "Now we shall eat pig! Now our bellies are good! Now we know where the big men live!" The hosts return this acclaim in similar fashion, excitement reaching its highest pitch as the guests prepare to depart. Young men bring out the *nama*, decorated for the occasion with coloured leaves and perfumed grasses, and as the visitors leave the flutes circle them continually, their shrilling almost drowning the shouts and laughter, the exchanges of compliments, and the expressions of appreciation. When the last of the guests has left, offerings of pork and salt are given to the flutes in the *zagusave*, and at night men parade them backwards and forwards through the group territory.

The weeks following this ceremony are devoted to caring for the pigs and preparing the highly elaborate decorations which will be worn at the dance. Groups of younger people set out on journeys which may take them as far as the Ramu Valley to procure bird-of-paradise plumes, vegetable dyes and bark cloth. Both sexes are busily engaged in making new clothing, plaiting arm bands and leg bands, and stringing shells and green beetles' wings for head decorations. At irregular intervals pigs are killed and offerings are made to the *nama*. The flutes sound each night in the settlements and surrounding gardens, rain alone preventing the men from bringing them out.

Women are not present at any of the ceremonies so far described: yet the festivals are for them, no less than for the men, the climax of social life. Reference has been made to the fact that they are acquainted with the decisions taken by their menfolk. Pigs are regarded as their special charge, and it is understood that a husband will consult his wife before he undertakes to kill an animal. Social recognition is also accorded the wives of those who supply the largest pigs. Such women are permitted to decorate themselves with male ornaments and to dance with the men on the concluding day of the festival.

As the manifold preparations for the pig-killing near completion, the tempo of ceremonial activities quickens. Special ovens (*semeni*) have been prepared in the village; firewood and stones have been placed in readiness, houses repaired and, in some cases, entirely renewed. Now, on successive days, the men play the flutes along the paths leading to the settlements of the guests, approaching closer on each occasion and then retiring. The climax of this gradual progress is reached soon afterwards on a day agreed to by both parties. Setting out from their own settlements after darkness, the men carry the flutes to the villages of their allies and play them ouside the dwelling of every man who has accepted a *nakahuni*. Each house is circled several times by the *nama*, to the accompaniment of loud shouts of acclaim, the donor of the pigs thereafter sitting down and taking refreshment with the man who has received his *nakahuni*.

Both hosts and guests then agree on a day for the next ceremony, which is known as *idza resa kimitune*. This takes place in the settlements of the receiving group. Pigs are killed, a large meal is prepared, and certain valuables are assembled by each man who has accepted a *nakahuni*. Consisting principally of lengths of bark cloth, large cowries and brightly coloured European material, these are destined as gifts for the donors of the pigs. The latter arrive as the ovens are about to be opened, proceeding in formal procession down the rows of houses and halting to shout their appreciation at every dwelling where the valuables are displayed. They then take up a position several yards distant from the hosts of the day while sugarcane and cooked foods are brought to them to eat.

Meanwhile, men of the second group gather round one of the open ovens. The gifts for their visitors are tied to the top of long poles which are then inserted upright in the ground. The cooked pigs are divided and placed in heaps at the foot of the poles. When all is ready, the spokesman for the gathering stands up to address the visitors. He again refers to the tradition of friendship which unites them and, having remarked on the bounty and wealth of the guests, calls each man by name to receive his gift of pork and valuables.

In the morning, a day or so after the *idza resa*, the pig-killing takes place. The animals are brought in and tethered near the dwellings of their owners, the largest specimens being decorated with cowries, cassowary plumes and necklets of smaller shells. Custom prescribes that such animals shall be killed by the man who is to receive it or else by an important member of his group to which this task has been entrusted. These people, accompanied by their wives, accordingly arrive in the settlements at about ten o'clock bearing bundles of freshly cut banana leaves and various greens. The pigs are led out one at a time and bludgeoned to death with a heavy club provided by the hosts. Shouts of triumph and appreciation from the visitors vie with the wails of women and the squealing of the animals. Eager bystanders rush forward to claim the valuables with which the pigs are decked, and in their grief, the women who have reared them throw away lengths of bark cloth, coloured material, tobacco and feather decorations. The animals are then prepared for the ovens, members of both parties sitting down under specially constructed shelters to dress them.

The festival concludes on the following day, when as many as a thousand people may be gathered together, for in addition to the groups directly concerned, members of neighbouring communities come to watch the dance and distribution. It is a brilliant occasion, lasting from early morning until late afternoon. Both parties put on the decorations which they have made in the preceding months, and they dance in each settlement belonging to the group which held the festival. They gather in the garden towards sundown and, while the singing continues, the pigs are brought forth in a seemingly endless procession, trussed to litters and carried shoulder high through the throng. Formal presentation of the animals follows gifts of smaller joints made in recognition of the dance the visitors have performed. Then as darkness falls, the guests return to their homes.

In the foregoing description, necessarily condensed, I have been unable to give full value to the months of preparation required by the *idza nama*, to the manifold subsidiary activities, and, above all, to the emotional intensity and vivid personal interest displayed by every man, woman and child throughout the period. Other occasions in Gahuku-Gama life also call forth strong expressions of individual and group emotion; but at no other time is the heightened tenor of life sustained for so long. Indeed, the conclusion of the festival finds people so exhausted that several days are required before they seem willing, or able, to return to the normal affairs of living.

Again, so many themes, and so many channels for the expression of cultural values are contained in the festivals that it is difficult to do justice, in the space of a short paper, to them all. A love of personal display, of dancing and singing, is a fundamental attribute of the people, and the *idza nama* stand alone in the opportunities they bring for each person to express his sense of design, his aesthetic appreciation of colour, his delight in rhythm. In the sphere of social relationships and values, it has been pointed out that the Gahuku-Gama here achieve the supreme expression of group unity. The cultural emphasis on warfare and on political ties, which, to a large extent, are responsible for a stable existence, are explicitly recognized and renewed in the context of a major group activity. More than this, however, the festivals are an affirmation of the bonds uniting members of the lineage, *dzuha,* clan and sub-tribe, expressing not only the aims and aspirations of each segment, but also the common purpose which underlies the larger organization. The benefits of group existence are given able demonstration, no less for those individuals who achieve a differential social recognition than for those who depend on their contribution. The virtues of industry, the prestige which accompanies wealth, the importance of values and sentiments which are basic to a particular way of life, to all those the *idza nama* lends support, attesting their absolute nature not in abstract terms which are capable of question but in a highly emotional group situation which their practical relevancy is impressed on every participant.

CONCLUSION

To the Gahuku-Gama the sacred flutes are a manifestation of the external supernatural force which watches over their well-being and destiny. The cult in which they feature shows the widest correspondence with the existing social order, with the system of group and inter-group relationships and the sentiments which underlie it. The support which it brings to the constituted way of life lies, however, not only in its linkage with the expression of fundamental cultural aims but also, by way of its supernatural association, in its confirmation of the absolute nature of group values and relationships. Male initiation and the great pig festivals give ceremonial expression to those ties of different kinds on which the continuity of group life depends. At the same time, the *nama* bring to these contexts the force of religious persuasions. There is not on the one hand a realm of human action and on the other a sphere belonging to the supernatural, for the recognition of social ties is a simultaneous acknowledgement of spiritual dependence, and, by means of this close identification, the accepted forms of relationships assume a transcendental nature. The affairs of men, their aims and aspirations, the bonds which unite them, are transposed to a higher sphere, becoming themselves a part of the eternal spiritual order, integral to it, reaffirming it and sanctioned by it.

The persistency of established forms may be seen to rest on the processes of cultural learning, on the conscious and unconscious inculcation and transmission of sentiments and values through successive generations, and on the demonstration of their practical relevancy in the manifold situations which confront the individual; but there is also an emotional element in group existence, a sense of belonging, an idea of the virtue residing in a particular way of life; in short, a concept of togetherness which itself supports the collective organization. And it is this emotional counterpart of social existence which finds expression through the sacred *nama* and which is continually renewed through the ceremonies in which they feature. The force which the *nama* symbolize is the power of society itself. Through them, a people express their faith in a particular way of life, and through them the validity of its constitution is reaffirmed and attested.

NOTES

1. The *nama* cult has certain essential similarities with the *koa* of the Kuman peoples of Chimbu. *Vide* J. Nilles, "The Kuman of Chimbu," *Oceania*, Vol. XXI, No. 1, pp. 60-61.
2. My field work was carried out as a Research Fellow of the Department of Anthropology, Research School of Pacific Studies, Australian National University.

3. Short notes on the Gahuku language are contained in A. Capell, "Languages of the Central Highlands," *Oceania*, [n.d.]

4. Gahuku-Gama is the name which the Rev. Helbig has given to the language spoken by the people. In my usage, however, it has social as well as linguistic connotations. Thus the cultural and linguistic uniformity of the group is not simply a construct from observed phenomena. It is also a reality to the people themselves, who, on the basis of differences from surrounding groups, have a theory or ideology of their own uniqueness. This awareness of cultural commonness—as Nadel has pointed out—is at the same time both a degree and a first stage of social commonness (see S. F. Nadel, *A Black Byzantium*, pp. 15-17). Gahuku and Gama are the names respectively of tribes situated on the northern and southern boundaries of the group. Coupling them in this way provides a convenient label for a social reality.

5. *Rova*, which is never concluded, must be distinguished from *hina*, fighting as a form of redress to be concluded amicably between otherwise friendly groups.

6. See "The Political System of the Ngarawapum," *Oceania*, Vol. XX, No. 3.

7. The Kuman of Chimbu, for example, are said to number between 60,000 and 80,000.

8. See Nilles, *op. cit.*, and Tischner and Vicedom, *Die Mbowamb: die Kultur der Hagenberg-Stämme im Ostilichen Zentral-Neuguinea*, Monographien Zür Völkerkunde.

9. The tribal name is invariably a compound formed from the names of the major segments. Thus sub-tribes Gama and Nagamidzuha give us the tribe Gama-Nagamidzuha. Gehamo and Gahuku together form Gehamo-Gahukuve, etc.

10. Cf. *dzuha nea*, seeds; *dzuha nouve*, to plant seeds; *gizasi dzuha*, the root portion of a banana palm; and, similarly, *gasi dzuha*, *masi dzuha*, the seed portion of yams and taro respectively. The *dzuha* is also referred to as *naga* (*ha'makoko naga none*), from *naga*, the generic name for vines.

11. Local bamboo is generally used, though special flutes are also obtained from the Ramu area.

12. In groups where the men's house no longer exists, the flutes may be hidden in the roof of an ordinary dwelling. In other instances they are destroyed at the conclusion of the ceremonies. The pieces are scattered in the cemetery and a new pair manufactured on the occasion when they are next required.

13. According to Nilles, *op. cit.*, 60-61, some of the *koa* flutes of the Kuman are similarly named, though in the names of others he professes to see an original totemic significance. All the Gahuku-Gama names which I collected are onomatopoeic, and it does not seem possible to infer a totemic origin.

14. In point of fact, enquiries undertaken by my wife show that women are well aware of the manner in which the tunes are produced.

15. Trial and error also plays a part in the manufacture, successive pairs being made and discarded until a satisfactory combination is achieved.

16. Nilles states that amongst the Kuman blowing another man's *koa* is equivalent to stealing his property, but that it may be done to insult him or as a means of retaliation (*op. cit.*, p. 61).

17. I have reported the rites and the age groups in my paper "The Gahuku-Gama of the Central Highlands," *South Pacific*, Vol. V, No. 8.

13

POLITICAL ASPECTS OF THE MOKA CEREMONIAL EXCHANGE SYSTEM AMONG THE KYAKA PEOPLE OF THE WESTERN HIGHLANDS OF NEW GUINEA[1]

Ralph Bulmer

In the stateless societies of Melanesia, systems of ceremonial exchange have political functions analogous to those performed by major religious cults among peoples at a similar level of organization in, for example, West Africa.[2] Malinowski's classic account of the Kula system of S.E. New Guinea[3] has been criticized because insufficient attention is paid in it to political aspects.[4] The Hiri of the Motu people of the Papuan coast has also not been described in these terms. With regard to the ceremonial exchange systems of the Western Highlands District, however, two authors, Vicedom[5] and Elkin,[6] have drawn attention to the political implications, though not treating them in detail. Since no concerted account has yet been given of the political functions of any New Guinea exchange system, I describe these in this first publication on the Moka among the Kyaka rather than economic or moral aspects of this institution which could otherwise equally well provide the starting point for extended discussion.

I take politics to include the constitutory principles and interrelationships of the main formal groupings in a society (with which Radcliffe-Brown, Fortes and Evans-Pritchard are largely concerned[7]) as well as the competition for power and the process of policy-making, to which some recent authors have suggested that it should be restricted.[8]

"Moka" is the pidgin English and English term for the ceremonial exchange festivals of the Metlpa, Enga and Gawil peoples of New Guinea.[9] This derives from the Metlpa usage "Moka" or "Moga"; the Central Enga call their exchange festivals "Te" and the Eastern Enga (or Kyaka) call them both "Te" and "Maku."

Reproduced by permission of A. P. Elkin, Editor of *Oceania*, and Ralph Bulmer from *Oceania*, 31:1-13 (1960-61).

The Kyaka, who number about 10,000, live on the north slopes of the Mount Hagen range, between the Baiyer, the Lai and the Ku Rivers, in the 6,000-3,500 feet aitituainal beit, where soil and climate combine to create very favourable conditions for horticulture. Sweet potato is the staple crop but a great variety of otner vegetables and fruits is also grown, and Kyaka horticultural techniques allow considerable leisure time for other activities. Their main form of livestock is the pig (in the periods I have spent among the Kyaka the pig population has probably approximately equalled the human population or slightly exceeded it) but they also keep a few cassowaries. Although many Kyaka have access to rich forest, hunting and forest collecting are not important sectors of their economy. Overall population density is about 140 to the square mile if forest areas which have not been cultivated within living memory are excluded in the estimate of space, but there is considerable local variation.

The Kyaka settlement pattern is one of dispersed homesteads and homestead clusters. Territorial units, with more or less clearly defined boundaries, are associated with named descent groups which are ideologically patrilineal; however, genealogical probing reveals that many members are there by virtue of one or more female links although these make almost no difference to their status if they have been brought up and have lived the greater part of their lives with the group. I call these descent groups, which are segmentary but which possess only incomplete frames, sub-subclans, sub-clans, clans and great-clans. The clan is characterized by (i) holding a single continuous territory with most of its boundaries fairly clearly defined; (ii) having rules of exogamy which apply not only to natal members in respect of each other but to natal members in respect of the children of daughters of natal members and to the children of daughters of natal members in respect of each other; (iii) having been the independent war-making unit in pre-contact days, and a group within which lethal fighting was most strongly disapproved; (iv) being the unit co-ordinating its members' performances in the Moka exchanges; and (v) being the unit collectively performing or potentially performing certain other cult and ceremonial activities.

In respect of clan territories men normally reside patrilocally and marriage is always followed by a period of virilocal residence which is expected to persist through the life-time of the partners, though in a small proportion of cases (about 10%) extended periods of uxorilocal residence later follow.

Clans include from about 20 to over 160 adult men. Many clans, including all large ones with over about 50 adult male members, are subdivided internally in terms of descent into named groups which we may term "subclans." Where more than two subclans are present within a clan these may be grouped according to some belief in the closer kinship of certain of their founders with each other than with others. Some large subclans are divided into named units which may be termed "sub-subclans."[10] Occasionally members of a single minimal named descent group, whether subclan or sub-subclan, may all be fitted on to one genealogy composited from information from its older members, but generally subclans are in turn internally segmented into a number of lineages of varying span whose members do not know how they are related to the other lineages of the sub-clan genealogically nor, in most cases, how they are descended from the eponymous subclan founding ancestor.

Further exogamic restrictions are sometimes phrased in terms of these sub-units of the clan, in that informants say that a man cannot marry into the natal subclan or sub-subclan of either of his grandmothers, but I am not sure how far in practice these apply to the named descent groups and not to lineages within them.

In terms of local organization, clans segment along lines which do not often coincide at all closely with their descent structure. Any clan with over 30 or so adult male members is likely to segment into a number of settlement groups each with from 15 to 40 adult males whose homesteads fall within easy range of a particular ceremonial ground or grounds and, generally, of a jointly owned men's house on one of these grounds. Such groups are readily identified or referred to by the name of their best known ceremonial ground.

These settlement groups, consisting of a core of male clansmen together with occasional co-resident affines and cognates of individual members, and wives, children and other dependents, approximate to local communities. They seldom have clearly defined territorial boundaries except where these coincide with the parent clan's territorial limits, though most of the land in the neighbourhood of ceremonial grounds and denser settlements will be associated unambiguously with one particular settlement group through its usufructory ownership by individuals and families who are members of the group. However, some of the land in its locality is likely to be held by men who are at present members of other settlement groups. Men can change their settlement group membership within the clan, though a man normally belongs to the same group as his father for as long as the father is still living. Underlying such movements is the fact that it is possible to obtain rights in garden land from clansmen other than one's close agnates on whom one has first claim. It is possible for a man whose lands or houses lie intermediate between two centres, or who has different areas of land and different homesteads near two different centres, to participate regularly in the activities of both groups.

In spite of the imprecision of its territorial and social boundaries the settlement group represents a real nexus of heightened everyday social activity, especially for women and children. People are as often identified by their settlement group place name as they are by a descent group name. Each settlement group has its acknowledged leader or leaders, the "Big Man" or "Big Men" *(numi)*.

Larger and more residentially dispersed settlement groups segment further into localized units of smaller scale but similar general nature, normally centring on one or more adjacent ceremonial grounds, with, possibly, a joint men's house; though often the personal house of a particular important man, sited on the ceremonial ground, serves the purposes of the group.

Kyaka refer to both settlement groups and subclans or sub-subclans as *akalianda mendake* ("Man-house one"). They justify this by saying that in the past each settlement group in fact consisted of one or two closely related named descent groups, but that things have become confused by movements in recent generations. However, it seems likely from what we know of the progressive territorial movement of most of the Kyaka clans in the remembered past that this is a rationalization, and that in the recent past at least the situation has in principle been the same as it is at present.

The effective segments of the clan or subclan defined by descent, as distinct from locality, can be conceived as either expanded families or lineages. These are clusters of elementary, compound or three-generation extended families whose senior male members, normally siblings or uncles and nephews, are linked (i) in their surviving interes´ ᵗn exchange transactions arising from the marriages of senior women of the group; (ii) in reversionary interests in each other's largely differentiated garden lands; and (iii) most importantly, in their collective duty to sacrifice to the ghosts of the previous generation of close kin, and especially to the ghost of their father or fathers.

Within this expanded family or lineage, the family or extended family, headed by an established adult man whose own father is dead, is an independent unit in landholding and exchange transactions, and within this unit, in turn, each individual male acquires from childhood on differentiated interests in pigs, garden-plots and exchange transactions.

Some Kyaka clans are linked by traditions of common patrilineal descent into units, which are generally named, like the clans and subclans, after their putative founding ancestor, and which we may call "great-clans." A great-clan is exogamous as regards its natal members, but marriage between a natal member of one clan within it and the child of a female natal member of another is quite permissible. In some cases the territories of clans comprising a great-clan are contiguous; in others they are divided by areas possessed by patrilineally unrelated groups. Within a great-clan certain component clans may have specially close links and may even enjoy a measure of joint interest in certain areas of land, though they will each have other areas exclusive to themselves. In theory member clans of a great-clan should not make war on each other, but in practice many such wars have taken place in recent generations. Great-clans do not normally combine for ceremonial or ritual purposes, though there is one Kyaka great-clan (the Kondeyen, comprising Ramwi, Kimbun and Kwunyengga clans) whose members perform a special cult at a joint fertility shrine which is believed to have been established by their founding ancestor.

The Kyaka rules of marriage, that one must avoid marriage with members of certain groups including notably one's clan or great-clan or mother's clan or grandmothers' groups, may alternatively be stated as that any cognate or affine except the widow of a kinsman is barred. Thus in terms of the existing set of kin relations each marriage creates a new bond between persons and families previously unrelated. The wedding itself involves a complex sequence of gifts, exchanges and feasts; and in later years further transactions of the same kind between the families of bride and groom, and between their descendants, follow on the birth of children, on the deaths of the spouses, and on the deaths of the children of the marriage, as well as on other formal occasions not related to life-crises. Thus cross-cutting the bonds of the settlement groups and clans is a mesh of individual and family bonds of affinity and cognative kinship.

Authority narrowly defined, or "ascribed leadership," only existed in pre-European Kyaka society within the extended family. However, individual men achieved and may still achieve positions of very considerable prestige and influence within their clans and even outside clan confines by their skill in manipulating pigs and valuables in loans and exchange transactions, by their prowess or former prowess in war, and by their forcefulness and shrewdness in debate of public affairs. If he has inherited or acquired by conquest land of any extent this also can be of advantage to a forceful man who can place other people in obligation to him by permitting them temporary use of plots or even by permanently allocating areas to them by gift or sale. However, performance in the Moka is perhaps the most important single criterion and index of influence and prestige. The Kyaka title of *numi* or "ranking leader" is explicitly stated by informants to be achieved when a man first becomes a principal in the Moka, and to be held only as long as he maintains this role.

The Enga Moka involves not only the Kyaka but the majority of Enga groups from beyond Wabag in the west to beyond Kompiem (Sau Valley) in the north, to the cultural and linguistic boundaries with the Waka and Gawil in the south, and in fact includes the Gawil or Kaugel people who are non-Enga speakers.[11] These peoples are all linked in the same cycles of festivals, though the character of the festivals changes as they proceed through the different regions, and changes presumably consistently with certain other features of the social systems of the participant groups. We are only concerned here with the Moka as it manifests itself among the Kyaka, but it is necessary to note, as a preliminary, that the Kyaka conceive that the cycles which they commence or terminate at the eastern end culminate or commence, as the case may be, in the west with the Mae (Central Enga), if not with groups even further away. The sequence of festivals moves along the river valleys and through the hillside belts of population, each clan organizing its main prestation, which may take place on one or several days, so that it follows on that of the clan to the east and is succeeded by the clan to the west (or vice versa), according to the direction of the particular cycle. The Metlpa Moka festivals do not, apparently, proceed in the same sort of cyclical order as the Enga ones do, each Metlpa group organizing a festival independently at a time best suited to itself.[12] However, many members of Metlpa clans near the Metlpa-Enga linguistic boundary are the individual exchange partners of Kyaka men and are thus involved in the commencement or culmination of the Enga cycles as well as in the Metlpa festivals. There is also a present-day tendency, at both eastern and western ends of the cycle, for clans which have previously not collectively participated to be drawn in to each succeeding cycle.[13]

Any particular cycle of the Enga Moka has three main phases of activity. In the first phase solicitory gifts (*kenju*) of legs of pork, live pigs, pearl shells, or axes are passed from partner to partner in the same direction as the main prestations were made in the previous cycle. These solicitory gifts are given individually, sometimes publicly and ostentatiously and sometimes privately, depending on their scale and on the social importance of the partners. Some of the objects concerned may be diverted and used by the recipients for purposes outside the Moka; others may be passed on and on through many hands.

The transmission of solicitory gifts over the entire area takes a period of at least several months, and normally more than a year. At the same time as these are being made, dancing grounds are being prepared and special houses built to accommodate the Moka-makers and festival guests and to display pearl shells. When houses and dancing grounds are ready, lines of pig-stakes are driven in, where the pigs at the main festival are to be tethered. This work provides occasions for food distributions and for the public transfer of the more substantial solicitory gifts. Large gatherings of men have the opportunity to harangue each other as to the scale of the gifts which they have given each other in the past and which they expect to give and receive in the future.

The second phase is that of the main prestations, or "true Moka (*Maku pilyamin,* "Moka they-make"), which are given in the opposite direction to the solicitory gifts, each giver of a solicitory gift receiving, in theory, a very much more substantial gift in return on this occasion. Unit gifts between important men normally number eight or ten pigs or valuables. Each clan's festival is preceded by a few days or weeks of frantic efforts on the part of its members to assemble plumes and other dancing regalia on loan from kin in other groups who are not simultaneously dancing. Each clan's actual festival performance is divided into two sets of trans- actions. In the first sets, gifts are given between fellow-clansmen (*yanggo pilyu*). In the case of a big clan these may take place on one or several separate days and on several different dancing grounds. Partners outside the clan are involved in these transactions in so far as pigs ultimately destined to them are formally shown to them at this stage, and they may "hold the tethering-rope" of the pigs marked to them as a public recog- nition of this. Then, when these transactions are complete, the total wealth of pigs and shells is mustered on one large dancing ground, displayed, and distributed to partners outside the clan. In this final distribution only the ranking men, the *numi,* make the presentations, which are both on their own behalf and on behalf of their followers.

The formalities of gift-making are very ostentatious. The givers, heavily and specially decorated with plumes and paint, individually dance up and down the lines of tethered beasts, striking the animals and shouting the names of recipients. There is extensive, excitable and aggressive speech- making by donors, recipients and other important men only indirectly interested in the immediate proceedings, and in the background is a large contingent of clansmen and their wives and children, dancing in full ceremonial regalia. In the earlier part of the day beast and shells are lined and relined, marked and remarked, and each person present through whose hands they are to pass acknowledges them and many in turn explain whom they are going to hand them over to. When the pigs, cassowaries, shells and other valuables finally change hands, names of recipients are called out and these have to run forward one at a time to the donors, jump with heels together and knees bent before them, shout *angke!,* a cry of recognition or thanks, and then, in the case of a gift of livestock, run back to the side- lines dragging or pushing the generally reluctant creature with them. The whole occasion of the main festival is one of great excitement, generally good-humoured, but always potentially convertible to violence if individuals feel they are not getting their due and in the heat of the moment try to redress matters. Watching such a scene, I was reminded of the mixture of good-humoured excitement and aggression of football crowds. It must be emphasized here that members of each host clan, on the occasion of its festival, give to partners not in one *single* other clan, but to individuals in nearly all clans which lie in the geographically apposite direction.

The large gatherings at the festivals include not only donors and re- cipients, and their kin, but partners of partners and others even more distantly linked in the Moka chain, and also all those who have loaned plumes and other items of personal decoration to the dancers or their representatives.

The third phase of the cycle follows when the main gift-giving festivals have reached the last clans in the chain, to east or west. The pigs, or the majority of them, are then killed and cooked, and the pork is passed back once more from partner to partner in the opposite direction (*poro pilyu*). I believe there is not much formality about this phase of the Moka, though I have not observed it. Along the line some pork is consumed and other pigs are killed, but much of the meat travels for many days and through many hands, being recooked several times, before it is finally eaten. European medical personnel in the Baiyer Valley tell me that a frequent sequel to this third phase is an epidemic of gastric complaints which can be very serious.

The next cycle proceeds in the opposite direction. In the last decade there have been periods of three to four years between cycles; it is likely that intervals were longer in pre-contact days. Three to four years may be the minimum period in which the pig population can be built up to sufficient proportions to justify the exchanges.

We may now examine the relationship of the Moka to the wider social system in three of its aspects: the Moka as a corporate activity of the clan; the Moka and the internal structure of the clan; and the Moka and inter-clan relations.

The first of these aspects does not need extended discussion, although it is important. Clansmen take pride in the clan's corporate performance in the Moka and measure this against the performance of other groups. Even socially insignificant men with little or no direct part in the ex-changes lend their efforts in preparing the dancing-grounds, building the houses and helping the leaders in the breeding and assembly of pigs. They attend the meetings at which the preliminary arrangements are made as well as the main festivals, and many of them dance at the festival. The performance of the leaders of the clan in the Moka is also seen by its members as the performance of the whole group. The Moka can then be seen as elaborating the functions of the clan, a group which is already in a number of other contexts of major political importance.

I should add here that the only Moka festival I have actually witnessed, late in 1959, was apparently aberrant in the way the host-clan organized it. The cycle was then just commencing with the most south-easterly of the Kyaka clans, the Ramwi, and this group in fact performed its main cere-monial giving of gifts to external exchange partners in two divisions, and on two occasions some months apart. This undoubtedly reflected a fission-ary tendency in this large clan, but the occasion for the division was pro-vided by a concatenation of external circumstances which it is impossible to discuss in detail here but which included European pressure to delay the Moka and some special interference by the Administration in the leadership of this group. However, such a division of Moka-making by one clan seems to be unusual and it was noticeable in this case that the whole clan in fact combined to dance and generally participate as hosts on the occasion which I witnessed, though only half of it was making its gifts then.

Turning to the bearing of the Moka on the internal structure of the clan we may note that, just as the clan as a whole co-ordinates its festival performances, so do the settlement-groups, or "men's house groups" within it. In fact the Moka provides one of the few occasions when this unit formally takes collective action, though we have seen that in everyday affairs it is a very important *de facto* group. One index of this is the fact that the occasion for actually constructing its joint men's house is a forthcoming Moka. In between festivals this group, although termed in Kyaka "one man-house," may have no such actual building.[14]

To understand further the importance of the Moka to the internal structure of the clan we must examine the interpersonal relationships within the clan which are activated by the Moka, since the solidarity of the clan obviously depends in part on the very close mesh of interpersonal ties binding its members.

Three classes of interpersonal Moka relationships within the clan may be discerned: those between close kinsmen whose duty it is to assist each other in this as in other matters; those between leaders and followers or dependents other than genealogically close relatives; and those between distantly related men, most often members of different settlement groups within the clan, who are exchange partners not distinguished terminologically from exchange partners outside the clan (*pu minyingk*).

Close kinsmen within the clan, who are normally close agnates, are dependent on each other in a whole range of activities and in respect of property and of exchange transactions other than in the Moka. A single extended family (father and adult sons) is often spoken of as though it formed a single unit in marriage and other exchanges, though in practice the individuals' shares are always clearly differentiated. It is the duty of a young man's father and elder brothers, if they are Moka-makers themselves, to make him the initial gifts which enable him to launch out in the Moka.

Members of an expanded family, brothers or uncles and nephews whose fathers are dead, may also share, through inheritance, certain Moka partners, though their individual transactions with these are always clearly differentiated, and in general the component families are quite independent Moka-making factions. They often make each other Moka gifts, justifying this by reference to their kin ties, but they do not necessarily do so.

Apart from help mutually given by close kinsmen Kyaka men of any importance also depend on the support of more distant relatives and even of genealogically unrelatable members of the same and nearby settlement groups. Such support may range from full participation in the leader's domestic group (it is very convenient for a polygynist without adult sons to have a bachelor or widower living in one of his homesteads and assisting one of his wives with male domestic tasks in the gardens, with the pigs, and with firewood) to minor and occasional assistance in gardening and other tasks at hand. Such men are likely to be granted garden-land, temporarily or permanently, to share particular current gardens with the leader, either on his ground or theirs, and, often, to look after pigs for him in their homesteads. This help with pig-raising is of considerable importance in the Moka. These supporters of a leader are normally in a state of mutual obligation with him, having been helped by him with bridewealth payment and the like, or expecting help of this kind. Such assistance obligates them to channel through him such pigs of their own as they are putting into the Moka. However, a man of lesser importance may be obligated to two or more leaders, so it is not possible to look upon groups of leaders and followers as mutually exclusive segmentary units within settlement group or clan.

Thirdly, within the clan are the *pu minyingk* ("rope holding") "friendships" or "partnerships" between men of roughly equivalent status who are, most often, members of different settlement groups and who are distantly related if related at all in terms of known agnatic genealogy. These relationships are sometimes traceable ultimately to a tie of cognatic kinship, often through two ancestresses who were true or classificatory "sisters." Such friendships are not only activated in the Moka. *Pu minyingk* assist each other with other exchange transactions, are often invited to come and eat pork when pigs have been killed, would help each other with house-building and similar tasks, and might, if it were convenient, permit each other use of garden land and make gardens together.

It will be seen that all these three types of relationship within the clan which are activated by the Moka, between close agnates, leaders and dependents, and full exchange partners, are also activated in other contexts. Obviously, the ties between close agnates would be extremely important even if the Moka did not exist. It could be argued, however, that in the case of the other categories of relationship the Moka is the predominant strand, or weighting factor, and that though they would possibly exist even without the Moka, it is under present circumstances the Moka which lends them their primary significance. It could possibly be argued further that the heavy weighting of these two kinds of ties devalues genealogically calculated agnatic kinship outside the expanded family or lineage.

The bearing of the Moka on inter-clan relations may be considered firstly in terms of the web of interpersonal ties linking members of different clans; secondly in terms of the co-ordinated activities of the clans as wholes in the festival cycle; and thirdly as relating to the exercise of power and influence outside the clan by individual leaders.

We have seen that the rules of exogamy ensure that every Kyaka has close ties with one clan other than his own, that of his mother if he is patrilocally resident, or of his father if he is matrilocally resident and primarily identified with his maternal kin and clan. This relationship through the mother (or father) is a bond with a whole clan to all of whose members he is a "sister's son" or "cross-cousin" (or "son" and "brother"), though he is specially closely related to a particular family or expanded family within it. Also, he recognizes kinship links with the other sister's sons of his mother's clan, who will be widely scattered through the other clans in his social field, and with some of these he may maintain close personal ties. Further, almost every man is linked through wife or wives and sisters to certain members of at least one other clan and generally of several, as an affine.

Moka partnerships to a very large extent follow these lines of individual affinity and cognatic kinship. The most frequent Moka partnership outside the clan is between brothers-in-law or father-in-law and son-in-law, though these are often carried over into the succeeding generations so that they then occur between mother's brother and sister's son and between cross-cousins. Maternal parallel cousins are also frequent partners. However, not only in terms of frequency but of content the partnerships between affines tend to be the most significant. Also, on the basis of the limited case material at my disposal, it seems that if a man over-commits himself and is forced to let down some of his partners in order to satisfy others, he is most likely to abandon his cross-cousins and other cognates but honour his obligations to his brothers-in-law. Here affective sentiments between partners apparently play little part; the decision is, one may suppose, taken because of material necessity, to ensure the stability of his marriage, and the long-term benefits of the ties to his children.

The Moka then adds extra weight and content to the web of affinal and kinship ties between men of different clans, but particularly to the affinal tie.[15] In general terms it does not affect the categories of direct personal relationships outside the clan, but may affect their relative importance as categories, and in individual cases allows kinsmen to elaborate very greatly the obligations existing between them.

However, another point must be considered here. The fact that the Moka is a chain of exchange partnerships means that instead of a man being concerned only with the actions of his personal affines and cognates outside his clan, he is also affected and concerned by the partners of his partners, to whom his solicitory gifts are transmitted and from whom the main gifts are to come in return. Men are aware of the onward links in the Moka chain for several stages in either direction, and are aware of the indirect obligations entailed. If there is a dispute over a Moka debt, not only do the partners immediately concerned argue it out, but the "courts" are generally attended by several other members of the chain whose interests are involved. It is hard to document what bearing this recognition of indirect dependence may have on other situations where the indirect partners may be in conflict or require each other's aid. I have observed one case where one Government Headman (*Tultul* Lengke of Roepo Wapisuk) helped conciliate a marital dispute in which another headman (the Yalimakali *Luluai*), who was an indirect partner of his was involved, in such a way that the Moka partnership hingeing on the marriage should not be prejudiced. I think one may assume that in general disputes are less likely to be prosecuted to extremes where even indirect Moka interests are at stake than they otherwise might be. And the recognition of these indirect partnerships is specifically a function of the Moka and not of the kinship system as it would be if the Moka did not exist.

Similarly in its collective aspects the necessity for all Kyaka clans to participate and co-ordinate their activities implies recognition of a measure of collective interest and a period of peace while preparations are being made. In pre-administration (pre-*ca.* 1947) days, war not only prevented the actual festivals from occurring but also prevented the assembly of pigs for exchanges. Wars disrupted the pig-breeding cycle, and the settlement of wars and payment of wirgild demanded the expenditure of pigs which could therefore not, in most cases, be used in the Moka. Also, Moka and other exchanges could not take place between members of groups who had not made at least preliminary settlement of wirgild debts outstanding between them.[16] The apparent increasing frequency of Moka cycles in the post-contact period probably reflects as much the cessation of war as the increase in wealth which can be incorporated in the exchanges.

At the present time at least, the Moka is seen by some Kyaka as an institution in which they as a people have a collective interest. I heard a speaker in 1959, when plans for the 1960 Moka were being discussed, stress that the Wabag (Central Enga) Moka was on a tremendous scale, and that it was up to the local *kanyi wamb* ("in-between people," i.e. people between the Lanim and the Baiyer Rivers) to show that they would not be outdone and put on an even better display.

Lastly, there is the question of leadership or political influence outside the confines of the clan and [of the] bearing the Moka has on this. Although Kyaka acknowledge no personal authority beyond that of the father within the family or extended family, the ranking Big Men (*numi*) can exert influence over a much wider field, and there is or was, in pre-contact days before the appointment of Government Headmen somewhat confused the situation, in most settlement groups and clans a clear ordering of the three or four most important individuals. War and the Moka were the two widest fields in which individuals achieved their position. A man's exchange partners outside his clan and his net of supporters and partners inside it were necessarily complementary. Really important operators in the Moka have to be members of large powerful clans. Men who are outstanding in the Moka are renowned over a wide area, as were successful war-leaders in pre-contact days, who also had to be members of powerful clans. It is hard now to reconstruct precisely how Moka leadership and war leadership were related, but it seems that a man's most stable and valued Moka-partnerships were with members of groups whom he could hope to mobilize when necessary in the shifting inter-clan alliances which characterized Kyaka war-making. Further, war-allies outside the clan were mobilized both by stressing obligations of kinship and affinity as such, and by promises of substantial material reward for assistance. A man whose Moka credit was good could presumably expect to get allies on the second score more easily, for there would be little question about whether or not he would be able to recompense them.

SUMMARY

I have tried to demonstrate three main ways in which the Moka is of political significance. Firstly, the exchanges activate individual relationships of kinship and affinity already existing in the social structure, but throw extra weight on certain of these and create new extra-kin relations with significant consequences to the kinship and descent system as a whole. Secondly, the Moka is a particularly important field for individual enterprise in gaining power and prestige in a social system where leadership and influence are almost entirely achieved rather than ascribed. Thirdly, at the group level, the festival cycle periodically co-ordinates the activity of the whole of Kyaka society in a way no other indigenous institution does; and in this, in pre-contact days, it limited the physically and socially destructive expression of inter-clan hostility and competition in war.

NOTES

1. The substance of a paper delivered to Section J of the New Zealand Science Congress, Wellington, on 13th May, 1960. I am indebted to the Australian National University, the Wenner-Gren Foundation, and the American Philosophical Society for financing the field work on which it is based.
2. Cf. Fortes, 1945.
3. Malinowski, 1922.
4. Evans-Pritchard, 1951, p. 95. But see also Firth's rejoinder in Firth, 1957, pp. 222-3.
5. Vicedom, 1943, Vol. II, pp. 458-60.
6. Elkin, 1953, pp. 196, 199-200.
7. Fortes and Evans-Pritchard, 1940.
8. Smith, 1956; Barnes, 1959.
9. "Moka" is also used in pidgin English in some Highland areas to designate any major public prestation except bridewealth, and especially for wirgild payments.
10. I am conscious that this terminology is inelegant, though it is not without precedent (Reay, 1959, p. 28). The problem is to find a term comparable to "lineage" for a series of segmentary groups which lack the complete genealogical structure essential to a lineage system.
11. Bus, 1951, p. 817.
12. Vicedom, 1943, Vol. 2, pp. 451-72.
13. Concerning the western end of the chain, I use personal information from Dr. M. J. Meggitt, 1956.
14. It may be that in pre-contact days the settlement group men's house was also associated with cult practices not closely related to the Moka, but I lack information on this point. Nowadays each settlement group has its Mission hut, used in evening

prayer meetings on week-days. Churches used for Sunday services are shared by members of a number of contiguous clans.

15. It may be argued that in so far as it reinforces the importance of affinal against matrilateral ties, it is a further factor militating against elaborated lineage structure within the clan, since it is a well-established fact that matrilateral links within a system of patrilineal descent groups have in most cases an important role in the genealogical definition of segments. Further, the stress on the affinal link, which the individual or his family can *choose,* exercising their choice to their own advantage in the competition for status, is also part of a social pattern which favours achieved as against ascribed status.

16. Elkin (1951, pp. 199-200) describes wirgild and ally-compensation payments being made at the same time as the *Te* among the Central Enga. It appears that the Central Enga call both the Exchange Festivals and these other payments by the same word, *te,* though they do distinguish them. Kyaka in contrast reserve the words *te* and *maku* for the ceremonial exchanges and call wirgild payments *wandepa pu minyilyu* ("wandepa-tree rope I-hold").

REFERENCES

BARNES, J. A. (1959): "Politics without Parties," *Man,* Vol. 59, p. 4.

BUS, G. A. M. (1951): "The *Te* Festival or Gift Exchange in Enga," *Anthropos,* Vol. 46, pp. 813-24.

ELKIN, A. P. (1953): "Delayed Exchange in Wabag Sub-district," *Oceania,* Vol. 23, No. 3, pp. 161-201.

EVANS-PRITCHARD, E. E. (1951): *Social Anthropology,* London.

FIRTH, RAYMOND (Ed.) (1957): *Man and Culture,* London.

FORTES, MEYER (1945): *The Dynamics of Clanship among the Tallensi,* London.

FORTES, MEYER, and EVANS-PRITCHARD, E. E. (Ed.) (1940): *African Political Systems,* London.

MALINOWSKI, BRONISLAW (1922): *Argonauts of the Western Pacific,* London.

REAY, MARIE (1959): *The Kuma,* Melbourne.

SMITH, M. G. (1956): "On Segmentary Lineage Systems," *Journal of the Royal Anthropological Institute,* Vol. 86, pp. 39-80.

VICEDOM, GEORG, and TISCHNER, HERBERT (1943): *Die Mbowamb,* Hamburg.

APPENDIX

I spent thirteen months among the Kyaka between January, 1955, and March, 1956, and four months between September, 1959, and January, 1960. One main cycle of festivals took place, from east to west, in late 1954, another from west to east in 1957, while one from east to west had an interrupted start in October, 1959, and should be proceeding now in 1960. Thus the only actual main Moka festival I have witnessed was at the interrupted commencement of the cycle among the Ramwi clan in 1959. In 1955–1956 I gathered some miscellaneous but not very satisfactory information about Moka activities and partnerships, but this was a bad time to study this topic, as interest in it was then minimal. In 1959, however, very many days of the four months I was present were devoted by the local men to Moka preparations—the giving of solicitory gifts, building of special houses, driving in of pig-stakes, preliminary display of pearl shells, and so on. I was therefore then able to get a considerable amount of information about this aspect of the cycle. However, I have no direct observations of the third phase of the cycle, when the pigs are killed and the pork changes hands.

14

HEADHUNTING PRACTICES OF THE ASMAT OF WEST NEW GUINEA

Gerard A. Zegwaard

The inhabitants of the swampy areas of southern Netherlands New Guinea have won a reputation for their headhunting practices. Because these practices were carried out even in the Australian Territory of Papua, which caused the Australian Government to protest, the Dutch Colonial Administration was forced to establish the first police post in Merauke with the Marind people (1902). The Jaqai have been forced to stop headhunting only since World War II; and the Asmat (at present thought to number about 25,000) still continue the practice.

During my stay with the Asmat (1952–1956; I had been with the related Mimikan tribes from 1946 to 1952) I had ample opportunity to study their headhunting practices on hundreds of occasions, as I was the first white man to take up residence among them and there was no representative of the Dutch Colonial Administration to enforce the ordinances against headhunting that were carried out elsewhere.

Though we may expect that even with the Asmat headhunting will gradually decrease and finally vanish, it is worth while to analyze the ideologies from which this practice originated. For, even when the Asmat people will no longer hunt heads, they will have these ideologies.

Because it is impossible to mention in detail all the differentiations that occur in the various districts among the different tribes of the Asmat area, I shall limit myself to the coastal area, notably to the inhabitants of the village of Sjuru, at the mouth of the Utumbuwé river near Flamingo Bay.

It may be mentioned in passing that the Asmat have associated headhunting with cannibalism. I had many an opportunity to observe this, but this exposition may make it clear that cannibalism is not the objective of headhunting (as far as the Asmat are concerned), but only a subsidiary part of it.

I will first give the mythical origin of the hunting feast and describe the

Reproduced by permission of the American Anthropological Association and the Reverend Gerard A. Zegwaard from the *American Anthropologist,* 61:1020-1041 (1959).

ritual as taught in the past and executed by following generations. This mythical background was told to me by Warsékomen, elderly chieftain of Sjuru, an extremely clever man with a remarkable memory (he knew nine past generations of all clans in his tribe; in many instances I was able to check the correctness of his information against other sources). In his description of the myth he typically mixed the myth and the reality as experienced by him.

In the second part I will describe a number of customs and rituals that have a more or less close connection with headhunting, and the actual headhunting raid. In the third and final part I will attempt an explanation of the headhunting practice, in which we will meet with several factors that may have influenced the Asmat simultaneously, but not to the same extent.

1. THE MYTH BEHIND HEADHUNTING (As Told by Warsékomen)

There were two brothers. The senior was called Desoipitsj (*deso*— wound; *ipitsj*—man: man with wound) and the junior Biwiripitsj (*biwir* or *bewor*—many colored parrot: parrot man). Because of his physical condition the elder brother had always to stay indoors and the younger had to go out to support him. One day, returning from a hunting trip, Biwiripitsj brought home a pig. He cut off the head and thrust a dagger into the throat so that the point came out through the neck. The dagger was a sharpened cassowary thighbone. With the point of the dagger Biwiripitsj pinned the head of the pig to the floor of the hut, which was covered with bark. The elder brother had been watching and after some time remarked: "Bah, a pig's head is but a pig's head. Why not replace it with a human head? That would be something, I think." But the younger brother didn't like the idea at all. "What are you talking about? Besides, where could I get a human head?" (The story presupposes that just the two brothers are around.) The older brother insisted, and proposed: "Well, you can have my head." But the younger wouldn't hear of this and refused emphatically. However, Desoipitsj continued to argue and in the end succeeded in persuading his younger brother. Biwiripitsj thereupon killed Desoipitsj with a spear, cut into the throat with a bamboo knife as far as he could, and pressed the head forward until the vertebrae of the neck cracked. He then removed the head from the body. The loose head, however, was able to speak and it gave instructions to Biwiripitsj, who obediently executed the orders given by it.

(1) To begin with, the head of Desoipitsj taught Biwiripitsj the technique of butchering (*nao*). He was told to make a deep cut with a bamboo knife from the anus to the neck in such manner that the cut went through one side of the trunk to the armpit and from there went by the collar bone to the throat. He was instructed to make a similar cut on the other side,

but now from top to bottom. Through these openings he had to break the ribs with a sharpened palmwood stick (*om*) or with a stone ax (*si*). Then he put his hand underneath the chest, which could now be lifted easily and put aside. Arms and legs were first loosened, then cut off. Now Biwiripitsj took the entrails as in a bundle and removed them from the backbone with a vigorous jerk. Only the backside remained. The various parts, including the entrails, were placed in the fire and roasted. The upper part of the body and the arms were at once ready for consumption, but the lower part and the thighs had to be mixed with sago (a starch prepared from the pith of the sago palm) which had to be made in the form of long sticks, whereupon these too could be eaten. [Preparation of sago in the form of long sticks is often the usual way of preparation in the rest of southern New Guinea, but is done by the Asmat only on ritual occasions.]

(2) The second lesson related to the triumphant return of the men from a headhunting raid to their village, which was a prelude for the initiation rite of a young man. [Here we note how our informant, Warséko-men, unconsciously shifts from myth into reality; in the myth there was only Biwiripitsj, here Warsékomen and his men from Sjuru are in action.]

Biwiripitsj blew a bamboo hunting horn to make known the success of his raid. On the way home the "paddle song" was sung. But he had also explained how those who had stayed behind—the old men, the women, and the children—had to act. The eldest man was to ask the headhunters approaching on the river in their dugout canoes: "How did you get along? What did you accomplish?" Whereupon the leader of the headhunters, who meanwhile arranged their canoes side by side in battle array, was to answer: "I, Biwiripitsj, have been to the Islands river this night. I killed a man, a big man. The flesh lies in the canoe." From the river bank would come the question: "What is his name?" And the answer: "His name is Desoipitsj." That caused the people on the river bank to jump and howl, while the canoes covered the remaining distance at a tremendous speed. The women had adorned themselves with ornaments and were beside themselves, cheering and dancing in honor of the warriors.

Biwiripitsj showed them how the oldest brother of the mother of the boy who was to be initiated, had to submerge the decapitated head for a while under water and then run with it to the bachelors' house. [Pubescent Asmat boys are separated from their families and live in the bachelors' quarters, which serves also as clubhouse for the men.] Meanwhile the spectators sang a long-drawn "e-e-e-e-h" and sounded bamboo horns. Then the singers had to harmonize with Biwiripitsj and sing a song alluding to the pose of shame that had been assumed by the initiate. The mother's oldest brother had to pin the head to the floor of the bachelors' house near the fireplace, with a cassowary-bone dagger, so that it might dry partially.

(3) As the head was to play a principal part in the initiation of a son or a younger brother of the headhunter, Biwiripitsj now demonstrated the role of the initiate and at the same time the role of the mother's oldest brother. The latter made a mat and filled it with *eram* (magic) twigs. The initiate took the mat under his arm and walked out of the bachelors' house. He went to a canoe, put the mat on its bottom, and acted as if he returned to the place from whence the decapitated man came. He then apparently changed his mind and went back to the bachelors' house, after some water had been poured over his head. After entering the bachelors' house he sat down on the floor, lowered his head, did not look up, and paid no attention to what happened around him. He assumed the pose of one who is ashamed, a taboo pose.

The initiate, acted by Biwiripitsj, received the name of the victim—that is, of the elder brother, Desoipitsj. The Asmat call this name the *nao juus* or decapitation name, often also referred to as *owam juus* or bamboo name (after the bamboo breast-plate that is later worn as a substitute of the hunted head). The new Desoipitsj persevered in his pose of shame for several days. Now and then the bystanders tried to upset him, but he sat tight. In this way he was to make clear that he was going to be a determined, fearless warrior.

He was subjected to various food limitations—the same taboos that rule the lives of new-born babies—for example, fish with thorns (a form of sympathetic magic: to avoid harm in the future).

The mother's oldest brother held the head long enough above the fire to scorch part of the hair. The ash of this burnt hair was mixed with some of the blood that had been collected in a mussel shell when the victim's head was cut. The mixture of blood and ash was smeared on the head, shoulders, and body of the initiate and thus the identity between the initiate and the victim was effected. Whereupon the initiate was adorned by his mother's oldest brother.

The ritual of identification and adornment had to take place in the afternoon or evening following the raid.

As instructed by the talking head of Desoipitsj, the whole body of Desoipitsj junior was painted with red ochre [burnt earth from the interior]. Alternating black and white stripes were painted on the face with wet ash and chalk. The hair of the initiate was lengthened with sago-leaf fibers, made in curls; a piece of mother-of-pearl had to hang on his forehead; on the back of the head were placed two big tassels of cassowary feathers; in the septum was placed a beautiful open-work swine-bone or wooden nosepin, decorated with beads or Job's tears; around the arms, wrists, calves of the legs, and the ankles, belts of finely split rattan were attached, and in one arm-belt was placed a carved human bone or a cassowary bone [dagger]; across the chest and the shoulders was put a crossed band; on the abdomen a triton shell; around the hips a sago-leaf-fiber apron [otherwise exclusively worn by married women]; and on the back the bamboo plate or *owam*. The bamboo plates are at first worn on the back and later shifted to the breast. [The breast is the more prominent place, as shown by the fact that it is the privilege of the great headhunters to wear their ditty bag, *bilum*, on the breast, whereas lower persons wear it on the back.]

There are several plates. First, a bamboo lath, *bakar-owam*, about twelve inches long and one inch wide, with pointed tips; next, a combination of two or four shorter and narrower laths that are bound side by side, *owam pa*, and then another combination of still narrower but somewhat longer laths, arranged in such a way that they fill three-fourths of a circle (almost as the spokes of a wheel). The three types of bamboo plate are all used during the initiation; afterwards one type can be used as a common adornment on the occasion of festivities or warfare. Instead of the third bamboo plate a string of dogs' teeth may be used *(juur sis owam)*.

When the initiate had been invested with the bamboo plates, the *mbipitsjin* (the skin of the victim that had covered his nose and upper lip) was hung over the plates, after it had been dried above the fire. (This piece of skin is removed separately during the scalping.)

(4) In the next instruction, the head of Desoipitsj taught Biwiripitsj and all future generations how to handle the decapitated head. In the evening the head should be roasted; during the night it should be kept on some sort of loft; and in the morning it should be scalped. But in the actual case of the first Desoipitsj this process was put off until the end of the whole ritual, because he had to continue his instructions. The treating of the head of the victim was again to be the function of the mother's oldest brother.

The next morning the head was to be taken down from the loft and the nose-skin was to be taken off first. Then the jaws had to be removed. The brothers of the initiate's mother worked in turns according to their age. While cutting and carving they would comment on the victim's past actions; for example, while taking the skin off the mouth one would say: "Yesterday this mouth ate fish on the bank of the river; today it is dead."

A cut had to be made with a bamboo knife or a shell across the head from the root of the nose to the nape of the neck. Thus the skin could be torn off in two pieces toward the ears.

The jaw bone had to be thrown outside; those interested could take it. It was eagerly seized and used as an ornament on the breast of a boy or woman who had to participate in the initiation rite.

The preparation of the head went on. It was held above the fire so that the flames touched the temple and the back. Then a hole was cut into it with the narrow side of a stone ax. The ax had been decorated and had been named after the victim [initiate]. The brains were then shaken out through the hole and caught in a mat. The mucus that came out first was at once removed. The brains were deposited in an *an,* a vessel made of the leaf-sheath of a sago palm. The remaining bits of brain were scraped out with a bamboo knife. About midnight the brains, mixed with sago prepared in the form of long sticks, were eaten exclusively by the old men.

After the eating of the brains, the leaves in which the sago had been wrapped were put in the *eram okop,* the magic mat. Into this mat also went the inedible parts of the body: eyeballs, genitals and the like. [Information about the contents of the mat was whispered into my ear by Warsékomen.]

Thereupon the skull was painted with ash, ochre, and chalk, and then decorated with tassels of cassowary feathers, beads, and so forth. The nose was filled with resin, and a net was drawn over the whole head to facilitate attaching the ornaments. The decorated head was laid between the spread legs of the initiate, who meanwhile had been sitting on the floor of the bachelors' house in his pose of shame. In the myth the head of Desoipitsj was placed against the groin of the initiate. The head had to remain there for two or three days, and the initiate had to look at it incessantly. He could take food only stealthily, when no one watched him.

During these days the women of the celebrating community had to collect young pith of the sago palm, and each time they came home in the evening they had to announce their return by blowing bamboo hunting horns.

(5) One or two days later the ceremonies were continued according to the next instruction of Desoipitsj. Every villager had to adorn himself, and the canoes too had to be freshly painted with ochre and chalk. Everyone boarded the canoes. The initiate stood in the canoe of his relatives, and the skull was placed before him on the bottom of the canoe. The brothers of the initiate's mother were to stand in front of him; later they would squat. Like an old man, the initiate would lean on a stick on which was set a disk with a hole in the center so that a few inches of the stick would show above the disk. The initiate would hold the stick with two hands somewhere in the middle. Slowly the canoes, manned with drumming and singing villagers, began to move down the river toward the sea—to the west, to where the sun sets.

The initiate acted like a worn-out old man; he appeared to become weaker and weaker, the farther westward they went. After a while he began to lean on the shoulder of an uncle and finally collapsed and lay down on the bottom of the canoe.

At that stage he was lifted by one of his mother's brothers and, together with the skull, was immersed for a while in the sea. After he was hauled back into the canoe, all his ornaments were taken off and put in the magic mat; they were never to be removed from it. From this moment on, the skull was no longer used by the initiate; he had to hang it on the breast of a woman, who had asked the owner-hunter for this favor.

While singing, all turned back toward the land, to the east, to where the sun rises. When they reached the shore, they entered the tide-flooded forest to look for crabs. The initiate joined them, but he had to be careful not to break off the pincers of a crab, as that might cause the death of the headhunter.

The initiate now acted as a new-born babe, and then as a child who did not know how to handle a paddle. He acted as if he did not know the name of the river and its tributaries, or the names of the trees. But gradually he seemed to learn more and more. At every tributary his name was called and he answered with his bamboo horn.

Back again in the village he did not enter the bachelors' house, but went to the house of his family. There he was again decorated from head to foot, and now the bamboo plates were hung on his breast while all present sounded a long-drawn "é-é-é-é-é-h." Henceforth the initiate acted as a young man, full of vigor and admired by all.

(6) After the submersion rite there were a few days of rest. The next instruction called for a ceremony in the sago-woods. While the whole community watched, the brothers of the initiate's mother cut down a sago palm and removed the bark. The initiate looked on, together with the woman to whom he had handed the skull. Somewhere near the middle of the palm trunk a *gaba-gaba,* sago-leaf-stalk, was planted by his mother's brothers. By loosening the rind, except at the top and bottom of the stalk, they could bend the middle part so that an oblong hoop was formed.

First the woman with the skull approached and swung with a sago pounder through the opening of the hoop at the sago palm without touching it. She handed the pounder to the initiate, who in the same manner swung at the tree. Meanwhile the onlookers sang: "*Amus jene, amus jene . . .*" [sago pounder, sago pounder], following with the same song that was sung on occasion of the preparation of the head.

After this ceremony, everyone went in search of palm pith. The woman with the skull found palm pith for the initiate, who repaid her with pith that he had found. The woman also prepared some sago in the shape of a stick and gave a few pieces to the boy. Other pieces were put in the magic mat.

The ritual ended with the brothers of the initiate's mother decorating him once again.

The night after the sago-pounding ritual there was a dance in the bachelors' house, with drums providing the accompaniment. The following morning all lengthened their hair with curled sago-leaf fibers. For the last time the initiate and the skull were decorated for the final ceremony, which was to take place the next night. The skull was hung in the center of the bachelors' house. At night a fire was built in front of the house, and singers and dancers sat in groups in solemn silence. Then the initiate came out of the bachelors' house, carrying the magic mat under his arm and in his hand the richly decorated skull. The men carried shields which they moved up and down, toward them and away from them, while a song was intoned; the dance began and the initiate joined the men, swinging the skull. The songs which were sung during the preparation of the head and during the sago pounding were repeated.

This dance, which with some breaks lasted until dawn, completed the *nao pokmbu,* the headhunting and initiation festivity.

In the myth the head of Desoipitsj was at this time roasted and scalped, as described earlier, after it had once more emphatically ordered that in the future all should obey its instructions.

Warsékomen ended his description of the myth with this apologetic remark: "If Desoipitsj had not pressed the headhunting and butchering on his brother Biwiripitsj, we the people of the Asmat would never have been headhunters."

Additional remarks on the mythical procedures. Thus, in the myth, the headhunting festivity came down from Desoipitsj, who instructed his younger brother in everything connected with the festivity.

The first ceremony was the butchering. The method described above is also applied when a cassowary, pig, crocodile, or big lizard is slaughtered. Throughout New Guinea we find regional instructions on the slaughtering of animals, and these regional methods are faithfully executed on both animals and human beings.

The actions of both the headhunters and those who stayed behind are also regulated; they consist mostly of certain traditional songs.

The heads acquired are intended for the initiation of sons and younger brothers, nephews and cousins. At times it is hard for a hunter to decide who is to be favored. All the different sections of the village, grouped around the bachelors' houses, have claims and those who have treated the others expect a feast in return. Often the claims of the different clans would lead to altercations and sometimes to bloodshed. On such occasions the corpses of the headhunting victims would be the subject of fights, would be taken and retaken by the different factions. It has happened that village unity has been permanently damaged by such fights.

Young boys are the proper candidates for heads, but, in what seem abnormal circumstances, older males and even women may be favored. The pose of the initiate, acting as if he were the decapitated victim, has a special meaning. The informants emphasized repeatedly that the initiate is smeared with the ash of the burnt hair and with the blood of the victim. This is explained by the fact that the initiate assumes the name of the victim. This identity between victim and initiate will later prove very useful. When meeting the initiate, even after many years, relatives of the murdered person will always call him by his assumed name, the victim's name, and treat him as their relative. They dance and sing for him and give him presents. It is strictly forbidden to kill people from other villages who, because of their ritual names, are related to one's village. These people are often chosen to be negotiators. On my tours I frequently hired them to be my guides to tribes hostile to their community. More than once I witnessed persons with the adopted names of headhunting victims being enthusiastically welcomed by relatives of the victim, especially on our Mission station where we had visitors from all parts of the district. Cases are known of the killing of such people but it is considered a very serious breach of the taboo law, and violators were said ultimately to meet their punishment, for example by the extinction of the whole family by disease.

There are definite regulations governing what is to be done with the head and how the scalping, removal of the brains, and decoration of the skull have to be performed. It should be noted that the initiate is absolutely excluded from the cannibalistic meal, in which the brains are consumed. It is certain that only the head is taken to the bachelors' house (social and ritual center of the neighborhoods), where it must undergo the ritual treatment. The flesh of the body is distributed at once after the butchering, according to the traditional scheme, among relatives and friends; after the return to the village it is taken to their homes. Even the women and children get their share. The bones are for the dogs.

For a considerable time the skull must rest between the thighs of the initiate, almost touching his genitals; thus there is thought to be a relationship between the skull and the genitals of the youngster, whose initiation marks his entry into manhood.

The immersion rite is clearly a rite of passage, with a ritual death and ritual rebirth. A cosmic event—the daily course of the sun—seems to have suggested this ritual: a parallelism in which sunrise is thought of as birth and sunset as death.

The sago pounding and the nightly dance with the decorated skull need not be interrelated, as may be gathered from the lapse of time between these phases. It is possible that the ritual sago pounding is a later addition for it seems to be associated with the following myth, which was related in the form of a song in a bachelors' house of Sjuru on the occasion of the inauguration of that house in the Ar section (December 26, 1953): *omo Faitepi omo.* . . . (*Fait* is the name of a river, southeast of the Asmat area; *ep* is the mouth of the river; *om* is a club, used by those who have no axes, to uproot the soil around a tree and also to remove the rind from a trunk.)

Biwiripitsj [this name appears in many mythical stories] went with his wife and children to the river Fait to pound sago. Near the mouth (*ep*) of the river he felled a palm that was in full flower and with his rooting stick he removed the rind, beginning at the *umu* (part of the trunk where the branches begin) and cutting toward the *mopan* (the thick part near the roots). Biwiripitsj then called his son and ordered him to lie prostrate on the bare trunk of the tree. The boy did so. The father [according to some versions the mother] took a sago pounder and struck the boy's neck with force. The head, decorated with hair-lengthenings, was separated from the body and with a few jumps landed in a *jimemmut* tree, where it became entangled by the hair. Blood from the head trickled down the trunk. The chin pointed upward and the hair-lengthenings hung down. The father [or mother] struck again and again with the pounder and smashed the body. Blood and flesh were entirely mixed with the pith of the sago palm, and the entrails splashed high into the surrounding trees. When the mother began to work the pith, it proved to be very easy to knead. She rejoiced and said: "Before it was very hard to knead sago and wring it out, now it's extremely easy." The son, however, was not completely dead, for the head began to talk. He taught his father the songs that have to be sung at the decapitation festivities: the songs on the way home from a raid, at the arrival in the village, when shaking out the brains, and so on.

2. Customs and Rituals Connected with Headhunting

Ancestors' cult. Before we discuss the various ceremonies in detail, it will be necessary to indicate first the relation between war (in the form of headhunting) and other rituals. Almost every larger festivity or public ritual presupposes a headhunting raid. The festivities occur at regular, short intervals and generally last for several months. Often the festivities are organized at the same time or with a short interval in the various neighboring villages.

The main festivities are: (a) the celebration at the building of a new bachelors' house, (b) the festivities on the occasion of the carving and the erection of an ancestor pole, and (c) the weaving of masks, followed by a solemn mask dance. On the occasion of any of these celebrations the spirits of the dead are supposed to come back to the community of the living.

When celebrating the building of a bachelors' house, grubs of the sago beetle are gathered and solemnly poured down from a loft into a cylindrical basket of sago-leaf ribs (*gaba-gaba*). The basket (*samu mini: samu* is the name for the spirits of the decapitated, spirits without heads; *mini* means a straight basket), which may be five to seven feet long, is filled to the brim and taken apart after the ceremony.

In the case of the ancestor pole, the spirits are carved in wood—for example, on the prow of a canoe.

The masks too represent the spirits of the deceased. However, on each occasion (celebration of the bachelors' house, the ancestors' pole, the masks) the spirits are allowed to stay for just one night. Then they are terrified and attacked without mercy. Thus, it seems that all festivities have the same object: to drive away the souls, who are forced to migrate to the *safan,* the realm of the souls, beyond the sea.

These rituals revive the memory of the dead and their revengeful feelings. But there is more: when we try to find out which spirits seem to play a part in the rituals, we discover that they involve largely the spirits of decapitated people—in other words, spirits who have a special reason to be angry or who, when living, had proven that they were not to be mocked at; spirits who may harm the community. Even these spirits are urged to leave and to cross to hades. When they have received the satisfaction of revenge they are more easily induced to go away.

The names of these spirits are passed on to other persons who will take over their duties and functions, and thus it is made quite clear to them that they are no longer needed.

On similar occasions the neighboring Kamoro (in Mimika) tell the spirits that they are indeed excellent boar hunters or war-lords, but that the survivors can easily get along without them, because there are still good hunters and war-lords left in the community. In fact, the Asmat and Kamoro tribes have much in common, both in language and culture.

As headhunting appears to be a part of the big rituals and because those rituals aim at driving away the spirits, it may be inferred that headhunting is also practiced to get even with and to satisfy the spirits. Thus it is practiced to urge the spirits to retreat.

Therefore, such rituals are not foreign to the general frame of Asmat religion in which the spirits of the deceased play the predominant part; on the contrary, they are an integral part of the religion. New canoes, new houses, spears, paddles, breast- and back-bags, strings of dogs' teeth, and even domestic dogs and pigs are named after the dead. The ornamentation of the mentioned objects can be understood in terms of this attitude and it is not surprising that human figures—either realistically or idealistically represented—are the essential pattern of Asmat art. And in the mind of the Asmat, they are real, they live. All these objects are generally called *etsjo pok,* things that make great. They serve to kindle thoughts of revenge and may be given to others who, by accepting such gifts, bind themselves to cooperate in the retaliation.

On one occasion, after a murder occurred in Sjuru, one of the relatives of the murdered man gathered a bundle of fire-wood and gave it the name of the deceased. He kept the wood in the loft of the bachelors' house, and after some time offered it to people of the other sections of the village. Those who accepted agreed to help him retaliate.

In the bachelors' houses the posts, roofbeams, central beam, walls, and the like, are named after the fathers and the brothers of those who occupy the houses. In the newly-erected bachelors' houses, the walls would not be placed until the *fo mbufum* ritual had been performed, that is, until the new canoes (again named after the spirits of the deceased) had been publicly put into use by removing the mats which concealed the ancestors' figures.

The Asmat, therefore, is surrounded by *etsjo pok,* objects named after the deceased, which remind him of his duty of revenge. The etsjo pok are not limited to private property (canoes, private houses, paddles, spears), but include public property as well (bachelors' houses, masks, ancestor poles).

Ceremonials connected with headhunting. First there is the *firao wu* ceremony, which opens the celebration for the construction of a new bachelors' house. A pole or palm pith (*firao wu*), which must end in a thick knob, is cut with ritual paraphernalia. The pole is decorated and carried in procession to the canoe. The accompanying ritual is similar to that of the return from a headhunting raid: bamboo-horn blowing, singing of the paddle song, the loud reception in the village where the oldest man will ask: "What did you bring?" And the reply of the senior man in the canoe: "We have killed a big man, he lies in the canoe." The pole is carried into the village where the knob (*kus*—head) is cut off. This ritual is performed either before or after the headhunting raid. Mention may be made of a similar ritual among the Kamoro of Mimika, in which some people act as pigs and are "killed" in a mock killing; this is in preparation for a headhunting raid. After this ritual is over, the leader of the "pig men" declares that the headhunting raid will be successful.

Another ritual is that of the *eram asan* or magic trunk. When a new bachelors' house is inaugurated, the lower part of a thin tree trunk is smeared with some mixture. The kind of tree and the ingredients of the mixture are known only to the performer of the ritual. During the night, fires are solemnly built in the new fireplaces. One of the leaders holds the pole in the fire; burning of the mixture produces a smoke that has a penetrating smell. One of the components of that mixture seems to be cassowary fat. The performer conjures the *namjipi,* the souls of the enemies, who are much feared, and invites them to come and eat the smell of the mixture. (Namjipi is the name for the soul of a body that is not yet dead.) The intention of this performance is to bring about some sort of enchantment of the enemies. The Asmat are convinced that the souls of the living can leave the body when a person is sleeping. This happens in particular when the head is in an uncomfortable position, for in that case the soul (thought to reside in the head) is more inclined to leave and roam around until daybreak. If that soul, on its wanderings, eats of the smell of roasted pig or of some other things, its owner will be killed not many days later by the inhabitants of the village where his soul was a guest.

On one occasion I witnessed the ritual butchering of a pig in Sjuru; the namjipi souls of some enemies were called up in that manner so as to be destroyed.

There is a myth about two heroes, Beweró and Tasjim, who died because their souls had eaten of the smell of roasting meat in a hostile village the night before their death.

If a person sees the roaming soul of a friend, disaster may be averted if that friend is warned in time. The one who is warned must reward his friend with a present.

A third ceremony is what the Asmat call the *dewen atakan* (in some communities the *naan atakan*), which is performed on various occasions. The achievements of the headhunters are called out. They boast: "I killed a big man on such and such river; I killed a big woman on such and such river; I killed another man. . . ."

I heard the most detailed dewen when I traveled on several rivers which were unknown to my rowers. At every tributary (also at whirlpools, which are thought to be entries to the underworld) all the men were bragging about their achievements.

On other occasions only the most important headhunters get a chance to do their boasting—for example, at the first stroke of the ax in the carving of an ancestor pole, or when the long basket is opened in which the grubs of the sago beetle had been placed, or when new warriors are inaugurated. The foregoing indicates that the dewen is always performed in awkward situations, for on all these occasions the people are confronted with something new and all that is new is dangerous because of the new spirits connected with it. In the same situations, the neighboring Kamoro speak of a *kaipiri,* a condition to which one is new, so that one is more subject to the harmful influence of the spirits.

It is entirely in accordance with the general attitude of the Asmat to cope with the frightening situation by over-awing the forces behind it by bragging about themselves. According to Asmat tradition, even after death the deceased will, at his arrival in the realm of souls, tell hair-raising stories of wars and fights in which he was the hero. Ordinary wounds and scars are bragged about as having been received during such fights. The enumeration of achievements on headhunting raids may be seen as an attempt to make the spirits more cautious, and thus it is regarded as a means to safeguard both the person who calls the dewen and those who join him.

Toward the end or after the bigger festivities a *fo mbufum* may be organized. This is the solemn unveiling of the carved memorial prow of a canoe, named after some one who has died. The brothers-in-law of the deceased are the performers. They receive a long stick stuffed with the grubs of sago beetles and also a large ball of sago. They take this food into the new canoe, and row toward the hostile place where their relative was killed. Most of the time they do not go beyond the spot where the tributary river, on which their relative had been killed, branches off. There they make a small rack on which both the stick and the ball are deposited, after offering them to the soul of the deceased by a gesture toward the place where the soul is thought to dwell. A few grubs are dropped into the river. The Asmat intend this food to be eaten by the souls. The food is uncooked; the souls do the opposite of what the living do, and thus eat uncooked food. After the food has been brought away and offered, they remove the mat which had hidden the figure on the prow of the canoe from the eyes of women and children. The food is taken back into the canoes; at home it will be roasted and eaten by the brothers-in-law. The day of revenge is not far away: the ceremony of the fo mbufum is considered a threat.

Threats are expressed in various ways, mostly in the form of arrows or other implements of war, placed in conspicuous spots. A favorite method of frightening enemies and keeping war psychosis alive is inventing and spreading lies and using tricks to confuse the enemies and make them nervous. I was often in contact with tribes which were hostile to each other, and traveling (for which I needed rowers) became very difficult as a result of these lies and false stories. The *nao piri* (lie connected with headhunting) is sometimes concocted by the entire group in the bachelors' house. They appoint someone who can visit the hostile village without being harmed— for example, because his decapitation name (bamboo plate name) is from that village, or because his mother or relatives came from there, or perhaps because he was given by the village as ransom or in reconciliation. He is sent to spread some rumor, for example, that village A is going to move to river B to catch fish. Thus the inhabitants of village C will have a chance to gather sago in the part of their territory adjacent to the territory of A. If village C believes this story, its inhabitants will be attacked and possibly slaughtered by A. Before the man who has to spread the story leaves the bachelors' house, all men present eat a lump of sago with which they have rubbed his body. Sometimes this sago is mixed not only with his sweat but even with his blood, taken from a scratch made for the purpose.

In several communities there is a ceremony which the Asmat call *ai tes* (probably means: new ornaments). New spear bearers are inaugurated after being decorated. Sometimes they must stand for two days and are subject to numerous taboos. They must plunge into the river and are then covered with a cloud of chalk which is thrown over their heads. In the Islands River area, the ai tes ceremony is considered an indication that a village will soon be going on the war path. A related ceremony is that of the *bajip*, the public decoration of two youngsters on the occasion when they wear their triton shells for the first time. This triton shell is a very precious and important ornament and is worn on the abdomen by the war-lords whenever they are performing their duties.

Background and preparation for headhunting. There are many variations of the work preparatory to the actual headhunting raid. At times there is no preparation at all, because the Asmat avail themselves of an opportunity —for example, they kill their guests or people who ventured too far from home. Thus headhunting raids with a ritual preparation, planned to be large and to involve alliances, are relatively rare.

It often happens that visitors are cordially welcomed and treated but later killed, especially in their sleep. Such visitors may even be given presents and later attacked as they are leaving. They may be under the special protection of some family which may try to protect them but is defeated by the majority. This, of course, is a humiliation to the protecting family. After one such occasion in Sjuru, a warlord and his group broke away from the other clans and built a new bachelors' house at another spot.

Since headhunting is associated in the origin myths with the ancestors, who were the great leaders and instructors, every village has its own peculiarities. But the main background of headhunting seems to be safeguarding the territory and therefore the food supply. For, according to the origin myths, the prime function of the ancestors is the protection of the tribe's economic prerogatives. The origin stories do not account for the origin of the world (creation), but they do emphasize the fact that the ancestor selected a definite territory for himself and his progeny. As the Asmat live exclusively on the products of nature without cultivation, ownership of village territory is vital to them. The ancestor of the tribe taught men the use of arms to protect their territory. While the men form a protective ring, the women can pound sago, catch fish, and gather mollusks in the tide-flooded woods. The men scout the area, the women follow and begin work.

Each ancestor left to his tribe his special magic objects which are kept in a bag, *eram ésé*. Some have played a part in the life of the ancestor or his wife: a round stone, a flat disk, a string of dogs' teeth. Some were brought by the ancestor from his native land (mythological world): the tusks of a wild boar, the teeth or the gall of some serpent. Most of them are also mentioned in the origin myth. These objects are called *omer pok*, things to frighten with. Before an attack on the enemy they are used to frighten the enemy and to make him an easy prey.

Ornaments worn in war have the same function as ornaments used for festivities (which are similar to the war ornaments). These festivities are a kind of war, aimed at driving away the spirits. The sago palm is widely used on both occasions. It seems to be no coincidence, but a result of Asmat thinking, that the same words are used for the ornaments of men and for the blossoms of plants and trees. A man with all his ornaments reminds the Asmat of a tree, and especially of the sago palm, in full blossom.

Another group of ornaments (red ochre, white chalk, black ash, bones of bears, bones and feathers of the cassowary, human bones, nose shells, white-parrot feathers, tree-rat skins) are also symbols of strength and courage, which aim to frighten. The ornaments not only display these qualities, but cause them too. For the Asmat, ornaments are equipment and armament. They are not allowed to wear them when on a friendly visit, for this would be demonstrative and would in fact invite trouble. In the Agats district the breaking of this rule caused frequent fights.

The chalk used for decoration is mixed with pulverized leaves and makes the men brave. The chalk thrown at the enemy is of a different composition and aims to frighten. Furthermore, chalk makes "hot" and throwing chalk is a challenge. To "warm up" for an occasion, the Asmat eat the leaves of the stinging nettle (for example, when erecting a bachelors' house) and also a kind of ginger.

In the village of Biwar the men sat around the stone disk which the ancestor-mother had worn on her abdomen. By moving their bellies toward the disk while sighing, they hoped to participate in the courage of the tribal mother who had foretold that her offspring would have the ferocity of the serpent while the neighboring Atsj would have the ferocity of the saw-fish. These qualities can probably be explained as totemistic, for the respective Mother and Father of the two tribes possessed the qualities of the mentioned animals in a high degree, namely, slyness and brute force. One preparation for a headhunting raid by the Asmat is to draw the imprint of a cassowary foot on their soles, calves, and thighs. The same drawing is found on the new canoes and on the stone axes. To the Asmat the cassowary is the symbol of swiftness and strength.

Immediately before the attack, the leader of the headhunting raid addresses the sun and asks for courage for his fellow warriors and for fright in the enemies. Enemies are lured into an ambush with the collar bone of a turtle or with a forked bough. The warleader makes gestures indicating "come this way." During the night preceding the raid, sorcerers go to the village of the enemies to charm it from nearby. They blow water through a loop or throw it toward the enemy.

Shortly before the raid the *onam so,* the song of the clouds, is sung, at least in the Bismam villages around Flamingo Bay. This song was sung by the ancestors of the Bismam when they rowed down from the mountains to the coast. It tells of the inhabitants of the "world above," of the ancestors of all villages who live there (every village on earth has a parallel village in the world above); it mentions all those who are mad, crippled, deformed, charmed; it tells about the misers, the roughnecks, the lizards, the thunder-men, the light-men, the white-cloud men, the black-cloud men, the ant-men, the gnat-men, the spider-men, the wasp-men, the mantis religiosa men, the worm-men. Of all these people it is said *ae mira fenaoa* (archaic language, seeming to mean: they harm us). People of the world above, abnormal people, outstanding people, men of the natural phenomena, men of the insects and the lizards, annoy the inhabitants of earth. This is a striking resemblance to the neighboring Kamoro people who, at the end of the "kaware" festivity, organize a ritual war against the spirits that embitter their lives.

The "song of the clouds" sings of the spirits that set all sorts of traps for men, manifesting themselves in all forms, not only in abnormal and deformed persons (abnormality and deformation are ascribed to the presence of spirits in the body), but also in the animals that annoy people. In the Asmat way of thinking, spirits take the shapes of crocodiles, birds, mice, and fireflies. The spirits have hindered man in various ways and thus he became weaker and weaker; that is why man needs rejuvenation.

The second part of the "song of the clouds" is an enumeration of scores of trees of the species that grow on plankroots, which are the favorite abodes of the spirits, and also of scores of grasses and reeds. From these hiding places the spirits steal upon man, molest him, make him ill and weak.

Next comes the *é'so* in which the different parrots are mentioned. *Bewör [parakeet] araotsj-o tsja tsjem-a tamoranése ajua.* ("Younger brothers [araotsj-o] of the Bewör [etc.] to whose house will we be going tomorrow morning?") The Opet, Jür, Sokor and all kinds of parrots are sung of in turn. The text runs as follows: Each line puts the same question to a different group of parrots. (Warriors call themselves the younger brothers of the parrots.)

They continue by addressing the tree-kangaroo (*fatsj*) and different kinds of squirrels.

Parrots and squirrels are famous fruit eaters, as noted in songs and stories, and men about to go headhunting feel a relationship to these beings and call themselves their brothers. (Remember the parallelism between the human body and a tree, the human head and its fruit.)

The song is repeated many times and sung softly so that the singers can not be heard by the women and children, who are sleeping in the family houses.

In Sjuru a swine hunt was organized on the eve of the headhunting raid. The swine was butchered on an open space between the war canoes that were lined up in two rows on the river bank. The head of the swine was offered to the leader of the raid. The people of Sjuru believe that the mythical swine that lured the ancestors of the Bismam group to the earth traveled with them to the coast hanging beneath the prow of a canoe. This swine is believed to join the raid in the same manner, causing a short curved swell (resembling the tusks of a swine) with its growling. This swell will get the enemies into trouble. The Amberep, I was told, had the custom of having the women dance before the men go on a headhunting raid. One of the women would tie the head of a swine on her buttocks. The older men, watching this dance, were supposed to remark that it would be better to have a dance with human heads. (Recall the beginning of the myth of headhunting.)

Another example of the preparations for a headhunting raid is this: The men gathered in the bachelors' house want to know if the raid will be successful. A sorcerer smears his right hand with chalk mixed with pulverized leaves; he rubs the hand faster and faster and so vigorously that blood trickles down from it. That is what the men have been waiting for: there is to be bloodshed! The sorcerer gets wilder, he takes his right hand in the left and swings both hands through the air. He runs up and down the bachelors' house in a trance. Suddenly he runs to one of the men and gesticulates as if cutting off a head and cutting a body into pieces. He becomes rational again after holding his hand in the fire. That is the end of the ceremony.

On one occasion, Jisinamakat of Sjuru performed a pantomime. He imitated a woman who was ready to pound sago and was looking for her pounder, sieve, and bags. Then he imitated a man who was to accompany his wife, looking for his paddle, bow, and arrows. Jisinamakat showed how husband and wife walked to the canoe and went off to the sago woods. After this performance the men needed no more hints. At once they rowed to the Seper river and laid an ambush. Shortly after that two men of Amberep entered the sago woods; they were attacked and killed. Their wives who had followed at some distance managed to escape.

Had Jisinamakat only foreseen the coming of the Amberep people or had he caused them to come by means of his magic? The Sjuru people are inclined to believe it is the latter.

The headhunting raid. The headhunting raid proper normally takes place in the early morning, shortly before daybreak. The participants, exclusively men, are divided in three groups: leaders who only give advice and commands, archers who open the attack by shooting from a distance, and spearmen and shieldbearers who attack from close by and do the actual killing.

The leaders are old men, the seniors of the families. The archers are strong men of middle age, who distinguished themselves on former occasions. They also hold the bows and arrows of the others in reserve. The spearmen form a semicircle at the back of the village, waiting for the frightened villagers to take to the woods when attacked from the front by the archers.

After the headhunting party has approached as near to the enemy village as possible in their canoes (the villages are all close to the river), they go ashore and take their positions. Then someone makes a noise. From one of the houses some man will call: "Who is that?" The answer is: "Your husband, Sjuru" (where Sjuru is the attacker). As a result of the sudden attack, panic breaks out; women and children flee into the woods or try to get away in canoes. The men may also try to escape, or they may put up a brave fight, sometimes after feigning flight. For that reason the invaders have every reason to strike quickly. Conditions are not altogether in their favor and the fortunes of war may easily turn.

The young people among the attackers are given the best chance for renown and priority to enable them to prove themselves, but there are always some middle-aged men who want to increase their prestige. In exceptional cases a woman or child is spared. If a raider wants to keep a captured woman or child alive, he has to make this quite clear, as the killing will often turn into an orgy. Such a woman or child will be taken to the attackers' village to start or expand a family. When a village has a shortage of women, their abduction may be the sole objective of a raid.

The young man who has cornered his victim will say: "Fathers, brothers, the women of our village never took any notice of me. I'll take this woman home." Or: "Fathers, brothers, I want an *asé pitsua* (a dagger of cassowary bone, worn on the hip as proof of being a great headhunter)." One who wants a decoration of this sort has to kill.

The success of the attack is announced by blowing the bamboo hunting horn. As soon as a victim is overpowered the *kus jetet* begins: a wild outburst of joy which is at the same time a reaction to tense nerves. The victims are seized, beaten, pushed around, and generally ill-treated. The head of the victim is particularly subjected to torture. The victorious raider yells constantly: "My head, my head won in the raid."

It is imperative to discover the name of the victim. Usually some one knows the name, especially when the raid was not too far from the home village. If the name is unknown, the hunters may use a trick to find out what it is. In 1954 three men marked for killing were received in a certain village as guests, and when a song was intoned in their honor they were asked to give their names so that they could be mentioned in the song. They could then be killed.

Only when the raiders are in a hurry are the victims killed at once. Then, only the head and thighs may be taken. Ordinarily the victims are dragged to the place where the raiders left their canoes, and placed in a sitting position in the bottom of a canoe with their hands and chest hanging over a pole. Then the invaders set out for home.

Somewhere on the way they leave a sign for the relatives of the victims, a man's ornament or a woman's skirt, placed in a conspicuous spot. There is no reason to suppose that the female victims are raped (my informants denied that rape took place and I never found evidence of it in the many cases which I investigated) but they are stripped and, like the men, ill-treated in many ways.

The most lugubrious sign left behind was done by the men of Puér, who tied parts of the intestines together and hung them across a small river.

On one occasion I saw a sign composed of an arrow point, a red fruit, and some hair of the victim. The arrow point and fruit were intended to attract attention, and the hair of the victim was identification for the family members who had not yet discovered their loss.

The victims are beheaded one after another at the confluences of rivers or at river bends (places where living spirits are found). The beheading is done by persons with special skill for it; the butchering and the distribution of flesh are done in the manner already described. After the festive home-coming, the raid celebrations, *nao pokmbu* (as taught by Desoipitsj) begin.

3. EXPLANATION OF THE HEADHUNTING PRACTICE

In this part I will attempt to draw a conclusion from the accumulated facts and account for the headhunting practices of the Asmat.

The Asmat is not a philosopher and cannot explain his behavior. He lives almost exclusively in a world in which his activities are regulated by customs that have become traditional in his community. Only on rare occasions will he make a more rational decision; as a rule he does what is done by everyone else in his environment and because it is done by every-one else. He will explain his actions by referring to the *o nditsjür*, the ancients, the ancestors. This does not mean that the Asmat has no con-victions of his own, basic to his actions. Though most of the time he does not seem to be conscious of his motives, we would not be justified in assum-ing that he always acts without reason and is only directed by the traditional pattern of life. While comparing the different myths and stories, I dis-covered that changes in actions had taken place and are taking place all the time, and that such changes are the result of individual, contemporary think-ing, of which the people are themselves unconscious.

The practice of headhunting is complex and rather confusing, many factors simultaneously and consecutively contributing to its origin and con-tinuance.

Among the important factors are (1) the cosmology of the Asmat (or rather, the influence of cosmic events on their lives), but this has now lost much of its significance; (2) the economic demand, sago-gathering and its cult; (3) fear of the spirits, expressed in the ritual of expelling the spirits as a characteristic feature of both large and small festivities; and (4) the need of prestige on the part of the male population, the desire for fame and the urge to impress the women of the village. We will examine how these ele-ments are associated with headhunting.

There appears to be a definite association between headhunting and cosmic events though it is not possible to determine whether the Asmat are themselves aware of it. I have already noted the invocation of the sun just before the actual attack in order to get courage for the hunters and spread fear and confusion upon the enemy. The sun is often taken as a witness to an oath of vengeance or to strengthen a solemn statement. Many mysterious things are said of the sun and admiration is expressed when they say: *nambir apok,* the sun never dies. There is probably some identity between the sun and the tribal ancestors. A wide and colorful sunset glow is a sign of a big headhunting raid somewhere, its red being the blood of the victims. A man of Sjuru is called *jomes omer,* afraid of the evening glow, expressing contempt for his lack of courage. The initiate's immersion in the water parallels the solar cycle—the sinking in the west, submersion in the sea, and rising in full glory on the eastern shore. The usual time of attack is toward sunrise (though this may be for practical reasons). Some ornamentation (perhaps not all) seems originally to have been symbols of the sun, moon, and clouds: red ochre—light of the sun; white chalk—light of the moon; black ash—rain cloud.

Cassowary and human bones, used as daggers, resemble the crescent moon, as do the shells worn in the nose, the dogs' teeth, and the boar tusks. (The Asmat have one and the same word for crescent moon, dogs' teeth, swine tusks, and clitoris, *okos.*) The white parrot feathers which adorn the head and the spears may be considered symbols of light. Spear and sunbeam are associated in myth and song and in colloquial language.

The technique of butchering victims suggests the image of the slowly decreasing moon, the picture of gradual scooping out. After the moon is full, it is exposed to the rays of the sun, for she (the Asmat would say "he") has not set before sunrise. Every day the moon falls further behind and is more annoyed by the sun. The moon is pictured in myths as a man wounded in the foot, unable to get away. In the myth about the origin of headhunting, the victim was called "the man with the wound."

The technique of scooping out (beginning at the top and progressing slowly) occurs frequently in Asmat life: when pounding sago out of the palm, when cutting canoes, and shaping eating-bowls. The same is done when butchering pigs (or prehistoric monsters in the myths).

Again, the Asmat may not be conscious of the relationship between the sago cult and headhunting, but there is no doubt in my mind of such relationship.

The account of the origin of the sago palm relates how the hero, Biwiripitsj, sinks in a morass one night while on his way home. In the night, after a thunderstorm, a magnificent sago palm appears on the spot where Biwiripitsj disappeared. Biwiripitsj's head is found in the bud of the palm, his arms in the branches. We have already had the story of the boy stretched out on a felled sago palm who was smashed to death by his father (mother); the sago pith, mixed with the blood and pounded flesh of the boy, proved to be more kneadable—an important economic factor, as more flour could be produced from that palm.

The prominent place of the sago palm in Asmat life is shown by the fact that sago-leaf veins are frequently used to make ornaments and that many names of people are allusions to the sago palm. Such names show that these men were beautifully decorated, and thus had distinguished themselves as great warriors, for only great warriors are entitled to wear sago-palm decorations.

One of the initiation rituals took place in a sago wood and consisted of the ritual pounding of a stripped trunk. The myth states a relationship between headhunting and sago by recording how the son of Biwiripitsj was killed to improve the sago pith. The ceremony of the *firao wu* uses the pith of the palm as a symbol of the human body.

Headhunting is required for the bodily development of young men and for their sexual maturation. The Asmat is inclined to consider things having a similarity in shape or otherwise to be related, as a younger or older brother. He uses the same word for many things that resemble a sickle. Stars, flowers, and fireflies come also under the same name, because they show and hide their color alternately. Similarly, the human body is associated with a tree: the legs compare to the plankroots, the trunk to the human body, the arms to the boughs, the head to the top (often with the fruit that sits in the top). In the related Kamoro language, the word for head is *wé-éke,* fruit of man, for the human head also has a hard shell which protects the core, like the coconut. We recall that the raiders call themselves the younger brothers of the fruit-eating birds, fruit-gathering squirrels, and tree-kangaroos; the headhunting raider goes in search of human fruit: heads. After a raid the heads are tied together in a bunch and hung on the door post or near the fireplace; *kus fé* is a bunch of heads.

The decapitated head of a victim is laid between the out-spread legs of the initiate, almost touching the genitals of the boy who is about to mature sexually. I have repeatedly been told that after this ceremony the boys grew very fast. The ritual is connected in their minds with the growing of the boys. As the fruit contains the germinative power, for the Asmat observe time and again how a new sago palm grows from a fallen fruit, and as the human head is associated with fruit, the Asmat expect that the germinative power of the head (fruit) will be transferred to the boy's genitals by the ritual of placing it between his legs, and thus that it enables him to reproduce.

More than once I noticed decapitated heads hanging near little banana plantations, coconut groves, or sugar-cane fields long after the rituals were over. The head evidently was expected to stimulate the growth of those plants. At times there was a triton shell in lieu of the head.

When I discussed the health of the children with the chieftain of Sjuru (two out of three children die before reaching their first birthday), the chief remarked that many children are weak and feeble despite the fact that they eat plenty (quantity but no quality). Therefore the parents have to go for heads to make their children strong and healthy.

The murder of a relative arouses feelings of revenge, and the Asmat see warfare as retaliation. The brothers-in-law are insulted and stirred up by their wives, and have to band together in planning revenge in order not to lose their prestige. Thus revenge is one of the motives behind headhunting.

I have already pointed out how the big celebrations aim at driving away the spirits of the deceased, and numerous other customs do the same.

Immediately after someone dies, the women undress and wallow through the mud; the men smear themselves with clay, as a protection against the spirits. A layer of clay, especially in the armpits and groin, prevents bodily smells from being strong and saves people from detection by the spirits, who have a keen sense of smell. (Swine hunters do the same in order to approach the swine undetected.) Keeping bones and skulls of the deceased is another effective way of keeping the spirits at bay. A spirit cannot stand the sight of his own bones or skull. In places the deceased had frequented, signs (arrows and the like) may be placed to frighten away the spirit. Most burial customs can be explained in the same manner. When a death has occurred in a village, there is a temporary prohibition of drumming, singing, and yelling, so that the spirit will be led astray as to the whereabouts of the living. The larger rituals are influenced by the same fear of spirits. To some extent, a feast may be considered a war against the spirits, as it is connected with war against living enemies.

Perhaps the nocturnal ritual dance (during the initiation rite) when the decorated skulls are brandished, is also to be explained as an attempt at over-awing the spirits. The shields are moved up and down, forward and backward, indicating the direction which the spirits should take. This was the explanation given to me on one such occasion.

Attempts to overawe the spirits are frequent; the *dewen atakam* (enumeration of achievements) is one. The faked attack in several rituals, as at the erection of an ancestor pole and the mask dance, are other examples. In certain villages a very demonstrative fight was staged during the mask dance to impress upon the spirits that they should seek safety in flight. In another village the masked persons were "killed" in a mock killing in the bachelors' house.

The desire for prestige as a motive for headhunting is certainly significant, but headhunting would not confer so much prestige if it were not already important for other reasons. The motives for headhunting are many, and they are undoubtedly interwoven.

In Asmat society all prestige, and therefore all authority, is ultimately derived from achievements in war. It is impossible to be a man of social standing without having captured a few heads. A bunch of skulls at the door post is a measure of status. When distributing food on the occasion of a feast, it takes wisdom to give everyone the share proper to his rank and achievements. Successful headhunters enjoy many privileges: they are entitled to wear their ornaments as distinguishing marks; they can expect an extra portion of food when relatives return from a food-searching party; they need not exert themselves with heavy work; they are to be consulted in the meeting of men; they stand better chances with the women.

Out of a hundred proper names in the community of Sjuru, 75 proved to have some relation to warfare: "Our iron-wood tree," "Our flowering sago palm," "Man with the hot belly," "Man with the fierce look," "Our gall," "Man with a body like a *jo*-tree," "Arrows with sharp points." Such were names for heroes. But the unheroic had their own names, too: "Man that stayed home for fear," "Man that did not venture far from home," "Man that paddled away for fear," "Man that did not contribute to the list of achievements," "Man that never blew a raiding horn," "Man that was afraid of Asiwetsj (people along a river), "Man without ornaments," and so on.

It is impossible to compliment someone without referring to his achievements. The usual titles are: *juus aptsjam ipitsj,* man with soul, courage; *aretsjar ipitsj,* great man; *nao pimir ipitsj,* man of frequent killing; *kus fé juro ipitsj,* man with large bunch of skulls; *tsjesesema ipitsj,* good shot. Tnese names indicate social standing. Many times I and other foreigners were given these flattering titles.

Headhunting is not a necessary prerequisite for marriage. An Asmat can marry without having acquired a single head, even without initiation, but he will be constantly reminded of his nothingness. His opinion will not be asked in the bachelors' house; his own wife will pay little attention to him. When his wife wants to hurt him, she calls him *nas minu,* piece of meat; she declares that he is only meat, that he has no soul, no courage. The nas minu is the milksop, the spineless fellow, the duffer. He is not considered a real man; he belongs to the category of the women and children. He is not entitled to wear ornaments, has no share in the festive meals, stands no chance with other women. He constantly feels the contempt of the community; he is always the odd man out. As a result, he may work himself into a frenzy and go out and kill. Then he can look eye to eye with the other men and has the admiration of the women and children, for he has proven that he too has a soul.

Bravery not only assures a career in this earthly life, but it will secure an important place in the realm of the spirits as well. When the soul of the Asmat has crossed the big river (the sea), he is at once surrounded by a number of ancestors and relatives who had seen him coming. They will ask his name and how he died. He will tell them in glorious detail about his fights and the raids he was in; his wounds and scars will prove his story. In the realm of souls, as in the bachelors' houses, strong stories—real and imaginary alike—are accepted.

There is also a vague relationship between headhunting and sexual intercourse, which seems to follow from the manner in which headhunting contributes to manliness. Mention has been made of the cry of the headhunters at the beginning of the attack: "I am your husband from Sjuru." It seems to me that the enemy is called woman for more than one reason. But undoubtedly, headhunting is drawn into the sexual sphere. There is a story telling how some men were decapitated and how their heads were miraculously restored, but this was a secret that the women were not to know. When the secret was given away by a child, the men were unmanned and transformed into dolphins (which have a hole in the nape of the neck and a skull that shows a striking resemblance to the human skull).

5. CONCLUSIONS

The motivation for headhunting is indeed complex; as headhunting appears today, it must be understood in the light of all the factors taken together.

Evaluating the different factors we may perhaps conclude by saying, in Scholastic terminology: "the finis operis," the objective, is the rite of passage, the initiation; but the intention and goal of the headhunters, "the finis operantis," is revenge, acquisition of social position through prestige, and attainment of the ideal of perfect manliness.

15

THE PAGENT OF
DEATH IN NAKANAI[1]

Ward Goodenough

* * * *

The Nakanai people occupy a one-hundred-mile stretch of the New Britain coast between the Willamez Peninsula and Open Bay. Along most of this coastline rugged mountains rise from the shore, leaving only a narrow strip of lowland. The area is actively volcanic. It is subject to a rainy season between the months of December and March, the rest of the year being dry. The Nakanai are divided into several major dialect groups which are very closely related, but whose extremes are not mutually intelligible. Numerically most important today is the West Nakanai group, inhabiting the Hoskins Peninsula where we worked.

The Hoskins Peninsula is a semicircle of flat land bounded at the base by a chain of mountains and ridges. At one end of this chain is rugged Mt. Oto, while at the other is the active volcano, Mt. Pago, whose violent eruption in 1914 laid waste the entire peninsula and forced its people to abandon it for several years. At the apex of the peninsula the extinct Mt. Lolo raises its graceful, solitary cone. All but three of the twenty-two villages located here are near the beach. There are few water holes inland on the plain. Rain filters quickly through the porous volcanic soil and the underground drainage emerges in springs a few yards from the beach. To be close to water, therefore, most villages must be near the shore.

Each village consists of one or more hamlets. In former times the hamlets were separated by a few yards of bush, but now they tend to be consolidated in a single clearing, though retaining their separate social identities. Each hamlet contains several dwellings and a men's house set around a little square, every inch of which is kept completely clear of all vegetation except for a shade tree or two. The edge of the square is planted with betel and coconut trees. Normally, there are large shade trees at one corner of the square under which is the hamlet's feasting ground. In

Reproduced by permission of the University Museum of the University of Pennsylvania and Ward H. Goodenough from the *University Museum Bulletin*, 19:18-43 (1955). Revised by the author. The bibliography at the end of the selection has been added by the author.

279

former times, the rectangular dwellings were built directly on the ground with frames wooden and bark walls and roofs. Nowadays houses for sleeping are raised on piles and thatched with nipa palm leaves, but the old style houses sometimes continue beside them as "cook houses" in which the older people still prefer to sleep. It is in the latter houses that all valuables are still kept and in which most indoor living takes place. On the dirt floor of these houses are as many stonelined hearths as there are women (other than small children) in the household. Whether young or old, married or single, each woman cooks at her hearth for herself and such of her relatives as she helps to feed from the produce of her gardens.

Back of each village is a tract of bush—dense secondary growth within which the villagers make their gardens. A strip of virgin forest separates one village tract from the next. An entire village, or several hamlets within one, will mark off an area in its gardening territory, starting one or two miles back in the bush. Within this each participating hamlet takes a strip and fences it. Each man clears his own plot within his hamlet's strip and prepares the ground for planting. The woman who is his gardening partner plants it and looks after it from then on, harvesting the produce and cooking it. Since there is no way of storing food, the Nakanai are constantly clearing and planting new plots the year round, regardless of the season. A plot is planted only once and when harvested goes back to bush. In the course of time the garden strips move toward the coast until they come too close to the village, where, despite fencing, they are too easy of access to the village pigs. Then the community starts a new set of strips back in the bush and proceeds to work coastward again. After fifteen or twenty years it will return to the first garden site. While garden lands are not communal property, the people feel that since gardening involves only transient use of the land it is not a form of trespass on private property rights, though the owners must be consulted before clearing begins. Indeed, the owners are only too glad to have their land used, because this will keep it from going so far back into forest as to require a new primary clearing operation. Small bush, however thick, is easier to clear (whether the tools are of steel or of stone and shell) than is timber. Once cleared of forest, land acquires a value which can be maintained only by periodic use. Cultivated crops are numerous: taro (the staple), sweet potato, sugar cane, greens, yams, tapioca, cucumbers, tomatoes, pumpkins, beans, tobacco, and ornamental leaves worn by the women. Also planted are bananas, coconut, breadfruit, betel, and citrus.

Behind the garden lands is the virgin forest—tall trees whose deep shade inhibits the growth of underbrush. Here the men hunt for pig, cassowary, and small game. This too is the preserve of a pheasant-like bush-fowl whose meat and eggs are an important source of protein food in the local diet. These fowl lay their eggs in prodigious numbers in holes in the ground in a region of bare hot soil at the foot of Mt. Pago. The

Nakanai regularly collect these eggs (which are twice the size of a hen's egg) throughout the long dry season. Rights to the egg fields for gathering purposes have been the cause of much warfare between native communities in their vicinity. The eggs are gathered not only for immediate consumption but also for sale to communities too far away to exploit the fields directly. The Nakanai also keep domestic pigs and chickens. The only other domestic animal is the dog, which is used in hunting as well as being eaten.

The sea provides the other major food-stuffs in the form of fish and shell-fish. Those communities close to the egg fields have relatively poor fishing grounds, as it works out, while those more removed have reefs close to their shores which provide sufficient quantities of fish. The big rivers at either end of the peninsula are also important sources of fish.

Ordinary dress for the Nakanai women consists of a belt with a short apron of leaves before and another behind. The leaves used are grown in the garden for the purpose. Some of them are heavily scented. Women coming in from their work in the gardens bring a fresh supply of leaves which they don after bathing. Until their recent adoption of the cloth wrap-around kilt or "laplap," Nakanai men went naked except for bark-cloth belts, but when dancing they wore a "grass" skirt made from fibers of the mangrove root. The first donning of this skirt by a first-born son is a ceremonial event. If not given to elaborate clothing, the Nakanai make up for it in adornment. Both sexes cut and stretch their earlobes and put turtle shell or reed rings on the loops. They pierce their nasal septa in which they wear a bar of tridachna shell or a set of turtle-shell rings. On the upper arm and around the leg just below the knee go braided armlets ornamented with small white shells. Over the bicep goes a set of turtle-shell rings. Braided circlets of purple-dyed fibers are worn around wrist and ankle, and men may wear broad fiber gantlets beaded with small shells on their wrists. On the head goes a crown-like frame of cured pandanus leaf tubing supporting a brilliant display of feathers which are family heirlooms. Needless to say, most of this splendor is for special occasions only.

Tattooing has only recently come into vogue, but ornamental scarification of women's backs is an old custom. Nor is the hair allowed to go as nature intended it. In former times, it was dyed black and worn in matted ringlets greased and sprinkled with powdered red pigment. Nowadays it is trained by combing to stand up in a frizzly mop which is trimmed fairly short in modern New Guinea style and is alternately dyed black or peroxide orange depending on the individual's fancy of the moment. As a result it requires close investigation to discover that the Nakanai are endowed with naturally brown to black hair which ranges from straight through wavy to very curly in form. Other physical characteristics include from medium to dark brown skin, an average stature for males of 5 ft. 6 inches and for females of 5 ft. 2 inches, large teeth with about 90 per cent incidence of shovel-shaped incisors (a Mongoloid trait), large palates, heavy jaws, often rugged brows, and muscular build. The people impressed us as hard-working and vigorous, especially considering the debilitating effects of universally chronic malaria and hook worm.

The Nakanai are divided into about forty clans. These clans are matrilineal, by which we mean that a person belongs to the same clan as his or her mother (not father). Every clan has associated with it a mountain or height; a body of fresh water, be it river, stream or spring; one or more animals or fish which it is tabu for its members to eat; several cultural or other objects whose origin is associated with the clan's origin; and personal names of people and pigs. The Kevemuki clan, for example, which is currently one of the most important in West Nakanai, has the volcano Mt. Pago as its sacred mountain. The spring Kalea on its slopes is its sacred water, the chicken its tabu, and taro, fire, and the sun are its associated objects. Many clans share in the same mountain, spring, tabu, or objects. These clans are considered to be sub-clans of a single larger one. Thus Kevemuki has at least five sub-clans: Hahili, Kureko, Matapoo, Kalea, and Goau.

When someone sets out to clear virgin forest for a garden or to establish a new hamlet, the ground is thenceforth considered the property of his clan or sub-clan. If two men of different clans jointly establish a new hamlet, its ground is then the joint property of their two clans. Title to the property is administered by the matrilineal descendants of the founder or founders. Men do not normally take up residence in the hamlet associated with their clan, however, until after their fathers have died. Even then they may continue to reside in the hamlet of their father's clan for a variety of reasons. Each hamlet, therefore, tends to consist of a few older men of the clan or clans which own its ground, their sons, those of their sisters' sons whose fathers have died, and perhaps a dead brother's son who has decided to stay on rather than return to his own clan's hamlet. Each hamlet is composed, therefore, of a group of fairly closely related men with their wives and children. Their leader is ideally the eldest resident man who belongs to the owning clan, but his position is influenced by his wealth and his reputation as a giver of feasts.

Several such hamlets make up a community or village whose members are normally at peace with each other but which as a unit is chronically hostile to the members of other communities (prior to the white man's peace). Peaceful relations between communities were limited to visits between fellow clansmen and to festival and ceremonial occasions. The two most important foci of festival and ceremonial were and still are the masked representation of spirits—stretching over several months of the dry season (though not necessarily every year)—and the long cycle of feasting and dancing in honor of the dead—taking several years to reach its climax. Masked representation of the spirits is a community undertaking, while memorial feasts are privately promoted by individuals who stand to gain great prestige thereby. Of the two types of festival, that having to do with the dead stands first in drama and energy consumed. There is no festival of greater importance or interest to the Nakanai. This is why I have chosen to take it as the subject of this brief report.

When a man dies, everyone in the community assembles at his house. People from neighboring communities come also, the women in the lead and the men following, all singing a dirge. They sing all through the night. The immediate relatives of the deceased make handsome gifts to the chief representative of each mourning delegation from another community, normally the deceased's closest kinsman among them, who must then kill pigs and make a funeral feast on his return home. They bury the dead man at noon on the day following death—they have to wait until the ground has warmed up in the heat of the day. The man is buried in the floor of his house in a shallow grave with his head left above ground. (Nowadays bodies are buried in cemeteries.) His head is oriented toward the sacred mountain of his clan, from which his spirit came when he was born and to which it returns now that he is dead. His head is exposed so that his family may continue to behold his face. They are concerned about his feeling cold in the ground and build fires over him to keep him warm. This may continue for a few days only or until such time as the dead man's face has completely decomposed, and then the body is completely buried.

Meantime, the dead man's wife and sister are incarcerated in a small closet which is partitioned off in the house for the purpose—normally the house of a relative of the deceased. Here they remain in strict mourning for from one to two months, being allowed out only twice a day to perform their natural functions. During this time they may not bathe, must wear special clothes, including heavy wrappings of vines on the legs so that they can walk only in a waddle, and must refrain from eating pork, fish, or taro and from smoking tobacco or chewing betel. When the dead man's clan mates decide that they have mourned enough, they break down the partition and formally release the women. The widow may now cut her hair and do limited work, but she must still refrain from gardening for about two years. She is not free to marry again during this period, but must wait until her former husband's clan mates release her from all mourning. If she violates the mourning regulations they are likely to try to kill her.[2]

A few months after the body has been fully buried, a close male relative of the deceased (brother, son, or nephew) secretly exhumes it. He removes the humerus or upper arm bone, reburying the rest of the remains. He informs the other immediate relatives of his action and, if it appears that they have the means to undertake it, they decide to go ahead with the memorial festival. The man who took the arm bone paints it red, wraps it in red bark cloth, then wraps this bundle in old pandanus matting so that it will resemble many other bundles containing items of family wealth and hangs it with them from the ridge-pole of his house. Nothing is said to the community at all about his intentions.

He and his near relatives who are in on the secret set out to accumulate pigs. They buy them where they can and breed them to raise as many pigs as possible. They begin to give the young pigs to others in the village to look after. By this time, the elders in the community are aware that something is up. One of them discreetly inquires of a near kinsman of the deceased what is the meaning of the pig-breeding activities. The feast-maker then publicly announces that he has taken the dead man's arm bone and intends making a memorial festival.

This announcement is immediately followed by the ceremony of "hanging the bone." The feast-maker places the bone on a circular wooden tray which he suspends from the ridge-pole of the men's house in his hamlet. He hangs a set of ankle rattles, such as are worn in dancing, from the tray, so that any vibration of the men's house will cause them to make a noise. He kills two or three pigs and distributes meat to the several hamlets of his own village and to those of neighboring villages (how many depending on the number of pigs he feels he can afford to kill). On this occasion other persons in the village who cannot afford to make a memorial festival on their own come forward with the arm bones of their dead. They add their meager resources to those of the feast-maker in return for riding on his coat-tails. All noise and clatter in the vicinity of the men's house is now strictly tabu. Children may not cry, people shout, or women noisily dump their loads of fire-wood. No stones may be thrown at or near the house. Violation of the tabu is punished by the spirit of the dead man acting through a sorcerer hired for the purpose. These tabus are in force only for a few days, after which there is a second feast for "taking down the bone," though the bone is in practice left to hang in the men's house until the final memorial celebration. This second feast is bigger than the first one and all the men of the village take part in cooperative drives with nets for wild pigs. When they have caught several, the feast-maker kills two or three of his domestic pigs to add to the total. The night after this feast, the feast-maker takes his family's slit gong (hollowed log drum) and places it in the middle of the hamlet square just in front of the men's house. This is known as "placing the gong," and formally serves notice to all neighboring communities that they will be welcome to come here and dance.

The feast-maker thus maintains open-house for one or two years. When visiting groups of dancers come to dance to the gong he must provide them with tobacco and betel. If they stage an all-night dance around some formal theme, he must kill a small pig for them and provide them with food. These "theme-dances" require that all performers wear a particular type of ornament or call for the women of the host's hamlet to attack the dancing delegation of men with a particular weapon: water, sand, mud, or fire. Such attacks may end with an orgy in the bush. The visitors always name the theme. The style of dancing done on these occasions is not an animated one. A man in the dancing group sits astride the gong and beats it with the butt end of a flexible rod made from a heavy vine. Rhythms are varied but not complicated. The dancers mill slowly around the gong singing and moving their feet in a shuffling heel-and-toe step. The songs are short and are sung over and over again. In theme-dancing one song will be used for the entire night. Other hamlets from the feast-maker's village may enter into a dancing contest with a visiting delegation. Each group dances around a gong at either end of the hamlet square, singing its own song. Both groups keep going at the same time until one is too tired to continue further. Dances continue to be held around the gong until the feast-maker is ready to make the final grand festival. As the time approaches, the dances are more frequent so that dancing becomes almost a nightly affair for a month or two before the big day.

Meantime, the near relatives of the deceased continue to accumulate pigs, distributing the shoats to the other members of the community to look after. Ideally, on the great feast day every household head in the village should have a pig to kill. As the time approaches, the men go out and clear new garden plots which their wives and sisters plant. When these gardens are ready to harvest, the feast-maker announces the time for screening the hamlet's feasting ground. Behind this screen the men will rehearse their dances for the coming festival. No adult women are supposed to go within the screened area nor are first-born sons who have not yet been initiated into the dance. What goes on within it, however, is perfectly visible from the outside, the screen of coconut fronds being a no-trespass sign rather than an effective physical barrier. Screening the feasting ground is a formal act. On this occasion the feast-maker kills several pigs and all the men of the community have a small feast within the screened area. Cuts of pork are also lashed to carrying poles and distributed to as many other West Nakanai villages as the feast-maker feels he can afford. The present of pork informs these villages that they are invited to attend the great festival and to take part in its dancing. The present also provides meat for the feast of screening the feasting ground for dance rehearsals in these villages.

Every day the men of the host and guest villages meet in their respective feasting grounds to rehearse for the coming dancing. Unlike the previous dancing, the dances performed on the day of the big festival comprise a series of patterned movements executed in formation. They call for a double row of dancers. Those who perform as partners on the festival day thenceforth stand in a special relationship and can no longer address or refer to each other by name without paying a fine. The dancers go through various movements somewhat analogous to those in our own reels. There is considerable movement; feet stamp the ground in a variety of steps, noise of the stamping accentuated by ankle rattles. Rehearsal of these dances is accompanied by buying and selling of the rights to perform them. Such rights are privately owned. Whenever a dance is performed, its owner must kill a pig to reaffirm his possession of the copyright.

Men also start preparing the paraphernalia which the dancers will wear. Most of this work they do in the bush out of sight of women and children. The chief job is carving and painting the crocodiles, snakes, and lizards which will be manipulated by solo performers during the festival. Their relatives by marriage carry them on litters. A solo performer stands braced on the litter's platform while his carriers heave it up and down. His face is elaborately painted, and he wears the fullest of ceremonial regalia. All the time he is carried, his eyes are glued shut so that he cannot see. In this blind and tossed condition, he performs his act, in the course of which he is paraded around the village area for five to ten minutes.

There is a wide variety of these solo acts—all of them, again, owned under private copyright. A common type of act is one in which a carved wooden crocodile, lizard, shark, dog, or pig is mounted on a track or trolley. It is rigged so that the performer manipulates lines which make the carved animal move forward and appear to bite his face and then retreat from him again. Instead of this, a performer may hold an elaborately carved wooden "pillow" across his shoulders behind his head. Another stunt is to appear to eat some inedible thing such as raw taro, or a human bone. Still other stunts call for having a fire burning on the performer's lap, a spear seemingly run through his middle, snakes emerging from his mouth. Again, the performer may exhibit stalk-like protruding eyes or a greatly elongated tongue, or he may dress as a woman and carry a wooden doll-baby.

Prior to all of these acts, the performer must abstain from food and water for several days. He may eat and drink only enough to sustain life, and this only providing appropriate spells have been made first. The reason behind it all is love magic. Every stunt performed carries with it a potent love charm which is designed to make the performer irresistible to women. If he eats or drinks, he "cools" the charm and makes it impotent. The violent tossing he receives on the litter following his fast often results in physical collapse. Solo performing is a genuine ordeal.

The rehearsal period lasts for about two or even three weeks. The feast-maker ends it by killing a few more pigs and making another small feast. He sends cuts to all the villages to which pork was sent earlier, informing them that on the fourth day thereafter the festival will begin. One of the great concerns of the feast-maker is that there should be no rain on the festival day. He hires rain-magicians, therefore, to keep rain away, and foil the attempts of any jealous rival to spoil the festival by magically causing a downpour. When the rehearsal period ends, the women break down the screen around the feasting ground and rush in. First-born sons who have reached the age to be initiated into the dance go through a little ceremony of having the dancing skirt put on them at this time. They are then put in a line of dancers to follow as best they can. Their mothers, aunts, and sisters beat the ground at their feet with mats and throw food and wealth to the crowd in joy at the boys' initiation.

The festival itself lasts for three days. It is opened with a dance by the boys and girls of the feast-maker's village. A men's dance belonging to the feast-maker or his family follows. Visiting delegations from other villages then present dances. The morning of the second day begins with solo performances. In each the arm bones to be honored, elaborately wrapped in ceremonial bindings, are carried by young kinsmen (occasionally women) of the dead as they are being tossed on litters. Also tossed on litters or carried on the shoulders of relatives are first-born sons who received their dancing skirt at the close of the rehearsal period. These appearances are followed by dancing on the ground. The third day is a repetition of the second, with the more spectacular acts reserved for this time. The host village performs the last number to close the dancing. The feast-maker has the pigs (from forty to fifty in number) killed on the third day. The division of food to take home winds up the affair on the third afternoon, though informal festivities continue through the night and for several nights thereafter.

The atmosphere on these three days is one of intense excitement. The dancers and solo performers get ready for their acts in the bush just off the village square. The women of the village dance in the square just in front of where they will emerge. Then with much shouting and chanting they come out surrounded by friends, some beating hour-glass drums, and led by one or two men with brightly painted shields and long wooden spears. They rush about beating their legs with the shields and thrusting at shadow enemies with the spears. Running about the fringes there may be a woman with spear and toy shield lampooning the men. Clowning, regularly done by women, usually enters into the performance somewhere. All the spectators follow the solo performer's tossing litter about the village or throng around the rows of dancers so as scarcely to leave them room to perform. Sweat and paint stream down the dancers' bodies, turning to mud in the swirling dust. They wear fixed expressions—their gaze turned inward—as they struggle to call upon the last ounce of reserve to overcome their starvation and thirst and last out the dance.

After the festival, the feast-maker kills a pig to pay for "drilling the bone." The dead man's arm bone is drilled so that it can be mounted on the butt end of a spear. Everywhere men now go about their work with caution, and visiting other villages stops, for the spear with the attached bone must shed blood. To this end, the feast-maker presents the spear to one of the foremost warriors of his village. Under his leadership, a raid is organized. Raids against other villages continue until the spear takes a life. The warrior receives a pig, spears, and gold-lip shells in payment from the feast-maker, who takes back the spear with the bone. It will be used subsequently in fighting as an especially deadly weapon, but no further ceremonies attach to it.

There is no festival of greater importance or interest to the Nakanai than this one. The dancing and solo performances provide a tremendous spectacle. It absorbs the attention of the Nakanai as the World Series of baseball absorbs ours. But what this pageant means otherwise is not so easy to say. Presumably there have been beliefs about death, the life thereafter, and the relation of the living to the dead, all of which provided justifying reasons for taking the arm bone of the dead man, honoring it in some way, and finally blooding it on a spear. But what these beliefs are or were our informants either could not or would not say. Their stock answer was simply that it is something that has come down from their grandfathers. However frustrating this may be to inquiring anthropologists, the fact remains that there is little more that most of us could say about the reasons for doing much of what we do at Hallowe'en or Christmas. We have to have festival occasions, and these occasions must follow prescribed patterns if we are to enjoy comparing the way this year's festival was put on as compared with last year's. In this regard, the Nakanai are quite like ourselves. Their memorial festivals, moreover, not only honor important men who have died, but are the means by which the living prove themselves to be important as well.

Successfully to make a great memorial feast is to establish one's reputation through all of Nakanai as a leader among men. A leader must continue to promote such feasts when his kinsmen die in order to maintain his position. Memorial feasts, therefore, are an integral part of the social processes by which men gain public stature, and establish their right to represent their community to the outside world and speak with authority in it. There is no higher praise than to be called "foundation of the slit-gong," which we may loosely translate as the "source of celebration." The successful feast-maker, therefore, in honoring his dead, performs the most respected of public services. What, for reasons no longer remembered, started out as rites in honor of the dead have, in the course of time, been transposed into an expensive public entertainment which few men have the energy and resources to promote successfully and which has therefore become a means for gaining social recognition and influence. Private sentiment for the dead is felt, of course, by the immediate kin, but death also serves as the established excuse for a public celebration whose meaning must be found in the pattern of life in the larger Nakanai community.

Striking evidence for this conclusion is provided by the fact that the memorial celebration and events specifically leading up to it are the least modified of all Nakanai customs relating to death. Formal mourning has almost completely disappeared—only the food tabus continue to be observed. Burial is now in a cemetery instead of in the house. The arm bone itself is no longer taken, but some object intimately associated with the dead (e.g., cane, toy, leaf apron) has been substituted. Attaching the bone to a spear and shedding blood with it has, of course, gone out under European rule. What remains is the great celebration, the pageantry, the economic effort, the prestige—all of which show how important to the Nakanai are the social aspects of their mortuary customs.

NOTES

1. The work upon which this paper is based began in 1951 with a reconnaissance in Papua and New Guinea sponsored by the University Museum and the Department of Anthropology of the University of Pennsylvania. I returned to New Britain in 1954 with several graduate students to make a six months' study of the West Nakanai people on the central north coast of the island. Accompanying me were Miss M. A. Chowning, Mr. D. R. Swindler, and Mr. and Mrs. C. A. Valentine. The expedition was aided financially by the Department of Anthropology of the University of Pennsylvania, the American Philosophical Society, and the Tri-Institutional Pacific Program (TRIPP, a research program jointly administered by the Bishop Museum, University of Hawaii, and Yale University). Mr. Swindler's work was helped by a pre-doctoral fellowship from the Wenner-Gren Foundation for Anthropological Research, and Mr. Valentine's by a Fulbright Scholarship to the Australian National University. Our work was greatly helped by the extraordinary courtesies extended us by the Administrator of Papua and New Guinea and his staff, which included synchronizing a botanical survey of the Nakanai area by the Department of Forests with our study. We are especially grateful to Assistant District Officer Michael Foley and Medical Administrator A. V. Bell, both of Talasea, and in Nakanai to Patrol Officer and Mrs. Ernest Sharp, Miss Cynthia Smith of the Malalia Mission, Father W. Berger and the Sisters of the Valoka Mission, and Mr. Frank Maynard of Matavulu Plantation for their many kindnesses and cordial hospitality.

2. Men are subject to similar mourning restrictions on the death of a wife, but for a shorter period of time.

PUBLICATIONS AND MANUSCRIPTS RESULTING FROM THE 1954 EXPEDITION
TO THE NAKANAI OF NEW BRITAIN

Works preceded by an asterisk deal primarily or significantly with the West Nakanai.

A. PUBLICATIONS (as of December, 1969)

CHOWNING, ANN, 1966a, *"Lakalai Kinship." *Anthropological Forum*, 1: 476-501.
1966b, *"Lakalai Revisited." *Expedition*, 9(1): 2-15.

CHOWNING, ANN, WITH WARD H. GOODENOUGH, 1966a, *"Lakalai Political Organization." *Anthropological Forum*, 1: 412-473.

GOODENOUGH, WARD H., 1953, "New Britain Expedition." *Bulletin, Philadelphia Anthropological Society*, 7(2): 4-5.
1954, "Ethnographic Expedition to New Britain." *Bulletin, Philadelphia Anthropological Society*, 8(1): 1-2.
1955a, *"Effect of European Contact on the West Nakanai Tribe of New Britain in the Australian Territory of New Guinea." *Yearbook, American Philosophical Society*, 1954, pp. 175-176.
1955b, *"What Anthropologists Do." *The Pennsylvania Gazette*, 53(6): 8-13.
1955c, *"The Pageant of Death in Nakanai: A Report of the 1954 Expedition to New Britain." *University Museum Bulletin*, 19(1): 18-43.
1956a, *"Some Observations on the Nakanai." *Annual Report and Proceedings, 1954, Papua and New Guinea Scientific Society*, pp. 39-45.
1956b, *"Reply (to Frake)." *American Anthropologist*, 56: 173-175.

1956c, "Residence Rules." *Southwestern Journal of Anthropology,* 12: 22-37.

1961, *"Migrations Implied by Relationships of New Britain Dialects to Central Pacific Languages." *Journal of the Polynesian Society,* 70: 112-126.

1962a, *"Kindred and Hamlet in Lakalai, New Britain." *Ethnology,* 1: 5-12.

1962b, "Foreword," to D. R. Swindler, *A Racial Study of the West Nakanai,* pp. vii-viii, Museum Monographs, Philadelphia: The University Museum.

1963, *Cooperation in Change: An Anthropological Approach to Community Development.* Russell Sage Foundation. (Scattered examples from Lakalai).

1965, *"Personal Names and Modes of Address in Two Oceanic Societies." In Melford E. Spiro, editor, *Context and Meaning in Cultural Anthropology,* pp. 265-276, New York: The Free Press.

SWINDLER, DARIS R., 1955, *"The Absence of the Sickle Cell Gene in Several Melanesian Societies and its Anthropologic Significance." *Human Biology,* 27: 284-293.

1962, *A Racial Study of the West Nakanai.* Philadelphia: The University Museum (Museum Monographs).

SWINDLER, DARIS R., WITH J. MAVALWALA AND E. E. HUNT, JR., 1963, *"The Dermatoglyphics of the West Nakanai of New Britain." *American Journal of Physical Anthropology,* 21: 335-340.

SWINDLER, DARIS R., WITH R. T. SIMMONS, J. J. GRAYSON, AND N. M. SEMPLE, 1956, *"A Blood Group Genetical Survey in West Nakanai, New Britain." *American Journal of Physical Anthropology,* 14: 375-386.

VALENTINE, CHARLES A., 1960, *"Uses of Ethnohistory in an Acculturation Study." *Ethnohistory,* 7: 1-27.

1961a, *Masks and Men in a Melanesian Society: The Valuku or Tubuan of the Lakalai of New Britain.* University of Kansas Publications, Social Science Studies, Lawrence, Kansas.

1961b, "Symposium on the Concept of Ethnohistory—Comment." *Ethnohistory,* 8: 271-280.

1963a. *"Men of Anger and Men of Shame: Lakalai Ethnopsychology and its Implications for Sociopsychological Theory." *Ethnology,* 2: 441-477.

1963b, "Social Status, Political Power, and Native Responses to European Influence in Oceania." *Anthropological Forum,* 1: 3-55.

1965, *"The Lakalai." In P. Lawrence and M. Meggitt, editors, *Gods, Ghosts and Men in Melanesia,* pp. 162-197, Melbourne: Oxford University Press.

B. MANUSCRIPTS

CHOWNING, ANN, Lakalai Society. Ph.D. Dissertation, University of Pennsylvania, 1958. Microfilm, Ann Arbor: University Microfilm Libraries, Inc.

FLOYD, ALEX, Final Report on Ethnobotanical Expedition—West Nakanai, New Britain—July-August, 1954. Report to Department of Forests, Port Moresby.

GOODENOUGH, WARD H., Lakalai Kinship Terminology: A Componential Analysis.

GOODENOUGH, WARD H., AND ANN CHOWNING, A Lakalai—English Dictionary.

GOODENOUGH, WARD H., AND CHARLES A. VALENTINE, The Willaumez Languages of New Britain.

SWINDLER, DARIS R., The Dentition of the West Nakanai of New Britain.

VALENTINE, CHARLES A., An Introduction to the History of Changing Ways of Life on the Island of New Britain. Ph.D. Dissertation, University of Pennsylvania, 1958. Microfilm, Ann Arbor: University Microfilm Libraries, Inc.

Cargo Beliefs and Cargo Cults among the West Nakanai of New Britain. Dated Canberra, March, 1955.

Health in a Changing Society: The West Nakanai of New Britain. Dated Canberra, June, 1955. Revised and Expanded, dated Canberra, March, 1956.

Millenniums and Messiahs in Melanesia: From Primitive Religion to Cargo Cult in a Lifetime Among the Nakanai. Part I: Descriptive Section. Dated Canberra, 1956.

Chronology of Recorded Events in and Around New Britain with Special Reference to the Nakanai Area. Dated Canberra, 1956.

New Britain Vocabularies.

FURTHER READINGS

For additional accounts of child rearing and related matters, see Mead's early works: *Growing Up in New Guinea* and *Sex and Temperament in Three Primitive Societies.* Whiting also did an early full-length treatment, *Becoming a Kwoma,* and an article of relevance, "The Frustration Complex in Kwoma Society." Other pertinent materials, although not dealing specifically with child training, can be found in Bateson's *Naven* and in Burridge's "Marriage in Tangu," "Adoption in Tangu," and "Siblings in Tangu." Hogbin's other works on Wogeo should be consulted: "Adoption in Wogeo," "The Father Chooses His Heir," "Marriage in Wogeo," and "Puberty to Marriage." He has also published similar materials for Busama: "Sex and Marriage in Busama." Langness' "Hysterical Psychosis in the New Guinea Highlands" discusses some of the problems faced by males growing up in that region.

Read's "Morality and the Concept of the Person Among the Gahuku-Gama" gives much insight into native conceptions of human nature and the good life. Valentine's "Men of Anger and Men of Shame" is a thorough account of Lakalai ethnopsychology. Other materials dealing in some sense with personality include Bell's "The Role of the Individual in Tangan Society," Langness' "Sexual Antagonism in the New Guinea Highlands," Meggitt's "Dream Interpretation Among the Mae Enga of New Guinea" and "Male-Female Relationships in the Highlands of Australian New Guinea," Malinowski's encyclopedic accounts of the Trobriands, especially *Sex and Repression in Savage Society* and *The Sexual Life of Savages in Northwestern Melanesia,* and Mead's *The Mountain Arapesh,* Volume 1. Watson has written two long biographical sketches that should be noted: "A New Guinea 'Opening Man'" and "Tairora: The Politics of Despotism in a Small Society."

Those interested in religion and related subjects should consult Allen's *Male Cults and Secret Initiations in Melanesia* and Fortune's *Manus Religion.* Lawrence and Meggitt have edited a valuable collection: *Gods, Ghosts and Men in Melanesia.* There are also materials by Aufenanger ("The Kanggi Spirit in the Central Highlands of New Guinea" and "Descent Totemism and Magical Practices in the Wahgi Valley"), by Luzbetak ("The Socio-religious Significance of a New Guinea Pig Festival"), and by Newman ("Supernaturalism and Ritual Among the Gururumba," "Sorcery, Religion and the Man," and "Religious Belief and Ritual in a New Guinea Society"). In addition, there are contributions by Malinowski: "Baloma: The Spirits of the Dead in the Trobriand Islands" and *Magic, Science and Religion and Other Essays.* Hogbin has written on the religion of Wogeo, *The Island of Menstruating Men.*

Marriage is well represented in the literature. There are Bell's "Courtship and Marriage Among the Tanga," Hogbin's articles mentioned above, Read's "Marriage Among the Gahuku-Gama of the Eastern Central Highlands," Burridge's "Marriage in Tangu," and the Lanes' "A Reinterpretation of the Anomalous Six-Section Marriage System of Ambrym, New Hebrides." In addition to the papers in *Pigs, Pearlshells and Women,* edited by Glasse and Meggitt, there are also very good accounts in Blackwood's *Both Sides of Buka Passage,* Reay's *The Kuma,* Hogbin's *Kinship and Marriage in a New Guinea Village,* and Wagner's *The Curse of Souw.*

There have been several recent studies of Melanesian political organization, many of which have been published in the *Anthropological Forum*. In addition, the reader should see Read's early paper "The Political System of the Ngarawapum" and his "Leadership and Consensus in a New Guinea Society." There are important papers by Powell, "Competitive Leadership in Trobriand Political Organization," and Salisbury, "Despotism and Australian Administration in the New Guinea Highlands." There are also papers by Paula Brown ("Chimbu Tribes" and "From Anarchy to Satrapy"), Pospisil ("Social Change and Primitive Law"), Strathern ("Despots and Directors in the New Guinea Highlands"), Epstein ("Power, Politics and Leadership"), and Langness ("Political Organization"). The following should also be examined: Bromley's "A Preliminary Report on Law Among the Grand Valley Dani of Netherlands New Guinea," Pospisil's *Kapauku Papuans and Their Law,* Sahlins' "Poor Man, Rich Man, Big Man, Chief," Uberoi's *Politics of the Kula Ring,* and a long account by Kaberry, "Law and Political Organization of the Abelam Tribe, New Guinea."

The question of warfare in Melanesia has never been the subject of definitive work, but there are several references of interest. For the Highlands, there is a survey paper by R. M. Berndt, "Warfare in the New Guinea Highlands." Dani warfare (in West Irian) has been the subject of attention by Gardner and Heider in their *Gardens of War*. Schwartz has touched at some length on the subject for Manus in "Systems of Areal Integration." There have been papers by Aufenanger ("The War-Magic Houses in the Wahgi Valley and Adjacent Areas"), R. M. Berndt ("Interdependence and Conflict in the Eastern Central Highlands"), Fortune ("Arapesh Warfare," "The Rules of Relationship Behaviour in One Variety of Primitive Warfare," and "Law and Force in Papuan Societies"), Glasse ("Revenge and Redress Among the Huli"), Wedgwood ("Some Aspects of Warfare in Melanesia"), and Scheffler ("The Social Consequences of Peace on Choiseul Island"). Much data are included in the papers on law and political organization mentioned above. There is also a good, more popular account in Matthiessen's *Under the Mountain Wall*.

Subjects like cannibalism and headhunting, surprisingly, are not well represented in the literature. This is partly due to the absence of these two institutions at the time most anthropologists were permitted to work in the area, so that, not having seen them, workers are hesitant to write about them. There is one account of headhunting, "Some Head-Hunting Traditions of Southern New Guinea" by van der Kroef, somewhat similar to the one by Zegwaard included in this volume, but probably no account of cannibalism worthy of mention. Mortuary customs have been described at length by Powdermaker in "Mortuary Rites in New Ireland," by Vial in "Disposal of the Dead Among the Buang," and more recently by Paula Brown in "Chimbu Death Payments." This topic also is mentioned in many of the book-length accounts cited above—as are most of the other subjects treated in this part.

PART IV

SOCIAL
CHANGE

All societies change, but some seem to do so much faster and more dramatically than others. Melanesia serves well as a laboratory where rates and kinds of cultural change can be observed, described, and compared. In Melanesia, as elsewhere, the pace is quickening, and the problems accompanying change are becoming increasingly urgent. Some Melanesian societies are changing with such unprecedented rapidity that they are evolving not merely *From Stone to Steel* (Salisbury's title), but also directly to radios and automobiles. These societies are duplicating, on a smaller scale, many of the changes and conditions experienced by Western societies whose industrialization required several hundred years.

Since Ian Hogbin did the first full-length study of culture change in Melanesia, *Experiments in Civilization*, this topic has been a major focus of interest for many scholars of Melanesia. There was no lack of material which could have been included in this part. The three articles presented give a fairly balanced view and some idea of the range of variation.

Peter Lawrence's paper illustrates the most salient features of "cargo cults," the Melanesian version of a broader class of phenomena often referred to as "nativistic movements." Lawrence shows that such movements can be interpreted partly in terms of indigenous religious beliefs. He points up the emerging nationalism involved and the political aspects of such cults. He also gives a good picture of how Christianity is often reinterpreted in situations of culture contact and of how misunderstandings are bred of ignorance and suspicion.

Ben Finney, in a somewhat unusual case, demonstrates that the traditional systems of leadership and authority in the New Guinea Highlands were perfectly congruent with the demands of the Western achievement-oriented economic system and, as a result, allowed a truly remarkable rate of change. He describes how the roles of businessman and politician are analogous to those of the traditional leaders and suggests that cargo cults, so much more colorful and attention-getting, are not necessarily the only Melanesian response to contact.

The final paper in this volume, by A. L. Epstein, presents an example of more typical culture change and contrasts well with the case presented by Finney. Epstein focuses on continuity as well as change and shows that in spite of a long history of contact with Europeans, the Tolai on the Gazelle Peninsula have maintained a way of life that retains many of its traditional features. Some

of the indigenous institutions, particularly the "market" (*bung*), may have facilitated change; others, such as the native currency, are still maintained but
operate only in limited contexts. Other institutions have not stood up to the new
aspiration levels and conditions, and many familiar problems can be noted—the
threat of overpopulation, the pressure for land, the generation gap, and the
politics of rapid change.

Melanesia is no longer simply an exotic land of cannibals and headhunters,
slowly changing, and remote from the responsibilities of the rest of the world.
Perhaps with caution, it may be able to achieve a place in the wider world without repeating the mistakes of others.

16

CARGO CULT AND RELIGIOUS
BELIEFS AMONG THE GARIA

Peter Lawrence

The Garia are a small linguistic group of about three thousand people living some forty miles west-south-west of Madang, New Guinea, in foothills between the Adelbert and Finisterre Mountains. This paper is based on field work carried out among these people from April 1949 until July 1950 under a scholarship from the Australian National University. Its purpose is to deal with one aspect of the Cargo Cult as a contact phenomenon. It offers an analysis, preliminary to a wider scheme of field work, of Garia beliefs concerning the Cargo Cult and of their religious beliefs, and tries to demonstrate that, in this case at least, the one can be interpreted more or less consistently in terms of the other.

Various types of nativistic cults have been known in the islands of the southern Pacific Ocean since the end of the last century.[1] They have been reported from Fiji, the Solomon Islands, the New Hebrides, the Torres Straits, Papua and New Guinea. In Papua and New Guinea there has emerged a movement to which has been given the name of Cargo Cult. The most famous outbreak of this cult was the Vailala Madness which swept through the Gulf Division of Papua from 1919 to 1923.[2] To-day very few areas of New Guinea, especially those which have been in contact with Europeans for a long time, have remained wholly unaffected by the movement. Outbreaks were frequent before the Second World War, but during and after it they have become so numerous that they are causing considerable anxiety in missionary and administrative circles.

Cargo[3] is a collective noun used by New Guinea natives to describe the material culture introduced by the Europeans—such things as steel axes, steel tools, clothing, meat and tobacco in tins, rice in bags, aircraft, rifles, and so forth. Many Madang District natives believe that although cargo is the material culture of the Europeans, it is not made by them, but is derived from a specific deity over whom the Europeans have some means of

Reproduced by permission of the publisher and Peter Lawrence from *International Archives of Ethnography*, 47:1-20 (1955). The notes have been renumbered to run in sequence throughout the selection.

control. The Cargo Cult aims to acquire supplies of cargo for the natives by means of ritual ordained by the prophesies of certain inspired leaders.

The Cargo Cult cuts across racial and linguistic boundaries, for the desire for the material culture of the European, and hence for economic and social equality with him, is one of the unifying factors of modern New Guinea. Natives who in the past never co-operated as political groups with or even against their neighbours, are now beginning to express a new type of nationalism in the face of white rule. They speak of themselves as "We people of New Guinea," and vis-à-vis the European their loyalties are extended beyond the range of a single village, or group of villages, to embrace a whole administrative district, or even all those parts of their country which they have visited and know to exist. Hence particular prophesies and ritual attributable to any one leader are not always limited to his own immediate vicinity, but spread rapidly from settlement to settlement and eventually influence a wide area. This is facilitated by the use of Pidgin English as a lingua franca throughout most of New Guinea.

For several years after 1944 a very large part of the Madang District was disturbed by Cargo Cult prophesies. From what is known it is apparent that there is a widespread belief about the origin of the cargo held in common by many of the peoples of the District; but that the most important local centre of the movement has been the Rai Coast south of Madang. From there has spread practically every major innovation in prophesy and ritual. Since 1944 the Garia have been interested in about ten different cult prophesies. Of these only one was expounded by a leader from within their own territory; the others all originated either in Kein and Girawa[4] country or in the Rai Coast area. Yet although the two main leaders[5] whom they followed belonged to different linguistic groups, the Garia were able to participate, or at least to show interest, in the subsequent cult activities, because the prophesies on which these activities were based were consistent with concepts which they themselves had already formulated as result of their contact with Europeans.

During the period of my field research I did not witness Cargo Cult ritual in action. By the time of my arrival the major cults which had swept through the Garia area were matters of the past, and the people were not following the ritual current on the Rai Coast. Hence I directed my enquiries mainly towards the nature of Garia beliefs concerning the origin of the cargo itself. I knew well many natives who had participated at one time or another in several cults, and from them I obtained descriptions of the ritual involved and the prophesies on which they were based. I became friendly with a Kein native, Kaum or Komaibu of Kalinam, who from 1944 till 1949 was an influential cult leader. Finally, I myself became the centre of rumours which, given proper encouragement, might well have developed into a large-scale cargo cult.

CARGO CULTS IN WHICH THE GARIA PARTICIPATED

There is no space to describe all the ten cults in which the Garia were interested after 1944. But in order to illustrate the analysis which follows, three of the most significant have been selected.

My informants told me that some time before the middle of 1947 Polelesi, a woman of the Garia village of Igurue, claimed that she had had a dream in which she saw one of God's angels, who warned her of the coming of a Second Flood. She told her fellow villagers that they would be saved because God would send them a ship, and she advised the inhabitants of other Garia settlements to hurry to Igurue and make use of this means of escape. Many Garia did in fact take this seriously and left their homes, but some refused to panic. These people, said Polelesi, would be drowned or eaten by crocodiles. In a clairvoyant moment she proclaimed that she had seen God, Jesus Christ, angels and the spirits of the dead in the clouds above the mountains. She had seen a storehouse built there as well, and in it was cargo which would soon be brought down to the survivors by the spirits. She ordained special prayers to God and the spirits, and later when it began to rain she announced that this was a divine sign of the imminence of the cargo's arrival. She ordered everybody to sit outside and be washed by it as if it were a form of baptism.

This was, as far as can be ascertained, the only cult which originated within Garialand. The others described below were based on prophesies derived from elsewhere.

The first of these concerned Yali of Sor, a man who had achieved a position of considerable influence in his own area, the Rai Coast. His real history begins in 1942, when he joined a native military unit under Allied command. He served with distinction until he retired with the rank of Sergeant-Major in 1945. During the war he visited Australia, where he was shown munitions and other factories. It is said that he was very much impressed with the Australian scene and returned to New Guinea determined to better the lot of his people. After the war he was supported by the Administration in his efforts for native rehabilitation along the Rai Coast.

Yali's exact position in the Cargo Cult is still debateable. Whether he was personally responsible for the prophesies attributed to him has yet to be proved. But it is certain that after 1947 he was definitely regarded by the Garia as a cult leader. During August 1947 Yali went to Port Moresby for discussions with Administration officials. After his departure certain natives who styled themselves his lieutenants went through the Madang District bringing the people a new prophesy. According to my informants the version which they brought to the Garia villages was as follows.

During the war, said the lieutenants, Yali had been killed by the Japanese and had returned to earth as a spirit of the dead. First he had gone to Australia where he had seen the King, and from there to Paradise where he had seen God, who had asked him about conditions in New Guinea and had then told him to return to Australia with these instructions: he was to tell the King that God was sending him back to New Guinea in the shape of a man to improve the country and run it for the benefit of the natives. While Yali was in New Guinea, God would send the spirits of the dead to Sydney with cargo, which the King was to load in a ship and look after until such time as Yali should inform him that he wanted it. When Yali had completed his initial work, the ship would be sent to Madang under guard of the spirits of the dead.

Yali, they continued, had now gone to Port Moresby to meet the ship, which the King had personally brought up there. Soon Yali would bring the ship to Madang. He would return as a District Commissioner and distribute cargo to his followers. This cargo would include war equipment with which he and they would drive out the Europeans. But before it could be distributed the people must organise themselves into large villages or *camps,* and build special houses for Yali to live in whenever he visited them. These orders were obeyed. "Boss Boys", in theory superior to the Administration headmen, were appointed by the lieutenants to supervise the work of construction.

Although my informants told me that no particular ritual was authorised in the Garia villages at this time, it is said that in other areas prayers were offered to Yali asking him to invoke God for cargo. Moreover, in Girawa country a large ceremony was conducted by the native evangelists of the Lutheran Mission, at which several thousand Garia and Girawa natives were baptised. The purpose of the ceremony was said to be twofold. First, only baptised Christians would get cargo from Yali; and second, in the course of the new war against the Europeans many people would be killed. Baptism offered the only means of salvation in the life to come.[6]

The final cult to be described seems to have occurred at roughly the same time as the events outlined above. The cult ritual was based on a prophesy similar to that attributed to Yali. The leader was the Kein native, Kaum of Kalinam. This man first came into prominence in December 1944, when he is said to have claimed to have been given cargo by the spirits of the dead. He urged the people of his locality to pray to God and the spirits of the dead, to put out offerings of food for the latter and to build storehouses. The spirits would bring up cargo through the cemeteries and put it in the storehouses. Kaum claimed also that the Japanese (who had recently evacuated the area) would return to help the people fight the Europeans. He was arrested by the Administration and gaoled for nine months, but he returned to Kalinam at the end of 1946. He was now the established cargo leader of the area in which the Kein, Girawa and Garia peoples lived. On his return to Kalinam he inaugurated similar ritual, for which he was gaoled again for six months in March 1947. He was released the following September, and some time after that date started the third cult ritual now to be described in detail.

This ritual was said to have been staged in an Administration Labour Compound in Madang. Several informants admitted to having participated in it when living there as manual labourers. They told me that Kaum gathered the workboys together and told them that while he had been in gaol he had been killed by the police boys. He had gone to Paradise, where he had seen God and the spirits of the dead actually making cargo. God had given him a new name, Konsel,[7] and instructions for ritual. Kaum claimed also that his personal *oite'u* (or indigenous god) Kilibob had given him a special symbol, which seems to have been a small gun shell, and that he now was the equivalent of a District Commissioner. He had other workboys cook his food for him.

Seances were conducted as follows: in the evenings Kaum would set up a table in one of the compound huts and cover it with a white cloth. In the middle he would place his symbol standing on its base, and surrounding it, plates of food and tobacco. Encircling the plates of food and tobacco he would place flowers in bottles. After cooking food for Kaum the workboys would assemble. They would sit down, fold their hands and pray to Kaum thus: "O Father Konsel, you are sorry for us. You can help us. We have nothing—no aircraft, no ships, no jeeps, nothing at all. The Europeans steal it from us. You will be sorry for us and send us something." Thereafter Kaum would pray to God and the spirits of the dead in a similar manner. He would also address Kilibob's symbol and ask it to go up to Paradise and communicate with God.

When the seances were over, the workboys would leave Kaum to sleep near the table in company with a trusted lieutenant. Kaum used to claim that his symbol would then go up to Paradise and get messages from God and the spirits of the dead about the coming of the cargo. It would return during the night, and Kaum, who alone could understand its secret language, would commune with it. During this period he claimed frequently that he had dreamt of the souls of the dead, and also that at night they came up to eat the food put out for them on the table. He proclaimed that he would soon bring up a tidal wave to destroy the Europeans in Madang. Emissaries were sent out to the Garia villages to instruct the people to follow the ritual practised in the Compound, and to put up storehouses, to which the spirits of the dead, supervised by Kilibob, could bring the cargo. This cult ritual seems to have been disbanded about April 1948, when Kaum was transferred to the Rai Coast.

THE PRE-CHRISTIAN RELIGION OF THE GARIA

The above account emphasizes these facts: that God is believed to be the source of the cargo; that the spirits of the dead are believed to be able to bring it to the natives from Paradise; and that ritual is designed to induce

God to send it, and the spirits to deliver it. These three facts can be under-stood in terms of Garia pre-Christian beliefs about their gods and the spirits of the dead. How far such an interpretation will prove consistent with the religions of other Madang District peoples remains to be seen from further field work. At present it must be limited to the Garia themselves.

The Pantheon

The Garia believe that their world is the creation of a pantheon of gods and goddesses (*oite'u*)[8], through whom everything came into being. They are independent deities in their own right, and as such should be distin-guished from the spirits of the dead.[9] The gods and goddesses are consid-ered to have existed more or less always, and they are never spirits of former human beings. They are said to be snakes, animals, birds, or men and women of the bush.

In the beginning, various deities put down the ground in different places, gave birth to human beings, and invented the artefacts and ceremonies of importance to Garia society. They are thought still to be the tutelary deities of the places they created, and to preside over the artefacts and ceremonies they invented. In the case of the artefacts and ceremonies, the Garia say that at the time of the creation particular deities would appear to men in the course of dreams or visions, and tell them their open names (*olo wenum*), by which they could be known in everyday conversation. The deities would also tell men their myths, and instruct them in the physical labour necessary to perform the ceremonies or make the artefacts for which they were responsible. Finally, the deities would reveal to men their magic, that is, their secret names (*wenum minikoro*), the silent repetition of which would ensure their co-operation and the ultimate success of different undertakings.

Thus the traditional knowledge of the Garia is based ultimately on myths and secret names revealed to men by the gods and goddesses. The texts of the myths as they exist to-day always refer to the origin of particular arte-facts and ceremonies, and establish their connection with pertinent deities. The myths are regarded, therefore, as guarantee of the existence of the pantheon.

Every deity has his or her open and secret names. Each patrilineal descent line is equipped with a full set of secret names of deities covering the basic necessities of existence—gardening, hunting, and pig raising. The deity and the open name may be the common property of all the descent lines of a locality, but each descent line will know the deity also by secret names which are its own exclusive property. The secret names are a possession of men in which women do not share, and the rights to use them are usually inherited from father to son. A boy learns about them during his initiatory period, which lasts from puberty until marriage.

There are broadly speaking two stages in training for magic—the observance of taboos, and the learning of the secret names. During his initiatory period a boy must observe stringent food and sex taboos. He may not eat certain bush animals and birds, and contact with women of childbearing age is forbidden him. These taboos are designed to make him strong and to help him get command over the gods of sorcery and love. Provided that he observes them properly, he will begin to learn the secret names of the deities towards and after the end of his initiatory period.

Although everybody in Garia society has an equal chance of becoming proficient in magic, it is only some people who are able to master all the many secret names, and to demonstrate successfully that they have done so. Such persons emerge as the big men (*kokai apu*) of Garia society. They are regarded as prominent sorcerers, and become leaders in such activities as gardening and initiatory ceremonies. Practically all personal prestige and authority depend ultimately on proficiency in magic, that is, in the use of the secret names of deities.

Before embarking on any activity of vital importance but doubtful issue, a big man must breathe[10] the secret name of the presiding god or goddess. Before general taro planting is carried out in a garden, the garden leader will take a specially prepared taro shoot, breathe over it the secret name of Ibinime the taro goddess, and then throw it into a hole. This ceremony is performed in each plot. Again, before a dance at a pig exchange or initiatory ceremony, the dance leader will gather together all the ornaments of the performers and carry out similar ritual.

No food offerings are put out for the deities except occasionally for those who preside over hunting, and for those who are thought to live near gardens in the bush, and may protect them from wild pig. The normal approach to all deities is through the kind of ritual described above. The Garia explain the breathing of the secret names thus: "*je oite'u po nanunanu pululone;* I pull towards me the *nanunanu* of the god". *Nanunanu* is the Garia word for *thinking,* but in this context it is not *thinking* in an intellectual sense, but rather *thinking on* or *of,* or *having a proper concern for.* Similar to it is the word *eiyo, sorrow* or *compassion.* To pull the *nanunanu* of the deity means to make him *think on* you and lend his power to your undertaking. This alone will guarantee success. The breathing of the secret name is a means of direct control over the god or goddess, who *must* come to the aid of the practitioner. Failure to achieve the desired success, however, does not mean that the god, although properly addressed, is angry or for other reasons unwilling to help. It means that the magic itself is at fault, that the secret names have been inexpertly used, or that the practitioner has been improperly trained. Otherwise the god is under control and has no freedom of action or choice. The practitioner who can so control him at will is said "to have the *nanunanu* of the god—*oite'u po nanunanu tina.*"

The power of a deity would seem to have a very wide geographical range. For instance, many dances performed by the Garia originate from outside their own territory. The rights to perform these dances are sold from village to village. They include the right to use the secret names of the gods who invented the dances. Although the gods may belong to very distant areas, yet it is believed that their *nanunanu* can be "pulled" by dance leaders who live in Garialand. Again, I was told that labourers on the coast found sorcery and love gods resident in Garialand quite satisfactory for their needs.

Yet although the Garia buy dance magic from outside their territory and sell it to others, the secret names of the majority of their deities are rarely revealed to outsiders, even by the members of one descent line to the members of another living in the same settlement. These secret names represent the very strength of those who possess them, and are, therefore, a closely guarded secret. If other persons were to learn them, they could steal away the *nanunanu* of the gods to their own advantage, and weaken the control of the original owners. They could raise bumper crops and rear many domestic animals, but they would impoverish the original owners to a corresponding degree. Because of this belief I had to wait many months before any informant would admit even the existence of the pantheon and its magic.

The Spirits of the Dead

In the pre-Christian beliefs of the Garia there are three kinds of spirit or soul: the *enumu*; the *kopa*; and the *kaua*. The *enumu* is the soul of a man while he is alive; it lives within his body. After death it turns into a *kopa* or a *kaua* according to circumstances. *Kopa* are the souls of those who have died either natural deaths or through the agency of sorcery. *Kaua* are the souls of those who have died by means of physical violence.

The *enumu* ceases to exist after death and seems to have very little importance during life. *Kopa* and *kaua*, however, are very important after death. Neither of them is an airy substance like our own ghost or wraith. Both are essentially corporeal. They have flesh and blood, skin and bones, hair—in fact, all human physical attributes. They differ from living men only in that they are cold to touch, invisible to everybody except sorcerers, and, for about three generations, immortal. Being essentially corporeal, they can handle, steal and carry material objects.

Before the coming of the Administration and the Lutheran Mission the bodies of the dead were exposed in trees until the flesh had rotted. The bones were collected and kept by the sons of the deceased. This practice is now illegal, and bodies are buried in cemeteries near the settlements. According to the old belief *kaua* go to roam in the bush; *kopa* go to Warua, the Land of the Dead. But the *kopa* is not forced to live in Warua always. It may, if it so desires, wander round the bush by day, and by night visit its descendants in the settlements and bring them messages about future events. *Kaua* may do the same. Such visits are usually made in the course of dreams. Both *kopa* and *kaua* are said to keep the wild pigs in the bush. After living in Warua or roaming the bush for three generations both types of spirit turn into flying foxes.

Relations between living men are governed by the rules of kinship. A man is expected to behave towards his close living relatives in a certain way, but this he cannot do unless he has a proper concern (*nanunanu*) for them. His concern for them, and theirs for him, must be generated by the fulfilment of certain recognised mutual obligations. In the same way, the spirits of the dead are expected to *think on* and help their closely related living descendants. But, just as the *nanunanu* of the gods must be pulled by means of ritual and that of human beings by the fulfilment of obligations, even so the spirits of the dead have to be made to *think on* the living by means of various counter-services. In the past, during the dry season, when there was plenty of food in the gardens, the Nalisägege dance was performed to propitiate the dead. At the time of this and other dances the bones of the dead were decorated with red paint. Nowadays the formal weeping of female kin at the time of a funeral is designed to show the spirit that his relatives are still *thinking on* him. Again, the principal partners in a pig exchange will honour their dead fathers by secretly naming their pigs after them—in the past they would carry round their fathers' jaw bones at the time of the ceremony—and those participating in the dances held to celebrate the exchange are said, while dancing, to *think on* the spirits of their departed relatives. This will please the spirits, who will rejoice in the dance and its regalia, and regard these things as honouring themselves.

In return for these services, the spirits of the dead are believed to help their descendants. They will bring them such things as dance ornaments, which they steal from other people. They will prevent the wild pigs from destroying the gardens of their descendants, and will put them in their way to shoot in the bush. Conversely, an angry spirit can steal belongings and chase away wild pig from unrelated persons who have displaced him. Moreover, *kopa* can bring up wild pig to ruin the gardens of their human enemies. *Kaua* can turn into wild pig, and either attack such persons in the bush or invade their gardens.

From the above description of Garia pre-Christian religion two very important facts emerge. First, the religion is preoccupied almost exclusively with material welfare. It is concerned with the acquisition by human beings of material benefits in this world rather than of spiritual blessings in the next. The pantheon of gods and goddesses is a means by which the Garia control their affairs, for it is the ultimate source of all culture and knowledge. The dead, whose existence automatically orders itself, are honoured so that they may intervene propitiously in the lives of their descendants and bring them gifts. In a word, the spiritual element in religion, as we understand it, is hardly stressed.

Second, as in all Papuan and Melanesian societies, relationships are expressed and understood most easily in terms of the giving or exchange of material goods and advantages. The Garia extend this feature to three types of relationship in which they are directly interested: between god and man; between the spirits of the dead and man; and between man and man. In each case, the medium in which the relationship can best be described, and the end to which it is directed, are the acquisition or exchange of material benefits. But in each case, the relationship so expressed is made possible only when it is ensured that both parties to it *think on* each other in the proper manner. This is achieved on the part of human beings by means of ritual to the gods, proper services to the spirits of the dead, and the fulfilment of obligations to the living. In this way the social and economic system, as the Garia see it, will function smoothly.

The Influence of Christianity

It seems that Europeans first came into contact with the Garia a little before the First World War. Although the people were not as yet under administrative control, their young men probably began to seek European employment at about that time. As in many areas of New Guinea, the first reactions of the Garia to the white men was that they were spirits of the dead who, out of concern for their living descendants, had come bringing gifts.[11] This idea, with a few modifications, persisted for a while, but gradually gave way to a more important set of beliefs to be discussed later.

At the present time the Madang District has been divided into two rough areas for the purpose of missionary activity; the north around Bogia is predominantly Roman Catholic; and the south around Madang and the Rai Coast is predominantly Lutheran. The Garia belong to the field of the Lutheran Mission.

At the outset the Lutheran Mission made little progress beyond the immediate coast. It seems, in fact, that it met with considerable hosility. But after 1914 evangelical expansion proceeded at a much more rapid rate. Administration patrols began to open up the hinterland, and missionary influence followed in their wake. In 1922 a Lutheran station was set up in Girawa country, and from there the Garia were gradually brought under mission influence. By 1930 schools and churches had been set up in all the principal Garia settlements, and native teachers and evangelists appointed to supervise lessons and services. In 1937 a large baptism ceremony was held in the Garia village of Iwaiwa, before which all the native esoterica—the equipment for sorcery, initiation ceremonies, garden magic, and so forth—were publicly exposed and destroyed.[12] The inhabitants of the other settlements intended to follow this lead but were prevented from doing so by the Japanese invasion.

Apart from Administration officials, the Garia were brought into contact with two types of European, those who dealt in commerce and those who dealt in religion. The one offered them employment and hence limited access to cargo. The other brought them a new God. The utility of cargo to the Garia was soon apparent from the fact that European artefacts of steel, glass and cloth readily replaced their native counterparts of stone, bone, wood and bark. These goods became a medium through which relationships within the existing social framework were expressed. But they also became symbolic of something hitherto unknown, an unequal relationship in which the native was dependent on the European for his access to cargo.

Because the Garia were rapidly absorbing the cargo into their culture, they had to find an explanation of its origin. They could not see it made, and hence it is hardly surprising that they turned to their own concepts as outlined above, and interpreted the new material culture in terms of the new God introduced by the missionaries at roughly the same time. From what my informants admitted it seems quite possible that many Garia imagined that by accepting the new religion they would acquire the cargo as well. The one went with the other even as their own gods were inextricably bound up with their own external world. The cargo itself was seen as the proof of the validity of Christianity.

The Garia Interpretation of Christianity

That God should have been thought to be the deity of the cargo is consistent with Garia pre-Christian religious concepts. The Garia refer to God and Jesus Christ as *Kokai Oite'u,* Big Gods; they have granted Them the same attributes as their own deities. Moreover, a large proportion of the mission school work was based on texts drawn from the earlier books of the Bible. As these texts dealt largely with divine revelation and corresponded so neatly with the beliefs that they already held about the creation of their own world, the Garia sought in them an interpretation of the origins of Western Civilisation as they saw it. They made the following rationalisation.

In the beginning, they said, God created Paradise, the bush, all animals and food-stuffs. He put Adam and Eve in Paradise, and He made and gave them cargo. The two copulated in the garden, so God threw them out into the bush where they existed without cargo. There was no cargo in the world until the time of Noah. At this time there was a Great Flood, which only Noah and his family survived. As Noah had obeyed the word of God, He was sorry for him and sent him cargo. Now the three sons of Noah had access to it as well. Shem and Japheth went to the land of the white men and to Israel, and as they and their descendants continued to obey God's word, they continued to get the cargo. But Ham was arrogant before God, who was angry, threw him out and took from him his right to the cargo. Ham came to New Guinea. The people of New Guinea are the descendants of Ham, and as they have never obeyed the word of God as the result of his sin, they have no cargo.[13]

But not only did the Garia try to explain Western Civilisation in the same terms of divine revelation as they explained their own world, they also believed that, just as their own culture had never changed except through the agency of new gods who had introduced new artefacts, new ceremonies, and thus new knowledge, even so Western Civilisation had never changed since the time of its origin. Hence in Garia eyes Noah, Shem, Japheth, and the other early Israelites were exactly the same as the white men of to-day. They wore the same clothes, used the same tools and ate the same food. Noah's Ark was a steel ship of the same type as those which are seen in Madang Harbour.

The preoccupation of the pre-Christian religion of the Garia with material welfare reappears in their interpretation of Christianity. Disinterested in its spiritual content, the Garia translated the Fall of Man, the Curse of Ham, and even salvation itself into terms of this materialism. Through Christianity they looked only for a road, as they put it, to the cargo. The European was thought to possess special ritual knowledge by means of which he could get supplies of cargo from his God. This ritual knowledge was summed up in the phrase: *"Ausiapu Anut po nanunanu tina*; the white man has the *nanunanu* of God"*. The European could make his God *think on* him in the same way as the big man of Garia society could pull the *nanunanu* of his gods towards him by means of ritual.

The Garia crystallised their beliefs about Christainity in the following manner. God was the deity of the cargo, and His myth was their version of the Creation and the Flood. He lived in Paradise where He made cargo, to which, as the native evangelists had promised them, the souls of the faithful would have access after death. Paradise was near Sydney, and down from Paradise to Sydney there was a ladder. With God in Paradise were the spirits of dead Garia and dead Europeans. As they were essentially corporeal beings, they could help God make and handle the cargo. Supplies of this cargo, some of which were meant for the Europeans and some for the natives, would be brought down the ladder by the spirits of the dead out of concern for their descendants, provided that the correct ritual were performed. But the problem was to find the correct ritual.

The Search for Correct Ritual

My informants told me that when the missionaries first came, everybody thought that they had been sent by God out of His concern for the descendants of Ham. The Garia believed that if they now obeyed the word of God, He would send them cargo. It seems possible that at the outset they thought that the correct ritual to ensure this end consisted in putting themselves in a right relationship with God. They therefore banned all the ceremonies condemned by the missionaries—those based on magic—and substituted for them church services and school lessons. (This, perhaps, may be compared with the right relationship with the god of sorcery created by a youth by means of his observance of the pre-marital taboos.) As a result God would see that the people were obeying His laws and would *think on* them. They would acquire cargo through their own merit and His grace. One informant expressed it thus: "All the time we worked hard. We were baptised. We praised God and we listened to sermons." In private many people prayed for cargo.

Yet when garden magic, initiatory ceremonies and dances had been banned for several years and still the cargo did not come, the Garia attitude apparently changed. The failure could be partially explained by the belief that, as they were obeying the word of God, their share of cargo was being brought down the ladder by the spirits of the dead; but that it had to be shipped to New Guinea under the control of the Europeans, who out of sheer greed were removing the names of the natives from the boxes and appropriating the contents for their own use. At the same time, however, the Garia reverted to their own concept of human control over the deity. They ceased to believe that their own prayers alone were enough to persuade God to act of His own volition pleased by the merits of His devotees, and began to assume that the Europeans had a secret prayer of such efficacy that, whenever it was uttered, God was forced to send them cargo. Just as the secret names of their own gods were never revealed to others, even so this prayer was the hidden strength of the white men, the one thing they would not reveal to the natives, who by acquiring the cargo would become their equals. It was by virtue of this secret prayer that the Europeans were said to have the *nanunanu* of God, and because it had been kept hidden from the natives, the missionaries were said to have lied and closed the road of the cargo.

It was believed also that a good European was one who, remembering his brotherhood with the natives through Noah, would fulfil the obligations of the relationship by giving liberally of his own store of cargo, and ultimately by revealing the secret of its origin. My own case bears this out. I had shown myself liberal and friendly: I therefore remembered my brotherhood with the people. I was a European: I therefore had the *nanunanu* of God. It was believed, by some Garia at least, that eventually I would pray to God to send the spirits of my own and the Garia ancestors with cargo to Sydney. From there my living relatives would ship it to Madang, and from Madang it could be flown inland by aircraft. I was approached by several natives and asked to build an aerodrome for this purpose.

If the above analyses of the Garia pre-Christian religion and the Garia interpretation of Christianity be compared with the account of the three cargo cults given in a previous section, it can be seen why the people were able and willing to follow any leader, even from an outside group, who could convince them that in the course of some supernatural experience he had acquired the special quality of the European, the *nanunanu* of God, or that he had gained control of an indigenous god, who could act as an intermediary[14] with Him. In other words, they were willing to follow any leader who, they believed, had learned the correct ritual for coercing God to send cargo, and the spirits to bring it, in such a way that it could not be stolen by the white man. But this in itself raises an additional problem.

Among the Garia all important physical labour has its ritual counterpart. Indeed, without it all physical labour would be in vain. For instance, before each stage in the preparation of a new garden—the cutting of the scrub and trees, the building of the fence, the planting of the taro, etc.—ritual is performed to ensure the successful completion of the work in hand. In Garia eyes, work is a compound of physical labour and ritual—a compound because the one cannot be divorced from the other. Yet the Garia apply the term "work" to the ritual of the Cargo Cult, in which there is virtually no attempt to imitate the manufacture of European artefacts. Why is it that they believe that they can acquire cargo by ritual alone, when they recognise that both physical labour and ritual are necessary to produce one of their own artefacts?

We must remember, to begin with, the lack of correspondence between the Garia and European material cultures. The Garia do not work in metals and glass, or weave cloth. As has been remarked, they have no opportunity to see Europeans manufacture their own artefacts, and therefore have no comprehension of how these things are made. This is in marked contrast to the case in many African and Asian societies. What the Garia do see— or at least know about—is huge quantities of cargo brought in by ship and aircraft, and put away in storehouses. A native may buy small amounts of cargo, if he works for money, whereas a European, as far as he is aware, can procure as much as he wants merely by sending his servant to the store with a chit. No cash transaction is apparent. It is no exaggeration to say that the natives cannot appreciate that Europeans engage in any physical labour at all, and that consequently they imagine that the "work" by which they obtain their supplies of cargo is secret ritual. Therefore, in the Cargo Cult, ritual is inevitably stressed to the exclusion of physical labour.

THE NATIVISTIC ELEMENT

It seems that 1947 was a peak year of Cargo Cult activity for the Garia. They had been visited by Yali's self-styled lieutenants, and had shown considerable interest in Kaum's ritual in the compound in Madang. But after 1947 they became more sceptical of the prophesies which were propounded. At the same time they had become disillusioned with Christianity, for it had failed to produce the results expected from it. Moreover, although for a few years before the war they had given up the ceremonies ordained by their gods and goddesses, they had never discarded their faith in the existence and efficacy of the gods and goddesses themselves. It was believed that when Ham came to New Guinea after forfeiting his right to the cargo, he was given, for his share, control over the deities who invented the culture of the Garia. As all magic—that is, the secret names of the deities—had been condemned by the missionaries as the invention of Satan, the deities came to be known as Satans, and were in a sense incorporated into Christianity. They were still real and powerful in their own spheres; and they were bad only in that the culture they provided was inferior to that of the new God who replaced them. With the removal of mission influence after the Japanese Invasion in 1942, pagan ceremonies came back into practice and for a time co-existed with Christian belief and ritual. After 1947, however, the return to paganism gathered momentum, until the Garia were paying only lip service to the mission, and finally reverted almost entirely to their traditional ritual practices.

On the other hand, the Garia were not openly so hostile to the Lutheran Mission as the peoples of the Rai Coast were said to be at this time. After January 1948 it was noticed that in this area the mission churches and schools were being deserted, and that there was emerging, in contrast, new cargo ritual based exclusively on the pre-Christian religion. These activities are properly attributed to the influence of Yali.

My knowledge of Yali's prophesies at this time is necessarily second hand. It is based on conversations with Lutheran missionaries and with Kaum. I was told that sometime after his return from Port Moresby towards the end of 1947 Yali claimed that it had been revealed to him that the cargo had been invented originally not by God, but by a deity of the Rai Coast. This happened when the first missionaries arrived. These men had no cargo of their own, but by acquiring the lore of the Rai Coast gods they had lured them away to their own country, and had thus appropriated the cargo. In return they had given the natives their illusory God and Jesus Christ, who had nothing to do with cargo whatever. While the people believed in these two Christian deities, they would remain under the control of the missionaries. In order to neutralise this control, they must abandon the mission schools and churches, and return to the ways of their ancestors.

The causes leading to the rejection of the belief that God was the deity of the cargo need fuller investigation before the part played by Yali can be properly evaluated. However, I was fortunate enough to learn at first hand from Kaum his own new prophesy, which he had been spreading secretly among his intimates, and which he intended to proclaim to peoples of the Kein, Girawa and Garia area as soon as the time was ripe. The prophesy and ritual which Kaum had devised were similar to the prophesy and ritual said to have been instigated by Yali after January 1948.

Kaum spent from April till September 1948 on the Rai Coast. He returned to Madang, but was arrested and gaoled in March 1949 for further cargo activities. He returned to Kalinam at the end of 1949. It was then that I became friendly with him. By this time he had altered his beliefs to fit those current on the Rai Coast, for during 1950 he told me that he had given up all his previous faith in God and that in a series of dreams had learned that in the Kein-Girawa-Garia area the cargo had been invented by the god Kilibob.[15] Kaum told me that he had received special instructions for ritual. He had already acquired the god's symbol, the Arm of Kilibob—the same gun shell as was used in the Labour Compound. From his dreams he had learned the myth reproduced here.

"Kilibob and his brother Manup fought at Milaguk. Manup chased Kilibob to Sek Island. Kilibob challenged Manup to fight. He stood up in a warship. Manup shot with bow and arrow: Kilibob used guns and bombs. The fight went all the way to Jerusalem. They returned to Sek. Kilibob then invented all the cargo, and taught the other gods to make it. Manup had no food. His mother brought him some—banana and *aipika* seeds. She wanted to bring him rice, but Kilibob said, "Mother has given Manup taro and everything; he must not get rice.[16] He took ashes from the fire and blinded his mother, so that she was confused. Thus Manup got no cargo, but worked only at taro cultivation. Kilibob alone got the cargo. When Kilibob invented the cargo, the Germans came and saw it. They had no cargo of their own: they wore bark girdles (just as the natives had done). They liked the cargo, so they put down Kilibob and stole away his lore to their own country."

Kaum claimed that by virtue of his dreams and his symbol he had the *nanunanu* of Kilibob and the other gods. But, he said, the cargo would come in abundance only when everybody followed the instructions revealed to him. First, the people must avoid attending mission church services, which were a mockery because God and Jesus Christ were completely fictitious, and refrain from telling Europeans the secrets of the native gods, for this would only enhance the power of the Europeans. Second, Kilibob and the other gods must be lured back to New Guinea, and the spirits of the dead made to think on their descendants. The necessary ritual would include these features. Holding up the arm of Kilibob, Kaum would address the god, recite his myth, and invoke him to send cargo. Short bamboo flutes, as used in Garia initiatory ceremonies, would be blown to call on the gods generally. Long bamboo flutes—the type used in the Garia Nalisägege dance—would be blown to honour the spirits of the dead, and offerings of food would be put out for them as well. The spirits would bring up cargo through the cemeteries.

As has been mentioned, the ritual described above is similar to that said to have been performed on the Rai Coast during 1948-49. Some Garia settlements adopted it temporarily from that area, but soon gave it up, possibly because of mission influence, but more probably because they saw no appreciable results and feared Administration reprisal. Furthermore,

Kaum never openly proclaimed his new prophesy based on Kilibob. Even so it is doubtful whether the people would have followed him at this time, had he done so, because his prestige was definitely on the wane. On the other hand, the Garia could understand such a prophesy, and be interested —with proper encouragement even take part—in the ritual it involved, for the following reasons.

In the first place, as we have seen, owing to their disillusionment with Christianity, the Garia were in a mood to try any alternative means of getting cargo. In the second place, Kaum's new prophesy could quite easily have been accepted by the people, because it dovetailed neatly with the pre-Christian religious concepts which they already held. That the cargo should have been invented by an indigenous New Guinea god was no strange idea. It had to be proved only by the appearance of such a deity in the course of a dream or supernatural experience. Again, the claim that the early missionaries had lured away the gods and goddesses to their own country, was quite in keeping with the Garia belief that the *nanunanu* of their deities could be stolen by outsiders, even if they lived at a distance. Finally, the ritual which Kaum told me he would use, when he had proclaimed his new prophesy, was based on traditional ceremonies with practically all of which the Garia were quite familiar.

Conclusions

The material of this paper can be summed up under the following headings:

a) *Belief and ritual in the Cargo Cult.* It was seen in the account of their pagan religion that the Garia believe that their culture is the creation of a pantheon of deities, who are subject to human ritual control. The material culture of the Europeans is interpreted in the same terms. At first the Garia believed that God was the deity of the cargo. Later in one area there was a change of emphasis, and God was replaced by one of the indigenous gods. The Garia never formally adopted this belief for any length of time, but they could understand it, because it was based on essentially the same concepts as the other. It was the same belief set in a new, but familiar, mould.

The spirits of the dead were traditionally thought of as corporeal beings, which, if properly propitiated, would bring gifts to their descendants. The same concept reappears in the Cargo Cult. In the quasi-Christian belief the spirits of the dead are associated with God in Paradise. In the pagan belief the nature of their association with the cargo deity is less definite. But in both beliefs the spirits are regarded as being sorry for their descendants, and able to bring them cargo made by the deity.

The ritual of the Cargo Cult is, therefore, the same in essence as the ritual of the Garia pagan religion. It is devised to ensure the delivery of the cargo by making the deity and the spirits of the dead *think on* the devotees.

In the quasi-Christian ritual, special prayers are offered to God, sometimes through inspired human intermediaries, and sometimes with the aid of a local deity acting as an additional go-between. The rite of baptism also appears. Prayers are addressed to the spirits, and food and tobacco are set out for them. Again, in the pagan ritual, if Kaum's account be accurate, the principal god of the cargo is honoured by a special address, and the others by the use of short bamboo flutes. The spirits of the dead are honoured in the traditional dance which the Garia call Nalisägege. Food offerings are put out for them as well. In both types of belief the ritual is thought to be effective because of the special instructions revealed by the cargo deity.

b) *Leadership in the Cargo Cult.* In traditional Garia society leadership was based ultimately on the possession of the secret names of deities. These names were originally revealed to men in the course of dreams, and those who possessed them were said to have the *nanunanu* of the deities. This concept is extended to the Cargo Cult. The European is thought to have the *nanunanu* of the god of the cargo, and to be able to control him for his own ends. Before cult ritual can begin, the leader must demonstrate through the traditional medium of the dream or supernatural experience, that he has this particular virtue. In the cult ritual described, Polelesi claimed the *nanunanu* of God by virtue of a dream in which she had seen one of His angels. The Garia believed that Kaum had it because of his claim that he had died, seen God and been given a new name, and that he had in Kilibob an intermediary through whom he could communicate with God. The same sort of thing was believed of Yali. In the cult based on pagan beliefs, Kaum claimed the *nanunanu* of the cargo deity by virtue of his possession of the Arm of Kilibob, and of a series of dreams. He told me that Yali made the same sort of claim.

Again, the Garia believe that the spirits of the dead can appear to men in the course of dreams and tell them about the future. This belief reappears in the Cargo Cult. Kaum, for instance, often claimed to have dreamt of the spirits at the time of cult ritual. The dream[17] or supernatural experience in the Cargo Cult is the medium through which the leader establishes his connection with the cargo deity and the spirits of the dead, and hence his authority among his followers.

c) *The political implications of the Cargo Cult.* That the Cargo Cult is the result of culture contact and the unequal relations between natives and Europeans is obvious. Although *prima facie* their interests are adequately cared for by the Administration, the natives of the Madang District are bound to feel their inferiority both socially and economically. Nearly all commercial enterprise is in the hands of Europeans and Asiatics. The natives do not form a middle class. In the vast majority of cases, they are brought into contact with the new economic system, which has done so much to revolutionise their lives, in the capacity of manual labourers, and hence they do not have any deep insight into the processes by which it works.

On the other hand, the natives resent the inferiority of their position, and they wish to improve it. For them the cargo has become the symbol of the political power of the Europeans, and this power they feel they must combat. But for the achievement of this rational end they are bound to employ completely irrational means. Their own concept of power is based on supernaturally revealed knowledge, and lacking all other means of politically organised resistance, they inevitably fall back on this concept in their struggle against the Europeans.

Nevertheless, the struggle is a very real and important one, for translated into political terms the Cargo Cult is an embryonic nationalistic movement.[18] This is at once apparent in several of the prophesies of the cult leaders, who proclaimed that, when they had acquired cargo, they would wage war against the Europeans, or in some other way destroy them. From this point of view the Cargo Cult can be compared with such movements as the 'Masinga' Rule of the Solomon Islands and the struggles for political independence in other colonial territories. But deeper and more systematic research is necessary before this aspect of the Cargo Cult in the Madang District can be properly understood.

NOTES

1. For a general survey of these cults see Cyril S. Belshaw, *The Significance of Modern Cults in Melanesian Development, Australian Outlook,* Vol. 4, June 1950, pp. 116-125.
2. F. E. Williams, *The Vailala Madness, Papuan Anthropology Report* No. 4, Port Moresby, 1923.
3. *Cargo* is a common Pidgin English word, and is more properly spelled *kako* or *kago.*
4. The Girawa are a people living on the northern boundaries of the Garia. The Kein people live on the northern boundaries of the Girawa.
5. Some leaders are responsible for a number of different prophesies over a period of years.
6. Salvation was probably interpreted by the natives in terms of access to cargo in Paradise. See p. [306].
7. The exact significance of this name is unknown. One suggestion is that it is connected with the Native Councils which were advocated for New Guinea after the war.
8. The Pidgin English equivalent of *oite'u* is *masalai.*
9. In this paper, in order to avoid confusion, the word "spirit" is used exclusively to refer to spirits of the dead.
10. In the performance of this ritual the practitioner repeats the secret name to himself. Nobody else can hear it, but only a sound of breathing. Hereafter it will be referred to as "breathing the secret name".
11. This belief is perpetuated in the occasional use of the phrases, *Kaua po ulu* and *kopa po ulu,* the cargo of the *kaua* and the *kopa. Kaua po ulu* refers to anything of European origin which is red in colour. *Kopa po ulu* refers to anything of European origin which has a colour other than red.
12. For an account of such missionary activity as described in the above paragraph, see H. Ian Hogbin, *Native Christianity in a New Guinea Village, Oceania,* Vol. XVIII, No. 1.

13. Cf. H. Ian Hogbin, *op. cit.*, pp. 9-10, and *Transformation Scene* (Routledge and Kegan Paul, 1951), p. 242, where this belief is also mentioned. But the belief may well be more widespread in the Madang District than Dr. Hogbin's footnote on p. 284 of *Transformation Scene* suggests that it is around Lae.

14. Kaum employed this method of approaching God both in his Madang Compound cult ritual and in ritual staged earlier in Kalinam.

15. Kilibob has now ceased to be a mere intermediary between God and man, and appears as the actual source of the cargo. He originally came from the Nobanob area, where he previously featured in the Cargo Cult. Kaum borrowed him, basing his claim on the assertion that he had an ancestress from the Nobanob area.

16. Presumably because rice, unknown before the coming of the white man, was symbolic of the cargo.

17. Cf. F. E. Williams, *Orokaiva Magic* (Oxford University Press, 1928), p. 35, where the importance of dreams in the Taro Cult among the Orokaiva is discussed. The conclusions are applicable here.

18. Cf. Cyril S. Belshaw, *op. cit.*, p. 125, and J. Guiart, *Forerunners of Melanesian Nationalism, Oceania,* Vol. XXII, No. 2, December 1951.

17

BIGFELLOW MAN BELONG BUSINESS IN NEW GUINEA

Ben R. Finney

Economic accomplishment and political leadership were closely linked in the indigenous societies of the New Guinea Highlands. Highlands leaders, like those in many areas of Melanesia (Sahlins 1963; cf. Oliver 1955), were "big men" who gained their status largely by their own deeds rather than by virtue of their birth. In particular, personal achievement through wealth accumulation and the organization of group transactions involving wealth was an important if not prerequisite characteristic of the Highlands big man (Bulmer 1960: 5; Newman 1965: 44; Read 1966: 71; Reay 1959: 96; Strathern 1966: 357-358). Now, after three decades of Australian control, the development of cash crops, and the introduction of Western political institutions, this linkage between economic and political spheres not only persists but is expressed in modern institutions. A new generation of leaders, who achieve status in the market economy and seek elective political office, has developed in the Highlands. Today a large coffee plantation, a trade store, and a truck are the marks of economic accomplishment of ambitious Highlanders, and election to a Local Government Council or to the House of Assembly of Papua-New Guinea is the avenue they follow to modern political power. This paper explores the development of these modern leaders with data from the Goroka Sub-District, the most advanced area in the Highlands.[1]

GOROKA: CONTACT HISTORY AND ECONOMIC DEVELOPMENT

The Goroka Sub-District lies within the Eastern Highlands District of the Territory of Papua-New Guinea. It includes the Goroka Valley, one of a series of intermontane valleys which occur between 4,000 and 6,000 feet along the mountain spine of New Guinea, and adjacent Watabung, a small mountainous region just outside of the valley along its southwestern edge. About 62,000 people live in the Sub-District, including over 4,000

Reproduced by permission of the publisher and Ben R. Finney from *Ethnology*, 7:394-410 (1968).

inhabitants of Goroka township, most of whom are Europeans or immigrant workers from other areas of the Territory.

The Goroka area was unknown to Europeans until 1930, when gold prospectors penetrated the Eastern Highlands. In 1932 administration officers followed the prospectors into the region, as did missionaries a few years later. Pacification and missionization were interrupted by the war, during which minor Allied airfields and army camps were established in the area. Not until after the war was full administration control extended throughout Goroka, and intertribal warfare effectively curtailed.

With pacification and the re-establishment of civil administration Europeans once again evinced a commercial interest in Goroka. This time they were not after gold, but were interested in obtaining land for coffee plantations. The first land was alienated (by purchase to the Administration which then leased it to European planters) for plantations in the late 1940s, and in the following decade a minor land boom followed in which some 30 European plantations were established. Since the late 1950s, however, further land alienations for plantations have been stopped because of a change in administration policy concerning European cash crop development in the area.

The indigenous people of Goroka began planting their own coffee in the early 1950s. Although they had previously entered the money economy—as laborers for Allied forces, as plantation workers and as growers of vegetables and other minor cash crops—in terms of monetary returns and subsequent investment activity coffee planting was their real entrée into commerce. Stimulated by the example of European planters, a few Gorokans planted coffee in the early 1950s. When they began to get sizable cash returns, other local people took notice and started planting. Aided by a vigorous extension program of the Department of Agriculture, planting was underway throughout accessible areas of Goroka by the late 1950s. According to Department of Agriculture estimates, by June, 1967, indigenous Gorokan plantings exceeded 4,500,000 trees, and yearly production was more than 1,100 tons. This tonnage amounts to almost 10 per cent of the total (indigenous and European) coffee production of Papua-New Guinea, and indicates the significant place the indigenous Gorokan growers have won in the Territory's coffee industry.

The speed and enthusiasm which Gorokans, barely removed from the Stone Age, showed in taking to cash cropping is only one facet of their economic accomplishments. Another has been their ability to save their cash income, pool it, and invest it in various enterprises. Contrary to the thesis of Nurske (1962: 67) and other economists, who predict that emerging cash crop producers will tend to spend most of their newly gained income on consumption goods, the Gorokans have proven so far to be more investment than consumption oriented.[2] A major part of their income has gone into setting up numerous trade stores (over 450, or one for every 130 persons, are now in operation), buying trucks (at the rate of 40 or more a year), starting commercial cattle and pig projects, and even opening small restaurants. Investment in commercial enterprises has excited the Gorokans, and the bigger and more visible the capital asset—such as a five-ton truck or a roadside store—the more attractive is the investment. To twist Veblen's phrase concerning American *nouveaux riches,* the newly wealthy Gorokans can be characterized as being "conspicuous investors."

The rapid economic progress of the Gorokans has been promoted by a combination of favorable factors, some external and some internal to Gorokan society. External factors concern the suitability of coffee as a Highlands cash crop, Australian aid, and the relatively laissez-faire attitude of the Administration towards indigenous society. Coffee was the ideal crop to develop in Goroka both because the area's excellent soils and favorable rainfall pattern combine to produce premium-grade coffee, and because coffee's high value per weight ratio meant that it could be economically airfreighted to coastal ports for export. (Not until 1965 was the road to the coast improved to the point where coffee and other crops could be trucked out of the Highlands.) Administration aid, including extension services to indigenous growers, and the organization of an extensive road system for internal transport and the construction of an airfield for external transport, was crucial to Gorokan success in cash cropping. In addition, European plantations were sources of direct aid—as demonstration plantations, and as places where indigenous employees were trained, as workers, to plant, cultivate, harvest, and process coffee. Finally—and this factor is most important to consider in relation to capital formation and investment—neither missionization nor the imposition of administration control broke up or radically demoralized indigenous society. Although warfare was prohibited, and some domestic and ritual practices were discouraged, the main Gorokan social groups and their organizational features survived European impact.

Internal factors relate to land and time available for cash cropping, and the adaptability of traditional features of Gorokan life to the demands of economic growth. The Gorokans, living in a fertile region with a population density of only about 80 per square mile, had both the land and the time (particularly after steel tools replaced those of stone; Salisbury 1962) to spare for cash crop cultivation without seriously interrupting subsistence production. As for the adaptability of indigenous society, a number of observers have commented on the marked receptivity of Gorokans to economic innovations (cf. Howlett 1962: 216-217), but none has examined this receptivity in terms of how traditional features of the society have proven adaptable to commerce. To analyse this adaptation, and the role of individual Gorokans in the process, a cursory examination of Gorokan social, political, and economic patterns is first required.

GOROKAN SOCIETY

The Goroka Sub-District was not unified in pre-European times, but was composed of a number of separate and often hostile tribal groups. Some of these are well represented in the anthropological literature. Langness (1964) has written on the Benabena of eastern Goroka, Read (1966) on the Gahuku of central Goroka, Newman (1965) on the Gururumba of northwestern Goroka, and Salisbury (1962) on the Siane, a group located along the southwest border and extending into the neighbouring Chimbu District. It is all too easy, however, to emphasize the uniqueness of each of these and other Gorokan groups not yet studied, and to ignore the common patterns present in the area. There is enough traditional similarity in the area (Read 1954: 20, 34-35), which has been reinforced by the formation of Goroka as an administrative unit, to warrant discussion of basic Goroka patterns without detailing local variation. Although the people of the Sub-District lack a common name, and still tend to identify themselves by their local tribal or linguistic names, for convenience I refer to them as Gorokans.

The Gorokans live mainly in villages with up to 300 or so inhabitants. These consist of a row of houses including, except where mission pressures have been successful, one or more separate men's houses. Before pacification, villages were stockaded and located on ridges for ease of defense. Now many have been relocated on lower ground to be nearer roads and crops. Separating villages are garden lands, pig grazing lands, and now coffee plantations, as well as disputed stretches where conflicting claims render exploitation difficult.

Inhabitants of a village are usually members of a single clan or subclan.[3] These groups have an ideology of patrilineal recruitment, although in most cases it appears that a significant proportion of the men of the group may be non-agnates, having become attached to the group by marriage, as refugees, or by some other means (cf. Langness 1964). Below the clan and subclan levels are extended families of patrilineages, the importance of which varies from group to group. Above the clan level are larger groups, usually termed subtribes and tribes. These groups, although not compact residential units, are made up of clans which occupy a continuous stretch of territory. Their members acknowledge a common name, share a common tradition of origin, and hold pig festivals and other rituals together. The tribe is the largest permanent group. Confederacies of tribes may be formed in times of war, but these are temporary groupings. Normally each tribe is an independent unit, potentially, if not actively, hostile to other tribes.

While at the extended family or lineage level authority ordinarily went to the senior male member, above this level leadership generally followed the achieved status, big-man form mentioned previously. Although there is some controversy over the degree of despotism exercised by traditional big men (Brown 1963; Salisbury 1964), it can probably be generalized that, except perhaps for a few extraordinary leaders, the Gorokan big men struck a balance between acting for the general welfare and for their own personal aggrandizement (cf. Read 1959). They were leaders in a type of consensus politics in which suggestions and decision by discussion played a more prominent role than rule by fiat. The fluidity and informality of this leadership system was marked. A big man might be a leader for only a decade or so when he was at the height of his physical and economic powers, and a large and changing number of big men, with varying degrees of authority and number of followers, might compete or co-operate in the making and implementation of decisions.

Gorokan economic activities were based on subsistence farming, but also involved the production and distribution of special types of goods. Salisbury (1962: 39-111), in a detailed study of the Siane living on the southwestern edge of Goroka, divides their economic activities into three separate nexuses. Although similarly detailed comparative data for economic patterns throughout Goroka are lacking, Salisbury's scheme appears applicable to Goroka in general and is followed in the outline below.

Subsistence activities form the first nexus. The Gorokans had a simple technology based on stone and wooden tools, and were primarily farmers centering their activities around the production of sweet potatoes and other vegetable foods in individually owned gardens. The second nexus is that of "luxury" activities, involving the production and distribution of such items as tobacco, salt, palm oil, pandanus nuts, and fine stone for adze blades. These goods circulated mainly by means of personal transactions between friends, commonly in the form of presents to visiting acquaintances. Activities centered around "valuables"—pigs, ornamental shells, bird of paradise plumes, and other decorative items—form the third nexus. In contrast to subsistence and luxury activities, transactions involving valuables were public events marked by great excitement as items of wealth were pooled and exchanged between groups. Pig festivals and ceremonies marking marriages, initiations, births, and peacemaking were the primary occasions for these wealth exchanges.

The traditional values and institutions that have facilitated Gorokan economic change find their greatest expression in this third nexus concerned with valuables. The Gorokans valued wealth highly, and sought the prestige that comes from accumulating and managing wealth. This emphasis was particularly marked in the achievement orientation of the big men who played an entrepreneurial role in transactions involving wealth. In addition, Gorokans had the ability, acting as members of a group, to pool their wealth for specific purposes.

Prestige accrued to a man through participating in the exchange of valuables, as well as through accumulating them. Exchanges usually involved transactions between clans or subtribes, in which members of participating groups pooled their resources to make sizable and prestigious presentations. For example, in the Idza Nama festival of the Gahuku people of central Goroka, an event connected with male initiation and the affirmation of friendship ties within the tribe, each participating group made a great effort to gather sufficient pigs and other valuables to exchange with their ally (Read 1952). Held in the dry season, these events were preceded by concerted efforts of the participants to build up their pig stocks through breeding and feeding, and also by bartering gold lip-shells for pigs from other groups. A successful presentation of many pigs (Read 1954: 18 reports exchanges involving up to 140 pigs) and other valuables brought prestige to both the group and the individuals who contributed to the group pool of goods.

Prominent, if not dominant, in the exchanges were the big men of each group. As personally wealthy men they were usually major contributors, and as leaders they acted in an entrepreneurial capacity in the pooling of wealth. They were prominent in discussions concerning where and when an exchange was to take place, directed the drawing together of contributions from individuals to make a presentation for the group, and, in turn, took a leading role in distributing the valuables presented to the group (cf. Read 1966: 89-94, 203). Big men also often took the lead in organizing ordinary village activities like land clearing, fence building, and the erection of men's houses. The picture that emerges—that of men who made decisions, led others in work, and controlled the circulation of wealth—is one of strong economic leadership which appears to have found a modern expression.

BUSINESS LEADERS

The role of modern Gorokan businessmen as leaders in commercial development is closely analogous to the role of traditional leaders in the indigenous economy. How much this analogy rests upon adaptation of traditional patterns to modern ends can be judged by the following analysis of the ten leading businessmen of Goroka.

Participation by the Gorokans in coffee growing and other commercial activities is nearly universal among the population, but degree of participation varies from area to area and person to person. The ordinary participant in the cash economy, earning his money from a small coffee plantation and perhaps a trade store or some other enterprise, is referred to as a "businessman" (*bisnisman*) in Pidgin English (*tok pisin*), the lingua franca and commercial language of the Highlands. Those who stand out in the commercial economy, as being more wealthy and successful than the ordinary businessman, are known as "bigfellow man belong business" (*bikfela man bilong bisnis*). It is tempting to render this term simply as "big businessman," but a translation as "business leader" is preferable to emphasize their role as leaders in the commercial development of their people. Ten prominent business leaders were selected for intensive study on the basis of repute; they were the men whose names repeatedly cropped up in discussions with Gorokans as the main bigfellow man belong business in the area (Table 1). Nine of them come from Goroka, and the tenth

TABLE 1. GOROKA BUSINESS LEADERS

Name	No. Coffee Trees	Trade Stores	Trucks	Cattle	Restaurants
A	22,000	1, (1)*	1, (2)	6	—
B	18,000	—	—	—	—
C	12,000	—	—	—	—
D	7,800	(1)	—	—	—
E	7,500	1	2, (1)	—	1
F	6,700	(1)	3	20	—
G	6,700	2	1	—	—
H	4,500	1	—	—	1
I	2,000	1	1	14	—
J	1,400	1	2	—	1

* Numbers in parentheses indicate trade stores now closed or trucks no longer operating.

comes from just over the western border of the Sub-District. The latter man was included because he was well known in Goroka, and centered much of his trading activities there.

If the assets of the ten business leaders are compared with the general distribution of assets in the area, their high reputation can be seen to be justified. The mean number of coffee trees per indigenous grower in Goroka is probably around 400 to 450 trees, whereas the mean number of coffee trees of the business leaders is almost 9,000, about twenty times the general mean. Similarly, the business leaders' participation in other enterprises—trade stores, trucks, cattle, and restaurants—indicates their outstanding position. Although I would hesitate to estimate their net incomes, most business leaders probably gross over $4,500 yearly from their activities. The official estimate of an estate left by a Gorokan who died in 1966 should give some idea of the value of a business leader's assets. His estate, including coffee trees (but not the land on which they were planted), coffee processing facilities, cattle herd, operating capital (he was a coffee buyer), and a $6,600 life insurance policy, came to over $35,000. In an area where per capita cash income probably does not exceed $25 per annum, the wealth of these business leaders is outstanding.

The business leaders' reputations are therefore solidly based on wealth and control of extensive assets, but that is not all. Part of their renown comes from economic leadership apart from the enterprises they direct. Most of them have been the first in their immediate neighborhoods to engage in large-scale coffee planting and other ventures, and their enterprise has been the inspiration of their clansmen and neighbors. Many have also been free with advice and aid to others starting commercial ventures. The business leaders are proud of, and do not hesitate to speak about, their inspirational and tutelary role in local economic development, a process they call "business development" (*kirapim bisnis*) or "local development" (*kirapim ples*).

An examination of the backgrounds of these business leaders prior to their commercial careers indicates a significantly higher degree of formal school and work experience than is general among Goroka men of their age (Table 2). Five have attended administration or mission schools, and

TABLE 2. EXPERIENCE PREVIOUS TO CASH-CROPPING

Name	Schooling	Private Employ	Public Employ
A	8 years	mechanic	agricultural station employee
B	9 years	—	schoolteacher; clerk; prison guard
C	—	servant	Army service (World War II)
D	1 year	—	carrier; police
E	—	—	Headman (Luluai)
F	—	—	—
G	6 years	servant	medical assistant
H	—	servant	Headman (Luluai)
I	8 years	—	schoolteacher; agricultural officer
J	—	servant	—

four of these have had six or more years of schooling. All of those with formal education have worked for Europeans, either in private or public employ, for a time before starting their commercial careers, and four of the five business leaders without any formal education have also had employment experience. Significantly, the jobs held by these men were all a cut above the usual position held by their Gorokan contemporaries who have had employment—that of plantation laborer—and some of their jobs, such as schoolteacher, agricultural assistant, or headman, represented the highest positions to which local men could aspire in the 1940s and 1950s, the time period in question.

To maintain, in the light of their significant school and work experiences, that these business leaders represent modern versions of traditional big men, instead of the first prototypes of a Westernized elite, would seem paradoxical. However, this apparent paradox is dissolved with the refinement of this paper's thesis. It is not maintained that individual traditional big men have become modern business leaders. Indeed, that is a virtual impossibility since the traditional big men of pacification times are now either dead or too old to lead an active life. What is maintained is that modern business leaders follow the style of traditional big men in seeking and achieving eminence. They, like their predecessors, are ambitious and opportunistic men, and they have been attracted to European school and work experiences both for the immediate rewards of pay and knowledge and for the advantage to be gained in furthering their personal careers. In this circumstance the exploitation of modern opportunities is not opposed to, but combines with, traditional achievement behavior.

The ability of business leaders to combine traditional and nontraditional methods to their advantage is particularly apparent in their commercial undertakings. They all have exhibited, for example, a facility for obtaining land, labor, and capital for their various enterprises in ways involving both traditional and modern operations.

The initial major undertaking of business leaders, the setting up of a large coffee plantation, illustrates this facility. While in most cases land for the plantation was acquired in a traditional manner—through inheritance or by staking out unused lineage or clan land—one business leader (F) hit upon the innovation of renting land for cash. This method was probably the only way he could gain sufficient land for a plantation, as he had been orphaned in childhood and adopted by a woman of another clan, a situation which left him with minimal land rights. The recruitment of labor shows a more balanced blend of old and new methods. Three men were forced to recruit paid workers for the initial job of clearing land and planting, while the others mainly relied on clansmen and others for unpaid labor. The difference apparently stemmed from the status of the coffee planter—whether or not he was already a man of influence in his community.

For example, when H planted coffee in the late 1950s he was already an important man and was able to call on some twenty men of his clan to aid him. No cash wages were paid, but his acceptance of donated labor obligated him to future reciprocity. As H explained to me, he is continually involved in repaying (*bekim*) those who helped him:

When these people are in need I give them some money because they helped me with coffee. All right, now I help them well—by buying food when they are short, by buying meat, buying rice, and by giving pigs at a feast.

This type of transaction is a modern analogue of traditional big-man transactions in which followers provided a leader with support and he, in turn, reciprocated when they were in need.

Those business leaders who were not established leaders when they started their plantations were not able to recruit labor in the big-man style. Both B and C, for example, had been away from their respective communities during the war and for some years thereafter, and were comparatively unknown to their clansmen when they returned home to plant coffee. They were therefore forced to use capital obtained elsewhere (B used mainly savings from school teaching and vegetable sales; C used savings from panning gold) to pay for workers to clear and plant a large coffee plantation. Similarly, A, who is now the leading indigenous coffee planter in New Guinea, was obliged to recruit paid labor to start his plantation as he was too young at the time to have sufficient status to recruit workers in the big-man manner. At the age of nineteen he left his village to go to Kainantu, where he eventually operated his own pit sawing business, employing ten workers, and a gold panning enterprise, employing seven workers. Then, he relates:

Money from timber, money from gold, I pooled it and planned to develop a coffee station. At this time I had $1,980. I brought it to Goroka in 1958. Before in 1955 I planted a little coffee. This time I had money, and recruited twelve workers to develop the plantation.

However, once he had established his coffee plantation, and his reputation as a business leader, he was able to recruit workers by the same means H used, involving the promise of reciprocity rather than direct cash wages. Similarly B and C, after their plantations were established, were able to use labor recruited in a quasi-traditional big-man style.

All the business leaders except C have invested in one or more enterprises after developing their coffee plantations. Their main source of investment funds has been coffee receipts, not necessarily their own. Like entrepreneurs elsewhere, Gorokan business leaders have been adept at using other people's money. They have exploited the traditional facility for combining resources with a process of capital formation called "pooling money" (*bungem mani*) in which contributions are solicited from a wide range of clansmen, tribesmen, and other supporters. (One capital subscription for a truck involved the raising of over $3,000 from 784 contributors scattered in nineteen villages.) This is an informal process, without legal standing in Territory law, but nonetheless an effective means by which the Gorokans have been able to make considerable investments which otherwise would not have been possible.

All the investments controlled by the business leaders involve a mixture of personal financing and pooled funds. Some leaders, like A, who have had ample receipts from coffee sales, have used mostly their own funds for investment. (However, in late 1967 A was planning to ask for large amounts of pooled funds to supplement his own savings in order to set up a service station and restaurant.) Others, particularly those who have only a moderate coffee income, have used mostly pooled funds in their investments. Business leader I, for example, has put only $110 (out of a subscribed capital of almost $1,000) into the store he controls, and only $185 into the truck he operates. Nonetheless, despite his small contributions the businesses are firmly under his direction. I's leadership is accepted because of his entrepreneurial abilities in getting his clansmen to pool their money for investment, and because of his managerial abilities.

One of the most complicated cases of mixed financing involves the investments of E and J, who are, in effect, the majority stockholders in several enterprises. J runs a restaurant, has the most profitable trade store run by a Gorokan, and also operates a 5-ton truck that carries freight between the coast and the Highlands. At our first meeting he told me that the enterprises were all his, and that his career all started with "30 cents of self-rising flour". He then launched into a Horatio Alger story (virtually every business leader has his own) of how he used the flour to bake scones in his employer's kitchen (he was then a personal servant for a European), which he sold at the Goroka market. The profits, he related, were reinvested in more flour, and eventually, after ploughing back his profits for several years, he earned enough to start a store, then a restaurant, and then to buy a truck. However, after further investigation of his case it became obvious that, in addition to his own considerable savings, he had drawn on pooled funds from his fellow clansmen and had accepted major financial aid from E, who is the biggest coffee grower of J's clan.

A question which may be legitimately raised here concerns whether or not coercion is used by business leaders in drawing on the capital and labor of others. (Land might be added here, as business leaders are generally successful in gaining control of larger quantities of land than the average person.) This particularly applies to those leaders who were administration-appointed Headmen or held an elective office at the time they were building up their enterprises. Brown (1963) cites the use by Councillors in the neighboring Chimbu District of administration-derived authority to get constituents to work on personal projects. She uses this and other evidence to argue that administration-appointed Headmen and elected Councillors have been able to achieve, because of administration backing, a degree of despotic control over their fellow men beyond that held by traditional leaders. Among Gorokan business leaders who were or are Headmen or Councillors there is evidence that some have used their office to obtain labor services by making work on their plantations obligatory like administration-required work on roads and schools. However, this has not occurred in all cases, and where it does seem to have occurred the leaders have not been able to maintain the flow of free labor for long.

It would therefore be an exaggeration to think of all cases of unpaid labor, as well as capital subscriptions or land allocations, solely in terms of coercion. Such a view ignores the willingness of Gorokans to support voluntarily the more ambitious men in their midst with donations of labor, capital, and land, and the degree of self-interest on the part of the donors in these transactions. My argument is that many Gorokans have supported a business leader in the expectation that they will gain by his success. The benefits they derive, or hope to derive, may be conveniently divided into the categories of prestige, service, and profits.

To repeat an earlier point, the Gorokans are "conspicuous investors."

The formation of a large coffee plantation, the establishment of a trade store, and the buying of a truck all have an element of repute-building which is still so important to Gorokan society. While maximum prestige accrues to the owners or organizers of these investments, those who contribute toward the investments gain a measure of pride in being a member of a successful group led by a man of obvious repute. The situation as observed by me and described by informants appears to be a modern counterpart to the traditional situation observed by Bulmer (1960:7-8) among the Kyaka (Western Highlands):

Clansmen take pride in the clan's corporate performance in the Moka [a wealth exchange] and measure this against the performance of other groups. Even socially insignificant men with little or no direct part in the exchanges lend their efforts in preparing the dancing-grounds, building the houses and helping the leaders in the breeding and assembly of pigs. . . . The performance of the leaders of the clan in the Moka is also seen by its members as the performance of the whole group.

In addition to prestige, Gorokans contributing to a business leader's venture hope to gain benefits of a service kind. If, in a village far from any retail outlets, a leader asks for contributions to build a store, the money is often willingly subscribed because a store in the village means easy access to goods instead of a long walk to town or to a store in another village. Service benefits can be more than simple convenience, as can be illustrated by the case of the Watabung people. Because they were far from coffee mills, and could only be reached by a rough and perilous road, coffee buyers would seldom venture into their area to buy coffee. However, by helping F to finance a coffee buying and trucking business, which he operated in their area, the Watabung people gained an assured outlet for their coffee.

The question of profits presents a difficult problem, and one that is being debated by Gorokans. In the case of reciprocal rewards to contributors of labor, such as in the starting of H's plantation cited earlier, contributors have usually been fairly satisfied with their rewards and have continued to donate labor until their own small coffee plots provided them enough income to be independent of a business leader's largesse. Profits on pooled money are another question, however. Because of either the unprofitability of many investments (particularly trucks) or the refusal of business leaders to part with earnings, many contributors receive little or no monetary return on their contributed capital. Nevertheless, despite some disenchantment, the hope of "getting profits" (*kisim winmani; kisim profit-mani*) remains an incentive for the pooling of funds.

POLITICAL OFFICE

If these business leaders are to be considered as having carried over the Highlands pattern of the big man leader into modern life, they should qualify as political as well as economic leaders. In the main they do qualify, for all are considered to be big men, and most have sought to formalize and extend their political influence by running for elective office. Two types of elective office are open to Gorokans—membership in one of the three Local Government Councils in the Sub-District, and the two seats allotted the area in the Territorial House of Assembly. Seven of the ten business leaders in my sample have run for office in a Local Government Council, the House of Assembly, or both, and five have won office (Table 3). The political participation of Gorokan business leaders, as

TABLE 3. CANDIDATURE AND ELECTION TO PUBLIC OFFICE

Name	Local Government Council	House of Assembly
A	Councillor; President	Member
B	—	candidate
C	—	—
D	Councillor; President	candidate
E	Councillor; Vice-President	candidate
F	—	candidate
G	—	—
H	Councillor; Vice-President	Member
I	Councillor	Member
J	—	—

candidates and as office holders, is far above the average and therefore marks them as leading political figures, in a modern sense, in the Highlands.

This impression of a high level of political participation is heightened by examining what offices Gorokan business leaders seek. All those interested in running for any office ran for Member of the House of Assembly, and in the 1968 elections three were elected. (This includes H, who won office in a neighboring electorate.) There is less interest in being elected Councillor, apparently because this office is seen to have comparatively little power or prestige and to require inordinate amounts of time and energy that would have to be diverted from business activities. It is significant, however, that of the five who ran (all successfully) for office in a Council, four were subsequently elected either Vice-President or President of their Council. When business leaders do decide to participate in a Council, they apparently want to have a position of power in the group.

The three exceptions (C, G, and J) to the general rule that business leaders seek political office are worth examining. None of the three was taken aback by questions as to why he had not run for any office, for all felt themselves to be men capable of political leadership. While C, who is elderly and is virtually retired, expressed no interest in eventually running for office, both G and J consider candidature a possibility. Both, however, prefer to avoid political office at present. For example, G, in response to my query as to why he had not sought election as a Councillor, replied that he could not waste his valuable time on such an insignificant job, particularly since he wielded more power than the elected Councillors in his area. When J was asked about his non-participation, he replied that at present he was too busy running his businesses to be active in politics, but added that if his two younger brothers now receiving secondary education decide to return home to help manage his enterprises, he would then feel free to run for office.

DISCUSSION

The rapid rise of Gorokan business leaders to positions of modern economic leadership in their communities, and the subsequent dominance by some of their number of the major elected political offices in the area, would seem to be processes contrary to some assumptions concerning economic innovation and entrepreneurship, and modern political development, in developing areas.

Many social scientists, influenced by the writings of Weber, have tended to consider that major changes in the traditional norms and institutions of a society are a prerequisite for economic growth, or, alternatively, that entrepreneurial behavior and economic innovations are most likely to be adopted by dissidents or members of minority groups (Hoselitz 1961; cf. Barnett 1953: 378-410). Yet it is obvious that Gorokan business leaders are neither dissidents nor members of a minority, and that they have promoted change within the context of Gorokan society by transferring the traditional pattern of individual achievement to the modern context of cash cropping and commercial enterprise. This development should not, however, come as a surprise to anthropologists working in New Guinea, where the emphasis on individual achievement is so marked in traditional society. Indeed, of the first two anthropologists to work in Goroka, Read (1959: 435-436) foresaw the ready acceptance of innovations by ambitious and leading men, and Salisbury (1962: 137) virtually predicted their emergence as modern entrepreneurs.

That rapid economic and entrepreneurial development in New Guinea has been largely limited to only a few areas, notably the Gazelle Peninsula of New Britian, Goroka, and other accessible areas of the Highlands, is what should be surprising to anyone acquainted with the widespread distribution of the achieving syndrome over New Guinea.[4] Although sufficient data are lacking for a complete analysis of the problem, the Goroka situation indicates the importance of factors exogenous to the society in reinforcing local efforts towards economic development. Suitable crops and soils, good communication and marketing facilities, as well as an attitude on the part of administration and of European private enterprise which is at least permissive, if not actively supportive, of indigenous enterprise, are essential if the New Guinean penchant for achievement is to find expression in economic development. Where these exogenous factors are lacking, one often finds frustrated efforts at economic development, such as the Tommy Kabu movement in the Papuan Gulf (Maher 1961; Hitchcock and Oram 1967: 8-21), or, alternatively, the growth of cargo cults.

A comment on cargo cults is relevant here because the attention they have received in the literature would tend to lead the casual reader to believe that the cargo cult is the typical New Guinean response to modern economic oportunities, and that rational economic effort, such as is displayed by Gorokans, is an atypical response. Although it cannot be denied that cargo cults have been common in New Guinea, and that cargo thinking—the belief that cargo (goods, wealth) may be obtained by ritual action—is widespread there, the degree to which New Guineans in all areas are already engaged in cash cropping and other enterprises, or are desperately trying to enter the market economy, is also impressive. Indeed, in some areas one can almost talk about a competition between rational and cargo cult means of obtaining wealth, and it can be observed that where significant and reasonably rapid returns from cash cropping and commerce are possible, rational economic effort prevails over the cargo cult. Cargo cult outbreaks have occurred in the Highlands, but most have been short-lived, and none has reached the proportions of cult movements elsewhere in New Guinea (cf. Berndt 1952; Meggitt 1967; Reay 1959: 194-201; 1964; Salisbury 1962: 121). That cargo cults have not flourished in the Highlands may to a substantial degree be attributed to the demonstrable superiority in this favored region of cash cropping and other enterprises over cult activities as a means of obtaining modern wealth.[5] Here the latest comments of Lawrence (1967: 274-275), on the Madang area, long a stronghold of cargo cult activity, are pertinent, for he finds that now, with improved economic opportunities, the Madang people seem to be accepting economic development as a potentially satisfactory alternative to the cargo cult.

The political aspirations of Gorokan business leaders and their success in winning election to important offices are indicative of a general trend which, though most marked in the Highlands, finds expression elsewhere in New Guinea. It is evident, for example, that a substantial proportion of the members of the House of Assembly have some background in commerce, and that commercial success was the outstanding accomplishment of many of them prior to election.[6] This prominence of businessmen-politicians in the House of Assembly has caught many political observers unawares. Probably because of patterns observed in new African nations, where so many leading politicians are members of an educated and Westernized elite divorced from and often opposed to private commerce, observers were looking for signs of the emergence of a similar elite type of politician in New Guinea. For example, those directing the 1964 election study paid no systematic attention to candidates' commercial backgrounds and reputations, but focused major attention on the obvious variables of Westernization—education, church membership, employment or professional experience (Hughes and van der Veur 1965: 388-429; van der Veur 1964). However, actual field studies of the 1964 elections, like that of Harding (1965), clearly indicated that commercial experience and reputation was a crucial variable in many electorates and apparently led to a rather belated realization that business leaders were a force to reckon with in New Guinea politics (Bettison, Hughes, and van der Veur 1965: 508).

While it is probable that, with increasing modernization, members of a growing elite—which is being fostered by new educational opportunities, including the formation of a university, and the opening of professional and executive positions to New Guineans—will become more prominent in New Guinea politics, the New Guinea linkage between economic and political leadership may prove to be a highly resistant bond. Its continuance could take two forms: the unaltered dominance of local business leaders in politics, particularly in rural areas like Goroka where significant individual commercial success is possible, or the rise of younger political leaders with both an elite (in terms of education and general Westernization) and a commercial background. The latter possibility is not as unlikely as observers attuned to political trends in developing countries elsewhere might think, for in New Guinea an elite background and a commercial background may not necessarily be mutually exclusive. The semi-elite status (relative to other Highlanders) of some Gorokan business leaders, and their general desire for education (some have children enrolled in secondary school, and one has a son in the University of Papua-New Guinea) may be indicative of this possibility. Politics in New Guinea may, therefore, continue to have a bourgeois flavor, although this does not necessarily mean that politicians will be as conservative as their commercial backgrounds might suggest.

Gorokan political leaders, like those elsewhere in the Highlands, are already considered to be "conservative" in contrast to the "radical" leaders from the Papuan coast. This popular distinction is misleading and one-sided, for it only reflects positions on constitutional questions: while many coastal Papuan leaders are seeking early self-rule and independence, most Highlands leaders advocate a more prolonged maintenance of Australian rule. The Highlanders' attitude stems partly from their belief that an end to Australian rule will also mean an end to Australian aid, which they do not want to give up, and partly from their fear of dominance by the generally more highly educated and sophisticated Papuans. It does not necessarily reflect any inherent conservatism on their part. Indeed, if some of their ideas on economic development come to the fore, they may be considered to be anything but conservative. Although Highlands leaders seem preoccupied with "parish pump" politics aimed at obtaining better schools, more agricultural aid, etc., they are deeply concerned about continued European dominance of the region's major commercial activities—coffee processing and marketing, importing and exporting, wholesaling, long-haul trucking, air transport, and banking. Some are coming to believe, and privately advocate, that New Guineans should gain a greater share in, if not control of, these activities. If some day these leaders, acting with the confidence of the self-made businessmen they are, decide to act on this issue of overseas economic control, they may come to be considered the most "radical" of New Guinea politicians.

NOTES

1. Field data were gathered between February and August, 1967, while I was a Fellow of the Australian-American Foundation attached to the New Guinea Research Unit of the Australian National University. I wish to thank R. G. Crocombe for suggesting and making this research possible, and also A. L. Epstein, S. Epstein, J. Fernandez, P. Leis, N. Mellor, M. Reay, R. Salisbury, H. ToRobert, and E. Wolfers for the suggestions and criticisms they offered at various stages of this research.
2. Epstein (1965: 191) reports a similar investment orientation among the Tolai of the Gazelle Peninsula, New Britain.
3. This summary of social organization is drawn mainly from Howlett (1962: 45-50) and Read (1954). .
4. Comparative research on need for achievement (as originally defined by McClelland and associates) among high school students from areas in New Guinea which contrast in terms of indigenous economic opportunities and accomplishments is now being carried out by Ruth Finney as part of a general inquiry into indigenous attitudes and responses to economic opportunity. Preliminary results of this research tend to support the reasoning contained in this paragraph.
5. Cargo cults still occasionally flare up in the Highlands (I heard of three outbreaks in the Eastern Highlands during my stay there in 1967) but they are generally greeted with great skepticism.
6. Of the 38 indigenous Members of the House of Assembly in 1967 at least 23 had been engaged in major cash-crop activities or other commercial enterprises prior to election (cf. Members 1966, a booklet which contains partial information on Members' backgrounds).

BIBLIOGRAPHY

BARNETT, H. G. 1953. Innovation: The Basis of Cultural Change. New York.
BERNDT, R. M. 1952. A Cargo Movement in the Eastern Central Highlands of New Guinea. Oceania 23: 40-65.
BETTISON, D. G., HUGHES, C. A., AND P. W. VAN DER VEUR. 1965. The Papua-New Guinea Elections 1964. Canberra.
BROWN, P. 1963. From Anarchy to Satrapy. American Anthropologist 65: 1-15.
BULMER, R. N. H. 1960. Political Aspects of the Moka Exchange System. Oceania 31: 1-13.
EPSTEIN, S. 1965. Economic Change and Differentiation in New Britain. Economic Record 4: 173-192.
HARDING, T. G. 1965. The Rai Coast Open Electorate. The Papua-New Guinea Elections 1964, ed. D. G. Bettison *et al.*, pp. 194-211. Canberra.
HITCHCOCK, N. E., AND N. D. ORAM. 1967. Rabia Camp: A Port Moresby Migrant Settlement. New Guinea Research Bulletin 14: 1-126.
HOSELITZ, B. F. 1961. Tradition and Economic Growth. Tradition, Values and Economic Development, ed. R. Braibanti and J. J. Spengler, pp. 83-113. Durham.

HOWLETT, D. 1962. A Decade of Change in the Goroka Valley, New Guinea: Land Use and Development in the 1950's. Ph.D. dissertation, Australian National University.

HUGHES, C. A., AND P. W. VAN DER VEUR. 1965. The Elections: An Overview. The Papua-New Guinea Elections, 1964, ed. D. G. Bettison *et al.,* pp. 388-429. Canberra.

LANGNESS, L. 1964. Some Problems in the Conceptualization of Highlands Social Structures. New Guinea: The Central Highlands, ed. J. B. Watson, pp. 162-182. American Anthropologist 66: iv, pt. 2 (Special Publication).

LAWRENCE, P. 1967. Road Belong Cargo. Melbourne.

MAHER, R. F. 1960. New Men of Papua: A Study in Culture Change. Madison.

MEMBERS. 1966. The Members of the House of Assembly for the Territory of Papua and New Guinea. Port Moresby.

MEGGITT, M. J. 1967. Uses of Literacy in New Guinea. Bijdragen tot de Taal-, Land- en Volkenkunde 123: 71-82.

NEWMAN, P. L. 1965. Knowing the Gururumba. New York.

NURSKE, R. 1962. Problems of Capital Formation in Underdeveloped Countries. Oxford.

OLIVER, D. L. 1955. A Solomon Islands Society. Cambridge.

READ, K. E. 1952. Nama Cult of the New Guinea Highlands. Oceania 23: 1-25.

——— 1954. Cultures of the Central Highlands, New Guinea. Southwestern Journal of Anthropology 10: 1-43.

——— 1959. Leadership and Consensus in a New Guinea Society. American Anthropologist 64: 425-436.

——— 1966. The High Valley. London.

REAY, M. 1959. The Kuma. Melbourne.

SAHLINS, M. 1963. Poor Man, Rich Man, Big Man, Chief: Political Types in Melanesia and Polynesia. Comparative Studies in Society and History 5: 285-303.

SALISBURY, R. F. 1962. From Stone to Steel. London.

——— 1964. Despotism and Australian Administration in the New Guinea Highlands. New Guinea: The Central Highlands, ed. J. B. Watson, pp. 225-239. American Anthropologist 66: iv, pt. 2 (Special Publication).

STRATHERN, A. 1966. Despots and Directors in the New Guinea Highlands. Man 1: 356-367.

VAN DER VEUR, P. W. 1964. Towards Self-Government in Papua-New Guinea. Asian Survey 4: 991-999.

18

THE ECONOMY OF MODERN MATUPIT: CONTINUITY AND CHANGE ON THE GAZELLE PENINSULA, NEW BRITAIN[1]

A. L. Epstein

For some time now social change has provided a major theme in the anthropological literature, and many monographs have been devoted to analysing how tribal societies have changed as a result of contact with alien and technologically more advanced groups. Yet frequently what is striking in these situations is not so much the changes that have taken place in response to external pressures, but the tenacity with which many groups have clung to their traditional customs and institutions in the face of those pressures. The question perhaps is not how or why have these groups changed, but rather how is it that change has not been even more radical and far-reaching?

Continuity and change are, of course, relative terms with shifting frames of reference; they represent two ways of looking at the same phenomena. Whether we describe a situation in terms of change or in terms of continuity must usually be a matter of emphasis in the context of a given problem. It would seem that in some cases to place the emphasis on persistence may be more fruitful in posing comparative problems, as well as in shedding light on the dynamics of social adaptation as a continuing process.

The formulation of the problem in this way was suggested to me by the situation of the Tolai[2] people of the Rabaul District of New Britain. Because of the geographical situation of the Gazelle Peninsula, and the favourable ecological conditions it enjoys, the Tolai have had a more immediate experience of the contact situation than has usually been the case elsewhere in New Guinea. Indeed, since the arrival in the area of the first Europeans in the 1870's, the history of the Gazelle has been one of fluctuation and dis-

Reproduced by permission of A. P. Elkin, Editor of *Oceania,* and A. L. Epstein from *Oceania,* 33:182-215 (1962-63).

turbance. There has been a succession of imposed regimes, including the
military occupation of the area by the Japanese in the Second World
War, each with its own administrative policies and programmes. European
settlement was encouraged by the Germans, and large areas of land were
acquired for the establishment of plantations: to-day about a third of the
total area remains alienated land. The Germans, too, built the town of
Rabaul which became the headquarters of their administration in New
Guinea. To meet labour requirements Chinese coolies were introduced as
well as native labourers from other parts of New Guinea. Again, from the
very outset, there has been intensive proselytization by missionaries of
different denominations.

Together, and in their several ways, these various factors have constituted
a considerable attack on the traditional fabric of Tolai social life. Indeed,
we have here a situation in which one might have expected to find a high
degree of cultural erosion of the kind reported for the Madang area and
other parts of Melanesia. Yet, far from showing the symptoms of disrup-
tion, the Tolai are now commonly regarded as one of the most advanced
and influential of all the indigenous peoples of Australian New Guinea. It
is, of course, clear that great social changes have taken place in the area,
but what is equally patent is the way in which the Tolai have maintained
a way of life that remains, in many important respects, recognizably
traditional. The island of Matupit, with which this paper is principally
concerned, is an excellent case in point. Matupit has been even more exposed to external influences than most other Tolai communities. It lies
only a few miles out of Rabaul, and over the years has established close
links with the town; its people are more sophisticated than inland Tolai,
whom the Matupi[3] sometimes refer to disparagingly as "cowboys." Matupit,
indeed, shares many resemblances with Hanuabada, the Motu village near
Port Moresby. But whereas Hanuabada has been described as "a truly
urban native community" (Belshaw, 1957, p. 2), this cannot yet be said
of Matupit. Matupit does possess some of the features of a peri-urban
settlement; nevertheless it remains, as I hope to show, a distinctive Tolai
community. How are these differences to be accounted for?

One factor of critical importance in this context, as Watson (1958)
showed in his study of the Mambwe of Northern Rhodesia, is the question
of access to tribal lands. Belshaw himself comments that the traditional
economy has collapsed at Hanuabada, whereas many of the villages
around Rabaul are still predominantly agricultural in interest. An account
of the modern economy of Matupit would seem, therefore, to be a useful
point of departure for examining the dual process of change and continuity
operating there. The task of this paper then is threefold: (1) to describe
the range of economic activities on Matupit and the ways in which they
are organized; (2) to examine the relative contribution of each to Matupi

income in the context of the modern cash economy; and (3) to analyse some of the implications of the data for continuity and change in Matupi social structure.

THE GAZELLE PENINSULA AND ITS PEOPLE

The Gazelle Peninsula occupies the north-east corner of the island of New Britain. Lying roughly within a 20-mile radius of the modern town of Rabaul, it covers an area of some 300 square miles. To the south and west it is flanked by a broad valley which separates it from the rugged Baining Mountains. Geologically and ethnologically the mountain areas of New Britain are quite distinct from the north-east corner; save for sporadic contacts with an autochthonous people collectively referred to as Bainings, who live on the fringes of the area, the Tolai are thus effectively cut off from contact with the rest of the island.

Perhaps the most striking topographical feature of the Gazelle is its marked physical instability. It has been an area of violent volcanic activity, Blanche Bay itself having been formed as a result of some volcanic cataclysm in the past. Around Rabaul, within a zone a couple of miles wide and extending across the centre of the harbour, there are four active or dormant volcanoes, and several other points show evidence of fairly recent activity. Dr. George Brown, the first missionary to visit the Gazelle Peninsula, who was also a distinguished naturalist, has given a vivid and oft-quoted description of an eruption in 1878 when a small island suddenly emerged in the middle of Blanche Bay (Brown, 1908, pp. 240–5). According to geologists the island of Matupit probably arose quite recently in much the same way, though it has not yet been possible to date this accurately. Topographically, then, the Gazelle Peninsula is made up of hilly country with a narrow coastal fringe of lower land flanked, as already noted, by a valley to the south and west which separates it from the Baining Mountains.

The Tolai are a people of Melanesian stock who to-day number between 35–40,000. They are a large group by Melanesian standards, culturally and linguistically homogeneous, though customs and dialect still vary in some degree from one locality to another. However, no system of centralized political authority ever emerged, and Tolai political organization centred traditionally on the parish, a named locality with relatively well-defined boundaries, within which small and sometimes scattered hamlets provided the residential units. Matupit itself conformed to this general pattern, but because of its insular position and small size—its total area probably does not exceed 200 acres—it must always have more closely resembled a true village in the sense of a discrete physical and residential group. The whole island was divided into a number of named territorial sub-divisions, each for many purposes an independent unit with its own internal organization. Each village section in turn was divided into smaller named local units which were composed of hamlets of five or six households. On Matupit, as in other Tolai settlements, each hamlet tended to be the locus of a matrilineal descent group *(vuna tarai)* under the leadership of its big man *(lualua)*. Hamlets and parishes were linked together through a network of kinship ties, matrilateral and cognatic, which ramified and spread across the entire area of Tolai settlement, but these ties did not effectively challenge the assertion of local political independence. Parochialism, indeed, has always been—and remains—a marked feature of many aspects of Tolai social life, but since the earliest days of contact with Europeans it has been increasingly tempered by growing awareness of common interests and the extension of political authority (Salisbury, 1962). To-day the Tolai are grouped within four Native Local Government Councils, and there has been some discussion amongst the people themselves of combining to form a single council.

There is one other aspect of Tolai culture which calls for brief comment at this stage. In tropical regions which also have a history of volcanic activity it appears not unusual to find a considerable degree of ecological diversity, even within comparatively small areas.[4] This is certainly borne out on the Gazelle Peninsula, where the degree of localized production is quite striking. I shall return to this point in a later section. Here I merely wish to note how ecological diversity provided the basis for a complex system of trade even in pre-contact times. Trading was carried on by means of a network of markets *(bung)*; goods passed through a series of intermediaries from the coast to the more remote inland settlements and vice versa. The institution of the *bung* has survived to the present day, though on a much modified and extended basis. Rabaul has become a central marketplace for the whole area. On Saturday mornings all roads on the Gazelle Peninsula lead to the town, and settlements are deserted as the people make their way there by lorry, car or on foot.

Associated with this system of trade, and providing a medium through which transactions could be conducted, was the indigenous form of currency known as *tambu*. *Tambu* itself consists of tiny shells threaded together on rattan vine. The standard unit of measurement was the fathom—equivalent to two outstretched arms—and this in turn was divisible into smaller units, each with a distinct name. But the use of *tambu* was not confined to wholly commercial transactions involving the exchange of goods. *Tambu*, for example, was necessary for marriage; at each stage of the frequently elaborate preliminaries there were public presentations and exchanges of shell-money, while the bride wealth itself consisted of shell-money. Again, *tambu* had a necessary part at every stage of the activities associated with the male cult known as the *tubuan*. For the Tolai, however, the chief significance of shell-money lay in its relation to the cult of the dead. For the central aim of acquiring *tambu* was to accumulate it in the form of large coils containing anything from 100 to 1000 fathoms. Once *tambu* had thus been made up in the form of a coil, it would not normally be touched until the owner's death or the death of a close kinsman. Then, in the course of various mortuary rites, the coils would be cut up and distributed amongst all those present as part of a complex series of exchanges and counter-exchanges.

Tambu was acquired by individual effort and initiative; and it was individually owned. On the other hand, the members of a local matrilineage usually stored their *tambu* in a kind of lineage bank (*pal na po*) which was under the control of their *lualua*, or deposited it with some other recognized "big man." It was only through the control of large stocks of shell-money that one came to be recognized as a "big man." In turn, access to large resources of *tambu* enabled a man to organize ceremonial dances or initiate cult activities associated with the *tubuan* and thus to maintain and extend his prestige and influence. In short, *tambu* was in a very real sense the central thread in Tolai culture, giving it coherence and strength. It was so interlocked with every other aspect of their social life that a perceptive missionary, who arrived in New Britain in 1878, was able to observe: "Take away their money . . . and most of their customs become nothing" (Danks, 1887, p. 317). In spite of the changes that have overtaken Tolai society since then, in particular the extent to which they have become involved in a cash economy, *tambu* remains a vital institution and, in the field of economic transactions, operates side by side with cash. The present status of *tambu* on Matupit, and some aspects of its relationship with cash, will be discussed in a later section.

THE ISLAND OF MATUPIT AND THE WIDER SOCIETY (1875–1950)

Matupit itself is a small island, less than a mile in length and perhaps half a mile across at the widest points, which lies a few miles out of Rabaul, to which it is linked by a narrow causeway. It occupies a strategic position in Blanche Bay, astride the entrance to Simpson Harbour. There are reports of Europeans trading in these parts of New Britain in the earlier part of the nineteenth century but contacts between natives and Europeans remained sporadic and intermittent until about 1870. By this time German commercial interests in the Western Pacific were beginning to expand, while a growing demand for native labour, and the increasing number of vessels engaged in recruiting, forced ship-masters to cast their nets in ever-broadening sweeps. Within a short time traders, labour recruiters and missionaries were beginning to converge on the Gazelle Peninsula. Blanche Bay offers at first sight an ideal land-locked harbour, but for these early visitors its waters were too deep, and anchorage could only be found close in to the shore at Matupit Island. In the circumstances it was inevitable that the Matupi should be amongst the first of the Gazelle peoples to be brought into close and immediate relationship with the

Europeans. In 1873 two traders employed by the firm of Godeffroy & Sons of Hamburg made a brief sojourn on the island before their houses were burned down, their trade goods stolen, while they themselves barely escaped with their lives. George Brown, who established his first mission on the nearby Duke of York Islands in 1875, quickly appreciated the important position of Matupit. He thought it must always be the mission headquarters for this part of New Britain, though this in fact never happened. Within a few years, however, the German trader Hernsheim had established a permanent station on the island from which German vessels were soon carrying cargoes of copra direct to European ports. Romilly (1887) reports that at the time of his stay on Matupit between 1881 and 1883 there was already a small European community there. Following their annexation of New Guinea in 1884, the German flag was hoisted at Matupit. Land was taken up for building and stores, and one can still see the sites on which the European club-house and tennis-court stood. One large tract of land was made over as a gift to the Methodist Mission, apparently to prevent its being acquired by Hernsheim. Land and its acquisition by the Europeans have remained ever since a major theme in the relations of Matupi and successive Administrations.

The Matupi had to adjust to the new regime imposed by the Germans, and it seems that they did this quite rapidly. They were able to sell their coconuts to traders, at first for trade goods, and then for cash. The traditional economy persisted, but increasingly the Matupi were coming to participate in a much more differentiated system. They were set to work as labourers on the roads and on the wharf. Quite a number became seamen on German vessels, and there are still a few alive who can recall voyages around the turn of the century to India, the Philippines and even as far afield as America.

In 1910 the German Administration transferred its headquarters from Kokopo (Herbertshohe), across the bay, to what is now Rabaul. There a school was established to which native children came from all the neighbouring islands. Amongst them were some of the brightest youngsters of Matupit who, their training completed, were able to take jobs in the bank, as surveyors' and medical assistants, type-setters and printing operatives. One acquired a local reputation as a musician and some of his compositions have been accepted into the hymnal. German was taught, and amongst the older men at Matupit to-day there are still a few who remember sufficient of it to carry on a halting conversation.

These changes in the mode of livelihood were matched by noticeable changes in patterns of consumption. According to one observer, the younger native had by now acquired a taste for luxury. "He likes his tobacco, he enjoys tin-meat, he glories in European clothes, puts a keen value on umbrellas, mouth-organs, lanterns and the hundred and one knick-knacks he sees a white man has" (Lyng, 1914). The Matupi frequently like to recall that they were always in the van of those who were ready to accept the new ways and standards of the Europeans. Before the First World War it appears that some Matupi were already wearing European-style suits and clothes (Bürger, 1923, p. 154), though this practice must later have been abandoned.

With the outbreak of war in 1914, the Australians at once sent an Expeditionary Force to Rabaul. The Germans were ousted and a new regime—that of the "English"—established. The period of the military occupation, which lasted until 1921, and of the years immediately following, has frequently been described as one of stagnation. Whereas the Germans had invested very considerable sums in the Territory, no resources were now available for further economic development, and the existing economy was allowed to run down. From the point of view of the Tolai this meant that while there was still a market for the sale of copra, there were now fewer opportunities for advancement outside the traditional economic and social framework. The school at Namanula seemed to be paving the way towards the emergence of a native elite, but this path had now been closed, and education became almost the sole responsibility of the missions, which aimed primarily at achieving literacy in the vernacular.

In the middle twenties the expropriated German properties came on the market again, there was an influx of Australians, new businesses were being opened, and the social pace seemed to quicken. Then the slump came, and the price of copra dropped sharply. Recovery was slow, and it was not until the mid thirties that there were once more signs of a quickening tempo. Some years earlier gold had been found on the New Guinea mainland, and many Tolai were now working at such places as Salamaua, Bulolo and Wau. At home, especially in the coastal settlements around Rabaul, the links between town and village had been considerably strengthened. Indeed, the Matupi were being described in 1932 as having lost all semblance of native institutions (Cilento, 1932). They had become, it was said, a community of native pedlars and hawkers, boat-boys and laundrymen. The pattern of wants again appears to have become more sophisticated, though more interesting perhaps is the fact that Tolai were now beginning to emerge as entrepreneurs and were investing their money in copra-driers (of which there were at least four at Matupit), cars and trucks. At about this time one enterprising Matupi was advertising loads of firewood for sale through the *Rabaul Times*.

But once again what appeared to be a period of steady development and rising prosperity was interrupted by war. The Japanese landed at Rabaul in 1942, and thereafter much of the Gazelle simply became a vast Japanese garrison until the end of the fighting. Few Tolai recall the Japanese occupation with pleasure, least of all perhaps the Matupi. Indeed, the occupation bore more harshly on them than most other Tolai, for they had an army force encamped on their very land. Their garden areas

were confiscated and access to them prohibited on pain of death. The coconut plantations, on which most of their wealth was built, were devastated
and only now are the new palms beginning to come into economic bearing.
Equally, if not more grievous to the Matupi, was the serious depletion of
their accumulated stocks of shell-money. Much of the *tambu* was actually
destroyed by the Japanese, but great quantities were also used up on
clandestine trips to purchase food from more fortunately situated Tolai
communities. As the war progressed, Allied bombing attacks became more
frequent, and the population was shepherded to the slopes of Mt. Kabiu
(The Mother). The genealogies I took at Matupit recall the many who
died as the result of these attacks and the even greater numbers who died
from malnutrition and the lack of adequate medical supplies. It was the
central position of the island in Blanche Bay which earlier had led the
Matupi to prominence as one of the wealthiest and most advanced of the
Tolai communities. Now, by the same token, but in very different circumstances, it had exposed them to the full brunt of modern warfare. Their
homes, many of them already before the war permanent structures built
to a modern design, had been destroyed, together with much of their
possessions; their wealth had been dissipated. After the war the Matupi
received substantial sums from the Administration by way of compensation,
but even so it was largely a case of having to set to afresh and build again.

PRODUCTION: TRADITIONAL ACTIVITIES

All Tolai to-day require money, but there is a wide range of choice
available to them as to how they should satisfy this need. Some concentrate
on traditional activities, cultivating their gardens and selling the produce;
some grow cash crops; some have emerged as contractors and entrepreneurs, while yet others are in regular wage employment. But what is
perhaps most significant for an understanding of the Tolai's adaptation to
modern conditions is the way many are able to combine a number of
these activities at the same time. The nature of these activities, how they
are organized, and what they contribute in the way of income will be
discussed in this and the following sections.

In the coastal settlements fishing is one of the major traditional activities
of Tolai men. It takes a number of different forms, the particular mode
followed depending mainly upon the season, but also to some extent upon
local conditions. At Matupit, for example, the use of traps (*a wup*) is
confined to the season of the *labur* (the north-west monsoon) which
corresponds roughly with the period December-March. Seine fishing (*a
umbene*) is carried on in the *taubar*, the season of the south-east Trades,
roughly May-October. Fishing with line and bait (*a niil*) may be carried
out at any time, depending on the weather. Further round the coast, however, men may be preparing to launch their fish traps when the season
at Matupit is already drawing to a close. No deep sea fishing is practised.

Currents in the area are notoriously capricious, and an early traveller described the sea as one of the most dangerous to small sailing craft that he knew anywhere (Romilly, 1887, p. 2). Matupi fishermen therefore confine their activities to within the bay.

Fishing with traps is an elaborate process for which the initial preparations may be begun months before the season actually commences. The traps are owned individually, and each man who intends to set his *babau* during the season is responsible for making his own preparations. The trap itself may keep him occupied steadily for at least a month and sometimes much longer. But while a man is thus primarily dependent for success on his own efforts, he also requires the assistance of others at different stages. This is particularly, though not exclusively, noticeable at the time of launching. A number of different activities now have to be co-ordinated. The wicker-basket (*a peo*), which will serve as anchor, has to be filled with heavy stones; the long cable of bamboo by which buoy and trap are affixed to the anchor and held in position has to be prepared for loading on a canoe; and the trap itself, perhaps as much as eight feet in length, brought down from its cradle in the workshop to the beach. Three canoes and a working party of at least ten men are usually required to place the *babau* in its proper position at sea.

The necessity for co-operation finds structural expression in the groups known as *motonoi*, to one of which each person engaged in fishing attaches himself. The *motonoi* itself, upon which the group is based, is a small area of the beach specially set aside for the men engaged in fishing. Each *motonoi* has its own workshops and house where members of the group may foregather, where fishing gear may be stored when not in use, or fishing magic performed. The *motonoi* is taboo to all women and to those males who have not yet been initiated into the cult of the *tubuan*. Membership is not rigidly fixed, and a man may join whichever seems most convenient for him. In practice, the distribution and social composition coincide with the main territorial divisions recognized by the Matupi. Once associated with a *motonoi*, a man is expected to co-operate with other members, and they frequently take it in turn to inspect the traps of the group and bring the catch to shore. They are also expected to help in maintaining the house and, at the end of the season, to join in the custom of the *vevedek* when each member's total takings for the season, which he has hitherto stored and left untouched, are brought to the *motonoi* house and publicly counted; after which all participate in a communal meal.

Motonoi organization, as I have just noted, is consistent, and fits in very closely, with local organization, built up around small highly localized and independent units. A man is free to visit any *motonoi*, but insofar as trap fishing is concerned, the *motonoi* are quite independent and have little to do with one another. Seine fishing, however, seems to demand more extensive co-operation, and here the position is somewhat different. The manufacture of the *umbene* from indigenous plant fibres was a traditional craft which has now almost completely disappeared. It is much simpler nowadays to purchase a net from a European store. The nets may cost up to £60 and more, so that the Matupi tend to buy them on a group basis. Beyond this, effective seine fishing requires a more enduring form of team-work than does the *babau*. The net itself has to be prepared for use, and pumice weights and wooden floats have to be carefully affixed. The elaborate form of fishing magic, once a necessary preliminary, is now only rarely carried out, but a feast is still given by the owning group at which those who assisted in the preparation of the net receive their fees in *tambu*, while baskets of food and *tambu* are also distributed to the other guests who, by their acceptance, are now committed to giving assistance when the net is actually in use. When fishing is actually in progress, the net is carefully folded and placed in a canoe which stands at the ready on the edge of the beach. Look-outs on the beach or in the trees cry out as soon as they detect the movement of a school of fish on the surface of the sea. Immediately the canoe moves away from the shore in a wide arc, while two of the crew begin to let out the net. Meanwhile, all the younger men on the beach dive into the water and begin hauling the net into the shore until the catch is disburdened on the beach, and then sorted and counted. The net is gathered up again and the canoe returns to its station in readiness to repeat the operation. Thus at least twenty men are usually required to launch the *umbene* and land the catch. In fact, large numbers of men are generally available on the beach during the season and all of them lend a hand.

Seine fishing is also a continuing operation, and there are a number of tasks to be regularly performed. The nets are constantly torn by the struggles of the larger fish which find themselves trapped, and have to be repaired and maintained. Thus there has to be a nuclear core of men who accept the responsibility for looking after and operating the net. Seine fishing, therefore, has a corporate aspect lacking in the case of trap fishing. *Umbene* groups are formed in different ways. Frequently, the members of a local descent group combine to buy and operate a net; sometimes two or more such groups belonging to the same moiety, who recognize close links with one another and tend to co-operate over a wide range of activities, enhance those links through their joint ownership of the net. In other cases seine fishing is the joint enterprise of the *uruur*, primarily a local group composed of contiguous hamlets within a village. How far the *uruur* was a feature of the indigenous social organization remains uncertain: to-day it operates primarily in the field of church activities. During my stay at Matupit, a number of *uruur* had purchased nets which they operated exclusively to raise funds for completing the new Methodist church they were building in the centre of the island.

Seine fishing of this kind is bound up with the known movements of the fish. These pass close inshore at a limited number of points so that, unlike trap fishing, the *umbene* can only be successfully operated from a few *motonoi*. Indeed, during the 1961 season, when there were seven nets all told in use on the island, most of the fishing was concentrated on a single *motonoi*. This meant that the activities had to be organized so that each group had the opportunity to launch its net. Not surprisingly in the circumstances, quarrels broke out and a serious dispute arose involving different claims to rights of ownership and user in the *motonoi*. However, such disputes did not disturb the general co-operation of men from the different sections of Matupit in the actual operation of the nets. *Umbene* operations, indeed, provide one of the few situations where Matupi from all parts of the island come together and interact on a completely informal basis.

It is difficult to assess accurately over any lengthy period what the sales of fish contribute to Matupi income. During the 1960 season about 80 *babau* were launched, representing the efforts of just under 50% of the available adult males who were not in regular wage employment; but the numbers participating vary considerably from year to year. At the end of the *babau* season each *motonoi* or group of *motonoi* should conduct a *vevedek*, when the season's takings are counted, but not all do this. Table I sets out the total amounts recorded at three *vevedek* held at the end of the 1960 season.

TABLE I. INCOME FROM FISH-TRAPS RECORDED AT THREE *Vevedek*, 1960

Group	Number of Traps	Cash	Tambu
Reinatun	16	£A142 2 0	230 fathoms
Kikila	18	236 18 0	575 ″
Ranguna	12	187 12 0	306 ″
Total	46	£A566 12 0	1,111 ″

This works out at an average of about £12 and 25 fathoms of *tambu* per person for the 3-4 months season, though there were some who recorded totals of £25 and close on 100 fathoms. Moreover, the *vevedek* does not disclose the total yield that the Matupi derive from their fish-traps. Those who go out to help in inspecting the traps, or assist by hawking the fish around the streets of Rabaul immediately the catch is landed, receive a portion of fish for themselves and pocket the proceeds. Again, when the catch from the traps is brought ashore, many of the womenfolk gather to *pipiai,* that is to purchase fish with their own money or *tambu* in order to cook and resell it at a profit at the market. In this way the *pipiai* is an important source of a woman's independent income.

As Table I indicates, income from the *babau* takes the form of cash as well as shell-money, but it is impossible to say precisely what their respective proportions are of that income. Prices vary according to the type of fish, as well as with supply, and there is no fixed conversion rate between the two currencies which is valid for all transactions. However, we may use the price of the variety of fish known as *malabur* to provide a crude measure. The *malabur* are made up in bunches of 10-12 fish, each constituting one *tinur*. A *tinur* normally sells at 1/- or a *vuvuai na tambu*, about a quarter of a fathom. Assuming further for the purpose of the calculation that all fish caught in the traps are of the *malabur* variety, then it would appear that about a quarter of all fish caught in traps is sold for shell-money.

In the case of seine fishing, keeping a reliable check on sales and income is even more difficult. Catches vary enormously from day to day. Sometimes the nets are put out repeatedly in the course of an afternoon, but the catch is so small that the handful of fish is simply distributed amongst the helpers; at other times I have known a single bumper catch to yield over 1000 fish, worth more than £20. No *vevedek* is performed for the *umbene* as for the *babau*, but a season's fishing is normally expected to yield at least £100 and 100 fathoms of *tambu* for the owners of the net. One *uruur* had purchased a net in 1958 to raise funds to complete the building of the Methodist church; by the beginning of the 1961 season the bank account stood at £500.

Apart from fish there is one other product of the sea which retains some importance in the economy. This is a powder of slaked lime (*kabang*) derived from coral deposits. It has important uses in certain ceremonial contexts but is principally associated with the chewing of the pepper-plant (few Tolai ever move very far without a small handbag or purse, in the case of men worn on the arm, containing amongst other things a supply of areca nuts, pepper-berries and *kabang* in much the same way as amongst ourselves the regular smoker carries a packet of cigarettes).

A person wishing to manufacture *kabang* arranges for a work party of perhaps a dozen men and women to help in gathering the coral from reefs around Nordup and Talwat. When brought home to Matupit, this is left to stand for a period of up to three years until the smell caused by the various forms of marine life has disappeared. The coral is then ready for firing. It is gathered up in baskets and crushed. These are then carefully covered with leaves and placed on a raised platform in a special house, *a pal na kabang*, where a small fire smoulders continuously. This process may last as long as six months. When the powder is finally ready, a small number of women gather together to make the special packets, *a vaum*, in which the powder is sold at the market.

The production of *kabang* is thus a slow and somewhat tortuous business, and it may be that there are now fewer undertaking it at Matupit. Heaps of drying coral are to be seen lying all around the island, but I was told that in the year of my stay only three or four people had made trips to gather fresh supplies. Like certain varieties of fish, *kabang* is regarded primarily as a source of *tambu* rather than of money, and coral collected from one trip is ultimately expected to yield *kabang* worth at least 100 fathoms. This might seem to be a small return, but the importance still attached to its sale is shown in the fact that on a number of occasions when I made observations at the market about one in five Matupi women had *kabang* for sale.

No ecological survey of the Gazelle Peninsula has ever been carried out, but visitors to the area have frequently been led to comment on its general fertility. One of the earliest, Powell, who spent three years in New Britain between 1877 and 1880, observed that the soils seemed very rich, being formed of decomposed volcanic and vegetable matters. And he reported of a trip from Nordup to Blanche Bay that the land he passed through was nearly all cultivated, large crops of bananas, yams and taro being all around (Powell, 1884, p. 31). These were, and remain, amongst the chief items of Tolai subsistence. But the coconut also flourishes. Indeed, for the Tolai the palm is king among trees. "The coconut is majesty" (*a lama a luluai*), they say. In a traditional context it serves a multiplicity of purposes. It provides food and drink, while its oil gives Tolai cooking a distinctive flavour; and no feast is complete without *ku,* a coconut preparation which the Tolai liken to butter. Food apart, the different parts of the palm, at their various stages of development, are also important in mundane as well as in ritual and magical activities. In the context of the modern cash economy, in the form of copra, it remains the most important single source of income for the Tolai as a whole, which has been estimated at £600,000 in 1959 (Epstein, T.S, 1963).

The palm is long-lived and may continue to yield nuts for sixty years and over. Consequently, it may only be planted on land belonging to one's own descent group. In a community like Matupit where descent is matrilineal, marriage virilocal and residence patrilocal, there may be a considerable number of persons who have no claims to matrilineage land in and around the island—though they have legal entitlement in the local communities of their mothers—and to this extent are precluded from planting coconuts on any large scale. But for those who have full legal claims to land through membership of a locally based descent group, plantings of up to 1000 trees and more are not uncommon.[5] The Matupit of pre-war days is remembered as a land of coconuts, so thick in parts that at night the stars were held from view. Even allowing for the poetic imagery, this may not be too gross an exaggeration for already, some fifty years earlier, Powell had described the island as being covered with coconuts. However, during the last war most of the trees were destroyed and serious replanting did not begin again until 1948–50. It takes about 10-12 years before the palm comes into economic bearing, so that during my period of field work sales of copra were still few and intermittent.

Reference has been made earlier to the ecological diversity on the Gazelle Peninsula and to the degree of localized production associated with this. Taro, for example, grows well and in abundance in many parts of the Peninsula but is scarcely seen at Matupit. I am not certain whether this is related to soil and climatic conditions, as the Matupi sometimes allege. Certainly, they only grow it in very limited quantities, and their principal staple is the banana.[6] But bananas themselves are of many varieties, each with its own distinctive properties, and sought after for a different purpose. And here again local variation is important, for a particular variety that does well at Matupit may not prosper elsewhere, and vice versa. So one is confronted with the seemingly curious phenomenon of Matupi, who themselves grow bananas on a large scale, buying them on their own doorsteps from a Tolai-owned lorry which has come perhaps from Kokopo, across the bay. Inquiry will then reveal that they have bought a variety which is either out of season, or which cannot be grown, at Matupit. In a similar way, a lorry-load of Tolai sometimes arrive from a settlement such as Vuna Irima on the north coast to purchase mats which the Matupi women weave from the leaves of the *voivoi* tree (a variety of pandanus), which does not appear to grow in certain other parts of the Tolai area.

But the most interesting and, from the people's point of view, the most important instances of localized production are the results of certain environmental peculiarities associated with the presence of volcanoes. The Matupi, and a small number of other groups, share the monopoly of a kind of clay which when fired produces red ochre called *tar*. *Tar* has magical and ceremonial significance, and as it is smeared on the body when people take part in dances or other ceremonial occasions, it is much sought after. More important is the monopoly which these folk have in the *kiau na ngiok*. Around the base of Matupi Crater, and at other points in the vicinity, the soil is very hot, allowing the brush turkey or megapode to deposit its eggs deep in the earth. The ownership of these areas is distributed amongst the various matrilineages, whose elders control the right of access to the egg-lands.

Egg collecting, which goes on during the months May-September, is a hazardous though popular activity amongst the men. The Councillor and elders of Kikila, the largest of the three village sections, have sought —without a great deal of success—to restrict it to one day a week, partly to avoid fatal accidents which are more likely to occur when men go out on their own, partly to ensure that other activities, such as work in the cocoa gardens, are not neglected. On these days, most of the men of Kikila who were not employed elsewhere set out in canoes for the egg-grounds in the early morning, only returning to the island at dusk. Some of the womenfolk accompanied them, taking with them supplies of tea, biscuits, tinned meat and rice which they prepared on the spot and sold to the diggers for eggs or money. The work itself is arduous, and the degree of success variable. The younger and stronger men are frequently able to gather as many as 80 eggs in the day, the equivalent of £2, but the older men also profit, for they are able to claim a levy from all the eggs gathered on land belonging to descent groups of which they are the acknowledged local leaders.

THE MARKET

All the activities so far described, save for the production of copra, are traditional in the sense that they played an important part in Tolai economic life before the coming of the Whites. They are also organized through indigenous forms of social grouping. They were in the past, as to-day, not only a means of subsistence but also a source of revenue, formerly in shell-money, now mainly in cash. As noted earlier, trading took place between different local groups and was carried on through the indigenous institution of the market (*bung*). These were held regularly at various points throughout the area.

The institution of the *bung* persists to the present day, though in an adapted form and on a more extended basis. The Rabaul *bung* has become the central market for the whole area, catering now not only for Tolai but for all the different racial and ethnic groups represented in the Gazelle's population. The range of foodstuffs available is also more extensive since Tolai growers now produce a wide variety of fruits and vegetables mainly for a European and Chinese clientele. Again, while shell-money remains legal tender amongst Tolai, the bulk of transactions at the market-place now require Australian currency. Nevertheless, the *bung* remains essentially a Tolai institution. The market-place is maintained and looked after by the Rabaul Native Local Government Council—a Tolai body. But above all, the vendors, almost entirely women, are without exception Tolai.

For the women of Matupit selling at the market is one of their most important and regular activities. Normally between 25-40 Matupi women are present each Saturday at the central market-place to sell fish and eggs on behalf of their husbands or brothers, and produce or other items they have acquired by the custom of *pipiai* on their own. Other women from the island sell in the neighbourhood of Chinatown, or hawk their fruit and vegetables around the streets of the town, serving those working in shops and offices who cannot get to the market. Many Matupi women, indeed, buy at the market in order to resell in this way. The market-place is also open during the week when the Matupi, because of their proximity to the town, are usually the largest group present. Because of the numbers of women, and the fact that they leave the island at different times and by different routes, and do not all sell at the main *bung,* it was difficult to keep a tally on sales. However, I did one check at the main market for four

Saturdays in the month of August, 1960, and another for a week in June, 1961. In the latter instance, which included two Saturdays, 86 women (32% of adult females) were recorded as having sold at the market during the period. The gross takings were £A77 7s. 6d. and slightly over 100 fathoms of *tambu,* giving an average figure of just under a pound and a little more than a fathom per vendor. These figures were comparable with those collected in the earlier check where the average takings were £A2 6s. and 4 fathoms per vendor for the four Saturdays.

Cash Crops and Wage Labour

Traditional activities thus continue to play an important part in the economy. But they are carried on in conjunction with other sets of activities which link Matupit to a much wider economy. In a later section I shall attempt to assess the contribution of each to the total modern economy.

Reference has already been made to the importance of copra as a cash crop. However, a more recent and major development had been the encouragement given by the Administration to the Tolai to grow cocoa. Here again such factors as the availability of land and local ecological conditions have been important in determining the success of different groups in exploiting the new opportunity. The whole question of land resources and land use raises complex issues which I propose to examine in a subsequent publication. Here therefore I may merely note that the proximity of Matupit to Rabaul sets obvious limits to the possible expansion of the area of cultivation. Indeed, from the point of view of the Matupi, the growth of the town has not only already deprived them of much of their traditional lands, but it poses a continuous threat to their existing rights of user in the form of fresh demands on the limited resources left to them. Within these limits many Matupi took eagerly to the new crop. In the area of Rabuana, around the base of Mt. Mother, various groups in whom ownership of the land was vested combined contiguous blocks to form single plantations of between 1-5000 trees. But conditions of soil and shade turned out to be unfavourable, and time and again the Matupi have seen their plants perish. But they persevered and in 1961, some seven years after the original plantings had been begun, some of the gardens were just beginning to show their first fruit. In the area of Ranu, however, conditions appeared to be more favourable, and here growers were now beginning to record their first sales. All told there were 32 cocoa gardens at Matupit, with total plantings somewhere in the neighbourhood of 20,000 trees, though in 1961 only six gardens had reached the stage where it had become worthwhile for the growers to register with a fermentary. With cocoa then, as with coconuts, it was a period of marking time. The people were fully aware of the economic advances that other Tolai groups were making but consoled themselves by looking to the years ahead when they too would see the fruits of their labour.[7]

The heaviest demand for labour on the Gazelle Peninsula has always been from the European-owned copra plantations. But few Tolai ever appear to have found the work acceptable, and indentured native labour had to be brought in from other parts of the Territory (Rowley, 1958, p. 114). However, within Rabaul itself, which the Germans had built up as an important port and headquarters of their regime, there was always a certain demand for labour so that, because of its closeness to town, Matupit has probably had stronger links with the labour market than most other Tolai groups. In the past many Matupi worked on the wharves or as laundrymen servicing the ships when they came into harbour; a few also appear to have worked as domestic servants. But the educational services provided in the pre-war period were limited in the extreme, and there were still few jobs requiring even a modicum of skill and responsibility for which the Tolai could apply. To-day the position has altered very considerably. Not only is the range of occupations available much wider, but many of them call for some degree of special training. Table II sets out the present involvement of the Matupi in the labour market.

TABLE II. MATUPI MALES IN REGULAR WAGE EMPLOYMENT, 1960

Age	Employed Within the Gazelle	Employed Outside the Gazelle	Total	Total Population	%
15-19	4	—	4	35	11.4
20-29	42	39	81	132	61.3
30-39	36	10	46	107	42.9
40-49	9	1	10	42	23.8
50 and over	2	—	2	53	3.7
Total	93	50	143	369	38.7

No figures are available to indicate how far involvement differs from the pre-war period. But the difference in the kind of involvement emerges clearly from the occupations in which Matupi now engage, which are set out in Table III.

Table III brings out a number of points which serve to distinguish the Matupi—and possibly the whole Tolai—situation from that which typically prevails elsewhere in New Guinea and, indeed, in many of the other underdeveloped countries of the world. The proportion of Matupi who are absent from home at any given time is only 13.6% of all adult males, though if scholars and others in training institutions were included the figure would rise to 20.6%. Data on migrant labour rates for other parts of New Guinea are not readily available, but the Matupi figure would seem

TABLE III. OCCUPATIONS OF MATUPI MALES, 1960

Age	Within the Gazelle Peninsula						Outside the Gazelle Peninsula						
	Teachers	*Clerks*	*Artisans*	*Drivers*	*Miscellaneous*	*Total*	*Teachers*	*Clerks*	*Artisans*	*Drivers*	*Police; Military*	*Miscellaneous*	*Total*
15-19	—	—	2	—	1	3	—	—	—	—	1	—	1
20-29	4	15	17	1	5	42	7	3	6	1	18	4	39
30-39	4	7	10	11	4	36	6	2	1	—	1	—	10
40-49	—	—	2	2	5	9	—	—	—	—	—	1	1
50 and over	—	—	1	—	1	2	—	—	—	—	—	—	—
Totals	8	22	32	14	16	92	13	5	7	1	20	5	51

to be low in comparison with parts of the Sepik and some Highlands areas; certainly it is low when compared with labour migration rates in many of the African territories. A further point to be considered is the character of employment itself to which the modern Tolai go. The artisans, who include trained mechanics, carpenters and joiners, painters and plumbers, constitute the largest single category of Matupi in regular employment, and I shall return to them shortly. The clerks include those working for European firms and in various administrative departments as well as junior staff in technical departments of the Administration. Here the evidence points to the gradual emergence of a white-collar class, though the term is hardly appropriate to the Tolai, few of whom follow European modes of dress. Few Matupi now offer for regular unskilled employment at home, still less abroad. In the pre-war period some Matupi worked as unskilled labourers on the goldfields at Edie Creek and Bulolo. To-day, of the younger Matupi now serving in Papua and New Guinea, some are with the Pacific Islands Regiment, but of those serving in the Constabulary itself most are police-clerks and drivers, or belong to the police band. For the rest they are teachers, clerks or assistants in various Government departments, and tradesmen. In short, the Tolai who are abroad to-day would appear to stand out as an occupational elite frequently working in areas and amongst peoples much less advanced than their own.

The data presented in Table III are, I believe, fairly reliable as such, but there are a number of points at which they require qualification if they are not to mislead. In the first place the dichotomy between those in regular wage employment and those who gain their livelihood at home in the village is not absolute. Those who are employed in and around

Rabaul generally live at Matupit: their wives work in the gardens and they themselves do so on free days or in their spare time. And those who are absent in Papua and New Guinea may also continue to exercise their rights in land. One young man who had been in employment at the wireless station in Port Moresby for the past six years spent most of his time planting coconuts each time he came home on leave, against the day of his eventual retirement when he would settle down at Matupit. Few Matupi, indeed, are absent from home for many years. Many of those I had recorded as absent on my first field-trip had already returned a year later, while yet others had left in their stead. Contrariwise, the fact that a man is classified for certain purposes as a "villager" does not mean that he will not work for wages from time to time as the opportunity arises. To this extent Table III does not adequately represent Matupit's involvement in the labour market.

I have referred to artisans as forming the largest single category amongst Matupi in regular wage employment. Most of these are carpenters, yet they are only a small proportion of the total number of Matupi who have a working knowledge of carpentry and put it to use from time to time. Some were taught it at the Malaguna Technical School, some at a mission college, while others simply say that they watched their fellows and learned on the job. It would seem, indeed, on the Matupi evidence, that there is already around Rabaul a good deal of concealed under-employment. At all events there are usually plenty of men available in the village if one of their number should land a contract to build a house, a school or a church. Such contracts are sporadic in their incidence, but since many of the clerks in Works and Housing and other Departments of the Administration are from the island, the Matupi are in fact very well placed to gain them. In one month towards the end of my field work Matupi contractors had won five jobs to my knowledge, all employing men who did not work regularly for wages. Contracts vary in value, but the following is fairly typical. The contract was to build a house for a European school teacher at Raval. The arrangement was that all the materials would be provided, and the job was to be completed within four weeks. For their labour contractor and workers would receive £90. On this occasion there were seven members of the party, all belonging to the Seventh Day Adventist Church, and they set aside £15 towards their fund for building their new church. The work in fact took six weeks to complete instead of four, largely because they were held up for materials. All told, therefore, contract labour is not particularly rewarding, the average weekly wage probably falling short of the minimum wage of £3 which had recently been introduced for urban workers. On the other hand, traditional productive activities do not require any rigid timetable. Once the season's main food gardens have been prepared the men have considerable freedom of choice as to how they will spend their time. In periods of slack, therefore, working on contracts is particularly welcome as a source of cash. For many older Matupi such labour is seen as the solution to the problem of working for money without being absorbed completely into the wage-earning economy of the town, with its threat to the traditional ways of the village. On occasion they complained bitterly against the Administration for allowing Kerema from Papua to settle in Rabaul after the war. These people, it was said, created unfair competition since they were prepared to quote lower prices for a job than were Matupi contractors.

One kind of casual labour that was formerly more important was stevedoring. In order to improve the supply of labour to the docks a system of zoning was introduced for the Rabaul Council area, each village having its own representative or boss-boy. His task was to arrange for the lorry to turn up at the village at the right time to collect the workers, to ensure that sufficient workers were available to make it worthwhile for the stevedoring firm to send out the lorry, and to look after and maintain discipline amongst the workers while working ship. A great deal of pilfering went on, particularly of liquor and spirits, which led to much altercation and friction between the stevedoring firm and the Tolai labourers. The Matupi began to drop out, on their own view because there was too much trouble for which they were unjustly regarded as being responsible; another view was that stricter controls introduced at the docks made it no longer worth their while offering for this kind of work. Nevertheless, even now a lorry turns up from time to time to gather a gang of 30-40 labourers if there is a rush on at the docks, or when some individual Matupi has been able to land a contract to get a particular ship turned round. However, the Matupi attitude towards casual labour seems to be well summed up in the following incident. The main street of Rabaul was being relaid, and labour was required to cut down and remove the roots of the mango trees that lined the avenue. Some Matupi secured the job, for which they understood they were to be paid a pound apiece per day. And, indeed, on the Sunday, when 30 men turned out to work they received this amount. The lorry returned to Matupit to pick up the workers on Monday and Tuesday. On Tuesday evening they received their pay, which only amounted to a pound apiece for the two days. Presumably the Matupi had not appreciated that their work on Sunday was regarded as overtime for which they were being paid at double rates. But whatever the source of the misunderstanding, they made it plain that they regarded 10s. a day as inadequate recompense for the work, and told the European contractor not to send the lorry down again.

ENTREPRENEURS

Apart from the contractors just considered, amongst those who normally live and work in the village there are also a few engaged in small-scale business enterprises and running village stores, though there is at present probably only one who deserves the designation entrepreneur. Alfred had served with the Army in New Guinea during the war. Afterwards he returned to Rabaul where, as he said, he found the whole place in ruins. There were no stores, there was nothing. He took a job as taxi-driver with a firm, the European proprietor of which owned a plantation near Raluana. The inspectors had insisted on the clearing up of the plantations to avoid the spread of malaria. All sprouting coconuts lying around were to be cleared out. Alfred was allowed to take as many as he liked.—He fetched them over to Matupit. During the day he worked as a driver, in the evenings he planted coconuts. In one area he had planted 600, in another probably a similar number, though he had not counted them. In the intervening years he continued to work as a taxi-driver, while the coconuts developed. Now, after twelve years, his trees were at last coming into bearing. Recently, he had put up his own copra drier near his house. It is a makeshift affair. The boiler consists of old drums acquired from derelict army stores, while the structure is made of corrugated iron picked up around the place. The total outlay was no more than a few pounds.

As a taxi-driver he had made numerous contacts all over the Gazelle Peninsula. Now that he had the drier, Tolai from as far as Kokopo brought their coconuts to him which he bought at six for a shilling. He then processed the nuts himself, employing a couple of villagers at 30s. a month to assist, and sold to the Copra Marketing Board at £4 2s. a bag. He sold about 18 bags at a time, giving him a net profit of 25s. per bag, but unfortunately I was unable to work out his average sales and profits over any lengthy period of time.

In addition, Alfred had also recently opened his own store, which he and his wife looked after. One morning when I called in at the store he immediately thrust at me a cheque for £5 which he had received the previous day for working on a plumbing job. "You see this," he said, "if a man is prepared to work hard he can make money. All these complaints about tax! It's because the young men to-day are different. They don't want to work but to loaf around." He went on to explain the importance of standing on one's own feet, and how many businesses foundered on the custom of partnership (*tur guvai*). In this respect his practice differed from that of other Matupi store-keepers, and his was one of the few that seemed to be running successfully.

There were eight village stores open in Matupit in 1960, most of them operated on a *vunatarai* or *tur guvai* basis, that is to say a number of people, generally members of a local descent group or of allied descent groups, combined to raise the capital to purchase the stock. But store-keepers faced a number of handicaps. They were unable to buy in bulk, and as stocks ran low they purchased from Chinese shop-keepers at retail prices. Thus their own prices were frequently higher than in the town. And there were other difficulties which hindered success. In one store where I was able to take stock (see Appendix) and keep records of sales and purchases—which the store-keepers themselves never did—the turnover for the month amounted to £23, and the profits to £5. When I returned to Matupit on my second visit the store had closed down, mainly because of wrangling amongst the contributors. In another case four groups within one of the moieties raised over £100 to start their store in 1957. A young man who was crippled was placed in charge. But he was unable to make the regular trips to Rabaul to buy goods. For a time another man helped by going in on bicycle, but he grew tired and soon dropped out. The trips now had to be made by taxi or by hiring a lorry within the village, which cost about 15s. a time. Since they sometimes had to go to Rabaul as often as four times a week, the expenses soon began to mount. At first the business prospered, but soon those who had invested in the store began to insist on their right to buy on credit, and other kinsmen pressed their claims in a way the storeman found hard to resist. Faced with these difficulties, and finding little profit for himself in the undertaking, the storeman himself dropped out, and the shop was finally closed. In 1961 a sum of £375 was still deposited in the store's account at the bank, but there has been no discussion of its affairs, nor of the way the profits are to be distributed amongst the original investors.

INCOME AND EXPENDITURE

Of the variety of occupations by which the Matupi gain a livelihood some are primarily urban-based, some village-based, while some allow for simultaneous or alternate participation in both sectors. The account of economic activities presents evidence both of change and continuity, but for an appreciation of the dynamics of the situation it is necessary to consider the importance that attaches to each set of activities, and the factors which govern choice of occupation. Such questions arise as the relative contribution of the various activities to Matupit income. Again, how far are those who are not in regular paid employment able to meet their own subsistence requirements and, conversely, how important are village activities for those who are regularly employed? As between these two categories are there significant differences in levels of consumption and standard of living? And if such differences exist within the community, what implications do they have for the social structure? Related to these are a further set of questions posed by the co-existence of two systems of currency. What is the relationship of cash and *tambu,* and what kind of factors determine the use of one rather than the other?

Unfortunately, the kind of data needed to answer all of these questions was not readily available. In a relatively large community, where people were engaged in so many diverse activities at the same time, it was often difficult to keep track of what was going on, and much of the information that one would have wanted to obtain was impossible to get. I tried to overcome some of these difficulties by a sample survey. Since I was principally interested in the differences between those in regular wage employment and those who earned their livelihood primarily within Matupit, the population was first stratified by occupation, age and place of residence. Eighteen households were then selected at random from which I collected budgets of income and expenditure, covering the period of one month, together with property inventories. In order to contrast the relative financial rewards of regular wage employment in town and work in the village, I have used in Table IV data from only twelve households,

TABLE IV. INCOME IN 12 MATUPI HOUSEHOLDS, APRIL, 1960

Source of Income	Wage-earners				Villagers			
	Cash			Shell	Cash			Shell
Wages	£A91	4	5	—	£A3	10	0	
Sales:								
Fish		1	4	0	8 fathoms	15	2	6	8 fathoms
Eggs		3	2	6	—	20	11	0	—
Garden produce		2	16	6	4 fathoms	15	8	0	2 fathoms
Other		6	12	0	4 "	15	10	0	8 "
Gifts		17	3	—	2	17	0	—
Subsistence		5	7	0	—	13	14	9	—
Miscellaneous	—			—	—			69 "
Total	£A111	3	8	16 fathoms	£A86	13	3	87 fathoms

where the householders concerned were aged between 20 and 40 and, with one exception, were married men with families.

It would appear at first sight that urban work is financially more rewarding than earning one's livelihood in the village, the average income for the month for those in the regular wage employment amounting to £18 10s. 6d. per household (19s. per consumption unit) as against £13 12s. 2d. (11s. per consumption unit). Closer examination shows, however, that if urban workers were wholly dependent upon a cash wage their position would in fact differ little from that of villagers. There is, moreover, a considerable range in income of urban workers which is linked with the degree of skill and responsibility deemed necessary for the job. (One Matupi I knew, who does not appear in the sample, had recently moved into a job where he was earning £40 a month.) In other words, for most Matupi urban workers the financial advantages they enjoy over their village confrères are dependent on their ability to participate simultaneously in both sectors of the economy. Conversely, it also follows that the Matupi "villager" is much better off at home than he would be as a manual or unskilled labourer in the town. Amongst those who stay in the village there is also a range in income levels, but it relates more to individual effort and enterprise. One of the "villagers" in the sample, widely regarded as *a tena tamtavun,* an idle fellow, had an income for the month of just over £5; but another, a young man in his late twenties who had a reputation for industry, had a cash income of close on £25.

The contribution of traditional activities to the income of wage earners is, of course, much smaller than for "villagers," but it is nevertheless, as I have suggested, of key significance. Among the urban workers in the sample, one had set his *babau* during the fish trap season which was more or less finished when I began collecting the budgets. Others fished at night with line and bait or gathered eggs at the weekend. But while these activities are important in themselves, the participation of male urban workers in the village economy is principally achieved through their womenfolk. As noted previously, once the main food gardens have been prepared the men are left relatively free for other activities. The women go out regularly to weed the gardens; they collect food and fuel and bring it back to the village; and of course they sell produce at the market. The full importance of the role of the women does not emerge clearly perhaps from Table IV because one of the wage earners in the sample was still unmarried, while in another case the wife was in hospital throughout the survey.

In Table V I examine more closely the proportion of income devoted to

TABLE V. PROPORTION OF TOTAL INCOME DEVOTED TO FOODSTUFFS IN 12 MATUPI HOUSEHOLDS, APRIL, 1960

	Urban					Village					Proportion of Total Income	
											Urban	Village
Subsistence	£5	7	0 (	5	5)	£13	14	9 (	11	2)	4.8%	6.3%
Indigenous	8	17	6 (	9	0)	5	10	0 (	4	5)	7.9%	19.4%
European	30	9	3 (£1	10	9)	16	18	0 (	15	4)	27.4%	41.0%
	£44	13	9 (£2	5	2)	£36	12	9 (£1	10	11)	40.1%	15.3%

food, which I have divided into three categories: subsistence is home-produced food; indigenous types of food are those bought at the market or from Tolai lorries which visit Matupit from time to time; and European foodstuffs, traditionally unknown, which have to be purchased in shops and stores. I have not included for this purpose the wide range of items which Matupi buy, such as lemonade, ice-cream, cigarettes and tobacco, etc. These I prefer to regard as sundries, and treat separately elsewhere. The figures in brackets are per consumption unit.

The proportion of total expenditure on all foodstuffs is roughly the same in both categories. All Matupi find it necessary to buy certain traditional type foodstuffs which they do not produce themselves, or do so in

Table VI. General Expenditure in 12 Matupi Households, April, 1960

	Sundries			Clothes			Household			Transport			Church			Entertainment			Repayment of Loans			Gifts			Miscellaneous			Total		
	£	s.	d.	£	s.	d.	£	s.	d.	£	s.	d.	£	s.	d.	£	s.	d.	£	s.	d.	£	s.	d.	£	s.	d.	£	s.	d.
Urban c.u.	10	13	10	12	11	0	30	5	1	1	2	0	2	8	2	4	14	0	12	0	0	5	0	3	18	13	0	97	7	4
		10	10		12	8	1	10	7		1	0		2	3		4	8		12	6		5	2		18	10	4	18	6
Village c.u.	5	6	9	3	18	0	10	14	0	5	1	6	2	14	3		10	0		—			15	0	14	2	9	43	2	3
		4	4		3	2		8	8		4	2		2	3			4		—				6		11	6	1	14	11

insufficient quantities, mainly taro, Singapore (taro Hong Kong), yams and sweet potatoes, as well as many European foods. Tea with sugar, but without milk, and bread, usually without butter, form to-day the standard Matupi breakfast, and a hungry and impatient child is frequently sent off in the morning to a village store to buy a loaf of bread. Again, rice, tinned meats and fish are now standard items of the Matupi diet. The main differences between the two categories would seem to be that the "villager" with his lower cash income tends to consume more traditional foods, which are relatively cheap and last longer, than does the urban worker. Secondly, while both categories include many of the same European items in their diet, the urban worker tends to widen his choice. His regular purchases may include meat from the butchery, butter, tinned vegetables, ketchups and relishes, and his wife uses flour and dripping for cooking.

A similar pattern emerges from the consideration of general expenditure. In both categories the heaviest item, apart from food, is the household. Most Matupi have a considerable amount of kitchenware and utensils, but many urban workers also invest a great deal in furnishing their homes in a distinctly European fashion. Similarly, all Matupi lay emphasis on the importance of dress, and most males own large wardrobes of *lavalava* and shirts; but urban workers tend to have more, and prefer to buy the more expensive brands. They also tend to spend more on clothes for their wives and children. In order to achieve and maintain this higher standard of living they appear to have to live very close to their level of income. Indeed, the data on general expenditure set out in Table VI shows that their total expenditure exceeded their recorded income for the month. Questioning of informants on this score generally drew the response that the excess had been made up from savings. This was probably genuine. One man's expenditure was unusually heavy because his wife had to go to Port Moresby to undergo an operation; in another case large sums were spent on items for a new home, not yet completely finished, for which the owner had been saving for years. Nevertheless, it would appear that within the category of urban workers who are married and have families, savings must be low, except possibly for the few in the highest income brackets. Amongst the "villagers" there was none whose expenditure exceeded his income, but some also had heavy commitments during the month, and average savings amounted to only £1 5s. per household.

Changes in food habits and patterns of expenditure throw light not only on the standard of living of the Matupi but also on their changing wants and aspirations. But an even clearer picture of these emerges from the analysis of their property and personal chattels. Tables VII and VIII are based on the full sample of 18 households and set out average holdings of productive and non-productive property.

The Tolai as a whole are recognized to-day as the wealthiest of all indigenous New Guinea groups, but within the Tolai community itself

TABLE VII. AVERAGE HOLDINGS OF PRODUCTIVE PROPERTY IN 18 MATUPI HOUSEHOLDS

Age	Number		Tools, Equipment		Transport		Livestock		Savings	
	U	V	U (£A s. d.)	V (£A s. d.)	U (£A s. d.)	V (£A s. d.)	U (£A s. d.)	V (£A s. d.)	U (£A s. d.)	V (£A s. d.)
20–29	2	2	6 4 6	14 12 9	144 5 0	9 0 0	—	—	57 0 0	117 10 0
30–39	4	5	6 4 8	12 0 9	15 3 9	14 5 0	1 12 6	2 0 0	140 10 0	118 19 3
40–49	2	1	6 15 0	21 2 0	17 10 0	66 0 0	—	3 10 0	75 0 0	150 0 0
50–	—	2	—	25 14 6	—	23 10 0	—	20 5 0	—	58 0 0

TABLE VIII. AVERAGE HOLDINGS OF NON-PRODUCTIVE PROPERTY IN 18 MATUPI HOUSEHOLDS

Age	Number		House		Household		Clothes		Miscellaneous	
	U	V	U (£A s. d.)	V (£A s. d.)	U (£A s. d.)	V (£A s. d.)	U (£A s. d.)	V (£A s. d.)	U (£A s. d.)	V (£A s. d.)
20–29	2	2	281 0 0	—	83 7 6	37 16 0	40 16 0	14 19 0	80 6 0	18 0
30–39	4	5	164 14 10	41 14 9	74 10 1	37 12 7	31 19 10	21 2 0	27 19 10	8 2 5
40–49	2	1	112 10 0	14 0 0	49 6 3	46 15 0	27 7 6	17 1 0	7 4 6	16 0
50–	—	2	—	41 4 0	—	49 5 9	—	32 5 0	—	12 0 0

Matupit is clearly poorer than many of the inland settlements, such as Rapitok, at least in regard to holdings of productive property. To the casual observer this appears most strikingly in the small number of motor vehicles owned and operated by Matupi as against other parts of the Gazelle. During my stay there were only two lorries and a jeep on the island, though some of the younger men were now beginning to acquire motor-cycles. On the other hand, it is true of course that the Matupi have less need of motor transport than other groups. They are nearer the town, and there is still no regular demand for transport to carry copra to the Copra Marketing Board or to Chinese buyers, and cocoa to the fermentary. More significant, therefore, are the differences in cash savings, which would probably be low when compared with certain other Tolai communities. What is striking in the Matupi figures is the fall in savings amongst those over the age of 50, that is amongst the category of Elders. Most of these had received cash sums from the Administration as war damage compensation, though in no case did the amount exceed £265. The figures indicate how they have had to eat into their capital.

But if the Matupi are less wealthy in absolute terms than other Tolai, their holdings of non-productive property reveal the relative sophistication of their standard of living and way of life. There is a very considerable investment in housing. The cost of putting up a modern-style house at Matupit ranges between £100 and £400. Labour costs are low because a man can generally count a skilled carpenter amongst his kin and friends, and services here are given on a reciprocal basis. The heaviest expense, therefore, is the material—fibro-cement, timber, corrugated iron for the roof, and fittings and louvre-glass for the windows. On one occasion word was received that a large quantity of salvaged corrugated iron was for sale in Rabaul. All day the lorries plied back and forth, taking the many purchasers to town and bringing them back again with the iron they would store until ready to begin the building of their new homes.

"Urbanites" and "villagers" are equally desirous of putting up good houses, but few "villagers" have been able to build houses of the same quality as those of the younger men now in regular wage employment, nor do they furnish and equip them to the same extent. Homes belonging to the latter possess European-style furniture and crockery, a wireless set and, in a few cases, a paraffin refrigerator. Houses belonging to Elders, on the other hand, with one or two exceptions, are still built in a traditional way with local materials; kitchen utensils and household goods are numerous, but furnishing is poor. Within the home, then, there is a growing approximation towards European standards, but it is interesting to observe that for the present this does not extend to dress. As already noted, a great deal is spent on clothes, but the standard dress for all occasions is the *lavalava* or Samoan loin-cloth. Shorts are worn, but the Tolai who appeared in khaki shorts would be derided as a *wok,* a New Guinea native labourer.

The intense desire for European clothes characteristic of Northern Rhodesian Africans, which Godfrey Wilson regarded as an inevitable expression of their search for a civilized status, has no counterpart to-day among the Tolai (Wilson, 1941, pp. 2, 15).

CASH AND SHELL-MONEY

An interesting feature of the Tolai situation is that in addition to participating simultaneously in different sectors of the economy, they also operate simultaneously with two distinct forms of currency. Wages, of course, are paid in Australian currency, and no European or Chinese store accepts payment in shell-money. On the other hand, for certain transactions involving only Tolai, such as the payment of bride-wealth or initiation into the *tubuan,* cash is regarded as inappropriate and unacceptable. Between these extremes there is an area within which cash and shell-money serve as alternative media of exchange, or may be used in combination. Thus fish, slaked lime or other produce may be sold for cash or shell. The purchase price of a canoe, or payment for certain services, on the other hand, is usually in cash and shell. For example, a man who was called in to carry out the magical rites over a new fishing net received as payment 10 fathoms of shell, £2 and a basket of food.

To what extent can the relationship between the two currencies be expressed in terms of exchange rates? As I have already explained, there is no fixed conversion rate between the two currencies. A rate of 1 fathom = 2 shillings was set in German times, and is still sometimes cited by Tolai as a theoretical equivalent. In fact, however, once the shells have been prepared as *tambu,* they cannot be purchased for cash. Secondly, there is considerable variation in conversion rates for different items. Thus, for certain varieties of fish or taro the equivalent rate for a fathom of shell is 4s., for slaked lime about 6s., while for chickens it may be as much as 10s. These variations appear to relate to the operation of supply and demand in distinct markets. The situation is one which might appear to lend itself to the manipulation of the different exchange rates, but this does not occur to any noticeable extent, presumably because of the small size of the *tambu* market, and the ensuing risk of loss involved (Epstein, T. S., 1961, 1963*b*).

The relative significance of cash and shell in the economy cannot then be assessed in purely monetary terms. Cash and shell operate in an area of overlap, but they relate essentially to different spheres of value, using the latter term in a sociological rather than the technical economic sense. To take an example: a woman had bought two baskets of fish for £1 when the catch was landed at Matupit. She cooked the fish for sale at the market. When I asked how much she thought she would get she replied that she was selling for *tambu,* and did not know how much she would make. In fact she received 10 fathoms. Her brother, with whom I discussed the point, explained that had she sold for cash, she would have received £3 to £4 but added that since his sister wanted *tambu* she was not primarily concerned about profit. The same point was made more explicitly in a conversation with one of the few English-speaking Tolai, and a prominent man throughout the area. Money of course was necessary for so many things, he said, but *tambu* was something different. "You've read *Treasure Island*?" he asked me. "Well this is our Treasure Island. It is our treasure. If we didn't have *tambu,* we would not be Tolai; we would be a different people."

At Matupit, as we have seen, shell-money continues to be used in a wide variety of situations. At the same time, the evidence also suggests that it is rapidly declining in significance, transactions being increasingly monetized. The details on income presented in Table IV show that the total in *tambu* amounted to 103 fathoms. Of these, 69 were raised through a performance of the custom known as *a vavaleke,* and strictly speaking should not count as income. What happens on these occasions is that a pig is killed, cut up into small pieces of pork, and sold for *tambu,* all of those subscribing becoming linked in an elaborate set of debt-relationships. A further point that ought to be noted here is that the proportion of shell to cash in income derived from the sale of fish is very much lower than that which I worked out on the basis of the *vevedek.* Assuming that both sets of figures are reliable, I can only suggest that the divergence relates to the period covered by my budgets. At this time (April) the trap-season has more or less come to an end, and the egg season is only beginning. Cash from village activities is in short supply, resulting in a preference for cash over shell. At all events it is plain that at Matupit to-day the amounts of *tambu* entering the villages are relatively small.

This is further borne out by such data as I was able to collect on accumulated holdings of shell-money. These were not included under Savings in Table VI because I regarded them as insufficiently reliable. In some cases informants were unwilling to disclose the amounts they held, in others the mode of depositing *tambu* in the *vuna tarai* bank meant that informants genuinely did not know how much they held. None the less, it is interesting that among the younger men few claimed more than 40 fathoms, while of the elder men only one claimed more than 500. Compared with known holdings in other Tolai groups, these amounts are trifling.

The decline in the significance of *tambu* at Matupit is seen more strikingly in the qualitative evidence. There has been no *matamatan* (a large-scale rite associated with the cult of the *tubuan* and *duk duk*) at Matupit for many years. During my stay on the island the Elders discussed the matter on a number of occasions but their plans to "raise the *tubuan*" always foundered because of their inadequate resource in shell-money. For the same reason, the mortuary rites I witnessed at Matupit were usually brief and lacked the elaborate ceremonial I observed in other Tolai communities. On one occasion, following a *vevedek,* a number of the Elders initiated a discussion on the problem. They pointed out that their holdings were of old *tambu,* and no new *tambu* was flowing in. They then agreed that they should revive the custom of old of having a house for the storing of *tambu* at the *motonoi* itself: as *tambu* was acquired from the sale of fish from the traps it would gradually be bound into coils, serving as a reminder and an incentive to remain strong in the pursuit of *tambu.* But like their plans for "raising the *tubuan,*" this suggestion is likely to come to naught.

These discussions, together with other material I have presented, illustrate the value that many Matupi continue to attach to shell-money, but the whole position of *tambu* also illustrates many of the complexities at work within the present social system. The older men who wield authority in the village deplore the current poverty in shell-money. At the village meetings, which are a regular feature of the social life, they harangue the young men and exhort them to give up their idle and futile pursuits in the town for more rewarding work in the village. Yet, poor in *tambu* themselves as a result of the losses during the war, the Elders are unable to offer a more positive lead. They might conceivably have attempted to buy the natural shells for cash at their source of origin at Nakanai on the north coast of New Britain. This would have involved a very heavy expense which few could envisage, for the fact of the matter is that the Elders, too, are caught up in the struggle for cash, not simply for personal use, but for investment. Thus, under the direction of the Elders, many of the *umbene* fishing groups have neglected for some years the pursuit of *tambu* in order to raise cash exclusively for the building of a new church on which £3000 had already been spent, and which was still far from completion. Others again were looking to the future and were accumulating funds towards the purchase of transport.

The attitude of the younger people was perhaps even more complex. Men in regular employment have in fact few opportunities for those activities which produce *tambu.* Yet a number of them did find time in the evenings or at the weekends to prepare their traps for the *babau* season, or to plant gardens of groundnuts, now generally accepted as a pure *tambu* crop. Again, amongst those employed in some departments of the Administration who received rations in addition to a cash wage, many handed part to their mothers or other older women to sell for *tambu.* Yet all recognized that *tambu* could not compete with money, and there were some who said contemptuously: "What can you buy with *tambu?* You can't buy goods in a European store with shell-money, nor erect a modern-style house with it." Some of the more thoughtful Matupi, indeed, saw *tambu* as a symbol of a traditional social order which had to disappear. For these the pursuit of *tambu* was a distraction. It served to perpetuate the old way of life and the system of political authority that went with it, and so acted as a brake on their entry as full citizens into a wider society. One man in his late thirties with whom I was once having a long discussion in the vernacular on a range of modern social problems himself introduced the question of shell-money. After expounding his views he suddenly burst out: "*iau* hate *ra tambu.*" He used the English word, presumably being unable to find one in the vernacular sufficiently apt to express his feelings. Yet this same man had his own coil of shell-money which he stored with a classificatory mother's brother at Raluana because, as he told me on another occasion, he did not think it would be safe at Matupit. Contradictions of this kind are built into the very structure of modern Matupit: they are the product of opposing pulls operating in a situation of continuing change. Many Matupi would perhaps be happy to see the end of shell-money, but insofar as they continue to pursue certain traditional activities and remain linked by ties of interdependence with Tolai or other groups who insist upon the use of *tambu,* the need for shell-money persists. *Tambu* is sought for the payment of bride-wealth and for the proper obsequies of kinsmen, but it is also necessary for more mundane purposes. Other Tolai frequently insist upon payment in shell for certain types of foodstuff such as taro. Again, canoes are a necessity at Matupit; they are required not only for fishing but also for getting to and from the gardens on the mainland. Most Matupi canoes have to be imported from the nearby Duke of York Islands, where a person may be charged sums of up to 200 fathoms plus cash for a large canoe.

LAND, CONTINUITY AND CHANGE

Matupit to-day has many of the features of a peri-urban settlement. Space is confined, and houses are built close together. Matupit has its own churches and cemeteries, schools and village stores, and a large playing field where baseball and cricket are played in season. Each morning men and women leave the island by foot, bicycle or bus for their work in Rabaul, and only return in the evening. Many again go back to Rabaul at night to visit the cinema or seek the other diversions of the town. It was presumably conditions of this kind, already thirty years ago, which led Cilento to speak of Matupit as a community without semblance of native institutions. This view can be accepted even to-day as valid only within certain limits, for withal Matupit remains a distinctive Tolai settlement. Hamlets and village sections still correspond to the divisions on German maps drawn at the turn of the century, and the ownership of these lands remains vested in local matrilineages. The rules of marriage, including the rule of moiety exogamy and other prohibitions on unions between certain close cognates, are still rigidly enforced. A high proportion of marriages are still intra-island, and these cement the already complex set of ties which link together local lineages. Matupi interact more closely, and quarrel more bitterly, amongst themselves than with outsiders, but what is more important they regulate much of their behaviour in these relationships by reference to traditional Tolai norms and customs.

If this is a valid view of the situation, how can we explain this high degree of structural continuity and cultural persistence in a group so exposed to external pressures towards change? Further, since persistence occurs here within a framework of change, what part does it play in the continuing process of change itself?

One hypothesis which suggests itself is that, paradoxically, the very stability of Tolai institutions is a function of the unsettled conditions that have prevailed in the area since first contact with Europeans. On this view, their experience of different administrations, all of which have proved unstable and unreliable, would have bred a deep-rooted suspicion of all alien groups, and the feeling that security lay ultimately in maintaining their own way of life. This argument would seem to carry a certain amount of weight. Many Matupi Elders, for example, were noticeably unenthusiastic about the need for improved educational services on which the younger people were so insistent. This was attributed to the fact that in their own youth they had received training in the German school at Namanula only to find under the Australian regime that there were no jobs for them, and that their education had been wasted. Yet it would be a mistake to explain persistence simply in terms of withdrawal. The weakness of this view is that it does not take sufficient account of the fact that persistence is only one aspect of a process of adaptation to continually changing circumstances. What then were the circumstances to which the Tolai were required to adapt themselves? And how are these circumstances themselves changing?

For the Germans, the value of the Gazelle Peninsula lay chiefly in the opportunities it offered for establishing a flourishing plantation economy centered on the production of copra. Already before the German annexation the Tolai were selling their coconuts to traders, but now they were encouraged to increase considerably their plantings of palms. At the same time, the establishment of European plantations, and the introduction of indentured plantation labour from outside the Gazelle, created an enlarged market for foodstuffs. The response of the Tolai again was to increase production. It is worth noting that the reaction at Madang and elsewhere to these new developments was different; it is reported that the natives of Kaiser Wilhelmsland, far from increasing production, were hardly planting enough fruits, vegetables and bananas to meet their own household needs (Blum, 1900, p. 139). The explanation of this difference seems to lie, at least in part, in the kind of drives built into the indigenous social system of the Tolai. Thus it appears that so insistent were they on payment in *tambu* for their coconuts that traders were compelled to acquire supplies of shell-money from Nakanai. This situation had adverse effects upon trade, and in 1902 the Administration felt it necessary to introduce an ordinance making the use of *tambu* illegal in transactions between Europeans and natives.

For many years, then, the economy of the Gazelle Peninsula has been built around the coconut palm.[8] As a cash crop the palm has a number of advantages. It makes no great demands on time and labour. Amongst the Tolai the nuts are not gathered on the trees, as in some other areas, but are simply collected where they have fallen on the ground. Again, once planted it requires relatively little attention, thus freeing men for other activities. Finally, the palm is long-lived, yielding nuts for 60 years and more. Through the sale of coconuts and other produce the Tolai were thus able to participate in the new cash economy without being wholly absorbed into it. Economic development in the area posed no immediate incompatibility with the maintenance of the traditional way of life. As their wealth accumulated they were able to buy various commodities formerly denied or unknown to them. But they continued to live on the land, and draw their livelihood from it. Participation in the cash economy, indeed, buttressed the traditional system rather than disrupted it. For example, the palm, because of its longevity, might only be planted on lands to which one had legal entitlement as a member of a local descent group. This in turn served to perpetuate the system of political authority based on the control and administration of descent group lands and funds by the lineage elders. Elders would put their new wealth to the service of traditional ends and enhance their reputation and influence by organizing large-scale dances and other ceremonial activities. Even when Tolai began to go out to work, this did not have the disruptive effects that have sometimes been attributed to wage labour in other parts of the world. On the contrary, wage labour provided new sources of wealth in cash without breaking a man's ties with his village. What is more, the situation on the Gazelle was such that a man could operate simultaneously in the different sectors of the economy. While he was absent for a short period in New Guinea his interests in the land were protected by the other members of his *vuna tarai,* and if he worked in Rabaul he could continue to participate in the economic activities of the village.

In certain respects the situation I have just outlined remains true of Matupit even to-day. There, as we have seen, the people have retained their links with the land. Activities clearly recognizable as traditional still play an important part in their economic life, and these are organized through traditional groupings. However, it is also clear that this kind of adjustment must be closely bound up with the question of land resources. With the increasing drive towards even greater wealth, pressure on the land is intensified. In these circumstances, the attachment to land, which had hitherto provided the very basis of structural continuity, now introduces sources of incompatibility into the social system which appear to be tilting the balance in the direction of further change.

For the Matupi the question of land is already seen as their most critical social problem, and I hope to examine it more fully in a separate paper. Here I may merely repeat the observation made earlier that the proximity of Matupit to Rabaul means not only that the people cannot extend their area of cultivation but that the expansion of the town itself poses a continuous threat to Matupi rights of user. A number of factors further exacerbate the situation. The rapid rate of population increase in the post-war period poses a serious problem for the future (Epstein, 1962); more immediate is the heightened clamour for land set off by the introduction of a new cash crop in the form of cocoa. Nor is it simply that land is in short supply. The very persistence of the traditional system of land tenure becomes, in the changed circumstances, a source of aggravation. At Matupit the principle of matrilineal descent is associated with virilocal marriage and patrilocal residence, and operates to produce gross inequalities in the distribution of holdings. With the high degree of residential continuity at Matupit over the past three or four generations, there are now a considerable number of men who have no legal entitlement to land at Matupit. In the past the problem was less acute since a man also had claims on his father's group for land to meet his subsistence requirements, with a possible option to purchase the land on his father's death. Now, with increasing pressure on land, there is less readiness to sell on the part of the father's descent group; and, in any case, such plots would be inadequate for cash cropping on any substantial scale.

The extent of the problem of land shortage is masked to some extent by the high proportion of men in wage employment in Rabaul and on the New Guinea mainland, but it is not thereby alleviated. Urban workers maintain their ties with the village and continue to participate in its economy. As I sought to bring out in the discussion of income and expenditure, this is the only way by which Matupi workers can take full advantage of the opportunities for employment in the town. At the same time they are also keen to have land on which to grow cash crops. Some are fortunate in having land at Matupit so that they can combine these pursuits; some have been able to exploit ties of kinship with other Tolai communities to acquire blocks of land elsewhere; but these are a minority. In these circumstances the continued attachment to the land pulls the Matupi in opposed directions at the same time, and produces apparent inconsistencies in their behaviour. Thus in one instance where the Administration had been bringing pressure on the Elders to agree to the lease of certain lands, the younger men announced at the village meeting their rejection of the authority of the Elders. The Elders, they said, had betrayed them by agreeing to the acquisition of the land by the Administration. Here the revolt was raised in defence of rights which the young men claimed under the traditional system. In other situations the younger men argued that the only way out of the present dilemma lay in the scrapping of the traditional system of land-holding, and its replacement by some form of individual tenure. This of course would involve the passing of the authority of the Elders in whom control of the lands at present rests.

The position of the urban workers also introduces other sources of strain into the present workings of the social system. The post-war period saw a considerable step-up in the programme of secular education among the Tolai; many Matupi workers are now employed in more responsible positions than in the past, and earn relatively high wages. The result is, as the earlier analysis demonstrates, that wealth and political authority are no longer concurrent. Following the losses of the last war the older men have become poor both in cash and shell-money, and the wealth of the community, measured in cash, is mostly in the hands of the younger men in regular wage employment in Rabaul and elsewhere, who enjoy little influence or prestige in the village. But the really significant point is that wealth in shell and cash are put to very different uses. Traditionally, Elders put their wealth in *tambu* to use in organizing *balaguan,* large feasts which commemorated the deceased of the *vuna tarai* or in "raising the *tubuan.*" These activities involved heavy expenditure and the distribution of large stores of food and shell-money amongst the participants, but since they imposed at the same time an obligation to make return in due course they also gave rise to an elaborate series of debt relationships. The big man therefore was one to whom many people were beholden, and this in turn was the source of such political authority as existed traditionally on the Gazelle Peninsula. Wealth in cash, however, is not put to these purposes. As we have seen, cash expenditure amongst urban workers is for personal and private ends; for example, building a house and furnishing it in the European manner so far as means permit. There is, therefore, in this situation a tendency towards a power vacuum. There are many Elders at Matupit but there are no big men whose influence and authority are acknowledged beyond the range of their own local matrilineage.

These various strains within the social system find expression in the atmosphere of social unrest which marks the Gazelle Peninsula at present, and poses the need for further adaptation and change. The unrest is manifested in the spate of curious rumours that were circulating in the area during the period of field work and in the rioting that occurred at Rabaul shortly afterwards. The drive towards further change is reflected in the heightened political awareness amongst Tolai in recent years. Many have developed aspirations which can no longer be satisfied within a traditional politico-economic framework. They have come to see that many of their problems can no longer be solved at the level of the local community. This is probably more evident still at Matupit than elsewhere. At Matupit the nature of the problems, and the closer links which have been forged with the wider society, are reflected in a growing shift in interest and debate amongst the younger men towards national politics. On this view, it is not without significance that the first public expression by a Tolai of the view that New Guinea was ready for self-government, made on the occasion of an official visit by the Administrator to Rabaul, should have been voiced by a

resident of Matupit. Nor was it surprising, therefore, when a little later in
the first elections for the reconstituted Legislative Council at Port Moresby,
which on the Gazelle were conducted through the Native Local Government
Councils acting as electoral colleges, a number of Matupi workers should
have nominated and given their support to a Papuan on the grounds that he
spoke good English, had worked for many years in the Administration and
had some understanding of its workings, and so was a better qualified
candidate than any Tolai they knew.

APPENDIX

ITEMS OF STOCK CARRIED IN A MATUPI VILLAGE STORE

Item	Quantity Purchased
Mackerel pike (15 oz.)	4 dozen tins
" " (7 oz.)	4 " "
" " (5 oz.)	8½ " "
Mackerel (7 oz.)	2 " "
Ideal Milk	4 " "
Nestle's milk	1 " "
Corned beef	4 " "
Curry powder	6 packets
Toilet soap	1 dozen bars
Gillette razor blades	20 packets of 5
Matches	3 packets
Cigarettes ("Three Cats")	100 packets of 10
Cigarettes ("Craven A")	200 packets of 10
Pipe tobacco	1 dozen tins
Torch batteries	1 dozen
Washing soap	1 dozen bars
Exercise books	1 dozen
Pencils	1 "
Rulers	1 "
Twist tobacco	26
Rice	1 bag (50 lb.)
Sugar	1 bag (50 lb.)
Biscuits	1 case
Sweets	4 dozen
Kerosene	1 drum (44 gallons)
Fireworks	1 box

NOTES

1. The field work on which this paper is based was carried out in the period
November, 1959, to September, 1960, and April to June, 1961, under a Research
Fellowship from the Australian National University, Canberra. For critical comments on earlier drafts of the paper I am grateful to Professor Raymond Firth of
the London School of Economics, and to my colleagues in the Department of Social
Anthropology, University of Manchester.
2. The use of the term "Tolai" as a group name is a recent innovation; in the

past there was no single name for the various communities living on the Gazelle Peninsula. The expression "Tolai" itself is used in the vernacular of the Gazelle as a mode of address or greeting, usually where the kinship relationship or personal name is not known. It corresponds roughly to the use of "mate" or "comrade" in other cultures. The first reference to its use as a group designation that I have been able to discover occurs in an item contributed to the *Rabaul Times* by a Wau Correspondent in the mid-1930's. This leads me to believe that the modern usage came into being as a categorizing device, non-Rabaul natives seizing on the use of the greeting to designate a distinctive category within the heterogeneous native population then gathering on the New Guinea goldfields (cf. Mitchell, 1956). The term "Tolai" has now been fully accepted by the people of the Gazelle Peninsula.

3. The final "t" is usually dropped when referring to the people of the island, or when the term is used as an adjective.

4. I am indebted for this comment to Dr. H. C. Brookfield, Department of Geography, Australian National University.

5. Some time before my arrival on the island the Agricultural Department had sought to carry out a census of palms, but the Matupi refused to co-operate, and the attempt had to be abandoned.

6. Gardening activities will be discussed more fully in a separate paper on land and politics.

7. In order to meet the problems posed by mounting land pressure, now being exacerbated by the demands for larger holdings for cash crops, the Administration embarked upon an experimental re-settlement scheme at the Vudal on land acquired from the Bainings. This scheme, begun in 1953, soon ran into many difficulties and although in the beginning large numbers of Matupi applied for blocks of land there, by 1960 only a few had persisted, and were successfully working the land. A second scheme at the Warongoi appears to have been more successful. This was designed to help more those Tolai outside the area of the Rabaul Native Local Government Council, and only two Matupi have acquired blocks there. A small number of Matupi, however, have been able to exploit kinship and other links to acquire land for cocoa gardens in other localities where land shortage is less acute.

8. In the plantation economy of New Guinea in the pre-war period 231,922 of the 239,370 acres were planted in coconuts. Four-fifths of the plantations were on the Gazelle Peninsula and New Ireland (Reed, 1942, p. 218).

REFERENCES

Belshaw, C. S. (1957): *The Great Village,* London, Routledge and Kegan Paul.

Blum, H. (1900): *Neu-Guinea und der Bismarckarchipel,* Berlin, Schoenfeldt.

Brown, Rev. G. (1908): *Autobiography,* London, Hodder and Stoughton.

Bürger, F. (1923): *Unter den Kannibalen der Südsee,* Dresden, Deutsche Buchwerkstätten.

Cilento, Sir R. (1932): "The Value of Medical Services in Relation to Depopulation," *Medical Journal of Australia,* pp. 480-3.

Danks, Rev. B. (1887): "On the Shell-Money of New Britain," *Journal of the Royal Anthropological Institute,* XVII, pp. 305-17.

Epstein, A. L., and T. S. (1962): "A Note on Population in Two Tolai Settlements," *Journal of the Polynesian Society,* LXXI, pp. 70-82.

Epstein, T. S. (1961): "A Study of Rabaul Market," *The Australian Journal of Agricultural Economics,* V, pp. 1-18.

Epstein, T. S. (1963a): "European Contact and Tolai Economic Growth," *Economic Development and Cultural Change* (forthcoming).

Epstein, T. S. (1963b): "Personal Capital Formation among the Tolai," in *Capital, Saving and Credit in Peasant Societies,* ed. by R. Firth and B. Yamey, London, Allen and Unwin (forthcoming).

Lyng, J. (1914): *Government Gazette,* Rabaul, November 15.

Mitchell, J. C. (1956): *The Kalela Dance,* Manchester, Rhodes-Livingstone, Paper 27.

Powell, W. (1884): *Wanderings in a Wild Country,* London, Sampson Low.

REED, S. W. (1942): *The Making of Modern New Guinea*, Philadelphia, Memoirs of the American Philosophical Society, No. 18.

ROMILLY, H. H. (1887): "The Islands of the New Britain Group," *Proceedings of the Royal Geographical Society*, IX, pp. 1-15.

ROWLEY, C. D. (1958): *The Australians in German New Guinea*, Melbourne, Melbourne University Press.

SALISBURY, R. F. (1962): "Early Stages of Economic Development in New Guinea," *Journal of the Polynesian Society*, LXXI, pp. 328-40.

WATSON, W. (1958): *Tribal Cohesion in a Money Economy*, Manchester, Manchester University Press.

WILSON, G. (1941): *The Economics of Detribalization*, Rhodes-Livingstone, Papers 5 and 6.

FURTHER READINGS

There are several excellent books on cargo cults. Lawrence's *Road Belong Cargo* should be consulted, as should Burridge's *Mambu* and *New Heaven, New Earth*. In addition, there are Jarvie's *The Revolution in Anthropology,* Worsley's *The Trumpet Shall Sound,* Schwartz's *The Paliau Movement in the Admiralty Islands,* and Cochrane's *Big Men and Cargo Cults*. Articles on cargo movements of particular interest include R. M. Berndt's "A Cargo Movement in the Eastern Central Highlands of New Guinea," Salisbury's "An 'Indigenous' New Guinea Cult," Jarvie's "Theories of Cargo Cults," and Stanner's "On the Interpretation of Cargo Cults."

There are countless articles dealing with various aspects of change other than those involving cargo cults. For a few of special interest or relevance, see Belshaw's "Social Consequences of the Mt. Lamington Eruption," C. H. Berndt's "Social and Cultural Change in New Guinea," R. M. Berndt's "Reaction to Contact in the Eastern Highlands of New Guinea," van der Kroef's "Patterns of Cultural Change in Three Primitive Societies" and "Culture Contact and Culture Conflict in Western New Guinea," Maher's "From Cannibal Raid to Copra Kompani," O'Brien and Ploeg's "Acculturation Movements Among the Western Dani," Langness' "Notes on the Bena Council," Pospisil's "Social Change and Primitive Law," Salisbury's "Early Stages of Economic Development in New Guinea," Scheffler's "The Social Consequences of Peace on Choiseul Island," and Valentine's "Social Status, Political Power, and Native Responses to European Influence in Oceania."

For books dealing with change, see Belshaw's *Changing Melanesia* and *The Great Village*. There are, in addition, Mead's influential *New Lives for Old,* Hogbin's *Transformation Scene,* and Kouwenhoven's *Nimboran*. For more recent works of special relevance to the current situation in Melanesia, there are Maher's *New Men of Papua,* Rowley's *The New Guinea Villager,* and Fisk's *New Guinea on the Threshold*. For an interesting personal account of what it is like to leap virtually from the stone age into the modern political arena, see Kiki's *Kiki: Ten Thousand Years in a Lifetime*.

BIBLIOGRAPHY

ALLEN, M. R., 1967, *Male Cults and Secret Initiations in Melanesia*. Melbourne: Melbourne University Press.

Anthropological Forum, 1965, 1966, 1967, various articles on Melanesian political organization.

ARMSTRONG, W. E., 1924a, "Rossel Island Money: A Unique Monetary System." *Economic Journal,* 34: 423-429.

1924b, "Shell Money from Rossel Island, Papua." *Man,* 24: 161-162.

AUFENANGER, HEINRICH, 1959, "The War-Magic Houses in the Wahgi Valley and Adjacent Areas (New Guinea)." *Anthropos,* 54: 1-26.

1960, "The Kanggi Spirit in the Central Highlands of New Guinea." *Anthropos,* 55: 671-688.

1961, "Descent Totemism and Magical Practices in the Wahgi Valley (Central New Guinea)." *Anthropos,* 56: 281-328.

AUSTRALIAN NATIONAL UNIVERSITY, 1968, *An Ethnographic Bibliography of New Guinea*. Canberra: National University Press.

BARNES, J. A., 1967, "Agnation Among the Enga: A Review Article." *Oceania,* 38: 33-43.

BARRAU, J., 1958, *Subsistence Agriculture in Melanesia*. Honolulu: Bernice P. Bishop Museum Bulletin No. 219.

BATESON, GREGORY, 1958, *Naven*. Stanford, Calif.: Stanford University Press.

BELL, F. L. S., 1937-38, "Courtship and Marriage Among the Tanga." *Oceania,* 8: 403-418.

1955, "The Role of the Individual in Tangan Society." *Journal of the Polynesian Society,* 64: 281-291.

BELSHAW, C. S., 1950-51, "Social Consequences of the Mt. Lamington Eruption." *Oceania,* 21: 241-252.

1954, *Changing Melanesia*. Melbourne and Wellington: Oxford University Press.

1957, *The Great Village: The Economic and Social Welfare of Hanuabada, an Urban Community in Papua*. London: Routledge & Kegan Paul.

BERNDT, C. H., 1957, "Social and Cultural Change in New Guinea: Communication and Views about 'Other People.' " *Sociologus,* 7: 38-57.

BERNDT, R. M., 1952-53, "A Cargo Movement in the Eastern Central Highlands of New Guinea." *Oceania,* 23: 40-65, 137-158, 202-234.

1953-54, 1954-55, "Reaction to Contact in the Eastern Highlands of New Guinea." *Oceania,* 24(3): 190-228; (4): 255-274, 25: 231-223.

1955, "Interdependence and Conflict in the Eastern Central Highlands." *Man,* 55: 105-107.

1964, "Warfare in the New Guinea Highlands." *American Anthropologist,* Special Publication, Part 2, 66: 183-203.

BLACKWOOD, BEATRICE, 1935, *Both Sides of Buka Passage*. Oxford: Clarendon Press.

373

BOWMAN, R. G., "Northern Melanesia: New Guinea and the Bismarck Archipelago." In Freeman, ed., 1951. Pp. 157-172.

BROMLEY, MYRON, 1960, "A Preliminary Report on Law Among the Grand Valley Dani of Netherlands New Guinea." *Nieuw-Guinea Studien*, 4: 235-259.

BROOKFIELD, H. C., 1964, "The Ecology of Highland Settlement: Some Suggestions." *American Anthropologist*, Special Publication, Part 2, 66: 20-38.

BROOKFIELD, H. C., AND PAULA BROWN, 1963, *Struggle for Land: Agriculture and Group Territories Among the Chimbu of the New Guinea Highlands*. Melbourne: Oxford University Press.

BROOKFIELD, H. C., AND D. HART, 1966, "Rainfall in the Tropical Southwest Pacific." Research School of Pacific Studies, Department of Geography Publication G/3, Australian National University.

BROOKFIELD, H. C., AND J. P. WHITE, 1968, "Revolution or Evolution in the Prehistory of the New Guinea Highlands: A Seminar Report." *Ethnology*, 7: 43-52.

BROWN, PAULA, 1960, "Chimbu Tribes: Political Organization in the Eastern Highlands of New Guinea." *Southwestern Journal of Anthropology*, 16: 22-35.

1961, "Chimbu Death Payments." *Journal of the Royal Anthropological Institute of Great Britain and Ireland*, 91: 77-96.

1963, "From Anarchy to Satrapy." *American Anthropologist*, 65: 1-15.

BURRIDGE, K. O. L., 1958–59a, "Adoption in Tangu." *Oceania*, 29: 185-199.

1958–59b, "Marriage in Tangu." *Oceania*, 29: 44-61.

1959–60, "Siblings in Tangu." *Oceania*, 30: 128-154.

1960, *Mambu: A Melanesian Millennium*. London: Methuen.

1969, *New Heaven, New Earth: A Study of Millenarian Activities*. Oxford: Blackwell.

COCHRANE, GLYNN, 1970, *Big Men and Cargo Cults*. Oxford: Clarendon Press.

COULTER, J. W., "Eastern Melanesia." In Freeman, ed., 1951. Pp. 173-204.

DAVENPORT, WILLIAM, 1959, "Nonunilinear Descent and Descent Groups." *American Anthropologist*, 61: 557-572.

1964, "Social Structure of Santa Cruz Island." In W. H. Goodenough, ed., *Explorations in Cultural Anthropology*. New York: McGraw-Hill. Pp. 57-94.

DELEPREVANCHE, M., 1967, "Descent, Residence, and Leadership in the New Guinea Highlands." *Oceania*, 38: 134-158, 163-189.

EPSTEIN, A. L., 1964, "Variation and Social Structure: Local Organization on the Island of Matupit, New Britain." *Oceania*, 35: 1-25.

1968, "Power, Politics and Leadership: Some Central African and Melanesian Contrasts." In M. J. Swartz, ed., *Local Level Politics*. Chicago: Aldine. Pp. 53-68.

FIRTH, RAYMOND, 1936, *We, the Tikopia: A Sociological Study of Kinship in Primitive Polynesia*. London: Allen & Unwin.

1957, "A Note on Descent Groups in Polynesia." *Man*, 57: 4-8.

FISK, E. K., 1968, *New Guinea on the Threshold*. Pittsburgh: University of Pittsburgh Press.

FORTUNE, REO, 1935, *Manus Religion: An Ethnological Study of the Manus Natives of the Admiralty Islands*. Memoir No. 3. Philadelphia: American Philosophical Society.

1939, "Arapesh Warfare." *American Anthropologist*, 41: 22-41.

1947a, "Law and Force in Papuan Societies." *American Anthropologist*, 49: 244-259.

1947b, "The Rules of Relationship Behavior in One Variety of Primitive Warfare." *Man*, 47: 108-110.

FOSBERG, F. R., ed., 1963, *Man's Place in the Island Ecosystem: A Symposium*. Honolulu: Bernice P. Bishop Museum Press.

FREEMAN, O. W., ed., 1951, *Geography of the Pacific*. New York: Wiley.

GARDNER, ROBERT, AND K. G. HEIDER, 1968, *Gardens of War*. New York: Random House.

GLASSE, R. M., 1958–59, "The Huli Descent System: A Preliminary Account." *Oceania,* 29: 171-184.

1959, "Revenge and Redress Among the Huli: A Preliminary Account." *Mankind,* 5: 273-288.

GLASSE, R. M., AND M. J. MEGGITT, eds., 1969, *Pigs, Pearlshells and Women: Marriage in the New Guinea Highlands*. Englewood Cliffs, N.J.: Prentice-Hall.

GOODENOUGH, W. H., 1955, "A Problem in Malayo-Polynesian Social Organization." *American Anthropologist,* 57: 71-83.

1962, "Kindred and Hamlet in Lakalai, New Britain." *Ethnology,* 1: 5-12.

HARDING, T. G., 1967a, "Ecological and Technical Factors in a Melanesian Gardening Cycle." *Mankind,* 6: 403-408.

1967b, *Voyagers of the Vitiaz Strait: A Study of a New Guinea Trade System.* Seattle: University of Washington Press.

HARRIS, MARVIN, 1968, *The Rise of Anthropological Theory*. New York: Crowell.

HOGBIN, IAN, 1935–36, "Adoption in Wogeo." *Journal of the Polynesian Society,* 44: 208-215; 45: 17-38.

1939, *Experiments in Civilization: The Effects of European Culture on a Native Community of the Solomon Islands*. London: Routledge.

1940–41, "The Father Chooses His Heir: A Family Dispute Over Succession in Wogeo, New Guinea." *Oceania,* 11: 1-39.

1944–45, "Marriage in Wogeo, New Guinea." *Oceania,* 15: 324-352.

1945–46, "Puberty to Marriage: A Study of the Sexual Life of the Natives of Wogeo, New Guinea." *Oceania,* 16: 185-209.

1946–47, "Sex and Marriage in Busama, N.E. New Guinea," *Oceania,* 17: 119-138, 225-247.

1951, *Transformation Scene: The Changing Culture of a New Guinea Village.* London: Routledge & Kegan Paul.

1963, *Kinship and Marriage in a New Guinea Village*. London: Athlone Press.

1970, *The Island of Menstruating Men*. Scranton: Chandler Publishing Company.

HOGBIN, IAN, AND C. H. WEDGWOOD, 1952–53, "Local Grouping in Melanesia." *Oceania,* 23: 241-276; 24: 58-76.

HOWARD, ALAN, ed., 1971, *Polynesia: Readings on a Culture Area*. Scranton: Chandler Publishing Company.

HOWLETT, D. R., 1967, *A Geography of Papua and New Guinea*. Melbourne: Nelson.

JARVIE, I. C., 1963–64, "Theories of Cargo Cults: A Critical Analysis." *Oceania,* 34: 1-31, 108-136.

1964, *The Revolution in Anthropology*. London: Routledge & Kegan Paul.

KABERRY, PHYLLIS, 1941–42, "Law and Political Organization of the Abelam Tribe, New Guinea." *Oceania,* 12: 79-95, 209-225, 331-363.

1967, "The Plasticity of New Guinea Kinship." In Maurice Freedman, ed., *Social Organization: Essays Presented to Raymond Firth*. Chicago: Aldine. Pp. 105-123.

KEESING, R. M., 1966, "Kwaio Kindreds." *Southwestern Journal of Anthropology,* 22: 346-353.

1967, "Statistical Models and Decision Models of Social Structure: A Kwaio Case." *Ethnology,* 6: 1-16.

1968, "Non-unilineal Descent and Contextual Definition of Status: The Kwaio Evidence." *American Anthropologist,* 70: 82-84.

KENNEDY, T. F., 1966, *A Descriptive Atlas of the Pacific Islands*. Wellington: A. H. and A. W. Reed.

KIKI, A. M., 1968, *Kiki: Ten Thousand Years in a Lifetime.* New York: Praeger.
KOUWENHOVEN, W. J. H., 1955, *Nimboran: A Study of Social Change and Socio-Economic Development in a New Guinea Society.* The Hague: J. N. Voorhoeve.
KROEF, J. M. VAN DER, 1952, "Some Head-Hunting Traditions of Southern New Guinea." *American Anthropologist,* 54: 221-235, 576-577.
  1957, "Patterns of Cultural Change in Three Primitive Societies." *Social Research,* 24: 427-456.
  1959, "Culture Contact and Culture Conflict in Western New Guinea." *Anthropological Quarterly,* 32: 134-160.
LANE, R., AND B. LANE, 1956, "A Reinterpretation of the Anomalous Six-Section Marriage System of Ambrym, New Hebrides." *Southwestern Journal of Anthropology,* 12: 406-414.
LANGNESS, L. L., 1963, "Notes on the Bena Council, Eastern Highlands, New Guinea." *Oceania,* 33: 151-170.
  1964, "Some Problems in the Conceptualization of Highlands Social Structures." *American Anthropologist,* Special Publication, Part 2, 66: 162-182.
  1965, "Hysterical Psychosis in the New Guinea Highlands: A Bena Bena Example." *Psychiatry,* 28: 258-277.
  1967, "Sexual Antagonism in the New Guinea Highlands: A Bena Bena Example." *Oceania,* 37: 161-177.
  1968, "Bena Bena Political Organization." *Anthropological Forum,* 2: 180-198.
  1971, "Political Organization." In *Encyclopedia of Papua–New Guinea.* Melbourne: Melbourne University Press.
LANGNESS, L. L., AND THOMAS GLADWIN, in press; "Oceania." In FRANCIS L. K. HSU, ed., *Psychological Anthropology.* Rev. ed. Homewood, Ill.: Dorsey Press.
LAWRENCE PETER, 1964, *Road Belong Cargo.* Manchester: Manchester University Press.
LAWRENCE, PETER, AND M. J. MEGGITT, 1965, *Gods, Ghosts and Men in Melanesia: Some Religions of Australian New Guinea and the New Hebrides.* Melbourne: Oxford University Press.
LEEDEN, A. C. VAN DER, 1960, "Social Structure in New Guinea." *Bijdragen tot de taal-, land-, en volkenkunde,* 116: 119-149,
LUZBETAK, L. J., 1954, "The Socio-religious Significance of a New Guinea Pig Festival." *Anthropological Quarterly,* 27: 59-80, 102-128.
MAHER, R. F., 1961, *New Men of Papua: A Study in Culture Change.* Madison: University of Wisconsin Press.
  1967, "From Cannibal Raid to Copra Kompani: Changing Patterns of Koriki Politics." *Ethnology,* 6: 309-331.
MALINOWSKI, BRONISLAW, 1916, "Baloma: The Spirits of the Dead in the Trobriand Islands." *Journal of the Royal Anthropological Institute of Great Britain and Ireland,* 46: 353-430.
  1920, "Kula: The Circulating Exchange of Valuables in the Archipelagoes of Eastern New Guinea." *Man,* 51: 97-105.
  1922, *Argonauts of the Western Pacific: An Account of Native Enterprise and Adventure in the Archipelago of Melanesian New Guinea.* London: George Routledge & Kegan Paul.
  1927, *Sex and Repression in Savage Society.* London: George Routledge & Kegan Paul.
  1929, *The Sexual Life of Savages in Northwestern Melanesia: An Ethnographic Account of Courtship, Marriage, and Family Life Among the Natives of the Trobriand Islands, British New Guinea.* New York: Eugenics Publishing Company.

1935, *Coral Gardens and Their Magic: A Study of the Methods of Tilling the Soil and of Agricultural Rites in the Trobriand Islands.* London: Allen & Unwin.

1948, *Magic, Science and Religion and Other Essays.* Glencoe, Ill.: Free Press.

MATTHIESSEN, PETER, 1962, *Under the Mountain Wall: A Chronicle of Two Seasons in the Stone Age.* New York: Viking.

McARTHUR, M., 1967, "Analysis of the Genealogy of a Mae Enga Clan." *Oceania,* 37: 281-285,

MEAD, MARGARET, 1931, *Growing Up in New Guinea.* New York: Morrow.

1935, *Sex and Temperament in Three Primitive Societies.* London: George Routledge & Sons.

1956, *New Lives for Old.* New York: Morrow.

1968, *The Mountain Arapesh: Volume 1, The Record of Unabelin with Rorschach Analyses.* New York: Natural History Press.

MEGGITT, M. J., 1962, "Dream Interpretation Among the Mae Enga of New Guinea." *Southwestern Journal of Anthropology,* 18: 216-229.

1964, "Male-Female Relationships in the Highlands of Australian New Guinea." *American Anthropologist,* Special Publication, Part 2, 66: 204-224.

1965, *The Lineage System of the Mae Enga.* New York: Barnes & Noble.

1967, "The Pattern of Leadership Among the Mae Enga of New Guinea." *Anthropological Forum,* 2: 20-35.

NEWMAN, P. L., 1962a, "Sorcery, Religion and the Man." *Natural History,* 71: 20-29.

1962b, "Supernaturalism and Ritual Among the Gururumba." Ph.D. dissertation, Department of Anthropology, University of Washington, Seattle.

1964, "Religious Belief and Ritual in a New Guinea Society." *American Anthropologist,* Special Publication, Part 2, 66: 257-272.

O'BRIEN, D. A., AND A. PLOEG, 1964, "Acculturation Movements Among the Western Dani." *American Anthropologist,* Special Publication, Part 2, 66: 281-292.

OLIVER, D. L., 1955, *A Solomon Island Society: Kinship and Leadership Among the Siuai of Bougainville.* Cambridge: Harvard University Press.

PACIFIC PUBLICATIONS, 1968, *The Pacific Islands Yearbook and Who's Who.* Sydney: Pacific Publications.

POSPISIL, LEOPOLD, 1958a, *Kapauka Papuans and Their Law.* New Haven: Yale University Publications in Anthropology No. 54.

1958b, "Kapauka Political Structure." In *Systems of Political Control and Bureaucracy in Human Societies.* Seattle: American Ethnological Society. Pp. 9-22.

1958c, "Social Change and Primitive Law: Consequences of a Papuan Legal Case." *American Anthropologist,* 60: 832-837.

1963, *Kapauka Papuan Economy.* New Haven: Yale University Publications in Anthropology No. 67.

POUWER, J., 1960, " 'Loosely Structured Societies' in Netherlands New Guinea." *Bijdragen tot de taal-, land-, en volkenkunde,* 116: 109-118.

1964, "A Social System in the Star Mountains: Toward a Reorientation of the Study of Social Systems." *American Anthropologist,* Special Publication, Part 2, 66: 133-162.

1966, "Structure and Flexibility in a New Guinea Society." *Bijdragen tot de taal-, land-, en volkenkunde,* 122: 158-169.

POWDERMAKER, HORTENSE, 1931–32, "Mortuary Rites in New Ireland (Bismarck Archipelago)." *Oceania,* 2: 26-43.

POWELL, H. A., 1960, "Competitive Leadership in Trobriand Political Organization." *Journal of the Royal Anthropological Institute of Great Britain and Ireland,* 90: 118-145.

RAPPAPORT, R. A., 1967, *Pigs for the Ancestors: Ritual in the Ecology of a New Guinea People*. New Haven: Yale University Press.

READ, K. E., 1949–50, "The Political System of the Ngarawapum." *Oceania*, 20: 185-223.

1954, "Marriage Among the Gahuku-Gama of the Eastern Central Highlands, New Guinea." *South Pacific*, 7: 864-870.

1954–55, "Morality and the Concept of the Person Among the Gahuku-Gama." *Oceania*, 25: 233-282.

1959, "Leadership and Consensus in a New Guinea Society." *American Anthropologist*, 61: 425-436.

1965, *The High Valley*. New York: Scribner.

REAY, MARIE, 1959, *The Kuma: Freedom and Conformity in the New Guinea Highlands*. Melbourne: Melbourne University Press.

ROWLEY, C. D., 1966, *The New Guinea Villager: The Impact of Colonial Rule on Primitive Society and Economy*. New York: Praeger.

RYAN, D'ARCY J., 1955–56, "Clan Organization in the Mendi Valley." *Oceania*, 26: 79-90.

1958–59, "Clan Formation in the Mendi Valley." *Oceania*, 29: 257-289.

SAHLINS, M. D., 1963, "Poor Man, Rich Man, Big Man, Chief: Political Types in Melanesia and Polynesia." *Comparative Studies in Society and History*, 5: 285-303.

SALISBURY, R. F., 1956, "Unilineal Descent Groups in the New Guinea Highlands." *Man*, 56: 2-7.

1958, "An 'Indigenous' New Guinea Cult." *Kroeber Anthropological Society Papers*, 18: 67-78.

1962a, "Early Stages of Economic Development in New Guinea." *Journal of the Polynesian Society*, 71: 328-339.

1962b, *From Stone to Steel: Economic Consequences of a Technological Change in New Guinea*. Melbourne: Melbourne University Press.

1964, "Despotism and Australian Administration in the New Guinea Highlands." *American Anthropologist*, Special Publication, Part 2, 66: 225-239.

1966, "Politics and Shell-Money Finance in New Britain." In Marc J. Swartz, Victor W. Turner, and Arthur Tuden, eds., *Political Anthropology*. Chicago: Aldine.

SCHEFFLER, H. W., 1964, "The Social Consequences of Peace on Choiseul Island." *Ethnology*, 3: 398-403.

1965, *Choiseul Island Social Structure*. Berkeley and Los Angeles: University of California Press.

1966, "Ancestor Worship in Anthropology: Or Observations on Descent and Descent Groups." *Current Anthropology*, 7: 541-551.

SCHWARTZ, THEODORE, 1962, *The Paliau Movement in the Admiralty Islands: 1946–1954*. Anthropological Papers No. 49. New York: American Museum of Natural History.

1963, "Systems of Areal Integration: Some Considerations Based on the Admiralty Islands of Northern Melanesia." *Anthropological Forum*, 1: 56-97.

STANNER, W. E. H., 1958–59, "On the Interpretation of Cargo Cults." *Oceania*, 29: 1-25.

STRATHERN, ANDREW, 1966. "Despots and Directors in the New Guinea Highlands." *Man*, 3: 356-367.

TAYLOR, C. R. H. 1965, *A Pacific Bibliography*. 2nd ed. London: Oxford University Press.

THURNWALD, R. C., 1934–35, "Pigs and Currency in Buin: Observations About Primitive Standards of Value and Economics." *Oceania*, 5: 119-141.

UBEROI, J. P. SINGH, 1962, *Politics of the Kulu Ring: An Analysis of the Findings of B. Malinowski.* Manchester: Manchester University Press.

UNIVERSITY OF PAPUA AND NEW GUINEA, 1968, *The History of Melanesia.* Second Waigani Seminar. Research School of Pacific Studies, Australian National University, and University of Papua–New Guinea, Port Moresby.

VALENTINE, C. A., 1963a, "Men of Anger and Men of Shame: Lakalai Ethnopsychology and its Implications for Sociopsychological Theory." *Ethnology,* 2: 441-477.

1963b, "Social Status, Political Power, and Native Responses to European Influence in Oceania." *Anthropological Forum,* 1: 3-55.

VIAL, L. G., 1936–37, "Disposal of the Dead Among the Buang." *Oceania,* 7: 64-68.

WAGNER, R., 1967, *The Curse of Souw.* Chicago: University of Chicago Press.

WATSON, J. B., 1960, "A New Guinea 'Opening Man.'" In J. B. Casagrande, ed., *In the Company of Man.* New York: Harper. Pp. 127-173.

1967, "Tairora: The Politics of Despotism in a Small Society." *Anthropological Forum,* 2: 53-104.

1970, "Society as Organized Flow: The Tairora Case." *Southwestern Journal of Anthropology,* 26: 107-124.

WEDGWOOD, CAMILLA H., 1930–31, "Some Aspects of Warfare in Melanesia." *Oceania,* 1: 5-33.

WHITING, JOHN W. M., 1941, *Becoming a Kwoma: Teaching and Learning in a New Guinea Tribe.* New Haven: Yale University Press.

1944, "The Frustration Complex in Kwoma Society." *Man,* 44: 140-144.

WORSLEY, PETER, 1968, *The Trumpet Shall Sound: A Study of "Cargo" Cults in Melanesia.* 2nd augmented ed. New York: Schocken Books.

INDEX OF PERSONS CITED